BHIL REVOLT

A Century and a Quarter of Struggle

SUBHASH CHANDRA KUSHWAHA

Translated from the Hindi by
NARESH 'NADEEM'

NIYOGI BOOKS

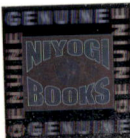

Published by
NIYOGI BOOKS
Block D, Building No. 77,
Okhla Industrial Area, Phase-I,
New Delhi-110 020, INDIA
Tel: 011-26818960, +91 7428978881
Email: niyogibooks@gmail.com
Website: www.niyogibooksindia.com

Text © Subhash Chandra Kushwaha

Editor: Subhrojyoti Mukherjee, Ritu Singh
Design: Nadeem Ahmed
Cover design: Amit Malhotra

ISBN: 978-81-992494-4-8
Publication: 2025

Every effort has been made to ensure the accuracy of the information presented in this book. The images used in this book come from either the public domain or from the public commons, unless otherwise stated.

All rights are reserved. No part of this publication may be reproduced or transmitted in any form or by any means, electronic or mechanical, including photocopying, recording or by any information storage and retrieval system without prior written permission and consent of the Publisher.

Printed at Niyogi Offset Pvt. Ltd., New Delhi, India

TABLE OF CONTENTS

	Prologue	5
	PART I	
ONE	Bhil Tribes: General Introduction	21
TWO	Khandesh and Its Bhils	32
THREE	British Policy Towards the Bhils of Central India and Khandesh	43
FOUR	Bhil Revolt and Its Leaders in Khandesh and Central India	58
FIVE	Bhil Revolts in the Khandesh Frontier Region and Maharashtra after 1858	109
SIX	Bhil Revolts Post-1833: Barwani and Alirajpur	126
	PART II	
SEVEN	Rajputana, Rewa Kantha and Mahi Kantha Agencies: General Introduction	173
EIGHT	Bhil Revolts and Their Heroes in Rajputana, Rewa Kantha and Mahi Kantha	185

PART III

NINE	Tantya Bhil: The Great Indian Moonlighter	261
TEN	Protection to Tantya Bhil and Punishment	322
ELEVEN	Tantya Bhil's Demise	330
	Epilogue	352
	Notes	358
	Selected Bibliography	374
	List of Newspapers and Journals	378
	Abbreviated Newspapers and Journals	383
	Other Abbreviations	385
	Appendix 1	387
	Appendix 2	390
	Appendix 3	400
	Appendix 4	403
	Appendix 5	405
	Index	410

PROLOGUE

Our perception of tribal communities has been entangled in an elite-accursed dichotomy and marred by the stereotypes of 'couth' and 'uncouth'. For millennia, history has ignored the truth that those who wrest natural resources from their natural possessors also deprive them of their human rights. When foreign hordes on horseback invaded what is present-day India and captured Bhil territories by means of their superior warcraft in the plains, they deprived the aboriginal inhabitants of the land of power by devious and deceitful methods. By means of economic and social theft, these invaders seized the natural resources of the land and the Bhil people's very means of livelihood.

History offers several instances illustrating the manner in which these so-called elites deprived the aborigines of their lands and forests. By obstructing the Bhils' access to education and other resources, they condemned them to ignorance and superstition, rendering the Bhil tribals, spread over approximately a third of India's territory, the very embodiment of social evil. It is also why superstitions reigned supreme among the Bhils, living as they did in ignorance—they had deep faith in witchcraft and punishing witches was part of Bhil culture. The desperate search for a livelihood and sustenance drove them to highway robbery and a guerrilla mode of existence, which further stereotyped them as a barbaric and delinquent community.

In the encounters with Rajput cavalries in the medieval ages, the Bhils found themselves at a disadvantage in the plains, with the swift horses of the Rajputs making short shrift of their resistance and forcing them to retreat despite their courageous struggles. Ousted from the plains, they sought refuge in the forests and hills from where they continued to fight their battles.

Deprived of the abundance of grain available in the plains, the mountainous areas, while they abounded in wildlife, offered limited means of subsistence. Hunger began to erode the community, exacerbated from time to time by natural disasters such as famine and drought. Faced with starvation, the Bhils took to violence and plunder instead of submitting to death. In the absence of agriculture as their means of livelihood, looting became the only means of survival, turning them into guerrilla warriors. Meanwhile, local princes and principalities increasingly deprived Bhil chiefs of their rights. A variety of taxes and cesses were imposed on forest produce, which the Bhils resisted from their strongholds in forests and hills. They began to assert control of the roads passing through their territories, leading to acts of violence. Nevertheless, in order to justify their oppression, the Rajputs dubbed them a barbaric, savage, cruel and criminal race.

This forced exodus up to the forests, hills and other desolate areas prevented this large community from entering the mainstream. Steeped in varna traditions, the Rajputs deprived the Bhils, whom they viewed as Shudras, of education. This kept the tribals mired in ignorance—they remained oblivious of their rights and dues. The Rajputs exploited the resources of Bhil lands, forests and hills on the strength of their superior knowledge base, including by the practice of deceptive religious ceremonies.

The tribals were divested of their lands by such crafty Rajput machinations as the concept of private ownership of uninhabited land stretching for miles. Having deprived the Bhils of their right and authority over land and water, the Rajputs brought these lands under their own control and thus, became owners in perpetuity. By the time awareness dawned, it was perhaps too late for the Bhils. These simplehearted people, living in the midst of nature, were oblivious to the economic deceit practised against them.

Consequently, most Bhil kings lost their power, with some demoted from kingship to the status of an ordinary *patel*. Even the few who continued to hold their fiefdoms were subject to taxes levied by the Rajputs, thus forcing them to accept Rajput suzerainty. Documents of the Bombay Government reveal that the hereditary rule of the Vasavas of Sagwara continued almost till India's independence. A privy purse was also sanctioned for the heirs of this family, even though Sagwara was regarded as a subject of the Rajput prince of Rajpipla.

By and by, the Bhil tribes were entered in the black book of time as an insurgent community. History had once known them as an extremely simple, peace-loving people true to their word. Bhils were known to be famous for their fidelity to the word given to their deities—in fact, their word carried more weight than written documents. They contracted loans from traders and moneylenders without any paperwork, and gave their lenders the first part of their produce every year as interest. The result was that they remained forever indebted to their wily creditors, even though they paid interest year after year. Till such time as a trader or moneylender decreed that a Bhil owed him, the latter was obliged to continue to pay, as a promise once given was the final word. When the Bhils of Rajputana, persuaded by Motilal Tejawat, took an oath to join the Eki (Unity), they remained within the Eki despite the many threats made, and atrocities committed, by the British.

Their simplicity, innocence and honesty can be gauged from a report in the 9 July 1868 issue of the *Bombay Gazette*:

> Once a thanadar imposed a fine of Rs 100 on a rich Bhil chieftain. As the chieftain was illiterate, he felt it was a very big amount. He asked the thanadar whether he would ever be able to pay this much money. He also pleaded that if only the thanadar gave him a chance to go home, he would bring him a drumful of money, which was buried inside his hutment, and said he had nothing more with him. The thanadar then accompanied him to his home. When the Bhil chief dug the floor and took out the drum, it had more than a thousand rupees.

Gordon-Cumming once declared that he had never lost a single rupee while wandering among the plundering Bhils for some nine years, even though he was often without a guard.[1]

Even as they divested Bhil kings of their chieftainships by depriving them of their hereditary rights, the Rajputs dangled before them the temptations of symbolic status. The Bhils were enticed with the promise that a Rajput ascending a throne would be considered king only after a Bhil chief had pierced his own thumb and, with his blood, anointed the king's forehead. This was yet another ruse to pacify the rebellious Bhils.

Rajput kings cared little about the human rights of Bhil tribes, forcing them to revolt from time to time. However, there is almost no information available about the insurgencies of that period. In this book, I have tried to highlight the Bhil community's struggle over a century and a quarter. This period roughly spans 1800 CE to 1925 CE; after 1925, a Bhil revolt is barely noticeable. One reason could have been the initiation of the Non-Cooperation Movement in 1920, which saw the common man's rise under the leadership of Mahatma Gandhi. At the same time, it must be said in all fairness that many native princes supported the Congress as well. Bhil communities actively participated in demonstrations and civil disobedience under the Congress. The struggle for emancipation from foreign rule pushed to the background the issue of liberation from the princely states, as the Bhils visualised their own emancipation as part of the national movement.

Bhil revolts before 1800 CE remain largely unknown because of lack of evidence or documentation. As a matter of fact, it was the systematic administration begun by the British and the meticulous preservation of their administrative documents that made possible the availability of information. Indeed, this book would not have seen light of day without British documents. On the one hand, the British entered innumerable facts in their gazetteers, which have been indispensable sources for a reconstruction of India's history; on the other, their official correspondence, newspapers and other written materials were stored in the archives of many countries around the globe, including India, Britain, Australia and the United States of America.

As for the Bhils, they continued to rebel and struggle against the British. In contrast, self-seeking Indian kings, caught up in their petty feuds and royal revelry, failed to successfully challenge the foreign threat. The Bhils did not commit any treachery or compromise with their self-respect. Although many in the Indian plains fled before the invaders, the Bhil communities, said to be savage and uncivilised, took to their bows and arrows to protect their soil and their independence. Dashing ahead with steely chests and their weapons, and raising high the blood-stained banner of resistance, the Bhils brooked no alien interference.

The colonial power commenced its manoeuvres for the support of Bhils even before it had established a firm foothold in Khandesh and Central India. On 1 November

1804, the *Calcutta Gazette* (hereafter *CG*) carried an item of news, praising the Bhils as a valiant community.

> The Bheels are very daring in their enterprises; not long ago, Captain Fallon's house was entered, although there was a guard stationed there; his was bedroom plundered of several articles within twenty yards of sentinel, who was over the colours of the Regiment, but they are so expert that they can elude the most vigilant eye.

On 16 February 1809, *CG* reported that Bhil chiefs and Arabs controlled all the mountain passes in Central India, except Barwani. However, when the British began their land settlements, educated and wily Rajputs, Brahmins, Banias and moneylenders had their names entered as owners of most of the land. Even as the Banias cornered trade and the business of moneylending, the uneducated Bhil, with no conception of ownership, was rendered landless and reduced to employment as the village watchman. The collective injustices inflicted upon the Bhils by the Holkars, Scindias (Shinde/Sindhiyas), the Nizam, Marathas and Rajputs of Rajputana compelled them to seek safety and join forces with the Pindaris and Arabs.

While this process, which turned the Bhils into savage rebels and compelled them to take to violence as their occupation, demands an incisive evaluation, our research organisations have done precious little. However, there are some studies at the regional level. Braj Kishore Sharma's work on the peasant and tribal movements in Rajasthan is invaluable. Both Charu Chandra Mukherjee's seminal study on Tantya Bhil in English in 1890 and Baba Bhand's in Hindi in 2001 are major works. A.K. Prasad, Arvind M. Deshpande, Ajay Sharika, Alf Gunvald Nilsen and V.K. Vashishth, among others, have made valuable contributions in English.

However, these publications mention less than a dozen Bhil chiefs. Yet, if the Bhil region in its entirety is taken into consideration, more than 200 Bhil chiefs resisted the British—but their names remain unknown. Chandra et al. (1989) briefly mentions the Koli and Santhal revolts, while the Bhil rebellion merits barely a sentence. The Bhil heroes of the Great Uprising of 1857 have been virtually ignored.[2]

This neglect of the history of struggle by an oppressed, illiterate and tormented community is troubling, because the Bhils consistently battled and made sacrifices till 1925. I have attempted to highlight the revolts in the entire Bhil region spanning Central India, Khandesh, Maharashtra, Gujarat and Rajasthan. I have also endeavoured to bring to the fore the struggles of Tantya Bhil and his comrades, with almost 90 per cent of this evidence culled from original sources.

Did the Bhils struggle or rebel against the Rajputs, Marathas and the British? Rejecting the self-appeasing viewpoint that links a struggle with 'autonomy', and a rebellion with subjugation, I choose the word 'rebellion' as more appropriate. Most British documents have used this word in the context of the Bhils. While a struggle may also be an inward one, against oneself, a rebellion must be manifested. A rebellion takes place against oppression, a loss of identity and a long period of exploitation, while a struggle may take place for personal and other reasons. The manner in which the Bhils were suppressed, tormented and deprived of their rights meant that rebellion for them was a life-and-death matter.

The present study documents the struggles of numerous important Bhil heroes, most of whom lie buried beneath the sands of history. These include Nadir Singh, Jagga Rawat, Gumani, Ram Ji, Hiria, Auchit, Kur Vasava, Mogir, Hatania, Kalia Chamar, Etcha Puggi, Omkar Rawat, Bangchund, Surajmal, Kunwar Jiva Vasava, Re Singh Nayak, Rupa Singh, Nilma, Ratania, Jugatia, Itiya, Shyamal Ji, Keera Singh, Devi Singh, Daulat Singh, Dalla, Deva, Anup Ji, Penchund, Khema Nayak, Kania Bhil, Kaji Singh, Bhima Nayak, Bhago Ji, Sitaram, Punja Dheer Ji, Putta Ji Nayak and Chitto Nayak, among 200 or more Bhil chiefs and warriors, most of whom are unsung thus far.

To cover the period of a century and a quarter under review, primary sources were preferred. British newspapers of the day, stored in the British Newspaper Archive, are the first authentic sources of information about hundreds of Bhil heroes. There are also references from foreign newspapers, for the first time, in this book.

The British viewed the forest-bound Bhil culture with a fascinated eye. Most British officers commented on Bhil life in British newspapers of their time. While at the British

Newspaper Archive, searching for references to the Bhil revolt against the British regime, I discovered numerous news items about the Bhil revolt in Khandesh, along with those of other tribes. As I was interested in the Bhil revolt, my curiosity deepened as my search through the digitised newspapers yielded more and more such references. The book, which had been originally planned to cover the Bhil revolt in Khandesh, eventually covered far more ground when research revealed the role played by Bhil heroes in revolts in the Rewa Kantha and Mahi Kantha regions.

At the outset of this study, it became increasingly obvious that a review of the Bhil revolt in its entirety was necessary to understand the history of Bhil heroes. The near-total absence of these revolts in the social histories written in Hindi induced me to take up this challenging task, even though it proved to be an expensive and trying endeavour. However, with inspiration provided by friends, and curiosity stoked by available documents, work on the book eventually started in 2017.

The book covers references to hundreds of newspapers in the British Newspaper Archive. While working through British Library catalogues, I came across several which had never been accessed at all. Much material was collected from there about the Bhil revolt in the village of Bari and about Kunwar Jiva Vasava, Kaji Singh, Bhima Nayak, Bhago Ji and Sitaram, among others.

Much material of importance was also gathered from the National Library of Australia, Sydney, where a number of newspapers yielded abundant references to the Bhil revolt. The Library also yielded Tantya Bhil's adventures, serialised in the *Leader* (Melbourne) and the *World's News* (Sydney). These have been made available for the first time. I was also able to access newspaper archives in the United States. The *New York Times* and some German newspapers, too, have been most helpful. Significantly, almost half the material used in this work was gathered from the British Library and the National Library of Australia. Some material was collected from certain important works in the National Archives, New Delhi, and the Madhya Pradesh Government Archives and Museum, Bhopal. For the first time, detailed information about Khema Nayak's relationship with Tantya Bhil has been made available to readers—it was he who had sheltered Tantya from the British for an extended period.

While a narration of the Bhil revolts that covered a very wide region—from Indore to Pune, and from Aurangabad to Udaipur—was indeed a tedious task that took almost four years, much of it during the pandemic, there is, nevertheless, a degree of elation that comes from highlighting the Bhil people's fights and their sacrifices, their history, and the role played by their innumerable leaders.

Apart from the original documents and foreign newspapers, two important works were also used. They are *The Life of Tantia Bhil: The Renowned Bandit-Chief* (1890), compiled from original records by Mukherjee[3] and *Jan Nayak Tantia Bhil and the Peasant and Tribal Movement: Source Material* (2001), in Hindi, by Baba Bhand.[4]

Besides the aforementioned works by Mukherjee and Baba Bhand, others works had also attempted to highlight Tantya Bhil's spirited rebellion. These include *Tantya Bhil* (1925) by Kirtibhanu Rai, 'Tantya Bhil' by Vishwanath Sakharam Khode in the Nimad issue (1930) of *Bani Khargon Patrika*, the Gallows issue (1888) of *Chand*, *Tantya Bhil* (1891), in Marathi, by Ramchandra Vinayak Tikekar alias Chhanuchhiri, *Tantya Bhil* (1928), in Marathi, by Nath Madhav, *Tantya Bhil* (1937), the Marathi play by Shantaram Gopal Gupte, *Tantya alias Tantya Bhil yanche Charitr* (1905, Hindi translation by Madan Mohan Joshi) and *Tantya Bhillaya Powada* (1905) by Bal Mohan Pathak.

The first part of the book covers a major part of Central India; the second is devoted to Bhil revolts in the Rajputana area, i.e., the Gujarat–Rajasthan of today. Some Bhil revolts took place on both sides of the Khandesh–Rajasthan border. They have been included in the first or second part, in accordance with their spread. The last part of the book is centred on Tantya Bhil and Khema Nayak.

The employees of the British Library, including Kathryn Mouncey, Andrew Gough, Mukund Miyangar and Debbie Horner, showed exemplary patience in comprehending my needs and making these documents available. Often, there was a hitch in the process, but they remained unperturbed and cooperative and deserve my deep gratitude. Without their cooperation, this book could not have seen the light of day. Jaya Ravindram, Assistant Director, National Archives, New Delhi, provided invaluable help in accessing documents.

I am also grateful to Gita Sabharwal, Deputy Director of the Madhya Pradesh Government Archives and Museum, Bhopal; Padam Singh Mina, Assistant Registrar and in-charge of documents at the Museum; and Deep Narayan Kushwaha, who made most of the documents speedily available to me despite the pandemic. Another employee, Bharat Singh Mandloi, who himself belongs to the Lala community, provided valuable information about Barwani. Mandloi also introduced us to Dr S.N. Yadav, a renowned historian.

A number of friends provided deeply valued assistance, both direct and indirect, during the writing of this book. I am especially grateful to Ashish Kumar, assistant professor of English at Christian Degree College, Lucknow, who helped in deciphering the handwritten letters of the colonial period. In India, the British started using the typewriter in the mid-19th century, and it became fairly common after 1880. As such, many of the East India Company's documents and other pre-1880 documents, being handwritten, were not easily decipherable. By rendering virtually all the Australian documents into Hindi, Naresh 'Nadeem' made my task that much easier. My elder son, Ankit, procured a copy of Mukherjee's book from the US. My wife, Asha, absolved me of the guilt of neglecting my family during the writing of this book; she also helped in the correction of errors. Vishal Shukla, a Faizabad-based journalist, helped decipher a handwritten letter of the East India Company. Chandrika and Ram Ji Yadav, sincere friends, offered their opinions on a draft of the book. Hari Bhatnagar, another friend, helped in procuring some manuscripts from the Bhopal Archives. During my sojourn at Bhopal, Hari and his wife, Priti Bhatnagar, were most cooperative. The book is now in your hands—and your opinions will be gratefully valued.

March 2021
Subhash Chandra Kushwaha

PART I

1
BHIL TRIBES: GENERAL INTRODUCTION

The history of Bhil tribes living in the territory spanning the ranges of the Vindhyas to the Narmada Valley—in Madhya Pradesh, Maharashtra, Gujarat and Rajasthan—goes back to hoary antiquity. As the aboriginal inhabitants of the land, the Bhils were its autonomous rulers in the past. Their history may be traced to pre-Aryan days, as reported on 12 November 1931 in the *Queenslander*. Owing to the deceit, trickery and fraud perpetrated on them, this primitive, uneducated and simple-hearted community was reduced from kings to commoners.

British scholars were the first to conduct in-depth studies of the Bhil warrior tribes with the courage to challenge feudal lords and British dominance. In order to perpetuate their own structure of power, the British studied the racial and social psychology of the Bhils and brought the independence-loving aborigines under their economic, administrative and religious dominance. In his reminiscences, John Malcolm regarded the Bhils of Central India as a special type of people and described them as older than the other peoples of the country.[1]

Raised amidst rivers, hills, waterfalls and wild animals, the Bhil tribals, the biggest tribe of South Asia, were renowned bowmen. Their dark complexion was a natural product of their life in the embrace of Nature, of their daily exposure to the weather's vagaries. They led simple lives in *palas* (villages), consisting of small hutments, with each village ruled by a chief. Strictly following the panchayati system, the Bhils preferred to lead simple and peaceful lives until foreign invaders turned them into rebels.[2]

This autonomous tribe, which rebuffed outside interference at all times, rejected change in their traditional socio-cultural life. Traditionally, Bhil chiefs had lived as independent rulers. Therefore, any Rajput or British attempts to subdue them were treated as assaults on their independence, compelling them to take to their bows and arrows and swords—it is from here that their bloodstained history began. They battled the British for a century and a quarter without capitulating, without respite, sacrificing lakhs of their people in the process. With little understanding of their obstinacy and determination, the British labelled them bloodthirsty, savage, barbaric, criminal, murderous and untamed. It was the Aryans who had deliberately dubbed the Bhils *mlechchha*.[3]

The Rajput onslaught forced them to fight to protect their lands and water, their forests and villages and their very identity. The lands they had once inhabited were originally far more extensive than the area which they populate today. Every hilltop, valley and mountain pass from Khandwa in

Madhya Pradesh to Aurangabad, Udaipur, Mumbai and Pune of the Bombay Presidency bears marks of their arrows and their bloodstains.

The Bhil tribes of India may be divided into two main groups—the Bhils of Central India, and those of Eastern India. The Bhils of Central India inhabit a wide swathe which once covered Khandesh, Central India and Rajputana of British times, i.e., Madhya Pradesh, Maharashtra (south-eastern parts), Gujarat (Rewa Kantha and Mahi Kantha) and the hill areas of Rajasthan (Rajputana) of today. In Eastern India, Bhils inhabit the north-western part of Tripura.[4] According to the Census of 2011, there are about 3,015 Bhils in Tripura. By some accounts, their ancestors settled there after they were displaced from Central India. According to an assessment made in 2020, some 12–17 lakh Bhils are also to be found in Pakistan. Their dialects resemble Rajasthani, Marwari, Gujarati and Sindhi dialects/languages. This book, however, does not include the Bhils of Tripura or Pakistan.[5]

According to the Census of 1901, there were 5,69,842 Bhils in Bombay (including Gujarat), 3,39,786 in Rajputana (including Ajmer and Mewar), 2,06,934 in Central India, and a total of 82,281 in other areas, taking the total Bhil population to 11,98,843 at the time.[6] In numerical terms, the Bhils are the third largest tribal group in India today, after the Gonds and Santhals. However, the Bhils rank first in terms of area as they occupy a vast territory.

Countless myths and fables surround the origin of the term Bhil. Several historians have repeated them, even though mythological tales have no basis. The word *viluvar* for bowmen, used by ancient Tamil poets, is derived from the Dravidian *vilu* or *bhilu*. People of the erstwhile South Canara district in Karnataka are called 'Bilawa' but while they, too, are bowmen, they do not identify as Bhils. As titles such as Turvi, Nayak, Garasia or Mukhiya are found among Bhils as well as Bilawas, it may be safely assumed that Bhil is a Dravidian term. Some historians do not associate this term either with Aryans or with Dravids.[7]

The term Bhil is found in both the *Ramayana* and *Mahabharata*. According to the *Ramayana*, when Ram was wandering through the forests in search of Sita, a Bhil woman named Shabari had offered him wildberries. Another tale records that Bhils were born of the union between Nishad, Mahadev's (Lord Shiva) son, and a forest woman. Nishad has been described as cruel and ugly. As he had killed a bullock belonging to his father, an enraged Mahadev had exiled him to the forests and hills. While such myths do not have much truck with reality, folktales do reflect folk life to some extent, and it could be assumed that Shiva might have been worshipped as these tribal people's deity. Their history of determination to fight for their society and culture, their traditions and customs, and for their rights, is absent in so-called civilised societies.[8]

In Sanskrit, the use of the term Bhil was first observed some 700 years ago to denote a strange kind of race, then living in the hills around the Narmada River, a barbaric people who depended mainly on vandalism. The same race is mentioned in certain verses of the *Mahabharata* as an origin tale.

The history of the Muslims of Gujarat and Malva, and the hill peoples of Mewar and Udaipur, reveals a court-type administrative system under a powerful head. Ancient documents also mention the existence of a small number of tribals in the sprawling ranges on the northern border of Khandesh. Much like the other tribes who settled in Mewar and Jodhpur, the Bhils had made their settlements in the Vindhya, Satmala and Satmula ranges, and on the banks of the Mahi, Narmada and Tapi (also known as Tapti) rivers, where Nature offered them ample protection. They depended on wood and timber as well as small enterprises for their livelihood. But when feudal lords seized their resources, the Bhils were compelled to plunder rich peasants in order to survive. According to the *Atlas* on 9 March 1861, the Bhils protected the roads passing through their territories and asserted their right to collect taxes from traders travelling on those routes.[9]

The Bhil cultural ethos is quite different from that of Hindu society. Their rites, from birth to death, and their ceremonies have differed from those of the Hindus. They perform no *shraddha* (Hindu funeral ceremony). During the Navaratri, a Hindu autumn festival, they remember their ancestors as 'Ancestor Ramana'. They offer meat and wine to their ancestors but consider any anniversary celebrations ill-fated, as reported in the *Tribune* (Melbourne) on 22 June 1916.[10]

On 26 July 1824, the *Star* (London) published Capt. Seely's observation that the cult of Hinduism had not reached Bhil tribals living in forested areas, and while they were excessively dark in comparison to the Hindus, they were more masculine.

The following are anecdotes of the Bheels, a horde of banditti, who are considered in Captain Seely as the aborigines of India:

Their haunts are in the wildest parts of India, where neither civilisation nor the Brahminical creed have ever penetrated; and they hold both in great contempt. They are generally of short stature, sometimes with curly hair and a thickness of the lower lip; of very dark complexion and more masculine in form than the Hindoos. Their habits are migratory; but wherever extensive forests or mountainous woody tracks are formed, parties of Bheels reside, and only quit their strong holds for plunder, or to engage as auxiliaries in a foray, to devastate and destroy that which contending chiefs cannot themselves accomplish.

According to a report in the *Times of India* on 10 October 1878, the British made attempts to bring the Bhils into the mainstream by recruiting them to the police and army. There were some marriage relations with the Rajputs, by which Hindu customs and rites gradually penetrated Bhil ranks. It was said that in the hill areas, 50 Bhils were enough to repulse an army of 500. They had even been known to walk

300 mil. at a stretch, as reported in the *Cumberland Pacquet and Ware's Whitehaven Advertiser* on 2 August 1824.

A Bhil king was called *gameti*, a village chief, *nayak*, and the sounds they made were called *kulki* (likely a part of their cultural expression, ritual, or communication). Bhils were organised in about 40 *gotras* (clans) and every clan had a specific deity, a totem tree and a totem animal. Every village had a *dholi* (drummer) who beat his drum at marriages and deaths. Every village had a *rawal*, whose main job was to organise a *kaita* (feast prepared at an individual's death). The Bhils of Manpur and Satpura did not intermarry. A hereditary king, called *turvi*, wore a sacred thread at an individual's death rites.

The Bhils of Rajputana considered themselves superior to Bhils of other regions. In 1901, about two-thirds of Rajputana Bhils lived in Mewar and Banswara. The use of Bhil blood to anoint a Rajput king was the custom in Mewar, Dungarpur and Banswara. Bhils born of Bhil–Rajput unions were called Bhilala and claimed superiority over other Bhils. In 1901, 1,44,423 Bhilalas lived in the Bhopawar Agency area of Central India. There, they were called Bhumiya, i.e., landowners. Omkar was regarded as the chief representative of the Mandhata (Bhilala) in the Central Provinces. The Bhilalas of Central India were divided into groups of various sizes, which did not intermarry.[11]

The Bhil religion and language have undergone many changes. Bhils have given up their own language and speak a corrupt dialect born of the Aryan languages of the area. The

Bhil dialect originated from the Gujarati language, but with Marwari and Marathi influences; in Nimar, in particular, it becomes a corrupted form of Marathi. This dialect called Bhili has several non-Aryan words, some of which appear to be borrowed from Mundari and some from the Dravidian languages. However, there is no evidence thus far to link the Bhils with the Kolari or Dravidian races. Their dialect resembles the languages of the Indo–Aryan family.[12]

As regards their clothing, even though Bhils once exposed most of their bodies, they wore turbans. Bhil women have been wearing the traditional sari for long, but without a blouse, while Bhil men now prefer turbans, pyjamas, jerkins and brass ornaments. Bhil chiefs did not wear crowns. They used bamboo to make their own bows and arrows for hunting and self-protection.[13] Bhil women performed arduous tasks in forests, hills and valleys and enjoyed greater freedom as compared to Hindu or Muslim women.[14]

On 22 June 1889, the *Congleton & Macclesfield Mercury* and *Cheshire General Advertiser* published 'The Bhils and Their Country' that commented on their general lifestyle:

> In the course of an interesting article on the Bhils, an aboriginal tribe of Central India, living in the rough country and jungle around the Vindhya Mountains, Sir Lepel Griffin says that from the earliest day of the Aryan conquest of India the Bhils have been looked on as wild animals, deserving of no protection or kindness. Since the advent of the British government, the condition of these simple and harmless

people has much improved, so that the poor Bhils are gradually becoming less and less savage. Their knowledge of woodcraft and of the habits of birds and beasts makes them invaluable to English officers. Unlike the orthodox Hindu, the Bhil has always eaten the flesh of the cow and the buffalo and other abhorred animals. In fact, he eats every wild animal except this monkey, which is universally worshipped in the form of the forest god Hanuman. The tiger is held in great respect, and the people are very unwilling to kill it, unless it is a man-eater. If a beast has thus become obnoxious, a trial is held with religious rites, and if the animal is found guilty, sentence is passed upon him; he is pursued, killed, and hung up on a tree over the main road as a warning to all evil-doers of his species.

The Bhils are noted for their endurance, for their capacity of living where others would starve, their indifference to the greatest changes of temperature. Not even to save his life will a Bhil tell a falsehood. Their most solemn oath is by the dog, their most valuable companion in the chase. They are gay and of a light-hearted disposition and take every opportunity of having a feast and a drinking bout. Their drink is made from the Mowra, a tree which abounds in Central India, the white flowers of which, when pounded and mixed with grain, form a palatable food, and when distilled by a simple process produce a highly intoxicating spirit. Their priests are not of any particular caste, but the office is a hereditary one. The deities most generally worshipped are the ordinary Vedic deities of water, fire, and the heavens, and each village has its presiding deity, who is a different personage in each village. Like Hindus they burn their dead, except unmarried children of both sexes, who are buried, as also those who die from smallpox. In case of cholera, they also bury the dead, believing that the smoke from the pyre disseminates the disease. The dead are worshipped and propitiated by offerings; tree worship is unusual; witchcraft and omens are implicitly believed in; charms of various kinds are universally used.

According to Haribhadra Suri, author of the pre-medieval tract, *Samraichchakaha*, the Bhils had no knowledge of the Hindu religion. Their gods were the gods of Nature, and they followed vastly different social and religious lives. The Bhils of Mewar also worshipped the first Jain Tirthankara Rishabh Dev, also called Kesaryaji. Their other deities were Babadev the horse, Kharo, Dhan, Moto Dharmi (the deity of sacredness), Bhais Dharmi (the deity of honesty), Nan Dev (the deity of maize), Mantonio Dev (the deity of vegetables) and Gawli (the deity of milk). Local deities of the mother earth like Khandoba, Kanhoba, Bahoba and Shitla Mata were also worshipped.[15] Contact with the Hindus encouraged them to accept Hindu deities and customs of worship.[16]

With the exception of Rishabh Dev, Bhil deities have no temples. Hereditary sorcerers of the community have been its advisers, while their bhagats or gurus have guided their religious rites. Tribal rules and regulations are strictly followed, with marriages within their own community. The *ghumar* dance of Bhils of Rajasthan is world famous, reflecting their deep passion for dance and music. *Ghoda nach* (horse dance) was customary at weddings. But with the passage of time, their society, thus far led by their chiefs, underwent seismic changes, according to the *Bombay Gazette* (hereafter *BG*) on 9 July 1868.[17]

The curse of caste has not escaped the Bhils, most likely developing in their community as a consequence of contact with the outside world. A Koli (Bhilala) did not accept water from a Bhil. Brahmins and Thakurs accepted water from high-status Bhil kings and Kolis but not from Bhil Nayaks. Interestingly, no such caste restriction is imposed with regard to hookah-smoking. The Bhils, too, have been divided among many such castes as ordinary Bhils, Nayaks and Kolis; in fact, they may belong to several castes, as reported by *BG* on 4 June 1851 and 9 July 1868.

The Bhils were divided into three categories based on their modes of living. Those living in villages were known as chowkidars or watchmen. Of a comparatively mutinous disposition, they owned no land; rather, well-to-do cultivators leased land to them in lieu of the watchman's job. The second category of Bhils cultivated their own lands or lived in towns or district headquarters, along with their *turvi*. Impoverished and mutinous of disposition, the third category of Bhils were generally hill-dwellers.[18]

2
KHANDESH AND ITS BHILS

Khandesh covered a sizeable part of Central India and was located to the north-east of Bombay. An administrative unit of British India, it was situated at the trijunction of present-day Gujarat, Maharashtra and Madhya Pradesh in the Tapi river basin. After the transfer of power from the East India Company (Company hereafter) to the Crown, it was deemed a district in place of a province. Touching the border of Indore (state) on one side and Pune on the other, it consisted of present-day Jalgaon, Dhule (Dhulia) and Nandurbar, as well as a part of the district of Nasik. Its frontiers touched Rewa Kantha and Mahi Kantha, now in Gujarat. In the second half of the 19th century, it was incorporated as Central Provinces and Berar, and made a district of Bombay Presidency. In 1869, the southern part of Khandesh was deemed the district of Nasik, while the remaining area was divided into Khandesh East and Khandesh West. Jalgaon and Dhule were made the capitals of these units, respectively, that later become the districts of Jalgaon and Dhule. The district of Dhule was once more divided in 1898, forming a new district, Nandurbar.[1]

A fertile and well-irrigated plain with an area of about 13,000 sq. mil., Khandesh's several low mountains gave birth to rivers or streams that flowed into the Tapi. As the whole region was covered with long mountain ranges and thorny bush, none but the hill tribes could live in this area. The Satpura range was the northern frontier of the province, interspersed with mountain passes. The Sukhen range in the west was steep and rocky and covered with dense bamboo forests. The Satmala (Chandore and Ajanta) ranges surrounded the province to the south, making the region highly inaccessible. As the entire province then lacked usable roads, accessing a village through mountain passes was no easy task.[2] Interestingly, no map of Khandesh existed until it was commissioned by Capt. John Briggs and executed by engineers over the next two years.[3] The boundaries of Khandesh, Western Nimar (Holkar territory) and Eastern Nimar (Scindia territory) met near Palgaon in Jalgaon district.[4]

Khandesh was part of the Maratha Confederation during the 18th and the beginning of the 19th centuries. It was ruled by the Nizam, Gaekwad and Maratha Peshwa by turn. The Treaty of Bhopal (1738) brought the Malva region under the Marathas, but after their defeat in the third Anglo-Maratha War in 1818, it was subsumed in British India.[5]

In 1872, the geographical spread of Khandesh extended from 200^0 8' to 220^0 7' of the northern latitudes, and from 730^0 42' to 760^0 28' of the eastern longitudes. Its total area was 10, 431 sq. mil. (20,099 sq. km.), with a population of

10,28,642.⁶ Its boundaries extended over 159 mil. (256 km) along the Tapi, while, to its north it was 57 to 89 mil. (92 to 144 km) wide. In 1830, the British made the first-ever assessment of the Bhil population at about 55,000.⁷

Besides the Bhils, Ahir tribes inhabited Khandesh in sizeable numbers. By some accounts, the total population of non-Hindu non-Aryan Ahirs displaced from Afghanistan was 1,04,894 in 1903. They had settled in Khandesh, Nasik, Kutch and Kathiawar. Ahirani, the Marathi dialect spoken by the Ahirs, was spoken by approximately half the population of Khandesh. The British considered the Gujjars the most intelligent and hardworking peasants of Khandesh, reported the *Homeward Mail* (hereafter *HM*) on 4 April 1903.

Khandesh continued to be a prosperous part of India from the 14th to the 16th centuries. The Deccan, i.e., the south, had been home to six Muslim capitals that had once ruled this region some centuries earlier. The province was made part of Akbar's empire in 1600, and that of the Marathas in the mid-18th century. The Arabs and Pindaris had ravaged the villages of the area into desolation, forcing the Bhils to escape to the hills.⁸

Several factors drew the British to Khandesh. The territory consisted of plateaus and forests. The fertile alluvial soil brought by the Narmada and Tapi was ideal for cotton cultivation, and was fully exploited by the British. Its dense forests abounded in lions, tigers and other wild animals, giving the British ample opportunity, as nowhere else, for their hunting pastimes. Maj. Oliver Probyn alone shot more than 100 tigers. He had joined the Company's Army in 1843 and was appointed superintendent of police (SP), Khandesh, in 1858. He was then commanding the Bhil Corps of Khandesh, as reported in the *Illustrated London News* on 11 August 1883. Newspapers of that period, such as the *Scotsman* on 9 September 1880 and the *Aberdeen Journal* on 22 July 1880, described the Bhils as a stubborn and wild people that no power could subdue. The British referred to them as the 'Rob Rays' of India and described them as natural cannibals and flesh-eaters, biologically resembling wild animals. Bhil tribes looted their victims as mercilessly as wild animals kill their game.

From 6 to 25 February 1779, Col. Goddard travelled through the Central Provinces on his way to Surat. He noted the fertile tracts and contented people of Khandesh and found that this was a province with ample grain production. He also observed that the tribals did not flee on sighting an army troop; rather, they voluntarily supplied them with provisions. Goddard observed that there were villages in succession for 80 mil. to the west, denoting prosperity. It was a prosperous region in Mughal times, during which the Bhils were masters of their territories. There was no outside interference—and they tolerated none.[9]

Other sources also indicate the prosperity of Khandesh. A number of markets took place at the beginning of Company rule. The taluka of Taloda, in Khandesh, held a weekly market on Fridays for all manner of necessities. Clothes were sold in Nandurbar and Ranala, while metal utensils, bullocks, horses, mules and other animals were sold in Songir. Gujjar, Maratha and Gujarati Banias, Marwaris, Bhils, Powras and Rohillas of Akrani frequented these markets. Powra tribals came there in large numbers to sell *charoli* or *chiraunji* seeds (*Buchanania latifoli*), mahua seeds (*Madhuka longifolia*), honey, wax, lac, gum and bitumen. As there was no road from Akrani, sellers brought their goods on pack animals or carried them on their heads. Taloda had a small market, where sal wood (*Shorea robusta*) was sold, a dispensary, and was home to the Banias and Marwaris. Intelligent and hardworking peasants, the Gujjars lived in the villages in the central or south-east parts of the province. Bhils formed the rest of the population and were divided into several categories, e.g., the Bhils of Taloda, or Nandurbar, or Nawapur. There were *patils* (moneylenders) who lent money at six per cent interest. By then, the Bhils had started to construct their *baru* (house) with roofs of reed. Mud walls and clay tiles were exceptions thus far. Bhils received loans at low interest but were trapped in a vicious cycle by Rohilla moneylenders. Drinking was common in Khandesh and signified high status. Minuscule sums were spent on clothes. The Gujjars of Nandurbar were the wealthiest, with houses of stone or brick. Their marriage ceremonies displayed extravagance, as reported in *HM* on 17 December 1900. The *Illustrated Sporting and Dramatic News* reported on 23 October 1915 that the Khandesh Ginning and Weaving Factory was established around 1888.

Most of the markets or cities of this province were situated in the eastern part. An exception was Thalner, located in the taluka of Shivpur, on the banks of the Tapi. The western part of Khandesh was neglected as the only usable road for trade in the province ran from the north-east to the south-west via Asirgarh, reaching the Ajanta mountain pass after crossing Khandesh East; still further, it ran to Daulatabad and Ahmednagar in the south. François Bernier, a renowned French traveller, who had travelled twice from Surat to Khandesh during Aurangzeb's rule, observed that Nawapur produced the finest rice in India. Burhanpur was an important city.[10]

The Bhils of Khandesh
The anarchy that prevailed in Khandesh during the initial years of British rule was absent in Mughal times. The decline of its prosperity dates back to 1802 when Holkar captured some territory from Muslim rulers and plundered the whole area, which was then deserted by the population. Some of these territories were claimed by the Peshwas and the Nizam. Nomadic Bhils then mingled with other inhabitants of Khandesh and began to guard the villages. These chowkidars later helped in the formation of the Bhil Corps. Bhils who could not find employment or a livelihood returned to the hills, taking to plunder once more.

An article carried in the *Times of India* on 6 September 1884 stated that the third generation of Scindias and Holkars had invited Pathans from Afghanistan to settle in Khandesh to provide security against the Bhils and other tribals. They were followed by the horse-riding Pindaris, who took advantage of the prevailing anarchy to plunder the area once a year. Arab traders had by then built fortresses to bring stability to the area. The British, therefore, had no option but to wage war to drive away the Arabs. According to Col. Graham, a British officer, fighting Pindaris was difficult enough in the plains but dealing with anarchist Bhils was the more arduous task. Graham observed that they had suffered much at the hands of Arab traders and Pindaris, as reported in the *Atlas* (hereafter *A*) on 9 March 1861.

> The bulk of the Bheel population in Khandesh, which is estimated at one eighth of the entire inhabitants of the province, is chiefly settled in Bauglan and to the North and Northwest, where they in general reside peaceably as Patels, cultivators and proprietors of the soil. In this portion of the province they are not so degraded, because they are not so completely destitute of all those claims that usually command consideration; they are not so exposed to want nor so inured to hardships, and therefore neither so reckless of their own or the lives of others, and possessing landed property, obligations as proprietors are imposed: the respect of others necessarily induces a certain degree of self-respect, and in proportion as these essentials are present or absent the Bheels are more or less civilised and inclined to live in peace and quietness. The most restless and troublesome are those dwelling immediately at the foot and amidst the recesses of the surrounding ranges,

who at different periods have either usurped or have been entrusted with all the passes leading into the country, and till lately have held charge of many of the most important fortresses in the plains. Their hive-like habitations, formerly crested the top isolated hill, where approach from every side was easily defended or immediately discovered, and these hovels not reared for permanent occupation but hastily put together to be crept into for a few months or weeks, were without regret abandoned on any occasion that induced the occupants to shift their quarters. Roving and restless by disposition, and skilful hunters by necessity, the woods and jungles supplied them with roots, berries and game; a successful foray filled their stores to overflowing, and as every man's hand was lifted against them, so the measure of wrath was fully returned by the tribe, whose powers of mischief far exceeded those of their numerous oppressors, and whose habits and locations enabled them to bid such a lengthy defiance to so many governments.

Turvi Bhils, who had embraced Islam in the Mughal era, lived in the north-eastern parts and were fairer in complexion. They were more inclined towards agriculture as compared to the other tribes but cooperated with the Pindaris during the days of anarchy. The Nahals, a dark-skinned and short-statured people, were barbaric, with different customs. Youngsters freely coupled with anyone and separated just as freely. Infants were raised by their mothers and adolescents by their fathers. Hirdhi Bhils were Muslims; they lived in the Jamuar and Bargaon parganas of the Ajanta range and were very quick to rebel. They, too, were regarded as barbaric and difficult to tame. In a sense, generically, all the tribes spread over Khandesh were called Bhils. As the article in *A* noted, the Bhils considered themselves superior to the other tribes from whom they had no qualms in accepting food but eschewed marriage relations.[11]

The Mutwari, Barda and Dorepi tribes lived in Akrani in the north-west and in the hill tracts of Dhadgaon. As they were adept at basket weaving and cultivation, they had grown distinct from other tribes. Generically, the term Khotil was used for all wild communities living in the Satpura range who supplied wax and gum to the plain dwellers. Those living in Dang, at the foothills of the Western Ghats, were called Dangchi. These tribes were considered more uncivilised as compared to other wild tribes. Living in the throes of crushing poverty and inclement weather, they were deeply superstitious and fatalist by nature, believing in good and bad omens, and were even known to temporarily abandon their villages because of ill omens. Drinking to excess, they believed that alcohol brought them in proximity to an energetic soul that destroyed their base tendencies in a raging fire.

The hill-dwelling Bhils also played a vital role in the war between the Marathas and Muslims. It is said that Khandesh was prosperous until 1798, when Bajirao assumed the title of Peshwa after the demise of Nana Phadnawis. But, in fact, its days of misfortune started when Yashwant Rao Holkar successfully staged a revolt. The government fell three times in two years as a result of the plunder by Maratha soldiers who devastated the area. The Maratha war of 1803 and the famine, whose horrors ranged from the Satpura hills to the city of Hyderabad, exacerbated the situation. From the plains, the Bhils escaped to the hills, never to return. This anarchy and chaos continued in the region for an extended period.

Organised, plundering Bhil gangs soon became a major headache for British officials. The hilltops were now controlled by Bhil chiefs, who brought smaller principalities under their control. This anarchy reached its peak in 1818 before the British occupied the region. The province of Khandesh, once known as the 'Orchard of the West', then had more than 50 infamous gangs who, with about 5,000 rebellious members, took to plunder for survival. The repeated deceptions and false assurances given by their former rulers were responsible for the Bhils' intense suspicion of and refusal to capitulate to the new government of foreigners.

Bhils inhabiting the entire Satpura range from Kukarmunda (Gujarat) to Burhanpur (Madhya Pradesh) continued to persist with their rebellion. Following the leaders of 32 gangs, Bhils of Satmala and Ajanta spread terror with swords and other weapons in the southern parts. Led by Govinda, a powerful Bhil chief, the minor chiefs of Pint and Abhona in Maharashtra were playing a bloody game in the Western Ghats. Although the roads here were not easily negotiable, they plundered villages and committed murders every day and stole cattle. The situation was so alarming that farmers abandoned the *taqavi* system of agriculture, in which the state or the zamindars advanced loans to the cultivators to dig wells, buy seeds, etc., in short, to improve agriculture, leaving their fields to the mercy of these marauding gangs. The once-fabled 'Orchard of the West' then lay devastated, reported the *A*, populated by just Bhils, lions and jackals.[12]

3
BRITISH POLICY TOWARDS THE BHILS OF CENTRAL INDIA AND KHANDESH

In British times, Central India was administered by the Central India Agency. It bordered the United Provinces of Agra and Awadh in the north-east, the southern frontier of Central Provinces in the east, Rewa Kantha in the south-west, and Panch Mahal in Bombay Presidency. Several principalities of Rajputana Agency adjoined it on the northwest. The Central India Agency covered an area of 78,772 sq. mil., with a total population of 8,62,878 in 1901, of which the Bhils numbered 2,06,934.[1]

The colonial attitude towards the Bhils was an amalgam of British education and elitist Indian notions. While they acknowledged the Bhils as the original inhabitants of the land, they continued to disparage them as barbarians, plunderers, robber bands, inhuman, etc. The British recognised the Bhils' strength and hence constituted the Khandesh Bhil Corps, Malva Bhil Corps, Gujarat Bhil Corps, Marwar Bhil Corps, among others. Their efforts to educate and civilise the Bhils were motivated by a policy to utilise Bhil valour and daring in British interest.

Before the British extended their jurisdiction to Bhil territories in Gujarat, Malva, Khandesh and elsewhere, they pursued a policy of appeasement of native Bhil warriors that began in 1806, as reported in an article in the *Lancaster Gazette* on 27 December 1806. They were convinced that this policy would be useful, too, in subduing native rulers, such as the Holkars, Scindias and Peshwas.

The British had little choice as they were well aware that but for the Barwani Pass, Bhil chiefs, along with the Arabs and other warriors, controlled all the other passes in the hill areas. Articles in newspapers, such as the *Calcutta Gazette* on 16 February 1809 and the *Sun* (London) on 15 September 1809, stated that it was impossible to cross these passes without the Bhil chiefs' permission.

In 1815, Capt. John Briggs was appointed junior assistant, Poona Regiment, and it was from his Poona (Pune) headquarters that he joined the military expedition against the Peshwas. In mid-September 1817, he was ordered by Sir John Malcolm to cross the Narmada into Holkar territory. The Holkar Army was then stationed in Mahidpur, near Ujjain. On 5 November 1817, the Company commenced its war against the combined Maratha forces. The war, in which the Marathas were defeated on 21 December 1817, claimed 3,000 jawans of the joint Maratha Army and 778 of the Company's soldiers. The two antagonists then signed the Treaty of Mandsaur on 6 January 1818 and as a result, Holkar, forfeiting his claim to the entire Satpura range, ceded it to the British. Nevertheless, the Marathas still held all the 19 forts in Khandesh.[2]

The Marathas were defeated in Astha on 19 February 1818 and were forced to flee Khandesh. On 27 February, without resorting to any major battle, the British Army, led by Briggs and Sir Thomas Hislop, captured the forts of Thalner (Maharashtra), Gaulna (a mountain fort in Khandesh about 87 mil. north-west of Aurangabad) and Chandore (Maharashtra). Chandore Fort housed the headquarters of Ramdas, a Holkar agent. In March 1818, Ramdas laid down arms before the Company and consequently, Khandesh became part of British India. On 16 May 1818, the British captured Dhaulkot Fort near Asirgarh, where they established the headquarters of the First Division of their Deccan Army.[3]

Although Khandesh was acquired by the British in 1818, they had to wait seven long years before their writ could run large. From the very beginning, Company officials adopted the policy of fraternising with the Bhils, on the one hand, and applying pressure, on the other, as reported in the *Scotsman* (hereafter *S*) on 9 September 1880 and in the *Aberdeen Journal* on 22 July 1880.

Briggs assumed charge as political agent (PA) in May 1818, a position he held up to 1823. The Khandesh administration was then under the commissioner of Deccan. Briggs established his headquarters at Dhule, which lay on the Bombay–Agra road. A letter from Briggs to Lt. Col. Neil Jardin on 1 April 1819 reveals that he was rather perplexed by the revolts of Bhil chiefs Ram Ji and his brother, Auchit. Jardin was asked to somehow capture the two unruly chiefs.[4]

Briggs soon discovered that all over Khandesh some 50 notorious chiefs, with about 5,000 supporters, were busily engaged in loot and murder. The governor of Bombay, Mount Stuart Elphinstone, suggested that Briggs drive the Bhils into the hills—but Briggs thought otherwise. He convinced Elphinstone that such an action would give the Bhils a refuge; in fact, he preferred to keep them in his sights. The captain did not see much difference in the deeds committed by Bhils of the plains and those of the hills. In 1818, Briggs reached agreements with several Bhil chiefs, including Ram Ji, assuring them of pensions if they cooperated in the maintenance of law and order.[5]

Grains were distributed among the Bhils of Nandurbar and in accordance with the agreement, Briggs sanctioned pensions to the Bhils of Chandore. Gumani (Gumania), Phegi Khan, Jiva Vasava, Rana, Devi Ji, Rahilia and Khundu, among others, all benefitted. In 1818, Gumani, of Sendhwa, received Rs 2,000; Jiva Vasava, of Chikli, Rs 3,000; and Rana Chandar Singh, of Budhwal, Rs 2,000. The chief of Gohali received Rs 1,300 in all—Rs 1,000 sanctioned by the Baroda state and Rs 300 by the British. The Kanti chief was pacified with a pension of Rs 37 annas 8 per annum, the Singpur chief with Rs 200 and the Nal chief with Rs 200. Ram Ji and Auchit each received a monthly pension of Rs 50, even though the yearly pensions sanctioned were Rs 2,000.[6]

The chiefs who did not support the agreement were arrested the same year. Dreaded chief Nadir Singh was arrested as a result of a friend's treachery. Ganga Nayak attacked the British Army near Chopra (Maharashtra) and was killed. Turvi Bhils attacked a police convoy but were repulsed. The chiefs of Erandol (Maharashtra) returned the pension sanctioned by the Company. Bhils from the hills looted the Thalner pargana in Maharashtra.

In 1819, the Bhils rebelled en masse. When the government arrested any of them, a new chief came to the fore—it was jungle warfare at its most basic. The Bhils also rejected the general amnesty. A troublesome Bhil named Cheel was arrested and hanged. In 1820, Dashrath, another chief, befriended Sheikh Dulla, a dreaded Pindari chief, and embarked on an indiscriminate spree of plunder. He overran and plundered a village in the southern hill tract and was eventually forced to surrender by Maj. Morin.

This anarchy continued in 1821, with military action proving a dismal failure. An attempt was made to ambush and kill Briggs as well. In 1822, the Bhils revolted under a chief named Hiria (Hiriya). Col. Robinson, who was deputed to crush the uprising, set their huts on fire and mercilessly killed all the Bhils he managed to capture. Hiria was compelled to live and die in exile.[7]

Briggs eventually reached an agreement with Gumani. The chief's band of 230 Bhils controlled Sendhwa Pass, the main route of trade between Khandesh and Malva. Briggs held up supplies through this route in order to pressure Gumani. But even after an agreement was reached, Gumani continued his depredations. His constant defiance of the agreement with Briggs caused him to remain an irritant to the British administration for several years. Briggs then launched a military campaign in the mountainous areas of the north and south with the help of some villagers and arrested Gumani, along with about 200 of his band. They were sent to Thane Jail. But the Company's court of directors at Bombay held the arrest of the Bhils without any specific charge to be a contravention of law. After Briggs was relieved of his charge in Khandesh and posted to Satara, the arrested Bhils were released. Upon release, they returned to the forests of Khandesh and slaughtered the villagers suspected of cooperation with Briggs.[8] The other tactics that Briggs had employed were to stop the supply of food grains from the plains, and to attack the hills which the Bhil chiefs had evacuated. Thus, the policy of brute force and violence used by Briggs to bring the Bhils under British control was a complete failure.

Nevertheless, by the second year of British administration, British soldiers, through their enterprise, had either arrested or killed several Bhil chiefs. Although the chiefs who survived were out of the British Army's reach, they had no security of life or property owing to the army's presence. An announcement was made assuring the Bhils that those who returned to their villages in the plains would be pardoned for earlier crimes and provided food—but not a single Bhil took the bait. In addition, information from the villages, where Bhils had been chowkidars, had also dried up. As the Bhils were the only reliable repositories of knowledge about Khandesh, running the administration without their support was impossible. At the time, the province had no full-fledged police system. News of dacoities, murders and burglaries trickled in every single day. There were about 100 complaints of the kind in just one month in the district of Nandurbar alone. The British attempted to use the hereditary chiefs of Turvi Bhils as army nayaks, but the experiment failed. Briggs had tried another tactic by sanctioning several marauding Bhil chiefs a pension, including some grain. But this too failed and ultimately, the British had to resort to military action. Soldiers were sent to guard the passes but soon had to be recalled—malaria had claimed two-thirds of the army. In view of this impasse, hereditary Bhil chiefs were once again entrusted with the responsibility of the passes, and their allowances were doubled. But this step, too, brought no improvement. Consequently, the four experiments made in four years were all resounding failures.

Col. Archibald Robertson, who succeeded Briggs, followed a more lenient policy by opening negotiations with the Bhils. The court of directors also favoured the policy of fraternisation—and it proved successful. Elphinstone, too, was hopeful that the personal influence of British officers would mould the Bhils into a disciplined army, or into peace-loving cultivators, and would prove far more useful than granting revenue-free lands or pensions to their chiefs. These new policies subsequently brought the desired results for Lt. James Outram and Maj. Owens, as reported in an article in the *Atlas* (hereafter *A*) on 9 March 1861.[9]

Accordingly, Elphinstone advised British officials to familiarise themselves with the habits, customs, etc., of the Bhils, in order to win them over, and to eventually employ them. Two Bhil agents (BA) were employed in Khandesh in Briggs' tenure—one each for the south and the west. These agents strove to bring the Bhils to cultivation by providing them with land and bullocks. Besides, several Bhils were temporarily deputed as armed guards at outlying posts. Robertson, appointed the first collector of Khandesh in 1824, was ordered by the court of directors in 1825 to organise a Bhil Corps in order to implement the policy of appeasement. Robertson also advised amnesty for some chiefs, and the grant of *taqavi* loans for agricultural operations, to which the Bombay Government conceded. On 22 April 1825, he selected 22-year-old James Outram, then an assistant in the 23rd Bombay Native Regiment, as PA, Khandesh. Outram was to discharge the task of organising a Bhil Corps. His brief was to select Bhils from various parts of Khandesh such that Bhils from any single area did not predominate. They were to be paid in grain; cash payment was allowed only on specific occasions.

As part of the Company's policy, which had realised at some cost that the Bhils of Khandesh were not easily controlled, diplomacy was deemed essential. Accordingly, in 1825, Khandesh was divided into three agencies. The first, Kukarmunda Agency, comprising the Mutwa Bhils included the chiefs of Nandurbar, Sultanpur, Pimpalner and Dhang. Bhils of the Ajanta range and its valley were included in the South Agency. Bhils of the Satpura range were included in the North-East Agency. Each agency was commanded by a British officer, who exercised legislative as well as administrative rights. Next, border posts were established in the hills, with individuals deputed from every agency. The third agency was entrusted with the task of adding numbers to the Bhil Corps, with Dharangaon as its headquarters.[10]

After effecting the said divisions, officials were issued the following instructions. The agents or employees deployed at various districts were to maintain peace and order in their jurisdictions and mediate between the Bhils and the government. They were to dispose of any complaints, monitor the chiefs' sanctioned pensions, apprehend criminals, punish them as per tribal customs, and keep the rebels in check, thereby minimising military expeditions. They were to register Bhils, keep an account of their livelihood, allot them fallow land and persuade them to live in colonies with certain restrictions. Another task was to prevent the formations of crowds and from gathering in a *hatti*. If the behaviour of certain chiefs was in question, their security or the revenue-free lands and livestock granted would be withdrawn. The officials were to motivate the village *patel*s for desired outcomes. An agent was required to keep an account of all Bhils in his area, monitor any rebels, and realise tax dues. Bhil panchayats were to be allowed in an agent's presence but dissuaded from pronouncing such punishments as imprisonment. Cooperative Bhils were not to be harassed, continued the article in *A*.

The Bhil soldier's salary was fixed at Rs 5 per month; duty away from headquarters attracted additional allowances. The government would provide them with uniforms and light infantry guns. Initially, not much work was expected from the new recruits. Discipline was first instilled so that, rid of their wayward habits, they could undertake onerous duties in the future. Attention was paid to their attire. Minor lapses were ignored; they were dismissed from service only for serious offences. By and large, the attempt was to adapt Bhil chiefs who followed traditional penal codes to European standards of discipline and teach them to become disciplined soldiers under British officers. They were to continue working as village police to strengthen law and order. Finally, as reported in *A*, the Bhils, now disciplined as the Bhil Corps, were used to enforce law and order in Bhil territories, thereby reducing the need for military expeditions.[11]

The third agency, led by Outram, was entrusted with the task of organising the Bhil Corps, assisted by a troop of the Bhil Infantry, with commissioned as well as non-commissioned officers. Khandesh was indisputably a challenge, but one to which Elphinstone had little doubt that Outram would rise. Outram soon realised that Bhil raids took place under chiefs who held sway in those areas. Consequently, he employed harsh measures to eliminate certain chiefs, thereby compelling the Bhils to respect British authority. Once he received cooperation from Bhil troops, he began to negotiate with the community, occasionally even going unarmed to live amongst them. If the community was known to be one of good hunters, Outram, too, was no less of a crack shot, thus earning him their reverence. After he had earned the faith of his corps, it was easy to fulfil his aims, as the corps diligently followed every order issued by him.

To start with, Outram had selected nine notorious Bhil chiefs to organise his Bhil Corps. The influence of those nine chiefs made it easy to recruit other Bhils to the corps, for which the chiefs also toured the province. The recruited Bhils were welcomed by the 23rd Regiment Camp of Bombay Native Infantry (NI) in Malegaon. While the Bhil Corps had merely 25 members on 1 July 1825, it numbered 62 in August and 92 by September. Outram also began to use younger Bhils in the corps, with the older tribals deputed as guards. They were first given swords and later armed with European weapons. By 1826, his corps numbered more than 600 sturdy Bhils, a capable troop which could be sent anywhere in the country.

It was Outram's personal charisma which was responsible for winning over the savage tribals of Khandesh in such a brief period. An article carried in *S* on 9 September 1880 noted that he wore a semi-divine halo for the Bhils of Khandesh and that he would always be remembered. His former sepoys frequently reminisced about their 'Outram Sahib' long after he was gone.[12] Outram's statue in Kolkata is a reminder of his contribution to the British cause.

The identical British policy may be observed in Salwa Judum. In other words, the British policy to equip Bhils with arms in order to suppress and control the community as a whole lived on in independent India as the means for the suppression of Adivasis.

The government pardoned the offenders who had surrendered and allotted them revenue-free fallow land for 20 years. Wherever any Bhil chief expressed a desire to lead a settled existence, the agents provided funds as well as agricultural implements and livestock. They were expected to take to cultivation after giving up plunder. But this help was not without strings—it was an advance of sorts, which was realised from agricultural produce. Meant to bring peace to Bhil territories, this strategy produced some beneficial results. Bhils settled peacefully in certain areas. By and by, as they began to have faith in the government, some of the rebels joined the Bhil Corps. Thus, Outram managed to draw the Bhils into the mainstream, forged close ties with them and won their confidence.

The Marathas, too, had wanted to exterminate the rebellious Bhils. In 1804, Balaji Lakshman had lured the Bhils to Kopargaon where his army, lying in ambush, had slaughtered them. Bhil children were stoned to death. This massacre, perpetrated by deceit, enraged the tribals. Outram later wrote that when 10 years earlier the Bhils had come to Dharangaon *kachahri* (court) to surrender, they were mercilessly slaughtered. Bhils were similarly massacred in Chalisgaon and Antur. The result was that Outram could mobilise very few Bhil youth for the Malligam camp.[13]

Utility of the Khandesh Bhil Corps
As the Bhil Corps had proved its utility, its numbers were swiftly increased. Its strength had reached 600 by the monsoon of 1827. All the tents and huts at Dharangaon, the Bhil Corps headquarters, had been occupied. The Bhils' loyalty developed as officers praised their jawans and treated them empathetically.

The Government of Bombay had not, however, specified the strength of the Khandesh Bhil Corps. The collector of Khandesh had suggested a corps of 400 jawans, with an increase in numbers as required. Outram had raised a corps of 600, without any specific order, and then further raised it to 700 in 1835. Its strength was further increased to 763 in 1842, and to 1,160 around 1850. Of these, 1,072 were Bhils, while the rest were foreigners or non-Bhils.

In 1827, before the monsoon set in, the brigadier of the East district held a four-day parade of the Bhil Corps. Here, an assessment was made of their military attire and other functions. Surprisingly, a marked improvement was noticed in these aspects in a remarkably short time in a community which had thus far been deemed savage and uncivilised. The Bhils deputed at sensitive frontier posts were summoned to the camp so that they, too, could be trained. Through the village chiefs, they were made to sign an agreement pardoning prior offences if they remained disciplined, practised cultivation with the assistance received as *taqavi*, and committed no new crimes. However, if they went back on their word or the agreement, they were to be punished for their past as well as recent crimes—a strategy that yielded good dividends. Chiefs were also paid regularly and only some violated the agreement.

Some *patel*s were allowed to cultivate revenue-free land, decided as a proportion of total village revenue. Thus, in villages, rebellious Bhils following the example set by the *patels* very soon became obedient peasants. In another three years, the remaining rebellious Bhils on the eastern borders of Satpura and Ajanta were settled in the southern parts of the province. A register was instituted for all Bhils. Every nayak and *tagla* was made to sign an agreement with regard to their rights, with all of them being paid adequately as an inducement to abide by the law. A darogha was appointed in every taluka to determine whether Bhils were in fact engaged in agriculture, agents toured the districts on inspection, and wayside robberies registered a decline.

Expected improvements and well-being were noticed within five years of the formation of the Bhil Corps, which was now a disciplined force. However, the creation of merely two corps for the southern province's several Bhil colonies failed to service such a sprawling region. But the jawans of Bhil Corps proved highly useful in adverse circumstances, fighting against internal as well as external threats. The corps was deployed in Gujarat as well, where their brethren were still creating disturbances. No less surprising was the reality that the corps, merely 800 strong, was now responsible for law and order in Khandesh, which was about a third of England in terms of area. The creation of the Bhil Corps was economically effective; its expenditure was minuscule as compared to the heavy expenses entailed by the salaries of British officers and soldiers, and the maintenance of their horses and large numbers of servants.[14] Outram's policies, thus, proved highly productive.

Despite his limited experience, Outram successfully discharged the onerous responsibility of subjugating Khandesh. He served as commander of the Khandesh Bhil Corps from 1825 to 1835 and was promoted as captain on 7 October 1832. In the north-east, Bhils of Adawad were in revolt in 1831, but Outram crushed the rebels in Sauda and Yawal. He arrested 469 suspects; 158 of them were tried and punished. An article in *S* on 9 September 1880 informed readers that during his tenure in Khandesh, Outram had killed 190 tigers, 25 bears, 12 wild bullocks and 15 panthers.[15]

Around 1827, rehabilitation of Bhils on the eastern border of Jamner was started by an engagement with agriculture. A Bhil Agency was formed in Kukarmunda as well but disbanded the same year. The Bhils appointed to the agency were brought under the second assistant collector and were used to maintain law and order in the western districts.

On the pattern of the Khandesh Bhil Corps, a Malva Bhil Corps was formed in 1837, under Capt. Stockley, with its headquarters in Bhopawar.[16]

4
BHIL REVOLT AND ITS LEADERS IN KHANDESH AND CENTRAL INDIA

The period from the beginning of the 19th century to the first quarter of the 20th century will be remembered as one of Bhil revolts in Central India, when Bhils were subjected to inhuman atrocities, and merits study. As a humanitarian aspect of history, such studies contribute to the creation of an exploitation-free society. Yet, very little has been done in this regard—the sad fact is that we belong to a caste-ridden and discriminatory race. History is still to make an adequate evaluation of the struggles endured and the leadership and sacrifices by the Dalit, the tribal, the impoverished peasant and other marginalised groups. Every act of these peoples, their struggles or successes, is regarded as something of secondary importance. Their histories, although golden and revolutionary, are relegated to the shadows, while traitors are unashamedly glorified as heroes.

The history of Khandesh, its social structure and its Bhil revolts can do much to expose the elitist, upper-class nature of Indian society and its caste-ridden mentality, which refuses to confer marginalised societies with equality. That the British were the only rulers to subject the Bhils to barbaric treatment is by no means accurate. Rajputs of the region were known to resort to far more cruel and inhuman behaviour vis-à-vis the tribals. British policy in Khandesh was motivated by economic interest by providing the Bhils with a degree of education and employment. The Bhil Corps was constituted in a move to strengthen their own hegemony. While local Rajput chiefs took pride in the fact that they were anointed with Bhil blood, there is no comprehensive account of the number of Bhils killed by Rajput princes or even by the British. The predominant refrain in historical accounts is that the Bhils were a barbaric, murderous, plundering people no better than wild animals. Whatever biases the British might have displayed, they did make studies, to an extent, of the deep-rooted causes which turned the Bhils rebellious. Except for the Mughals, the rulers of the region without exception drained the natural resources of Khandesh and deprived the Bhils of their means of livelihood. They exploited the water, land and forests belonging to the tribals and mercilessly slaughtered those who resisted.

In the very period when Indian princes were prostrating themselves before the British, Bhils, loathed as a dark and ugly race, were subjecting the British to stiff resistance. There are very few instances of a people sustaining their rebellion for almost a century and a quarter. They remained rebellious even when the Company, and later the British Crown, deployed powerful armies and used modern weapons against them. An analysis of the reasons for the plunder and murder committed by Bhils is essential to an understanding of revolts by the Bhils.[1]

In 1802–03, when the Company had not yet subjugated Central India, the region suffered a devastating famine in which large numbers of Bhils began to die of starvation. The appalling situation demanded immediate relief action from the then-existing principalities, which was not forthcoming—instead, the Marathas continued to plunder Khandesh. This Maratha attitude turned the Bhils increasingly violent. Every outsider was now an enemy—it was a question of life and death. They began to loot the wayfarers and traders passing through their territories in order to survive. Led by Bhil chiefs, this aboriginal community continued to fight even in the face of death. If a Bhil rebel died, another took his place. They committed crimes and then took to the hills. After Central India was subjugated by the Bombay Presidency, Bhils who were arrested were sent first to Bombay, and then to Malwan, Sindhu Durg, Ahmedabad, Anjar and Pen. Many died during these journeys. In 1823, according to J.G. Hancock, who was in charge of Bhil prisoners, three Bhil prisoners died while en route from Bombay to Sindhu Durg. In the same year, Chief Secretary W. Newham reported that 172 of the 238 Bhil prisoners sent from Khandesh had died en route. It was on account of the inhuman treatment meted out to them that several arrested Bhils broke free and absconded. On reaching their forests, they took up arms against the British.[2]

In India's history, the importance of the Bhil revolt in Central India and in Khandesh, in particular, cannot be emphasised enough. While it was a prosperous and content region in the Mughal period, it was subjected to all-round exploitation by the Marathas, Rajputs and the Nizam. When the British arrived, the indigenous principalities, with their cowardice, mutual envy and infighting, did not put up any determined resistance; rather, they succumbed one by one to British suzerainty. But for more than a century, the Bhils, with their guerilla tactics, continued to rain down their arrows and wield their swords against the British, who for all their superior armaments and mighty state power, fought a protracted, frustrating and often futile battle against them. The Bhil revolt was not just against colonial encroachment of their land, forest and culture; it was also against feudal lords. Their sacrifices were no less during the 1857 War of Independence. While the Bhil Corps were fighting for the British, other Bhils fought against the latter at numerous places. As for the various Bhil Corps, they rendered much help to the British in 1857.

Revolt of 1804 and the Peshwa's Misdemeanour
Till 1802, the Bhils had been leading a peaceful life along with other local inhabitants of the region. They were employed as village watchmen and extended much help to the police. Bhils living in bands moved into the forests during periods of famine and drought and returned to the plains when the situation improved. But the famine-stricken Bhils turned

rebellious in the face of the Maratha Peshwas' atrocities against them.³

The Bhils had built a very sturdy organisation. According to the British, they were reportedly so strong that most weapons proved ineffective against them. But Khandesh could not escape outside interference in the course of time—many powers had cast their eye upon the region. The Battle of Assaye on 23 September 1803 had debilitated the Scindias and the king of Nagpur. The Company now had a foothold in Khandesh. They defeated the Scindias at Burhanpur and Asirgarh on 21 October 1803 and forced the latter to sign the Treaty of Adgaon on 28 November 1803.⁴

To subdue the insurgent Bhils, Peshwa Bajirao appointed Balaji Sakharam Lakshman as the *sarsubedar* (governor) of Khandesh and Baglan and sanctioned him with authority to act with impunity against the Bhils. Egged on by one of his captains, Manohar Gosavi, Lakshman summoned a large meeting of Bhils at Kopargaon (Ahmednagar) on the banks of the Godavari, took them prisoner by deception and had them dumped in a well. The memory of this treachery of the highest magnitude was held by the Bhils for more than a century. The Bhils of Chandore range, too, were exterminated. In retaliation, in 1804, Chandore Bhils of Kopargaon encircled Lakshman and mercilessly slaughtered his army. In 1806, to avenge the aforementioned killings, the Marathas ordered Triayambak Dengle (or Dengalia) to organise a massacre of Bhils. Dengle was then in charge of the district. He slaughtered the Bhils at Ghevari–Chandgaon in Shevgaon (Maharashtra). Bhils were also massacred in Chalisgaon, Dharangaon (Maharashtra) and Antur (Maharashtra). Dengle also invited Naroba Patil from Karambha (Solapur) and placed him at the head of an army, which included 5,000–6,000 horsemen. In about 15 months, Naroba Patil slaughtered some 15,000 Bhils in Gangthari, in the Godavari basin. Dengle was hopeful that the tribals would be subdued by these massacres. But the relief proved short-lived—the Bhils revolted once again. Major cultivators and feudal lords of Khandesh were forced to enlist mercenary assistance from the Arabs, who had become moneylenders of the area and had also bettered their status. At the same time, tormented by the indigenous principalities, the Bhils, too, tried to strengthen themselves by forging cordial relations with the Arab merchants. Consequently, Bhil chiefs, Arab merchants and revenue officials began to collect various kinds of taxes from common tribals.

The Pindaris were a visible presence in the armies of Holkar, Scindia and the Nizam during the decline of Mughal rule. They had begun stray forays at the beginning of the 19th century. In the closing days of 1805, about 3,000 Pindaris looted Malkapur, led by Supkaram, who had served in the Holkar Army. A letter from Bombay, dated 20 March 1813, reveals that a large gang of Pindaris, armed with bows and swords, had attacked the entourage of J.F. Stevenson on the night of 3 March 1813. There is a reference to a Bhil king, Bhim Singh, who, supported by the Pune durbar, had captured Wahid Wali Khan Bangash and Dawood Khan in the first week of January 1809, and handed them over to Col. Wallace who was then in hot pursuit. Bhim Singh controlled Devra Ghat at the time. These events were reported in a number of publications—the *Kentish Weekly Post* (or *Canterbury Journal*) on 1 May 1804, *Morning Advertiser* on 22 March 1806, *Calcutta Gazette* on 16 February 1809, *Saunder's Newsletter* on 4 October 1810 and *Star* (London) on 13 December 1813.

In 1816, Dengle, jailed for the murder of Gangadhar Shastri, escaped and began a war against Peshwa Bajirao after enlisting the support of the Bhils of Ahmednagar, Nasik and Khandesh. Gen. Smith was deputed from Shirur to protect the passes in the Chandore range.[5]

In 1816, Pindaris and Bhils formed an alliance in Khandesh. The Pindaris had entered through the Asirgarh Pass in the eastern mountain ranges, guided by Muslim Bhils. On the orders of the governor of Bombay on 16 October 1817, Lord Hastings and Lt. Davies had persuaded the Nizam's Army to drive the Pindaris away.[6] Till then, the Pindaris had been plundering the area, protected by the immunity offered by Bhil chiefs. As reported in the *Bombay Gazette* (hereafter *BG*) on 14 August 1816, Pindari leader Bakhsh plundered Dhulkot in 1816, along with a Bhil chief, and then took refuge in the hills of Berar. The main cause of worry for the British was that their continued presence in Central India would prove to be impossible if local Bhils and Pindaris continued their alliance. Therefore, they left no stone unturned to oust the Pindaris.

No comprehensive accounts of Bhil chiefs in the east exist, but it is known that Juba, a Bhil chief, had repeatedly plundered 16 villages in Nasirabad (Maharashtra).[7] Motivated by self-interest, Dengle incited the Bhils to rebel in 1818, and then again in 1819.[8] He had escaped Capt. Briggs in mid-June 1818, but Briggs continued to pursue him, accompanied by Capt. Swanston's cavalry. Dengle was captured in Ahirgaon (Maharashtra) on 29 June 1818 in possession of gold and silver worth Rs 60,000, ornaments worth Rs 5,000 and four horses. He was incarcerated for life in Chunar Jail.[9]

Nadir Singh Bhil, 1802–1820

There is a reference to a rebel Bhil chief, Nadir Singh, in and around Mhow in November 1818. A report in the *Madras Courier* on 8 December 1818 states that he cooperated in the capture of those who had raided Maj. Gen. John Malcolm's camp.

Nadir Singh, a Bhilala, was the chief of Bhils in the western parts of Mandu, where his family had held the chief's position for centuries. The Mandu governor had sanctioned him special powers to punish the Mankurs—tribal plunderers. By 1802, Nadir Singh had become a notorious rebel of the Vindhya hills. He was allotted four villages in 1805, in the hope that he would bring in some revenue. An agreement on 8 October 1819 stipulated that Nadir Singh would pay Rs 251 within three months, or else he would be evicted from the allotted villages. Nadir Singh had enjoyed the support of Yashwant Rao Holkar but after the latter's demise, his relations with the Holkar kingdom deteriorated. He plundered the plains, leaving desolation in his path. By the time the British arrived in Central India, Nadir Singh had become another name of terror in the southern parts. He commanded 600–700 rebel infantrymen and owned 200 horses at the time Mhow Cantt. was established. In view of his status, the British preferred compromise as the more prudent strategy. Led by his nephew and son, Nadir Singh's men were pressed into the service of the British.[10]

At one time, Nadir Singh had about 2,000 followers and held undisputed sway in Malva for over 15 years. Although the British pardoned him for most of his crimes, there were some which could not be ignored. Malcolm's letter to the Secretary, Sir Charles Metcalfe, on 9 May 1820 reveals that two traders and a Bhil guard had been abducted, hidden in Nadir Singh's house in Sailana for three days, and then mercilessly slaughtered. Malcolm had ordered an enquiry. Nadir Singh was then summoned to Nalcha. Meer Nabi Bakhsh, a subedar of the 14th Regiment, and Maj. Wilson cooperated with Malcolm in the operation to apprehend Nadir Singh. With foresight, Malcolm had gathered about 50 Bhil chiefs from Nalcha and the neighbouring areas and warned them that the army would annihilate all Bhils if the culprit was not apprehended in three days. The chiefs cooperated, and Nadir Singh was found guilty of three murders. He was arrested and sent to Allahabad Jail. Bhiman Singh, his son, then aged 14, was appointed chief in his father's place. Nadir Singh had been receiving a salary of 2,564 Hali rupees per annum from the Holkar kingdom. An agreement on 8 May 1820 stipulated that Bhiman Singh would receive the same amount. Through another agreement, reached on 4 October 1820, Bhiman Singh received the village of Kheri for Rs 150 per annum, as remuneration for the protection of Durjanapur Ghat.[11]

The Peshwas continued to oppose Company rule even after it had established a foothold in Khandesh. On 27 June 1818, the *Royal Gazette* reported that, led by Dengle, about 1,000 Bhils reached Kalyan and Junnar (Maharashtra) from Sangamner, where they created disturbances. The defeated Peshwas had incited the Bhils and Ramosis to cut off the roads and plunder various areas. As it served their own interest, the Bhils cut off the road to Bhora Ghat, which prevented mail from reaching Bombay. Aided by a powerful army, Gen. Smith had the road reopened and deployed an army troop in Ahmednagar for future security. However, Lt. Ennis, an officer of Bombay Engineers, deployed on survey work on the Shirur-Mundhwa road, met an unfortunate end. The road Ennis was working on was cut off as well. He had been advised to return to his station but refused as he had faith in his guards. The Bhils attacked him sometime during the night and led by Dengle, surrounded him in the morning. His jamadar and 25 jawans promptly defected to Dengle's band. Ennis' death was reported in an article carried in the *Evening Mail* on 30 April 1818.

Revolts in 1819-1820

Gumani Nayak

Gumani Nayak controlled the Sendhwa Pass along Malva-Khandesh road, the chief trading route even before the advent of the British, from where he collected taxes for the Holkar kingdom from traders passing through. Customs officials, too, collected customs duty at the pass, part of which was shared with Gumani. On 5 March 1818, Capt. Briggs entered into an agreement with Gumani. The latter accepted Brigg's conditions but did not go to meet the PA. Even though the Company had sanctioned him an annual pension of Rs 2,000, Gumani violated the agreement four times between October 1818 and January 1819 and stole cattle in the village of Chopra. His plea was that Scindia's officials had not given him his dues. Briggs instructed the *mamlatdar* (revenue officer) of Chopra to do so and Gumani was also given the right to maintain a small army, although his annual pension was reduced to Rs 1,200.[12]

With no administrative control in sight, 1819 proved challenging for the British. Equipped with arms, Bhils were committing plunder everywhere. Khundu, Rup Singh, Ram Ji and Auchit, who was once the chowkidar in Turkheda (Gujarat), controlled the western hills. Jardin was particularly harassed by these Bhil chiefs. A letter from Briggs on 1 April 1819 informed Jardin that Ram Ji had promised to abstain from plunder if he was granted a pension. In accordance with an agreement, Ram Ji and Auchit were each sanctioned a monthly pension of Rs 50. Similarly, Phegi Khan, Java (or Jiva Vasava), Dev Ji Nayak, Raillia and Khundu were also granted pensions. However, any attempts to persuade Turvi Bhils to enlist in the police corps were in vain and the British Army marched against the Turvi Bhils of Kanai. Jardin conducted a military operation against Kama.[13]

Cheel Nayak

Cheel Nayak, chief of the Satmala Bhils in the south, raided Dharangaon towards the end of January 1819. To British officials investigating the incident, his excuse was that he had received merely Rs 175 instead of his annual entitlement of Rs 648.

> It is necessary to tell you that I was not getting my dues from the villages which I raided. We'll give up raids if you ensure our rights. First you ensure our dues and, if we then commit any plunder, you do summon us. By not making any arrangement for our livelihood and leaving us dependent on grass and leaves, you have left no other alternative before us.[14]

However, Briggs, refusing to concede to Cheel Nayak's demands, ordered the army to apprehend him—the chief had no option but to surrender. He was arrested at the beginning of June 1819, imprisoned and later hanged to death.[15]

Dashrath Bhil and Kaniya Bhil

Muslim Bhils of Meer Khan and Adawad controlled the eastern regions. In Rawer (Maharashtra), Kaniya Bhil received assistance from Dashrath and Dhan Ji, chiefs of Lasur in Maharashtra. Around 1820, Dashrath revolted against the Company, with support from Pindari chief Sheikh Dulla. These chiefs had devastated the fertile lands between the Tapi and Satpura by their raids. Along with about 1,200 Bhils, Jandhola, Jukaria and Mohan surrendered before Maj. Morin. Yet, negotiating Sendhwa Pass was still impossible. The Bhils attacked Nawapur. Pal Ji Deshmukh was captured and killed. Along with about 400 Bhils, Kur Vasava of Sagwara plundered Nawapur and Kukarmunda, and then escaped. Morin managed to crush them and forced the chiefs of the south to surrender.[16]

Kaniya Bhil, a powerful chief in the eastern part of the Satpura range, had rebelled when he was denied his dues. In 1818, his band comprised 650 Bhil warriors and Sebandis. Briggs ordered a settlement, but Kaniya ignored all British proposals and continued his plunder. This episode brought Briggs to the realisation that mere settlements with Bhil chiefs would not suffice. He wrote to his superior officers suggesting direct action as the only viable alternative. Thus, Khandesh was in utter disarray when Briggs was posted out in 1823.[17]

From Aurangabad, a *risala* (troop of cavalry) was sent on 24 November 1819, led by Capt. Davis, to secure the valleys and passes of Khandesh. A battalion was summoned from Kopargaon as well. Both troops launched joint attacks on Bhil *hatti*s but found not a single soul. The troops subjected the tribals to a blockade to starve them into surrender. There was no let-up in chaos in 1821 either—military operations were simply not yielding any results. The villages around Parola were disturbed. Some 12.4 mil. (20 km) from Dhule, Parola was a prosperous town of weavers where a fatal attack was made on Briggs, whose death was reported in *BG* on 22 December 1819.[18]

Hiria Bhil, 1822

In 1822, after a lull of some months, three gangs began plundering the prosperous plains of Bhadgaon and Erandol, involving the Nahal Bhils of Satpura as well as bands led by Hiria Bhil and Saibu. Briggs did his best to curb them but to no avail. Anarchy prevailed in the region when Briggs was posted out.[19]

At the beginning of 1822, a British troop halted at Neemuch near the Madhya Pradesh–Rajasthan border. Despite constant raids by Bhils in the forest areas, Lt. Hepburn set out with his troops and walked overnight to reach a Bhil stronghold. The army encircled the Bhils after taking stock of the situation, and the Bhil chief was killed after a fierce battle in which some jawans of the British Army also lost their lives. Most of the Bhils were taken prisoner. In April 1823, Col. Robinson managed to oust the Bhils and destroy their habitations.

When the collector of Khandesh took charge, the Nahals of Satpura and Bhils of Ankush, Bhadgaon and Erandol were plundering the area. Rusola had been captured and Punia was killed. Although the massacre of captured Bhils continued over the next two years, new chiefs rose to replace those killed. Sahib Khan had joined hands with the Bhil rebels. While Anand, a Bhil chief, had been captured, Gumani was still at large. But Rup Singh, Yashwant Singh and his brother had been captured. Gumani, too, was apprehended at last and jailed. An article carried in the *Hereford Journal* on 30 January 1822 stated that the army continued its patrols under Maj. Deschamp.[20]

Revolt in Bari, 1824

On 14 December 1824 in Bari, a small Bhil village in Alirajpur, Bhils clashed with mounted police of the Fifth Regiment near Local House, an opium farm established by the British Government near Ujjain. It was believed that opium was being supplied from Ujjain to the port of Trankal in Gujarat. The first tranche was dispatched on 28 October 1824, with an escort to secure the route. A letter written from Bhopawar by Maj. I. Gough, commanding officer (CO) of the Fifth Regiment's Local House, informed the local agent Capt. Spears on 16 December 1824 that Naib Risaldar Mirza Azim Beg was on escort duty along with mounted police, and the party was returning from Trankal Port after delivering the opium. Harassed by the shortage of fodder and high grain prices, they had decided to take a shorter route. The naib risaldar had contacted the local administration for military help, which was denied. On the morning of 14 December, they reached Bari from Rajpur via Jobat. They were scheduled to reach the town of Kanas on the same day through a mountain track that passed through a forest that would shorten the journey by seven *kos*. From Bari, they hoped to hire a guide to lead them through the forest. Spears had already deputed two policemen in Bari, whom the risaldar could easily have used as guides. Unfortunately, there followed an altercation between Omkar Rawat, the *patel* of Bari, and the risaldar, when the latter demanded a guide. When the villagers saw their chief being subjected to insult, they used the war drum to summon their fellow Bhils. At the drumbeat, a large crowd gathered and began to rain down arrows, resulting in the death of the jamadar and dafadar. As soon as the *patel* was freed, the Bhils halted their attack. The risaldar and his party retreated to Rajpur, but Bhils from several villages had by then gathered in the hills and blocked the Bari–Kanas route. Subsequently, a battalion arrived from Rampura to defuse the situation.

The episode was thoroughly investigated and Spears' report was sent to G. Wellesley, resident (Res.), Indore, via a letter on 27 December 1824. For the investigation, the captain went to Bhopawar on 21 December, where he was met by the king of Alirajpur, accompanied by Omkar Rawat and his brother, Rao Singh Rawat. Spears also recorded the statements of Hira Singh, Ram Bakhsh Singh and Puran Singh, sepoys of the Sixth Local Battalion in Rampura. On the basis of their statements, Spears concluded that the behaviour of the risaldar and his troops was unjustified. As two policemen had already been deputed at Bari, the risaldar ought to have sought their help. He had no right to humiliate and arrest the *patel*. After submitting his report, Spears sought instructions from Wellesley. In order to save English honour, Wellesley imposed a fine of Rs 200 on the villagers of Bari, which was distributed to the families of the dead jawans for their last rites. No further action was taken against the *patel* and Bhils of Bari.[21]

Revolt by Shivram Nayak, Re Singh Nayak, Govind Mang and Other Bhil Chiefs in Baglan: Historic War at Mulher Fort (Nasik, Maharashtra), 1825

The Baglan revolt was led by Goda Ji Dengle, a relative of Triayambak Dengle. On 1 April 1825, the *mamlatdar* of Baglan sent a letter to A. Robertson, collector of Dhule, along with a letter received from the *mamlatdar* of Lohaner.

> Just today, news came from Mulher that some 25 Bhils have gathered in the valley below the fort, and that Bhils are still coming in from all directions. This poses a great risk to the villagers of Mulher and surrounding villages. I have sent 10 men and a Jamadar to Mulher, but it is impossible for 20 or 25 persons to face a huge Bhil crowd. Our taluka has no horseman or *sebandi* (local guard). I have put 15 men to guard the cash chest. Kindly send 50 persons and horsemen, along with local guards, at once.

On 4 April 1825 from Dhule, Robertson wrote to William Chaplin, Commissioner of the Deccan, at Pune (see Appendix 1 for the letter), apprising him of large Bhil crowds in the villages of the *mamlatdars* of Baglan and Lohaner, based on their letters to him on 1, 2 and 3 April. While the letter of 1 April mentioned 25 Bhils, that of 3 April put the number at 500; they had collected on the western side of the fort. Robertson assured Chaplin that 25 horsemen had been immediately dispatched from Kukarmunda, along with local Bhils, to strengthen the Baglan *mamlatdar*'s position. That such efforts would compel the rebels to flee the fort did not seem improbable but even if they did not, they were likely to be weakened at least in Dang (Gujarat). In response, Robertson instructed the CO, Malegaon, and Capt. Rigby of Kukarmunda, to send to Baglan any forces they could muster to help curb plunder by the Bhils on the other roads.[22]

In 1825, Goda Ji Dengle issued a call for the restoration of Maratha rule in West Khandesh, with support from the Bhils of Baglan, whom he had already convinced by deceitful means. The misled and manipulated Bhils rose in rebellion against the British Army for the restoration of Maratha rule, notwithstanding the fact that several chiefs involved in the uprising were receiving allowances from the British Government, e.g., Re Singh Nayak and Govind Mand, among others. In March 1825, the revolt assumed horrendous dimensions in the western districts of Khandesh, and its leader Shivram (Sevram) declared that he would incite all of Khandesh. He had produced a counterfeit document before the king of Satara and managed to rally the Bhils of Baglan. With an 800-strong band, Shivram had been plundering the areas near Antapur. He captured Mulher Fort, from where he conducted his insurgency, and unfurled the Peshwa's flag atop the fort to signal the battle for the restoration of the Maratha Confederation's glory. British troops were summoned from Surat, Jalgaon and Ahmednagar to crush this revolt and to defend Jaikheda, the main town of the district of Mulher. The government's treasury, which was only 12 mil. from the rebel stronghold, was swiftly relocated to a safer place. From Malegaon, 200 jawans of the 11th and 23rd Regiments were dispatched, as reported on 6 January 1858 by the *Glasgow Herald* (hereafter *GH*). The manner in which the anti-Bhil proponents of Maratha rule managed to manipulate the Bhils' support for their own devious agenda certainly merits deeper investigation.

On 6 April 1825, a troop led by Outram reached Jaikheda from where the rebel stronghold was barely 35 mil. Outram received intelligence that in numerical terms the enemy was now in an invincible position. After some thought, he prepared to take the fort by surprise and informed Ensigns Whitmore and Paul of the 11th Regiment of his plan. His men moved forward at dusk. Whitmore and Paul were instructed to stage a mock invasion of the fort from the front with 150 jawans. With the remaining 50 jawans, Outram would attack the fort from the rear. Before dawn on 7 April, both contingents had climbed the hill. Rebel strength was difficult to assess in the dark but appeared to be concentrated at the front where Whitmore and Paul were set to stage the mock invasion. Then, without any warning, Outram attacked from the rear—and this assault was a resounding success. Rebel leaders, including Shivram, were killed, and some escaped to the other hills. As there was a very real possibility of the rebels regrouping, the British Army pursued them for almost 50 mil. over the next 36 hours, killing several rebels on the other hills as well. Many were taken prisoner, while others abandoned their weapons and escaped to their villages to eventually engage in cultivation. The Bhil chiefs of Bundi and Sutwa were also at loggerheads with the British.[23]

A letter written on 10 April by the muqaddam of Antapur to the *mamlatdar* of Baglan reveals that Antapur was plundered on the night of 9 April when Bhils had kidnapped Ragghu Ramchandra Pant and his family members as well as a trader. A letter on the same day from the muqaddam of Taharabad to the *mamlatdar* of Baglan also confirms that Bhils had devastated Antapur.[24]

On 2 April, Gopal Narayan, the muqaddam of Lohaner, wrote a letter from Saptshringi to Krishna Ji Nilkanth, the *gomasta deshpande* (record-keeper).[25] Nilkanth wrote back on 13 April. This correspondence reveals that Bhil chief Re Singh Nayak had been sighted, along with 50 Marathas and 400–500 Bhils in Babulan, a small village near Mulher. He had first plundered Antapur, and then moved on to nearby Virgaon, where he had wounded three or four individuals. The band had also beheaded about 300 animals and looted Kanshi, Pimpali and Koradi. At Dhamauri, near Antapur, the rebels had plundered all the stored grain and then proceeded to Mulher Fort, which was commanded by Atta Ji Rao, a sepoy. The correspondence mentions the pensions from the government received by Re Singh Nayak, Govind Mang and other Bhil chiefs.

It is widely believed that Outram, Rigby and Owens followed the policy of persuasion and tact to quell the Bhil rebellion. Outram's efforts brought several Bhils to the British Army, while others preferred the peaceful life of cultivators, having been assured of *taqavi* loans.

Dhur Singh, Dev Chand, Shobhania, Rania, Pandya and Bawa Ji, 1826

Being commercially important, Sendhwa Ghat was perpetually targeted by plundering Bhil chiefs. In 1826, Bhil chiefs Dhur Singh and Shobhania blocked the Sendhwa Ghat route. At about the same time, Bhil bands looted Borgaon and Sultanpur, near Mehkar. One gang of 30 Bhils was led by Dev Chand. The troop dispatched to suppress Dev Chand put him and all other gang members to death near Sultanpur. A troop was sent against Shobhania as well, but his band and he fought back with determination. Later, Rania, a Bhil chief who enjoyed the government's patronage, arrested Shobhania, who was sent to Dhule Jail where he died in captivity. Pandya, another Bhil chief, was captured, while Bawa Ji was murdered. Revolts by the Bhil chiefs of Dang and Lohara continued in 1826.

Lt. Bennet's Murder, 1826

In June 1826, Lt. Bennet, a young officer, was murdered while asleep in his tent at the village of Nawur (or Nur), in Ahmednagar. The Bhil band included a chief who had been arrested earlier at Jalna (Aurangabad district) and had then turned anti-British. This fact came to light when seven members of a gang of 11 were captured in 1829. A beautifully carved knife with an ivory hilt was recovered from one of the band—this British-made knife was one of the objects stolen from Bennet's tent—who confessed to the murder when he was subjected to interrogation. He held that he had been unjustly punished by Canning, the resident commissioner (RC) of Aurangabad and had ever since harboured a visceral dislike of all Europeans. That evening, he had plundered Nawur with his band and spotted a tent on open ground with the young British officer asleep within. He beat Bennet black and blue, which led to the latter's death. The incident was reported in the *London Evening Standard* (hereafter *LES*) on 3 February 1829 and in the *Monmouthshire Merlin* on 3 March 1854.

Khundu and Mahadev, 1827

In 1827, Bhil chiefs Khundu and Mahadev joined hands to form a band near Sendhwa and plundered the village of Borwadi. A small troop of Bhil Corps was sent to fight the raiders. In that intractable mountainous terrain, the Bhil Corps launched an attack against the band. The rebels resisted but when they escaped to the plains, an army troop, led by Outram, gunned them down. The dead included a chief and some of his supporters, and the looted property was recovered. The situation remained relatively peaceful in 1828 and the area witnessed the least cases of plunder in 20 years.[26]

Bhil Chief's Revolt in Dang, 1830

Forest-dwelling Bhils often plundered Dang in 1830. Outram organised a campaign against them with a large contingent that included the Bhil Corps, four NI regiments, some troops of Poona Irregular Horse, and 13 other officers. Within a month, he managed to arrest the Bhil chief of Dang. The latter's supporters escaped to the forest. While the campaign did prove the worth of the Bhil Corps, forest fever (malaria) gripped all the officers. Four of them died, while the others, terrified, left Khandesh—only Outram remained, as reported in *BG* on 13 April 1863.

Hatania, 1833

Hatania's revolt around 1833 was one of great significance. After Outram was promoted to captain, his most important battle was against Hatania. Bhils of the Barwani region, in the Satpura range to the north of Khandesh, had revolted in 1833 and plundered the village of Barwani, led by Hatania. Outram pursued them and arrested Hatania, for which he received much praise from the Bombay Government on 27 June.

Mogir, 1833

The Bhil-occupied regions of Rajasthan and Gujarat adjoined Khandesh. In mid-1833, Mesarabad, in the Neemuch Cantt.

area close to the Rajasthan–MP border, was the site of a horrendous battle between the Bhils and the 37th Regiment of Bengal NI. The latter was commanded by Capt. Henry Bowden-Smith, who was sent to Neemuch in October 1833 when a local opium agent was killed, following a request made by PA Capt. Pasley to Brig. Coming of Neemuch. The killer of the opium agent was Mogir, a Bhil chief, who belonged to Mowah, located in the dense forests and hills of Banswara (Rajasthan).

On 21 October 1833, Bowden-Smith set out from Neemuch, accompanied by 50 jawans of the Bhil Corps and 12 jawans of the Second Local Cavalry. After travelling 36 mil., they reached Pratapgarh from where, at about 8 pm, they set out for the rebel chief's village. Reaching Mogir's hideout at 1 am, on 24 October, they surrounded the village while it was still dark.

Mogir's large band attacked the army and police with arrows. The retaliatory firing ordered by Bowden-Smith killed and injured several villagers. Bowden-Smith and his native subedar urged Mogir to surrender, but he ignored their calls and continued to rain down arrows from his hideout. The battle left Mogir and his brother injured, while a nephew was killed.

The injured Mogir was transported to base camp in a cot carried by his men who had also been captured. But the Bhils were agitated.

When Bowden-Smith was descending a narrow pass, they felled a tree to block the passage, showering arrows from both sides of the hill to free Mogir. The Bhils numbered 1,000, but Smith's party now comprised just 37 individuals. The attack killed three jawans and one sepoy, while 11 sepoys were injured. Bowden-Smith received two arrow shots, one of which was to his head.

Sensing the gravity of the situation, Bowden-Smith set the captured Bhils free, abandoned Mogir and with his jawans still fighting, descended 1.86 mil. in two and a half hours to Pantawal.

When they reached the plains, the cavalry managed to scatter the Bhils. Bowden-Smith estimated about 2,000 Bhils camped on the surrounding hills, where they remained till 3 pm. He then travelled to Pratapgarh via Morin Pass where he was helped by the local chief and reached Neemuch on the evening of 29 October. Bowden-Smith died of his head wound at Neemuch on 2 November.[27] The episode was reported in the *Hampshire Advertiser* on 19 April 1834 and in *LES* on 17 May 1834.

Ahmad Bhil, 1836

The Mhow area continued to be plagued by the Bhil rebellion at the beginning of 1836. By then, Arabs had joined hands with the Bhils. From Mhow, a troop with two officers, 30 army personnel and 12 sepoys was dispatched to crush the uprising. The army raid killed Ahmad, the Muslim Bhil chief. One British officer suffered injuries, as reported on 8 October 1836 by the *Naval Military Gazette and Weekly Chronicle of the United Services*.

Revolts in Dang, Pimpalner and Sultanpur, 1840

The district of Dang, now in Gujarat, was then administered from Khandesh. It was a predominantly Adivasi area, ruled by chiefs of Bhil tribes in British India. Pratap Singh, the chief of Amli, mutinied against the British in 1840, ordering his Bhils to plunder villages under British control. This open revolt infuriated officials, and the magistrate sent him a summons. But when Pratap Singh refused to respond, the British had little choice but to summon the Bhil Corps and cavaliers from Dharangaon, more than 60 mil. away. The army unearthed the chief's hideout and arrested him along with his family and other Bhil rebels, besides confiscating their weapons.

In 1841, a large number of Ahmednagar Bhils plundered the government treasury at Pimpalner. The Bhil Corps sent to subdue the rebels met with partial success. The corps pursued the rebels and took some prisoners, while others managed to escape.

Bhamania, a Bhil chief, rebelled near Sultanpur in 1841 and raided a village. The Bhil Corps was sent to arrest him and he was shot dead in an encounter with the Bhil agent on the banks of the Narmada. His men were arrested and sent to Dhule Jail.

Bikarai and Bangchund, 1842

Turvi Bhils plundered Sawda (Sawhda) and Yawal in 1842. They were led by Bhil chiefs Bikarai and Bangchund. They fought valiantly against the British, but Bangchund was killed, while Bikarai was arrested.

Revolts by Mamlatdars of Various Forts, 1844

Lal Ji Sakharam, 1844

The Company and Scindia, at loggerheads over certain territory in Khandesh, entered into a treaty at Gwalior in 1844, which returned Yawal, Chopra, Pachora and Lohara to the British. Yet, tensions persisted and the *mamlatdar* of Yawal fortress, Lal Ji Sakharam (Lala Bhau), refused to surrender. He deployed his employees and a 300-strong army, mostly Bhils, to defend the fortress. Bell, the collector, sent troops from Asirgarh and Malegaon as well as the Bhil Corps under Capt. Morris. The army reached Sakli and Bhalod, on the two sides of Yawal, and camped there. Sakharam surrendered the fortress in April 1844, only when an officer of Scindia brought him information about a proposed treaty. The British had to face similar challenges in Lohara and Pachora. The Western Bhil Agency was re-established in view of the Bhil Corps' usefulness. Houses for Bhil jawans were constructed in Nandurbar.[28]

Penchund, 1846

On 9 May 1846, intelligence received from Mhow indicated that the Bhils of Malva had revolted. Murder, loot and arson ruled the region. A few months earlier, the Bhil chief Penchund had been involved in an encounter with a 20-strong troop led by the subedar major of the Malva Bhil Corps. Bhil revolts had spread in all directions in the preceding few years ever since the 5th Irregular—the Red Coats—had been withdrawn. To teach Penchund a lesson,

BA Lt. Evans and 150 jawans of the Bhil Corps, accompanied by the 5th Irregular, raided the chief's village near Dhar on 7 May 1846. A dafadar, several army personnel and six Bhils were killed in the fierce skirmish that followed. Risaldar Sahib Ali Khan's performance in the battle was disappointing. On 25 June 1846, the *London Daily News* reported that this first field test of the Bhil Corps, in the opinion of British officials, had proved unsatisfactory.[29]

Kunwar Jiva Vasava, 1846

In 1818, the Mehvasi Bhil chief, Vasava, ruled Chikhli (Maharashtra), before the advent of the British in Khandesh. According to Capt. Briggs, Vasava's forefathers were chiefs from the hills. They owned lands and firewood forests in the Rajpipla hills, where the family commanded 84 villages. Several zamindars were their subordinates and traders passing their way paid them taxes. Briggs invited Kunwar Jiva, Vasava's son, to join the Company's service. As the most important Bhil chief in the Chikhli area, Briggs had authorised him to collect taxes and to maintain a small contingent of 11 horsemen and 40 infantrymen. He was sanctioned a pension of Rs 3,000 every year. But a Bhil agent's interference in Kunwar Jiva Vasava's jurisdiction provoked his revolt against the British in 1846. Infuriated, the British withheld his pension. An army was dispatched to subdue him and a bloody skirmish followed. Several jawans were killed on both sides, but Jiva was eventually captured and sentenced to 10 years rigorous imprisonment (RI). His son,

Ram Singh, and nephew, Son Ji, were also arrested and later sent to Pune to be educated.[30] In 1854, Kunwar Jiva's throne passed on to Ram Singh, who proved incapable. Although the latter's pension continued, he was divested of the right to maintain a cavalry and infantry.

When the British observed that Bhils following Islam were far more rebellious, they fanned Hindu–Muslim discord in Khandesh. There were riots in Burhanpur in 1849. Attempts were made to divide the Bhils along communal lines.[31]

Revolt against Land Survey in Jalgaon, December 1852

The Bhils were not born robbers, or looters, or violent. The *Halifax Courier* (hereafter *HC*) on 22 January 1853 proffered its candid opinion in an article on changes in the behaviour of Khandesh Bhils. It held that the farmers of Khandesh were unable to grasp the Company's plans to implement the new revenue arrangement and fixed rate of taxation. Moneylenders, whose prosperity depended on farmer loans, were threatened. Those with land believed they would have to pay more taxes after settlement, leaving both moneylenders and Bhil landowners agitated.

The measurement of agricultural fields began in 1852. When a team led by Revenue Commissioner Davison began to fix slabs in fields as demarcation, the peasants of Sawda, Rawer and Chopra reacted violently. A troop was sent to assist Davison, but Bhil resistance was so forceful that the government had to temporarily postpone the land survey.

Davison set up camp in Rangaon, on the banks of the Tapi, 5 mil. from Sawda. A few days later, the survey was restarted with the army's help. But thousands of peasants surrounded the tents put up by the survey team, raised slogans and grew restive. While British officials beat a hasty retreat, local officials, including the *mamlatdar* and *mahalkari* (revenue official), tried to reason with the peasants but were attacked.

On receiving this intelligence, Mansfield, the collector headquartered at Dharangaon, ordered Maj. Morris, along with the Bhil Corps, to the spot to ensure the implementation of the government's order at any cost. Unmoved, the peasants of Erandol refused to provide their bullock carts to the army. The *mamlatdar*'s messengers were held up and a subedar major was held captive in Erandol. Along with 500 jawans of the 11th and 16th Regiments NI as well as two companies of the Bhil Corps, Morris arrived at Erandol. To break through the cordon put up by peasants and jagirdars, the army occupied the entry point of the town. The jagirdars of the area—viz., Deshmukhs and Deshpandes—were arrested.

A detailed letter about this revolt was written from Dharangaon on 15 December 1852 and published in *HC* on 22 January1853. It stated that the 11th NI had reached its headquarters in Dharangaon on 15 December and was to march to Bodwad on the following day, where it would join forces with an army troop commanded by Morris. But on 8 December 1852, leaving his Dharangaon camp intact, Morris moved out in haste, taking nothing along except his weapons. He had received intelligence of an uprising in Erandol where Bhils had encircled an army troop and also attacked the cavalry. From Bodwad, the combined army marched to battle, with a troop of the Poona Horse in the vanguard, followed by gunners and the 11th Regiment, with the Bhil Corps bringing up the rear. On reaching Erandol, army officers proposed peace and a truce was attempted. The army read out a declaration, which pacified the Bhils, who agreed to return home. However, British officers arrested 32 ringleaders and sent them to Dhule. It was then learnt that Bhils were gathering again at Tornale and more disruptions were anticipated. In view of the Bhil revolt in the entire Jalgaon area, no cartman was prepared to enter Khandesh to transport cotton to Bombay, even though it was the season for cotton harvest.

Although the government had captured Erandol, the peasant revolt continued in Sawda and Faizpur where the rebels had formed parallel governments. Panchayats were formed to look after local administration, revenue collection, and law and order. Maj. Morris and Capt. Wingate reached Faizpur on 15 December 1852, as did Mansfield an hour before dawn on 16 December. They discovered that the rebels had surrounded the whole town, with rebel peasants guarding the entry points. The army arrested the ringleaders, and a troop subsequently marched to Sawda where the leading rebels had taken shelter. They, too, were arrested. Later, they were released on a bond and instructed to return to their villages. To settle the issue,

Mansfield held a durbar at Sawda two days later to convince the landowners of the necessity of the survey.³² Overall, jagirdars and landowners had played a leading role in this rebellion.

The Khandesh peasantry included mainly Bhil and Gujjar tribals, both prone to rebellion. Revolts were rampant in 1853, during Company rule, and in 1858, under the British Crown. After Khandesh came to be controlled by the Company, its wealth was mercilessly exploited.

Revolts against Land Tax, 1853

In January 1853, the peasants of Khandesh revolted against the enhancement of rents by the Company. They hounded the Company's revenue collectors and refused to pay the land tax. In view of the spreading revolt, the Company summoned the army, stationed at all its headquarters, to Khandesh, which included cavalry, infantry and artillery. The army immediately started the work of suppression. On 3 February 1853, a letter published in the *Daily News* (London) (hereafter *DNL*) clearly points to the involvement of about 22,000 peasants in the revolt, a rather large number in view of the population then. It was as if all of Khandesh had risen in rebellion. Titled 'Khandesh Revolt and Indian Agrarian Discontents', the letter may help better understand the peasant revolt in Khandesh. It held that the Khandesh peasant revolt was caused by the unjust land-tax policy of the Company, which was exploiting the peasantry (see Appendix 2 for the text of the letter).

Revolts in 1857

During the countrywide Great Uprising of 1857, princes of Central and Western India, including Khandesh, remained loyal to the British. However, Bhils of the area were in constant conflict with the British and the Bhil Corps. The Marathas and the Bhil Corps proved useful to the British. However, the 1857 Uprising did exert its influence on the Bhils, who did their best to defeat the British through joint efforts. Worthy of mention in this context are the contributions of Kaji Singh, Bhima Nayak, Bhago Ji, Mawasia, Khala Nayak, Dular Singh and Kalu Baba. While Bhago Ji controlled the Satmala range, Kaji Singh held the Satpura hills.[33]

During the Uprising, the Khandesh Bhil Corps was of immense help to the government in subduing the rebellious Bhils of Khandesh. At roughly the same time, yet another battalion of the Bhils was raised but, in view of the Uprising, was kept inactive for three years. It was ultimately transformed into a police unit in 1891.[34]

Bhago Ji's Revolt, 1857; Captain Henry's Murder

Around 1857, when the Bhil revolt was raging in southern Nasik and northern Ahmednagar, around 3,000 rebels were led by Bhago Ji Nayak, who had earlier organised the Bhils in the Nizam's territory. Bhago Ji, formerly a police official, had been tried in 1855 for rioting and preventing police proceedings, and jailed. A year after his release, he left his village, Nandur Shingote (Nasik) in the Sinnar subdivision of Nasik to form a band of 50 Bhils, which included women, and turned a hill on the Pune–Nasik road into his stronghold. Lt. J.W. Henry, SP, reached Nandur Shingote on 4 October 1857. Bhago Ji then engaged in an encounter with Col. T. Thatcher and A.L. Taylor, the inspecting postmaster. Led by Henry, 30 constables and 20 revenue messengers joined the battle with swords.[35]

The encounter on 4 October is of historic importance, as it presents a comprehensive picture of Bhil strength and sway in Central India and the extent of their harassment of the British Army. The SP's death enthused the Bhils and the revolt in Ahmednagar continued throughout October 1857. Pathar Ji Nayak gathered some 100 Bhils in Rahuri, but the deputy collector persuaded them to disperse. Maj. Montgomery (later appointed Lt. Gen.) was now deputed in place of Henry.

On 18 October 1857, Bhago Ji's men engaged in an encounter with Col. Machan of the 26th NI in the hills of Shamsherpur, in Akola. Machan was joined by Lt. Graham, on special police duty. Civil servant F.S. Chapman was wounded. Capt. Nuttall replaced Graham and in an intelligent move, organised a corps of Kolis, traditional enemies of the Bhils. Accordingly, Jav Ji Nayak Bomla, chief of the Bomla community, was appointed chief of the Koli Corps.[36]

When the Bhil revolt was raging around Nasik in 1857, the 26th NI was dispatched to crush it, aided by troops from other stations. A 1,500-strong Bhil contingent had occupied

Sinnar, and another, near Sangamner, was in an invincible position. At Nasik, terrified traders had closed down the markets amidst confusion and disarray. According to the *Poona Observer* (hereafter *PO*), a group of 400 Bhils had plundered the village of Palasner, in Ahmednagar district. On 7 November, they dismantled telegraph wires, blocking mail from Mhow. Along with 800 Bhils, Bhima Nayak occupied a small fortress near Sendhwa Ghat. In view of the grave situation, the army was summoned from Dhule and Palasner. These events were published in the *Morning Post* (hereafter *MP*) on 16 November 1857, the *Dublin Evening Post* on 17 November 1857, and the *North Briton* on 18 November 1857.

Bhima Nayak finds mention in the history of the 1857 Uprising. It is believed that he met Tantya Tope in Nimar and helped him cross the Narmada. As reported in the *Homeward Mail from India, China and the East* (hereafter *HMICE*) on 11 June 1862, Bhima was the guardian of the Sendhwa region and traders or Britishers could not safely pass through without his consent.

Towards the end of 1857, a horrific Bhil uprising took place at Kondhar, which was close to Nandgaon, on the Malegaon road, 12 mil. south-east from the Chandore district headquarters. The Deccan Field Force was summoned from Ahmednagar to Aurangabad. The force marched from Aurangabad on 31 October but was repelled by the Bhils at least twice or even three times. Maj. Montgomery, SP, Ahmednagar, planned military action to clear the route. Lt. Stewart, of the Sixth Infantry Hyderabad (Nizam Infantry), and several other officers were deputed to help, arriving from Bolaram at Aurangabad on the morning of 7 November. In addition, Montgomery's command included jawans of the Fourth Rifle, 19th and 21st NI, and some policemen. By then, the Deccan Field Force had already made three futile attempts to repulse the Bhils, with army jawans killed at every attempt. These incidents find mention in *HMICE* on 29 December 1857, the *Norwich Mercury* on 24 February 1858, and the *Manchester Courier and the Lancashire General* on 27 February 1858.

From Akola on 3 December, Capt. Nuttall, along with 160 infantrymen and 50 horsemen, marched to Sulgana where the Bhils had put up a front. On 6 December, while he was en route, he was informed that Pandu, a thakur, accompanied by some Bhils, had raided the treasury at Traiyambak at the instigation of a local Brahmin. By the time Nuttall reached Sulgana, Bhil rebels had gone into hiding in the hills near Traiyambak. The thakur and the Brahmin were captured after a search. Chapman, who was district in-charge, was convinced that the revolt at Traiyambak was instigated by local Brahmins. The arrested Brahmin was hanged to death the next morning.

On 12 December came the news of a revolt in Pent principality. The village of Harsul had been plundered, some documents destroyed, and a moneylender murdered. At Harsul, Nuttall arrested some of the rebels and then made his way to Pent where Rs 3,000 had been looted from the treasury. Subsequently, the rebels escaped to the hills on the Dharampur border. But a crowd of 1,500 to 2,000 had gathered on the surrounding hills to get those arrested by Nuttall freed. Their strength was further increased when Bhago Ji Nayak and 60 of his men, armed with guns, arrived from the district of Sulgana. By then, Lt. Glasspool had also reached the spot with 30 jawans of the Fourth Rifles.

While some jawans were taken captive by the rebels, Bhauraja, the chief rebel, and 15 of his men could be hanged only after army officers Walkor and Boswell arrived on 19 December. On 20 December, Walkor, Boswell and Nuttall proceeded south with 50 policemen from Ahmedabad. The next day, the rebels were joined by Wasir Hira, and 50 jawans of Poona Horse clashed with 500 rebels. In the encounter, 13 horsemen were killed or injured, three were taken prisoner, and Mahipat Nayak, Bhago Ji Nayak's brother, was killed.

On 20 January 1858, a force dispatched from Hyderabad arrived at Mandwar (Nandgaon). Montgomery arrived as well to support the Deccan Field Force. In the fierce battle that ensued, he was badly injured. A number of his jawans were killed, and he had to beat a hasty retreat. Stewart, too, was seriously injured and died soon after. Thatcher then decided to recall the army. The battle had injured 15 jawans, including Lt. Davidson of the 19th NI, and Lt. Chamberlain. No information is available about Bhil casualties. Soon thereafter, news of another Bhil gathering was received from Kornaur, near Aurangabad.[37]

Bhago Ji Nayak and Bagga Ji, 1858

At the beginning of 1858, a police party, led by Capt. James Fox Pottinger, of the 17th NI, and SP Capt. Arthur attacked Mahadev Dungar, west of Chandore. The army had moved out of the hill fortress at Kopargaon at 2:30 pm but without their tents or bags. Marching for 44 mil., they reached Jategaon via Wagla on the evening of 14 February. Bagga Ji, the *patel* of Wagla, was a supplier of arms to the Bhil chiefs. Arthur took some Bhils captive, who eventually deposed against the Bhil chiefs. Jategaon was some 8 mil. from Wagla and near Mahadev Dungar where Bhago Ji Nayak had put up a defensive shield after carefully selecting the location. It had an escape route to one side, while the hills were closely guarded by his men.

On 15 February, Pottinger discovered the precise location of the rebels and planned joint action. Since the area was forested, they took their time and attacked the Bhils at an opportune moment on 17 February. As the British had attacked after meticulous preparation, some Bhils were killed. Others escaped, leaving their women and children behind. A nayak and three privates were British casualties; Bhago Ji Nayak was still missing. News of these events was carried in the *Yorkshire Gazette* on 20 March 1858, MP on 5 April 1858 and the *North Wales Chronicle* on 10 April 1858.

The Bhils continued to plunder the Bombay–Indore route. On 9 April, the *Montrose, Arbroath and Brechin Review; and Forfar and Kincardineshire Advertiser* published a report on Bhil chief Raja Singh's raid on traders, who were on their way to purchase opium worth Rs 7 lakh. With daring, near Sendhwa Ghat, he searched a train wagon carrying the royal artillery. Although referred to as Raja Singh, he was also known as Khwaja Singh or Kaji Singh.

Battle at Dabakovari, 11 April 1858

A letter from an officer of the Satpura regiment, detailing the battle against the Bhils and other rebels of Khandesh, and their defeat in April 1858, is reproduced below. It was written from Silavad on 15 April 1858 and published in *PO*.

THE RECENT ACTION IN KHANDESH

We have just been favoured with the following letter received from an officer with the Satpoora Field Force, giving an interesting account of their recent victory over the Bheel and other insurgents in Khandesh:

Rilawud, 15th April, 1858—The centre column of the Satpoora Field Force, commanded by Major Evans of the 9th Bombay N.I., arrived at Barwanee on the 11th instant, after a most difficult march from Shada. Along the route we found all the villages deserted and most of them burnt to the ground. Wood, grass, and water were in abundance, but everything else we had to take along with us on bullocks. The scenery is very grand; from the valley of the Taptee the country is a mass of magnificent mountains covered with dense jungles intersected with precipitous ravines.

On our arrival at Burwanee the left column under Captain Sealy were ordered off to Dabakowree, and the next morning (the 11th) a combined attack was to be made on the enemy who were in a strong position only six miles due South.

At daylight, each column commenced its march. So much for the plan, and now for the result. Our column (the centre), under Major Evans, duly started, and we were soon in the midst of the strongest passes. I ever scrambled through; fifty of the sort of men we afterwards came across could have closed it against three times our force. When we had gone about three miles, our flanking parties came across some of the enemy's scouts, but they made off over the hills to report our arrival. On coming to a small plain we halted to refresh, when someone called out that the enemy were in force in our front; and sure enough they were occupying the spurs and ridges that intersected a kind of hollow of large extent, and which falls into the Nerbudda.

We were loaded; the Rifles and Bheels were thrown out in skirmishing order, and we pushed on; and very rough work it was. We soon came within shot, and as the enemy seemed inclined to the right, gradually closing in on them; the firing soon got very hot, and it was clear we were gaining on the foe. Many now began to escape by their right flank, and to prevent this Major Evans ordered the troop of Poona Horse round to a small open space where cavalry could act, and they did their duty well.

We had now well got into the thick of it, when to our delight we saw shells from another column hitting on the opposite side of the great ridge up which we were forcing the enemy. We gradually worked up the slope—an awful undertaking it was—what with the excitement, the heat, and the labour of climbing, the thirst was fearful, not a drop of water to be had. On topping the ridge we found Langston's column at the foot of the south side of the ridge, and they met the enemy retreating, and had a great deal of sharp skirmishing. It took us from eight am till three pm before we could entirely subdue the enemy, as they defended the great rocky ridge with wonderful resolution, using the clusters of rocks as so many little forts, resting their matchlocks on them till we got close, and then they made a final stand, sword in hand.

One spot in particular, on the top of a steep crest, gave us much trouble; but after a time Lieutenants Hanson and Sibthorpe, of the 9th Regiment No. 1, and Scott of the Bheel Corps, followed by a party of the 9th N.I., crept up the slope, and made a rush for the rocks: they lost four men in the attempt, but had the satisfaction of killing every man in the place—23 Makranees.

Another very plucky feat was performed by Bassevi of the Artillery. He was a well-dressed fellow, who he thought must be a Chief, and made at him up hills; he came up with him and closed, and they had a regular set-to; Bassevi got a severe cut on each arm, and gave his friend a severe wound on the forehead; they then seized each other and rolled down the hill.

Some of the Golundauze soon rescued Bassevi and shot the fellow, who was a strapping big Makranee.

Dr. Shepherd, you may fancy, had his hands full; he himself was wounded slightly during the engagement. It is too sad sending a force like this with only one medical man. Just imagine what would have been the result if Shepherd had got knocked over! The miserable supply of Doolies was also much felt; but he got litters rigged up of bullocks' packs, and the sepoys themselves acted as Dooly-wallahs for their wounded comrades.

We are now halted here to lay in supplies, and we wait till we hear where the public in general look upon as a contemptible body of naked Bheels, we found at least 3,000 strong, well-armed and very resolute, and principally Makranees and Welaeetees of sorts—a collection of the most desperate villains, who have escaped from Dhar, Mundesore, and other parts of Central India. We counted 170 dead but from the rugged and jungly state of the position, many must have escaped our notice. Of the number killed there were 82 Makranees and Welaeetees of sorts; 18 Siddees; 19 Mussulmans; 58 Bheels, and 11 of unknown caste. We made prisoners of 50 men and 400 women and children.[38]

From a letter published in the *Age* (Melbourne) on 7 January 1858, one may surmise that the British Army suffered great losses on account of the sturdiness of the Makranis and Vilayetis. A news item in the *Derby Mercury* (hereafter *DM*) on 26 May 1858 reported that five jawans had been killed and 36 injured; these included five officers. The horror of the battle is evident in an article carried by the *Inquirer and Commercial News* (Perth) (hereafter *ICN*) on 14 July 1858, which reported that while the Bhils were decisively defeated in this battle, 71 British soldiers were either killed or wounded.

Various newspapers—*Jackson's Oxford Journal* on 22 May 1858, the *Oxford Journal* on 22 May 1858, and *DM* on 26 May 1858—reported variations in the figures of those killed and injured in the battle on 11 April 1858. But their substance is similar—indicating that it was fought against the Bhils in the Satpura range under the command of Maj. Evans. Of the 35 army personnel killed, five were officers—Capt. Briggs, Lt. Basevi, Lt. Blair, Lt. Atkins and Capt. Clarke. The 36 injured included Lts. Lewis, Dartnell, Sewell, Holroyd, Fowler, Laurent, Fox Prendergest, Simpson and Dr Cruickshank. The Bhils had also attacked another army troop at close quarters, leaving 60 killed or injured. Rebel casualties were estimated at 1,100. Briggs's coachman received gunshots in both legs and his horse, too, was injured, reported *ICN* on 14 July 1858.

Putta Ji Nayak

Putta Ji Nayak had been a major nuisance for the Khandesh and Nagpur administrations. The British Government had organised a search for him on a war footing during the 1858 battle, but he proved elusive. A few months hence, he was seen in Bharwuttea. He surrendered unconditionally to the Poona police when both his sons were captured but urged the government to free them. After his surrender, he was incarcerated in Joonere Jail. On 14 July 1858, *ICN* carried Putta Ji's speech to the officer to whom he had surrendered, as follows: 'I'm Putta Ji Nayak, who you could never apprehend. Now I'm giving myself voluntarily. Arrest me and hang me to death as soon as possible but, for God's sake, release both my sons.'

In the last week of May 1858, publications such as *GH* on 28 May, the *Dundee People's Journal* on 29 May, and the *Edinburgh Evening News* on 25 May, among others, reported his surrender as that of a valorous warrior who had given himself into British custody to save the lives of his innocent children.

Raghunath Singh Mandloi and Sitaram Bawa, 1858
At Barud, a hamlet 6.2 mil. west of Khargone, Jagirdar Raghunath Singh Mandloi revolted against the British and Holkar, threatening Bhils who refused to participate with excommunication. When Raghunath was evicted from his jagir, Daulat Singh Mandloi was appointed jagirdar by Holkar. Later, the government created a police post in Barud. However, some 200 cart-owning banjaras, belonging to Nimgul, Valkhad, Nandri and Devdi, continued essential supplies to the insurgents who numbered around 3,000.[39]

On 6 October 1858, Capt. K.H. Keating, political assistant (PA), wrote to Robert Hamilton Burnett, Agent to the Governor General in Central India (AGGCI), then camping in Julwania. Keating had marched to Mandleshwar on 29 September, accompanied by mounted police and Risaldar Farzan Ali. They found the road from Palasner to Khurampura totally deserted. The Bhils had, in fact, marched to the city, blocking traffic from Sendhwa to Palasner and Khurampura. About 2,000 to 3,000 Bhils had gathered near Julwania under Sitaram Bawa, a Hindu nayak. According to intelligence received, about 700 Bhils were to raid Rajpur on the morning of 30 September. The Bhils had plundered the police post at Balsamund and stolen the ammunition. They had also looted 10 maunds (approximately 373.242 kg) of opium from the carts of opium traders.

At 8 am on 11 April, a fierce battle took place between the British Army, led by Maj. Evans, and the Bhil chiefs, which continued till 3 pm. After the battle, Capt. Cumming sent Jamadar Bagga Singh to Nangalwadi to negotiate peace with the Bhils. As per the agreement, the Holkar state was to disburse the Bhils' outstanding pensions. The Bhils desisted from plunder for 15 days, despite which the Holkar state failed to honour the agreement to give Sitaram and his Bhils their due. On 12 September 1858, Sham Ji Nayak informed Cumming's bailiff that they had received nothing, even though several months had elapsed. Cumming forwarded the information to Keating, but it reached the latter only on 4 October, by which time Sitaram had raised the banner of revolt.

On 1 October, Keating, accompanied by a troop of 100 jawans and 150 men of Holkar Horse from Bhopawar, marched to Bijagarh where Sitaram was camping. Keating had recorded that this was only a stopgap arrangement, and that enduring peace would be possible only when Sitaram and his followers received their dues from the Holkar state. He dispatched the *sadr amin* (judicial officer) to Mandaleshwar to bring peace and also requested the deployment of capable officers at Khargone and Rajpur.[40]

At the end of September 1858, the fortress of Bijagarh, 29 mil. from Mandaleshwar, was the stronghold of rebel activities led by Sitaram. On 25 November 1858, the *Falkirk Herald* reported that Sitaram had revolted against the Holkar state and had occupied the fortress with his supporters and 40 horses. He had fortified his position by amassing a great deal of supplies within the fortress.

On 8 October 1858, Keating raided the fortress with 30 to 40 cavaliers, taking advantage of the absence of Sitaram's supporters, who had left either to plunder Barud or to fetch supplies. He then laid siege to the fortress. Sitaram fought valiantly, but it was a losing battle because few of his men remained. Ten of his men were killed, and 16 were arrested. Keating shot Sitaram dead and as per British policy, the latter's severed head was brought back to the camp. The surviving Bhils escaped when they heard the news of their chief's death, abandoning 65 horses and mules, some bullocks, and some opened and unopened bags. They also left behind Nana Bakhsh, an old enemy of the

British. Critically ill and unable to move, he died en route to Mandaleshwar.

On 9 October, Keating offered Raghunath Singh Mandaloi a compromise, which was accepted. He then returned to the fortress and initiated action, as it appeared that the late Sitaram's followers had regrouped. Some 45 to 50 Bhil men and women were arrested from various villages, and more were expected to be apprehended. One publication recorded that all the Bhils from nearby villages came to beg forgiveness—and were indeed pardoned—except for Bhima Nayak, the chief rebel. He had been pardoned just one year earlier but had violated the terms of truce by escaping with his band, now reduced to four or five. British officials hoped that Keating, who was then in Dhutwara, on the banks of the Narmada, just 5 mil. from Bhima Nayak, would be successful. Various publications—*HMICE* on 19 November 1858, the *Downpatrick Recorder* on 27 November 1858, and the *Lancaster Gazette* on 27 November 1858—reported that the campaign had secured the road to Sendhwa. For the action against Sitaram Bawa and his band, the Bombay Government's board of control passed a resolution on 28 October 1858, congratulating Keating and his team.[41]

In March 1859, Keating, in an encounter with Bhima Nayak's band in Khandesh, succeeded in subduing the rebels. Keating's sepoys were able to capture the band, which had scattered, by keeping the Bhils hungry and thirsty and produced them before Atkins at Shahada. This episode found mention in various newspapers, such as the *Glasgow*

Daily Herald on 24 March 1859, the *Royal Cornwall Gazette* on 25 March 1859 and the *Preston Chronicle and Lancashire Advertiser* on 26 March 1859. Bhima Nayak's surrender to the king of Bikaner in April 1859 was reported by the *Daily Post* on 20 April 1859.

Rebel Activities in Shirpur, 1858
Bhils of the Shirpur region continued their rebellion in 1858 by blocking mail from Mhow and stealing cattle. Nor did they spare the bullocks drawing government carts. They seized the horses from mounted travellers on the Sendhwa–Mhow road, dismantled the telegraph lines between Shirpur and Poona and plundered and set on fire three villages. On 8 October 1858, an article in *BG* stated that the 23rd Bombay Light NI had been dispatched to Shirpur on 4 October to quell these disturbances.

Bhil insurgencies raged round the year in Sultanpur, Pachora, Yawal and Shirpur. It was in the midst of these happenings in Khandesh that Tantya Tope assumed leadership of the revolt in 1857. On 3 November 1858, when the British were alerted about a troop led by Tantya Tope that had crossed the Narmada and was approaching Khandesh, they strengthened the security of Asirgarh and Burhanpur.[42]

Bhomia Bisen Singh, 1857–1858
The armed revolt by Bhils of the village of Sarai Talab during the 1857 Uprising has gone unnoticed. In this incident, a band of about 40 Bhils, instigated by four Makranis, set

fire to the Gujari dak bungalow. Led by Bhomia (minor zamindar) Bisen Singh of Bharudpura, most of the Bhils involved were his own men. After the event, Bisen Singh escaped to Tanda. On 23 February 1858, a letter from the deputy Bhil agent (DBA) and PA informed AGGCI Robert Hamilton Burnett that when Jamadar Bagga Singh had been sent to arrest Bisen Singh, the latter had placed his turban at the jamadar's feet, indicating that his prestige now lay in the jamadar's hands, then collapsed and died. Bisen Singh's body remained there till the next afternoon—there was speculation that he might have been poisoned. With his last breath, he had accused Jamadar Sardar Muhammad of his murder. Four Bhils of the village of Sarai Talab were tried for the murder. One was declared innocent and acquitted, but the cases of the other three were referred to the AGGCI, who sentenced them to death. Subsequently, two others from the same village received a similar sentence.[43]

Thus, Khandesh remained disturbed in 1858 as well. In 1858, Maj. Oliver Probyn was appointed political supervisor (PS) and SP, Khandesh. An exceptional administrator and army officer, Probyn had served in the East India Company's Army from 1843 to 1856. In June 1860, with cooperation from Atkins, Probyn destroyed the stronghold and confiscated all the property of a Bhil chief who was then controlling the Satpura range. When the Bhil revolt resurfaced in Bombay Presidency in 1881, Probyn's services were invaluable. According to *HMICE* on 7 August 1883, and the *Illustrated London News* on 11 August 1883, he understood perfectly how to subjugate and civilise the savages.

Revolt by Man Singh and Bhikhari Nayak, 1867

Probyn was appointed captain in 1867, with the additional charge of BA, Khandesh. His letter of 11 June 1867 informs Khandesh magistrate, L.R. Ashburner, that Man Singh, s/o Dhan Singh Nayak, was the rakhwaldar of the taluka of Balwari, and Bhikhari, s/o Dashrath Nayak, hailed from Dhawali Pass. The families of both had been receiving allowances from the Holkar state for years. But when these allowances were stopped, both Bhils, who controlled the territory between Chopra and the Satpura hills, had approached British officers, demanding intervention. Holkar's agent accused Bhikhari of ignoring the extended territories. Bhikari had then been receiving monthly allowances of Rs 75 from the Holkar state, Rs 30 from the British, and Rs 30 from the taluka of Chopra for the security of the roads and ghats. The Holkar state offered Bhikari a reduced allowance, which his Bhil followers and he declined. Bhikhari's band comprised 40 individuals, of whom 30 were village guards. He had also deployed three guards in the Holkar state and two in British territory.

Dhawali was one of the few passes through which traders took their camel caravans from Khandesh to Holkar territory. For four generations, Man Singh's family had been receiving Rs 75 a month from the Holkar state, which had been withheld for nine months, and thus both nayaks were ready to revolt. British officials believed that both Bhils ought to be given their due for their protective duties.[44]

The regions from Khandesh to Rajputana witnessed a severe drought in 1860–1861 and once more in 1868–1869. The talukas of Chalisgaon, Nandgaon and Malegaon were worst affected, according to a report in the *Birmingham Daily Post* on 12 January 1869. While some episodes of plunder by Bhils in the western and northern areas of Maharashtra, Gujarat and Rajputana were reported in this period, the Bhil revolt was comparatively insignificant in eastern Khandesh. The Nimar region and its neighbouring districts witnessed Tantya Bhil's reign of terror from 1878 to 1888. An article carried in the *Burton Chronicle* on 3 June 1869 stated that the Bhils' rebellious tendencies had been partially controlled by the success of the Khandesh Bhil Corps and also as most Bhil chiefs had been rehabilitated. An expansion of the railways had helped in this endeavour as well.

5
BHIL REVOLTS IN THE KHANDESH FRONTIER REGION AND MAHARASHTRA AFTER 1858

Bhil revolts continued in the regions of Maharashtra that adjoined Khandesh, Mahi Kantha and Rewa Kantha. The entire Bhil region was under the jurisdiction of the Bombay Government, which also controlled the action taken against these revolts. District borders were usually disregarded when joint action was undertaken in the areas surrounded by hills.

In 1826, Dev Chand Bhil as well as the Bhils of Bodwad, Naoor and Jalana had created disturbances in the taluka of Sultanpur, which once again appeared to be in rebellious mode by 1840. No less important are Bikarai and Bangchund, chiefs of the Sawda and Yawal regions. Kunwar Jiva Vasava of Chikhli rebelled in 1846, and the Bhils of Sultanpur in 1851. In the Jalgaon area, Bhil peasants revolted on the issue of land tax. Bhago Ji Nayak struggled in Nasik and Ahmednagar in 1857; he was also in communication with Kaji Singh and Bhima Nayak. Yashwant, Har Ji Nayak and Putta Ji continued the revolt in Ahmednagar in 1857–1858.

Bhago Ji, Yashwant, Appa Nayak and Har Ji Nayak
Distancing themselves from Ahmednagar in 1858, Bhil rebels moved to Nasik, Khandesh and the Nizam's territory, which they plundered. Bhago Ji and Har Ji resumed their raids in the Ahmednagar area in April–May 1859. On 5 July 1859, Capt. Nuttall had an encounter with a large Bhil crowd at Ambhore, 8 mil. south–east of Sangamner, where the Bhils had put up stiff resistance. But 23 jawans of the Koli Corps engaged them in battle, killing 10 Bhils, included Yashwant, Bhago Ji's son. Three Bhil chiefs, including Har Ji Nayak and Appa Nayak, were taken prisoner.[1]

Appa Nayak was tried for sedition and sentenced to be executed by the high court on 17 September 1862, which was commuted to life imprisonment by the governor general at the high court's recommendation. He belonged to Malegaon in the taluka of Sinnar and faced several other charges. All his property was confiscated.

Between July 1859 and November 1860, first Bhago Ji, then Bhago Ji and Mahadia Nayak together, laid siege with arms to the Ahmednagar collectorate. There were charges against them of battling the British Army at Ambhore Pass and plundering villages in the Konkan district. Appa Nayak was charged with participation in the battle of Mith Sagare, as reported in the *Bombay Gazette* (hereafter *BG*) on 14 January 1863.

In the two preceding years, Bhago Ji had been the cause for much trouble to Sir Frank Sauter, SP, Ahmednagar, which was part of the Nizam's territory. In 1859, Bhago Ji's band was once again spotted in Ahmednagar district. In October 1859, a Bhil band was observed trying to join the chief in the Nizam's territory. On 26 October 1859, Bhago Ji looted goods worth Rs 18,000 in Korhala (Kopargaon) and later led a daring raid on Chalisgaon. On 11 November 1859, Ahmednagar police, led by Sauter, engaged in an encounter with Bhago Ji's 51-member band.

Bhago Ji had been previously employed in the Ahmednagar Police Corps. When he turned rebel, he managed to influence many Bhils to follow his lead. His intelligence was so effective that he invariably managed to evade police encirclement. The government was forced to depute the 26th and 4th NI Poona Horse to assist the Ahmednagar police and the Coolie Corps apprehend him; a trained artillery troop was also deployed in the hill regions.

On 11 November 1859, Sauter laid siege at Mith Sagare, near Sinnar, making Bhago Ji's escape impossible.[2] The skirmish at Mith Sagare was reported in articles carried in the *Morning Post* (hereafter *MP*) on 24 December 1859, and *Homeward Mail from India, China and the East* (hereafter *HMICE*) on 30 June 1888.

When the head of the village of Panchala, in Mith Sagare, informed Sauter that Bhago Ji and his men were resting on the river bank 5 mil. away, Sauter arrived post-haste. In the skirmish that followed, his horse took three bullets and collapsed under him. On 11 August 1888, the *Illustrated London News* (hereafter *ILN*) reported that even though a sword had pierced his jacket, Sauter continued to fight with one hand in the battle that raged for four hours. An officer, four sepoys and six horses of the NI lost their lives, while 15 jawans and six horses were wounded. Four members of Bhago Ji's band were arrested, while 46, including Bhago Ji, were killed.

After the battle, Bhils from the Nizam's territory, awaiting Bhago Ji's arrival, dispersed when they heard of his death. One of Bhago Ji's relatives, an influential Bhil leader, had set out from Sonai to help Bhago Ji but lost no time in decamping to Khandesh when he received news of the latter's death. He was captured en route but was pardoned as he had not committed any crime.[3] Mention of these incidents was made in *MP* on 24 December 1859, in *HMICE* on 23 December 1859 and 30 June 1888 and in *ILN* on 11 August 1888.

Sauter's heroism was much exaggerated subsequently. One newspaper commented that Capt. Henry's killer was finally punished for his revolt. On the same day, i.e., 11 November 1859, after the battle, Sauter sent a telegram to A. Bettington, Commissioner, Police (CP), Bombay:

> I have the pleasure to report that I came up with the rebel Bheels under Bhagoji Naik at noon this day and succeeded in shooting and cutting up the gang to a man. Fifty-one bodies and Arabs composing the gang fought with great obstinacy and I regret to say that this service has not been performed without loss—A Jamadar, two sepoys, and a sowar of the police killed, several men and horses wounded. My own horse

fell under me, pierced with three shots. I now start to hang Bhagoji Naik at Nandoosingoba (Nandur Shingote), the spot where Captain Henry was murdered.

On 23 December 1859, *HMICE* reported that in accordance with their policy, the British took Bhago Ji's body to his village, Nandur Shingote and in an unambiguous message to the Bhils, hanged him precisely where he had earlier killed Capt. Henry. Sauter was later rewarded and appointed CP, Bombay, as reported by *HMICE* on 7 July 1888. On 11 August 1888, *ILN* published the news of his death from a heart attack in Ooty on 4 June 1888 while recuperating from his wounds.

Revolt in Nanded, 1860: Itoba and Sukram
With reference to the *Poona Observer* (hereafter *PO*), *HMICE*, on 6 October 1860, described an encounter between the *ziladar* (minor tax official) of Nanded and a Bhil band at Devgaon, in Maharashtra, towards the end of September 1860.[4] Capt. Davies was informed that Itoba Nayak, Sukram Nayak and certain other chiefs were together vandalising Devgaon and had also killed an orderly and a nayak of the police. Davies immediately instructed Haidar Beg, *ziladar* of Nanded, to assess the situation and call for military help from Hindoli, if necessary. Accordingly, Beg set out from his Nanded headquarters on the same night, with 125 men; mainly Sindhis and Deccanis, including 40 cavaliers, while the rest were from the infantry. After a 120-mil. four-day

journey to Rampuri, Beg attempted to discover the enemy's whereabouts. He then travelled another 40 mil. to Devgaon. The Bhils offered stiff resistance but Beg, who had more men as well as cavaliers, overpowered them. Some 60 Bhils were injured. Beg arrested another 44, including four chiefs; they, too, had sustained injuries. Twelve of Beg's jawans were injured and a horse was killed.

On 3 or 4 July 1860, a band of 25 Bhils plundered the shops of two Marwaris in the village of Chas in Ahmednagar district. Armed with guns, swords and scimitars, the band was led by a son of Bhago Ji Nayak. Looting goods worth Rs 1,600, they beat up the Marwaris but killed no one. The Assistant Superintendent of Police (ASP) conducted a search only to find merely Rs 35 in the possession of three Bhils. This incident was reported in *HMICE* on 4 September 1860.

Plunder in Shelgaon, 1860: Hiri and Buhiri Punished
The village of Shelgaon was subjected to a major raid on the afternoon of 9 November 1860. Committed by 18 to 20 individuals armed with guns, swords and maces, they were mostly Bhils and some thakurs; two women were also involved. Apparently, some moneylenders had committed atrocities against the Bhils and one Jayram had lodged a police complaint but without naming anyone. Goods worth Rs 1,980 had been looted and the victims' account books destroyed. The police rounded up the accused, including Hiri, Buhiri and five thakurs. The case came up for hearing

at the sessions court of Bombay on 17 April 1861, and one Ganesh Hemchand deposed against the Bhils. Sessions Judge C. Forbes held all the accused guilty, as reported in *BG* on 10 May 1861.

Execution of Mahadia and Five Other Bhils

Many Bhil revolutionaries associated with Bhago Ji Nayak actively participated in the revolt of 1857 against the British. One of the most notable among them was the famous Bhil leader, Mahadia, who was declared a rebel in 1857. He was a close associate of Bhago Ji Nayak. Due to this association, on the morning of 17 October 1861, he was hanged along with five other Bhil revolutionaries.

Mahadia was accused of the brutal murder of a Bhil named Yashu, whom he killed for being a police informer. Yashu's wife and children also spied on Bhil revolutionaries and passed information to the British.

The execution took place in Nimnapur Yarli, about 15 mil. northwest of Ahmednagar, the site of Mahadia's last alleged crime. A large crowd of Bhils and villagers was intentionally invited to witness the hanging, which the British hoped would instil fear and deter future rebellion. A British officer is quoted in the *Times of India* (hereafter *TOI*) on 23 October 1861 to have remarked: 'Such spectacles are necessary to make others realise the consequences of siding with rebels.' This execution marked a major setback for the Bhil revolt, especially in Khandesh, where Mahadia had significantly challenged British control.

The Ahmednagar area witnessed some peace by 1861 for which the Koli Corps must be duly credited. But once their purpose was achieved, the British disbanded the corps in 1861.[5] On 30 December 1861, *BG* carried a report on an incident at the end of 1861, in which a Bhil band attacked a troop of the Malva Bhil Corps near Nimar, killing some jawans and injuring others, after which they ravaged the area and set the camp on fire.

The Bhils plundered a village near Malegaon Sadar (Maharashtra) and set the cavalry station on fire. On 21 December 1861, the Poona Horse and 6th NI were dispatched to deal with the situation, according to a report by *BG* on 24 December 1861. A departmental letter written to the acting secretary of the Bombay Government on 24 February 1862 discloses that actions were initiated against the Bhils on the Bombay road in view of their continuing rebellion.[6]

The Bhil revolt continued in Khandesh in September 1862. An army troop commanded by a British officer was dispatched from Mhow but was unsuccessful in that mountainous and forested region because it was the rainy season. On 22 September 1862, the *Mercury* (Hobart) reported that it had been decided to tackle the Bhils after the monsoon.

Revolts in Toranmal Hills, Jhand and Dang, 1862
The British introduced several Bhil chiefs to cultivation, hoping that the latter would desist from insurgency and join the mainstream but were only partially successful in the

endeavour. Many Bhil chiefs still yearned for freedom. When faced with police pressure, the disappointed Bhils gathered at Toranmal, the highest part of the Satpura range, from where they continued their rebellion. Toranmal was about 29 mil. from Sultanpur. Maj. Keating, PA, Nimar, deputed his assistants, Lt. Cadell, Lt. Hanson and Lt. Hall, to launch a campaign against these Bhils. Shyamal Ji, chief of Toranmal Hills, was captured, and Keating brought him to Probyn to present his grievances. Shyamal Ji asked for an assurance that his jagir would be restored to him, but the officers gave no promise to this effect. Disappointed, Shyamal Ji escaped from Probyn's camp but later surrendered unconditionally to Cadell in March 1862, stated *BG* on 5 March 1863.

The Jhand forest (Madhya Pradesh, Gujarat) situated on the Rewa Kantha border was also part of the Panchmahal district on the Malva–Gujarat border. The British Government had brought the entire area under its control in 1861. Naykara Bhils were then in revolt, which was judicially contained. A Brahmin agent of the Peshwa, who was leading the rebellion, was soon arrested near Alirajpur by the officers of Nimar, according to a report in *BG* on 5 March 1863.

Dang (Gujarat) witnessed Bhil unrest in January 1862 on account of local factors. The forest of Dang lay in the Sahyadri Valley, between British-held Nawapur and Gaekwad-controlled Langur district. It was then ruled by five major and two minor Bhil chiefs. Their autonomous jurisdiction had continued on account of their resistance. But both the Gaekwad state and the British had their eye on the teak growing in abundance in the region. The Bhil agent of Khandesh initiated action against minor chiefs in 1852 with a view to acquire this valuable resource.

Of the major Bhil chiefs, Shripat had been killed, while his eldest son lived but briefly. Devi Singh ascended the throne, provoking a revolt by his elder brother who agreed to give up his claim only if their uncle, Uday Singh, was appointed instead. When Uday Singh died, his son, Kira Singh, succeeded him. But when Kira Singh injured two persons in a dispute, he was arrested and imprisoned for two years. From jail, he was shifted to the mental asylum of Colaba, from where Devi Singh engineered his escape in April 1860. Upon release, Kira Singh returned to his depredations by plundering the neighbouring villages with his former comrades. Devi Singh first issued him a warning, which was ignored, and eventually killed him. The government dispatched the Khandesh Bhil Corps to contain the unrest. Devi Singh absconded and together with his brother, Daulat Singh, began his own ravages. A reward was soon announced for his arrest. When he could withstand the pressure no longer, he surrendered to the magistrate of Khandesh. His brother was also arrested, along with some supporters, after which peace was restored in the Khandesh-Rewa Kantha frontier region, according to a *BG* report on 5 March 1863.

The Bhil chiefs of Dang continued the battle for their rights to the forests. The autonomous authority at three areas in Gujarat—Sagwara, Kirli and Wajpur—they had ruled independently for centuries, although Gaekwad, employing deception, had begun to occupy their villages by sanctioning them annual pensions. The British, however, preferred the Dang chiefs to remain independent for entirely selfish reasons. In 1857, a railway contractor acquired the forests of Dang on lease from the Dang chief and began to fell trees. The lease, sanctioned by Gaekwad, was objected to by the British who had appropriated the area from the Scindias in 1861. When the lease ended on 31 May 1863, the British Government intervened and the British forest conservator issued a fresh lease. Gaekwad later complained to the Bombay Government.[7]

Revolt in Maharashtra Khandesh Frontier Region, 1879
Of the four main tribal groups active in Bombay Presidency in 1879—mainly from the Koli, Ramosi and Bhil tribes—one was that of the Ramosi, led by Hari Maka Ji who belonged to Kalambi in the Satara district of Maharashtra. His band had committed several robberies in Satara in January. When he was apprehended in March by the Solapur police, Tatya Maka Ji assumed leadership of the band with help from his brothers, Babia and Ramakrishna. Tatya was killed at the end of that year, while Ramakrishna and the others were arrested.

The second major group was led by Daulatta, who had organised several robberies in Poona, in February–March 1879. When faced with pressure from the Poona police, he slipped into Thane district where he carried out two major robberies. He was killed by Maj. Daniel in an encounter on 17 March after he had returned to Poona. Four of his comrades were also killed, and 11 injured. A prominent member of this group was a Brahmin, Vasudev Balwant Phadke, who was at one time a clerk in the revenue department. After Daulatta was killed, Phadke moved to the Nizam's territory where he gathered a band of Rohillas. He was soon arrested by Daniel in Kaladagi district.

The Kolis of Purandar Ghera, led by Krishna Sable and his son, Maroti, had carried out raids in Poona district and nearby areas. At the end of 1879, with cooperation from the Khandesh police, Maj. Wise and Insp. Syed Jamal arrested this band near Bhusawal. Ten Kolis were arrested in the hills near Saswad.

The fourth group was one of Bhils, led by Tukia and Aniya. For reasons of safety, they were headquartered in the Nizam's territory but were active in the Khandesh and Ahmednagar districts under British control. The Central Provinces reported 161 robberies that year; 81 of these were committed by the four groups, stated a report in *HMICE* on 17 February 1881.

Wise eventually arrested or killed these tribal rebels in and around Poona. By the end of 1879, 10 such groups had been apprehended in the Saswal hills area, and two near Bhusawal. On 29 January 1880, *HMICE* reported that these tribal rebels of the south were led by Tantya Bhil.

According to a report carried in the *Field* on 2 June 1883, the British Army in 1883 was continuing with its anti-Bhil campaign in a part of Aurangabad district adjoining Khandesh.

Jangia Nayak, 1887
The southern areas witnessed Bhil revolts at the beginning of 1887. Bhil chief Jangia rebelled in Dasala, 104 mil. from Aurangabad. Charged with several cases of murder and robbery, he had invariably managed to evade the British. He was eventually arrested by Lt. Ford in Dasala and handed over to the Nizam's officials, as Dasala was under the Nizam's jurisdiction. The British entertained high hopes that he would be suitably punished. On 25 April 1887, *HMICE* reported that news of disturbances from nearby areas had ceased after Jangia's arrest.

At the beginning of 1888, a large group of Muslim Bhils of Khandesh, associated with Tantya Bhil, entered the district of Nimar and executed two raids. Their leaders were tried after they were arrested by the Nimar police. Some were given death sentences, while others were sentenced to long imprisonments.[8]

Dashrath Bhil, 1890
Like Tantya Bhil in the Narmada river basin, Dashrath Bhil was a terror in the Mahanadi basin. But Naylor, SP, Bilaspur, liquidated his band and arrested him following a few encounters. On 16 July 1890, the *Colonies and India* reported that although Dashrath had carried out several robberies, he had not committed murder and hence, escaped execution.

Bhola Ji Bhil, 1898

C. Hankin, Inspector General (IG), Nizam's police in Aurangabad, reported that Bhil chief Bhola Ji or Bhola Singh, with his band of 100 Bhils, had offered stiff resistance to a large police–army contingent on 11 and 12 May.

Bhola Singh originally belonged to Karjat and after several raids there had moved to the Nizam's territory. His band carried flags which they used to issue signals. Troops of police, Rohilla and Arab soldiers were sent from Pachora on the night of 11 May and after marching for 10 mil., approached the Bhil band before dawn on 12 May. The Bhils opened fire when they heard the sound of hoofs, killing a Rohilla jawan. A heavy exchange of fire took place at first light. But despite the Bhils' belief in Bhola Ji's miracle, which would turn enemy bullets to water upon touching their flags, they suffered an ignominious defeat. While 64 Bhils were taken prisoner, 14 managed to escape. Their aim now was to attack Aurangabad Jail to free their comrades.

Of the 60 members of Bhola's band who raided Borgaon, 33 were apprehended. When the Bhils escaped towards Parbhani, there was yet another encounter with police in the Sohale hills where another 11 were captured. The group then took refuge in the Ahirmal hills. Later, they carried out a robbery in Malegaon, where a jamadar and two jawans were shot. Here, the band captured and beheaded Itoba Bhil, Hiria Bhil, Yadia Bhil and Ramchander, who they suspected were police informants, before returning to the Ahirmal hills.

The band also tried to loot government funds sent from Mahalgaon to the tehsil office. Bhiva and Wadiya, members of the band, killed Bhavo Singh Bhil, a police informant. Another suspected informer, Dagaria, was killed by Wadiya and Ramjai. The government tried and punished the captured Bhils, reported *HMICE* on 5 September 1898.

The Curse of Famine, 1899
A severe drought in Khandesh and Rajputana in 1899 came as a harbinger of death. On 21 November 1899, the *North Devon Gazette* reported on the acute starvation that forced desperate Bhils to agitate against traders and moneylenders in order to survive. The uprising was more prominent in Rajputana than in Khandesh.

Driven to desperation by hunger, Bhils on the Gujarat–Madhya Pradesh border rose in rebellion in hundreds from the villages and forests around Sunth and Rampur. In the Western Malva Agency, Bhils raided a village in Sailana (Madhya Pradesh), a small principality near Ratlam. Burdened by the levies imposed on their villages and by rising food prices, they urged traders to sell grain at fair rates. But their demands were ignored, and they resorted to plundering stored grain and livestock.

On the night of 21 September 1899, a band of 200 Bhils raided Kheria Rundi, a Gujjar village, looting all available grain and some 150 buffaloes. At Sailana, local police and horsemen, supervised by the thakur of Roati, as well as 100 local Bhils, pursued the band for about 25 mil., raining bullets, killing some and injuring others. Yet the rebels, without abandoning any grain, animal or injured comrade, escaped to the hill forests of Jhabua. As soon as they had reached safety, they staged a counter-attack, killing seven sepoys and six horses belonging to the thakur and then melted back into the hills. A troop of NI was sent to Panchmahal to manage the situation but ravaged by drought and hunger, the Bhils continued their depredations. Only traders and the affluent were content at the time, stated *HMICE* on 14 April 1902.

Bhil raids continued in the Khandesh–Gujarat frontier region in 1901. The Malva Bhil Corps was deployed to control the Bhils of Jhabua (Madhya Pradesh) and Dahod (Gujarat). A Bhil band from Dahod attacked the Pitol thana and freed a comrade. Despite being pursued by the Jhabua police, the rebels managed to reach their destination in British territory.

Khandesh, too, suffered a drought from 1888 to 1903. Deficient rainfall led to poor cotton crops in Ahmednagar and Nasik, among other places, except in Khandesh—in 1900, Khandesh alone accounted for 77 per cent of the crop. On 9 January 1900, the *Manchester Courier and Lancashire General Advertiser* carried a report on the desperate condition of the Bhils who were now starving to death, their carcasses strewn in thoroughfares and dumped in the ditches and old wells of Khandesh.

Kanhaiya Bhil, 1901

A telegram sent from Secunderabad (Hyderabad) on 5 July 1901 reveals that the Nizam's court had, in mid-

1901, pronounced the death sentence on Kanhaiya Bhil for his involvement in robberies, killings and plunder at Ahmednagar, among other places. He was incarcerated in the Nizam's jail and tried for the murders. Between 1899 and 1900, Kanhaiya had carried out several raids in Ahmednagar district at a time when a severe drought was ravaging Khandesh, Rajputana and Ahmednagar. The British police made several futile attempts to capture him and when pressure mounted on him in Ahmednagar district, he escaped to the Nizam's territory. Finally, the Nizam's police apprehended him in the Hyderabad area, with cooperation from Stevenson, a British informer, and tried him in the Nizam's court. The Bombay Government commended Stevenson for his cooperation and rewarded him with Rs 500, stated *HMICE* on 29 July 1901.

Jaora Jail Revolt, 1922–1923

In 1922–1923, 45 Bhils were lodged in Jaora Jail. With help from their comrades on the outside, the incarcerated Bhils staged a revolt, while those on the outside raided the jail and overpowered the security guards. Telephone wires were snapped, and all the prisoners made good their escape. The army, which had been summoned to contain the situation, opened fire on the escaping prisoners. In all, 16 Bhils were killed. The survivors, too, were seriously injured, reported the *Pall Mall Gazette* on 12 June 1923.

6
BHIL REVOLTS POST-1833: BARWANI AND ALIRAJPUR

The study of Bhil revolts in Khandesh, Barwani and Alirajpur in separate chapters has been a challenging proposition. All these areas were adjacent to and also dependent administratively upon one another. Barwani and Alirajpur shared borders with Khandesh and Gujarat and were ruled by Rajput thakurs who were, in turn, controlled by the British. Internally, these states remained autonomous until India's independence. After the British had established a foothold in Khandesh, the army-supervised process of Bhil settlement gathered momentum in Barwani from 1833 onwards. The Bhil chiefs were agitated at the time and the British soon realised that they would not be pacified until the Barwani state restored their rights. The situation demanded a balance between oppression and the establishment of a security system. When, by the end of the 1830s, the Bhils had not received their due rights (an agreed upon share in fixed revenue), they perforce took to vandalism. At the beginning of the 1840s, colonial policy concentrated on using arms against rebellious Bhils. In the middle of the decade, British officials inspected the forests of Barwani and investigated the claims of Bhil chiefs. However, as the Rajput king remained indifferent, their raids continued. As a result, the second half of the 19th century saw two major insurrections in the Nimar region—one in Barwani and the other in Alirajpur.[1]

Kaji Singh Nayak and Bhima Nayak

The Bhil revolt raged in Barwani from 1833 onwards following the arrest of one Hatania. The rebellious activity of Kaji Singh Nayak, a rakhwaldar of the British Government, too, had posed a challenge to the British. Both Kaji Singh and his relative Bhima Nayak turned rebel following a dispute about wages. They were active in the villages of the Dasana hills, Dahi, Bhikalda and Kukshi from where the road turned unsafe. Capt. Hutenison, BA, then suggested to the AGGCI that Lt. G.S. Dysart be entrusted with the responsibility of controlling the Bhils in the Bhikalda and Dasana regions.[2]

The state of Barwani had a total of 134 villages, 26 of which were earmarked for other members of the royal family or for religious purposes. The remaining 108 villages provided a revenue of Rs 25,000 per annum. In the whole area, which was mountainous and forested, the Bhil population was about 700–800 and Bhil chiefs received monthly wages in accordance with their traditional rights. They were in a superior position as compared to the Bhils of such neighbouring areas as Dhar, Alirajpur and Holkar. As Khandesh was British territory, British officers launched a campaign against Kaji Singh, variously referred to as Khaji, Kajar and Khajya Singh.

Masefield, collector of Khandesh, had pardoned Kaji Singh on many occasions. As a member of the Bhil Corps from 1831 to 1851, Kaji Singh was known to be loyal and his conduct irreproachable. His task was to guard the 40-mile stretch of the Sendhwa–Shirpur road, and he was put in charge of the local police force. In other words, he was the *rakhwaldar* (guard) of Sendhwa Ghat. Not a single robbery or murder was perpetrated on this stretch in his 20-year tenure. It was because of his loyalty and courage that the collector had pardoned some of his minor misdemeanours. Kaji Singh had served faithfully under Maj. Graham, Maj. Morris, Capt. Rose and Maj. Kier.

In 1851, Kaji Singh was tried and sentenced to 10 years RI when a Bhil offender succumbed to a severe beating administered by him. However, in 1855, following strong recommendations from Capt. Rose and certain other officers, he was released. In June 1857, he was entrusted with the security of the northern pass but by then he was so thoroughly disenchanted with the British that he turned rebel, although the possibility of there being other contributing causes cannot be ruled out. It is possible that with the coming of the Great Uprising of 1857, he had sensed widespread anti-British discontent. His associates, Bhima Nayak and Mawasia Nayak, had also turned rebel. However, no evidence is available to support the contention of certain writers that Kaji and Bhima had directly joined the 1857 Uprising, although some evidence of a minor involvement of Bhima's uncle exists. Kaji's and Bhima's sons had also turned rebel on the grounds that their rights were not being honoured.³

Kaji Singh and Bhima Nayak were related through marriage; Bhima, married to Kaji's sister, was a powerful Bhil chief of Barwani. The king of Barwani had been using him in the interests of his own rule. When Brahmangaon on the banks of Narmada, which the king of Barwani regarded as his own territory, was usurped by the Holkar state, he instigated Bhima to plunder the village. According to the *kamadsar* (caretaker) of Brahmangaon, Bhima arrived at the village of Datwara on 18 August 1857 with 500 to 700 of his men and plundered the village from 10 am to 11 pm. Holkar territory, Khandesh, Barwani and the Bombay Highway suffered the same fate—he now was the hero of a large territory between the Vindhya and Satpura hills.

On 27 September 1857, Bhima wrote a letter to the *wahiwatdar* (patron, used here for the British Res.) of Baroda: 'I didn't plunder village Datwara of my own sweet will, as you suspect. I was told to do so by Maharaja Yashwant Singh of Barwani, Bhudhagir Baba and Daulat Singh Mama. They told me to plunder any place but Barwani.' He added that he was told to plunder Datwara as it belonged to Barwani. 'They gave me fifty rupees and a robe of honour, but the king didn't help me after his goal was achieved. And now that the king is complaining to you about me, I've decided to loot my area too and to keep aloof from the raja...Act not on any complaint against me as I have been a man of the king and whatever I did, I did on his bidding. Therefore, instead of ordering me to provide compensation, you get it from the king. If you wish that I should not plunder your areas, kindly arrange for the payment of my salary.'[4]

In September 1857, Bhima Nayak attacked Lt. Kennedy as a warning to the police officers of Khandesh. He had, at the time, described himself as a representative of the (then-tottering) Mughal ruler of Delhi. The British made all efforts to apprehend him for his insolence and when they failed in this endeavour, they announced a reward of Rs 1,000 for his arrest.[5]

Two Bhil chiefs of Khandesh had also joined forces with Bhima Nayak. Telegraph services often suffered disruption on this route. Through his letter on 22 October 1857 to the assistant GG, Masefield had suggested that the 90-mile stretch of Sendhwa road be regularly patrolled by the Irregular Mounted Police and ordinary policemen. He recommended that the Holkar kingdom guard its own borders as well.[6]

On 29 October 1857, Bhima Nayak, Kaji Singh and a few other chiefs, together with a contingent of some 1,500 Bhils, jointly raided and plundered Shirpur. Capt. Birch's pursuit for 56 mil. proved futile. On 1 November, Kaji and Bhima plundered two villages merely 6 mil. from the headquarters of the British district. At the same time, Khala Nayak plundered a village in Sultanpur taluka. The Bombay Government learnt, probably based on information from some jagirdar, that a large Bhil crowd was gathering in Patoda taluka. Another 400 Bhils were soon to arrive from

Sinnar to plunder the area. An appeal was made to the collector to take necessary precautionary steps.

Kaji Singh soon began to plunder the villages in the foothills and blocked Sendhwa Pass. More and more anti-British rebels continued to join his ranks, including soldiers from the Holkar Army. Next, he plundered government treasure, which was being sent from Indore to Bombay.[7]

Kaji Singh and Bhima Nayak had been looting the government treasury since 1857. On 17 November 1857, a 1,500-strong Bhil contingent had looted Rs 7 lakh at Sendhwa Ghat on the Bombay–Agra road. A few days later, opium and mail, loaded on 60 bullock carts, were looted at Bijasan Ghat, and telegraph wires were snapped. The Bhil band then swarmed downhill and raided villages in the Sultanpur area. Meanwhile, Bhago Ji Nayak and his band, also seething against the British, had come to their aid. Arab mercenaries, who had been laid off from the army of Dhar, also enraged with the British, joined forces with Kaji Singh.

Maj. Evans tried hard to reach an understanding with Bhima and Mawasia but in vain. Kaji Singh, Dular Singh, Daulat Singh (Kaji's son) and Kalu Baba opened up a joint front against Evans. At 8 pm on 11 April 1858, a bloody battle took place between the British Army and Bhil chiefs at Amba Pani and continued till 3 pm. Besides their traditional weapons, the Bhils also employed muskets. About 1,500 Bhils joined this battle in which Bhima Nayak was ignominiously defeated, a number of British officers injured, and an Indian officer killed. Some 65 Bhils, including Dular and Daulat, were killed, and 170 injured. Helping their menfolk, some 400 Bhil women also joined the battle; they were arrested and sent to Dhule Jail. A part of the funds looted from Sendhwa on 17 November was later recovered by the army. Pleased, the Bombay Government announced cash rewards for the jawans; 57 Bhils were tried and punished, as reported in the *Bombay Gazette* (hereafter *BG*) on 12 June 1863.[8]

In a letter to AGGCI Robert Hamilton Burnett on 28 June 1858, Lt. W.J. Cumming, then Acting Political Agent (APA) of Nimar, informed the former that Rs 40,000 of the funds looted by Bhils on the Sendhwa Ghat road in November 1857 had been recovered by the police and as per Hamilton's order, five per cent of that amount had been deducted and the remaining returned to the concerned trader. The Satpura Field Force had also recovered about Rs 1,20,000. A sum of Rs 3,500 recovered from the district of Barwani had been deposited in the Mandaleshwar treasury. The letter indicates that there was no intention of returning this amount to the traders.[9]

The secretary to the Bombay Government informed Hamilton by letter on 20 November 1858 that 165 guards had been arrested on suspicion of collaboration with the Bhils in the loot of the treasury at Sendhwa Ghat earlier that month. Of these, only five guards were injured in the skirmish. The rest were sentenced to 14 years RI, which was later reduced to five.[10]

In view of the joint revolt by Kaji Singh and his accomplices, two companies of the 26th NI were dispatched from Shirpur to Dhulia on 18 May 1860, commanded by Capt. Boudich, an able officer. Atkins and Probyn were already in position accompanied by 150 jawans of the Bhil Corps, reported the *Homeward Mail* (hereafter *HM*) on 6 August 1860.

In 1858, Kaji Singh reached an understanding with the British that he would take responsibility for any of Bhima Nayak's misdemeanours but wanted an assurance that if he were to turn in the latter to them, he would neither be arrested nor sent to the Andamans, nor hanged; rather, he would be allowed to live under police protection. If Bhima ever escaped into the hills, it was Kaji's responsibility to hunt him down.[11]

Capt. E.H. Thomson, PA, Nimar, wrote to the AAGGCI expressing his failure to understand why Kaji Singh, a paid *rakhwaldar* of the British, had entered Holkar territory from Khandesh. Kaji had promised to capture Bhima but had failed. Thomson suggested that the British ought not to trust him but send him back to Khandesh. In a semi-official letter, Ramachandra Rao, a minister in the Holkar Government, commented: 'Khajya Nayak has committed plunders in Khandesh and had escaped with his family to Barwani. Lt. Dysart fears that there may be a mass revolt by the Bhils. But it won't happen. Other Bhil chiefs don't like Khajya's activities. Muwasia and Nurla Nayak, Bhima's paternal uncle, are not prepared to help him.'

In view of past services rendered by Kaji Singh and Bhima Nayak as well as their hold on the Sendhwa Ghat road, the government condoned their 1857 rebellion and entrusted them with the security of Sendhwa Ghat once more. However, when Capt. Keating later took charge of Barwani in October 1860, he refused to grant any amnesty. Keating wrote to J.C. Wood, acting BA, Sardarpur, that Bhima had bribed office employees to get an amnesty order passed. He pointed out that Wood had approved the amnesty proposal on the basis of an 8-month-old letter from the AAGGCI, but after Keating assumed charge of Barwani, he had discarded the arrangements as per the old letter and issued fresh instructions. Keating stressed that he had refused amnesty to Bhima with the AAGGCI's permission. Bhima had been informed that the earlier promise would not be honoured. Both Keating and Capt. Thomas were convinced that Bhima had bought the policemen's support by bribing them. Keating informed Wood that the latter would find the same situation prevailing in his own office, revealing that Bhima had access to British offices as well, stated the *Homeward Mail from India, China and East* (hereafter *HMICE*) in its editions of 4 September 1860 and 11 June 1862, and the *Newcastle Courant* (hereafter *NC*) on 24 August 1860.[12]

On 4 July 1860, the *Jam-e-Jamshed* reported that Kaji Singh and Bhima Nayak were plundering carts and their passengers on the road running parallel to the Wasind–Mhow train route. It appeared that around 1860, the two rebel chiefs were active between Wasind and Indore, raiding their prey in separate units and then re-grouping. The villages between Dhule and Sendhwa in the dense forests behind the hills were their meeting places as well as where they had supporters. Kaji Singh had injured and insulted some employees of an executive engineer on the Agra road as well. He had seized whatever money they had and escaped into the Satpura hills, thumbing his nose at the British once again, continued the reports in *HMICE* and *NC*.

Kaji Singh plundered yet another caravan transporting government funds on 15 June 1860. Various newspapers—*HM* on 6 August 1860, *HMICE* on 4 September 1860, and the *Geelong Advertiser* (Victoria) (hereafter *GA*) on 12 September 1860—had reported the incident, but their reports were conflicting. On 23 June 1860, for instance, *BG* reported that a caravan of 12 camels was transporting government funds worth Rs 2,60,000 to Indore and that a week after the incident, Kaji had gone to meet Bhima in Boond. Bhima had, by then, raided a few villages on the Sendhwa side and had amassed Rs 8–10 lakh from traders, which enabled him to maintain a large army. On 2 July 1860, *BG* reported that after the raid, Kaji had taken refuge in the hills, lying low; he was also known for snapping telegraph wires and plundering small railway stations. On 11 June 1862, *HMICE* estimated the treasure at Rs 4 lakh, while another newspaper reckoned its worth at Rs 2,70,000. British newspapers thus carried varying versions regarding the amount of funds, the number of camels, and the amount plundered from the government or from traders.

The most authentic information, however, comes from a letter from Lt. Probyn, Western BA and ASP, Khandesh on 22

June 1860 to Lt. Dysart. With a caravan of 12 camels, traders were on their way to Indore to purchase opium. On 15 June 1860, near Sangvi, Kaji captured the camels and escaped into the hills with the funds. The camels were carrying merely Rs 2 lakh. As Kaji and Bhima were chiefs of the area, the government suspected their involvement. But Kaji had by then entered Barwani territory through the Satpura passes, where he joined Bhima and Madho Singh (Madho Nayak), chief of Salun and guardian of the Gohan post.

A large police posse was deployed to apprehend the looters. From his Barwani camp on 25 June 1860, Dysart wrote to AGGCI Sir R. Shakespear Bart, expressing the government's apprehension about the possibility of Arabs and Makranis from the north of the Narmada joining forces with Kaji. The government ordered all the nearby states to maintain a strict vigil.

The police hunted for the rebels in Malegaon, Dhule, Mhow and Indore. On 29 June, Atkins and Probyn learnt that Kaji was in hiding to the south-west of Niwali in the Satpura hills. From Shirpur, Atkins took along jawans from the Light Field Force, Khandesh Bhil Corps, Poona Horse, Khandesh Police, Poona Irregulars and others familiar with the terrain of the Satpura hills. Maj. Baugh and Lt. Diester commanded 300 cavaliers supplied by the king of Indore as well as the 6th and 9th NI regiments, while Capt. Davison, assistant director of the transport train, and other British officers led massive teams. The mountainous terrain was an obstacle; rain also affected their march. After an arduous trek of some 100 mil., they camped for four days at Khul, near Niwali, from 1 July onwards, from where they launched a surprise attack on the rebels. Kaji's comrades fought valiantly but were forced to flee. Kaji, too, managed to escape with his chief supporters.

Probyn and Atkins pursued Kaji Singh and his men for 8 mil. By then it was evening, and it had begun to rain after a dust storm, making the pursuit even more exhausting and challenging. Once they missed Kaji by a mere whisker. But before the British force could apprehend or fire upon his band, they escaped on their horses to seek refuge in the dense forests and valleys. Before it was dark, carbine attacks had already killed two Bhils and injured three. A Bhil group gathered up their dead and wounded and made good their escape, although they left behind part of the looted money, two fine swords and a double-barrelled gun belonging to Kaji Singh. Madho Singh, his chief collaborator, was apprehended. The force also recovered some costly Persian carpets, bullocks, buffaloes and mules—but not Kaji Singh.

However, the officers did manage to apprehend Bhima Nayak's uncle, chief of his territory during the 1857–1858 uprising. His notoriety was so widely known that a large force, comprising jawans of the Bhil Battalion and the Indore Regular Cavalry, was deployed to escort him safely to the Mandaleshwar fortress near Khul.[13] Reports of the incident were carried in *NC* on 24 August 1860, in *GA* on 12 September 1860 and in *HMICE* on 4 September 1860 and 11 June 1862.

It was eventually decided that a campaign against Kaji Singh was best launched after the monsoon. The campaign could not have hoped for a more seasoned leader than Col. Evans, of the 9th Corps—the corps' experience in the Satpura hills in 1858 was invaluable. But as the corps was then stationed in Mhow, it could launch the campaign only after the rains, stated *HM* on 6 August 1860, and *NC* on 24 August 1860.

The government had announced an award of Rs 2,000 for Kaji Singh and of Rs 500 each for Madho Singh, Bhima Nayak, Nimla, Ratania and Seva Bhil. Of the lot, Madho Singh was now dead. A letter written by A.R. Grant, acting magistrate of Khandesh on 26 June 1860 to AGGCI Bart, discloses that as Kaji Singh had rebelled in 1857–1859, the government had withheld his salary for the period. While escaping from Sangvi with the looted funds, he had written to the *mamlatdar*, complaining that his salary was inadequate. Grant, however, was not in favour of clemency.[14]

A letter from Bhima Nayak warned Grant that he would capture any sepoy who brought the latter supplies and that he was now prepared to take the Barwani soldiers and police posts hostage—ironically, he also asked Grant to take care of himself. He said that he had been ordered by the government in Delhi (the Mughal government) to behead every European and their employees, and he expected to succeed in his mission after the festival of Dussehra.[15]

Keating apprised AGGCI Bart by a letter on 2 May 1861 of a convoy of traders that had been obstructed near

Sendhwa but that contradictory news had been received about the incident. He had also learnt that Bhil groups were to plunder other such convoys. Such funds being transported in this manner had been looted twice in the preceding three years, with several other aborted attempts. The letter stressed that the practice of transporting such wealth on the Sendhwa road without adequate security ought to cease.[16]

Kaji Singh's Martyrdom

Till his death, the British regarded Kaji Singh as a traitor and worked ceaselessly to apprehend and punish him. To this end, they solicited the support of every loyal Bhil chief. Eventually, on 3 October 1860, a Makrani and his men murdered Kaji Singh and as per British policy, brought his head to Shirpur. Pahlad, Kaji's son, was brought there as well in an iron cage. According to a report in *HMICE* on 9 November 1860, the British believed that such punishments would compel Kaji Singh's comrades and other rebels to either surrender or to go underground but nothing of the kind happened. They had evidently underestimated the emotions of the Bhils, whose rebellion continued unabated.

A letter dated 30 April 1861, addressed to the governor of Bombay, available in the India Office, London, reveals that Rohiddin, a Makrani jamadar, accompanied by a police team from Khandesh had murdered Kaji Singh and also captured his son. Kaji had been pardoned twice, yet revolted against the British. Reaves described him as 'a traitor and pest of Khandesh and the Northern frontier' (see Appendix 3).[17]

Attack on Shyam Ji Nayak and Hingona, Bhima's Martyrdom
Bhima Nayak and his nephew Mawasia were the most dreaded rebels of Barwani in 1857. After perpetrating several robberies at the beginning of 1858, Bhima approached Col. Stockley for clemency, which was granted. Despite the grant of clemency, he continued his raids. In the first week of May 1858, Bhima was summoned to the British camp for discussions and arrested. At Kusumbia on 5 May 1858, he informed Maj. Cumming that he had not received his salary for 11 months, compelling him to commit the first raid.

> I asked Jagga, the Maharaja's man, for my pending salary and he promised payment in four days; he even gave me 50 rupees. I then had nothing for food. I borrowed two maunds of jowar from Bhura Maru of Balkuan. Eight or ten days later, I looted Kantool in Khandesh. I did all this at the king's bidding, but Jagga deceived me. Hunger forced him to plunder some villages. I met Hutenison in June 1857 and helped him get his salary; I also wrote to Himmal Lal, an official of the raja, for it. I don't know about the activities of Daulat Singh (Kaji's son). At the time of the Amba Pani battle, I had 200 men with me but we were half a kos from the site. I was not involved in the battle of Dhaba Bawdi and I had no hand in the loot of the treasury, nor did I get anything from it. I looted Datwada at the bidding of Hanumant Rao of Nisarpur.

Following Bhima's statement, Cumming pardoned him yet again. However, a few days later, he informed the government that Bhima was once again uncontrollable. Cumming sent Bhima's nephew to persuade him to surrender, but the effort failed. As reported in *BG* on 16 September 1867 and in the *Englishman's Overland Mail* (hereafter *EOM*) on 23 September 1867, Keating arrested Bhima towards the end of 1858 and for the third time, he was lodged in Mandaleshwar fortress.[18]

On 24 February 1859, a letter from H.L. Anderson, secretary to the Bombay government, apprised Sir Hamilton Bart, agent of the governor general of the secret department, Central India, Indore, of Keating's attacks on Bhima Nayak's comrades. On 1 April 1861, Keating informed PA Grant via a letter that when he assumed charge of Barwani in October 1860, he had had a cart road constructed via Goin Pass to enable access to the area vandalised by Bhima in 1857. A police checkpost was established after the road was constructed. While it made the supply of items to Bhima and his comrades more difficult, the police's task became easier. On 18 February 1861, Bhima wrote to the *patil*s of his intention to join the army but threatened to return a year later to destroy their villages. It is believed that he had 30 to 40 men with him when he crossed the Bombay–Indore road to go east. Keating immediately informed the king of Khargone, who refused to take action, even though his force was more than adequate, all the while maintaining that Bhima Nayak had not encroached on his territory. Keating could only hope that Bhima's resources would soon be exhausted. The police of Khargone continued to search for him in the southern hills and had built two police checkposts on the western border. Keating told Grant that, whenever commanded, he was ready to cooperate in the search for Bhima Nayak to the west of Asirgarh.[19]

Some of Bhima Nayak's men and his mother, Sursi, were held in custody at Mandaleshwar so that pressure could be brought to bear on him. Bhima's mother breathed her last there on 28 February 1859. The prisoners revolted on 22 August, attacked the guards whose weapons they seized and occupied the fortress. APA Capt. Helms immediately requested cannons from the Holkar state, but the light cannons, which arrived by 5 pm, were ineffective. Helms took a bullet and died. In order to keep the siege going till more cannons arrived from Mhow, Bart and Lt. Scot deployed the 19th NI around the fortress. But the prisoners escaped from the rear around 10 pm, along with Rs 7,69,629 from the treasury. Of the absconders, 26 were later caught and tried. Seven received the death sentence, and 11 were deported. No information is available about the remaining eight.[20]

At Mandaleshwar, Bhima Nayak was sent to a makeshift school every day to enable him to become literate and civilised. Keating imposed no restrictions on him. Some six weeks later, though, on 24 November 1859, he escaped at night through a window and resumed plundering his former territories. As Kaji Singh was now no more, there was no one left to mediate. On 31 December 1859, Keating wrote to inform the AAGGCI that Bhima had instigated Itiya to rebel against the thakurs of Muthwara. Meanwhile, he had already dispatched 50 sepoys from Alirajpur and Barwani, along with two troops of the Malva Bhil Corps to Muthwara. One troop of the Bhil Corps had already reached Muthwara on 26 December 1859, where 30 members of Itiya's band were sighted but managed to escape. Thus, Bhima Nayak was still at large even after a reward of Rs 500 had been announced for his capture. Keating received a message sent through the thanadar of Chikli that Bhima was prepared to surrender but with conditions. Keating, however, insisted on an unconditional surrender, as Bhima had thus far not honoured any previous conditions.

On 24 January 1860, Cumming wrote to SP Atkins that he believed it would not be possible to capture Bhima and Itiya without assistance from the other Bhil chiefs. From Solapur on 24 February 1860, the CP wrote to the judicial secretary of Bombay that favourable weather ought to be awaited before launching a campaign in the Akrani and Barwani forests in order to capture Bhima, references to which may be found in reports by *BG* on 16 September 1867 and *EOM* on 23 September 1867.[21]

Bhima's band was in the vicinity of Semli in December 1860, where five Muslim adults and an adolescent arrived to serve him. As Kaji Singh had been killed only recently, the band suspected treachery. They tied all the six servants to trees and ran them through with swords. Bhima was not a party to the killings; he had wanted to release them.

On 26 March 1860, Grant informed Keating that Bhima had personally led the attack on the village of Hingoni, his last major raid. Regrettably, he had escaped through Khargone, leaving no trace. The reward for his arrest was raised from Rs 500 to Rs 1,000 and still later to Rs 2,000. But the Bhil community, ever protective of his safety, maintained total secrecy. Certain British officials favoured clemency for Bhima's petty misdemeanours as, in their view, he had not committed any major crime or murder, but the government dismissed the suggestion. On 11 March 1861, Cumming informed Bart that the Makranis of Alirajpur were providing Bhima with help and supplies. He suggested that arrests be made at Alirajpur in the presence of Meer Sahmat Ali, adding that this would help apprehend Bhima. It was his belief that Bhima had hidden slabs of silver underground, which he was using to meet the expenses of his comrades and to evade the police, continued the reports in *BG* and *EOM*.[22]

According to Lakshman Brahmin, Bhima's priest, Shyam Ji Nayak had joined the band just two days before the raid in Hingoni—Shyam Ji had, in fact, planned the raid. According to Buddhu, Bhima's syce, Shyam Ji had joined Bhima specifically for the Hingoni raid. Shyam Ji was, in fact, the *rakhwaldar* of Bombay–Agra road for which he received a pension from the Holkar state. He had been deeply aggrieved ever since this pension was withdrawn. After the Hingoni raid, he returned home. Keating was convinced that Shyam Ji would rejoin Bhima if the Holkar state failed to restore his pension. He believed that the Khandesh administration needed to issue a 15-day notice before initiating action against Shyam Ji and strongly urged that until that was done no funds be transported on the Bombay–Agra road. Every bullock cart laden with opium was to have two armed guards, and a caravan of 15 such carts. Here, too, it is evident that the dishonour of the Bhil chiefs' rights was the primary reason for their rebellion.[23]

In 1866, DBA Lt. Blowers deployed men of the secret police as woodcutters in the hills. During the monsoon of 1866, they discovered Bhima Nayak's hide out, where he had buried two guns acquired from the king of Barwani. On 2 April 1867, policemen found Bhima asleep in a hut on the slope of a hill, his bow and arrows beside him. He was arrested after a minor scuffle with four policemen and incarcerated in Sardarpur Jail. The *EOM* on 23 September 1867 and *HM* on 21 October 1867 carried reports on the incident and Bhima Nayak's trial by the government. Sentenced to life imprisonment, he was sent to Port Blair Jail where he died on 29 December 1876.[24]

During Bhima Nayak's trial, the issue of sedition against Barwani state arose once more. His brother, Seva, pleaded that they had turned rebel as their rights had been disrespected. Starving, the Bhils had raided Kantool, and 20 days later looted Datwada, after which they returned to Dhaba Bawdi. Bhima agreed with his brother's contention to an extent but also emphasised that his claim to innocence regarding his rebellion had been jeopardised. After the revolt of 1857 had broken out, the king of Barwani had ordered Mawasia and Bhima to bring about 200 Bhils, but Bhima alone went to meet the king. Bhima said he was prepared to help the king, provided his revenue village was restored to him. When the king dismissed his claim on the grounds that it was an inappropriate moment for such a discussion, Bhima moved to the hills and raided the village of Balakwada in retaliation. When the king refused any help in response to Bhima's frantic message that his men were starving, they perforce began their plunder.[25]

Bhima's wife Nandi and his son were lodged in Indore Jail from January 1865 onwards. Although innocent, they were kept in custody to create pressure on Bhima to surrender. On 31 May 1867, when Bhima was incarcerated in Sardarpur Jail, the agency surgeon of Indore wrote to the AGGCI to petition for his release.[26]

Other Bhil Leaders of Barwani

Around 1858, the Bhils of Dasana, Dahi, Chikalda and Kukshi were raiding the villages and roads of the area. Both the BA and PA were of the opinion that Bhil insurgencies in the Vindhya ranges would continue unabated until the Bhils of Chikalda and Kukshi were subjugated.

A letter from the CO, First Cavalry, to the AGGCI on 11 January 1859 discloses that Daulat Singh, Kalu Nayak, Brahma Singh and Mohasa Nayak were then hiding in the Dasana–Sultanpur forests. Fifty mounted rebels had crossed the Narmada to raid Banswara. Mohasa Nayak had joined forces with Brahma Nayak.[27]

It was the British administration's firm conviction that if the Bhil chiefs of Barwani had vandalised Khandesh, it was because of Kaji Singh and Bhima Nayak. Around 175 chiefs plundered the village of Kheir, in Sultanpur taluka, on the morning of 28 May 1860; they were led by Rustam, Nimbia and Athar Nayak, belonging to the village of Doba Duggar. Earlier, on 3 May, the same band had plundered Tilari Padav near the village of Kheir. Yet another raid took place in Sultanpur when Probyn was still in Pansemal. It was Probyn's belief that, possibly, Isram Nayak and Bhima Nayak had instigated those raids. Both Probyn and Atkins were convinced that about 400 Bhils from Barwani had entered Khandesh and were regularly ravaging the region. In view of the continuing disturbances in the area, Atkins wrote to Grant on 1 June, requesting him to requisition the services of Poona Horse, adding that these ought to be placed under Probyn's control in the Sultanpur and Thalner talukas. In a letter on 10 June 1860, Bart disclosed that he had dispatched 100 armed jawans of the Bhil Corps. Bart held that the king of Barwani would have to compensate for any losses if he was incapable of controlling the chiefs. But the Bhil Corps was unable to capture Ratania or Nimla, although the former's house was razed to the ground and 50 of his livestock confiscated.

The Bhil struggle continued well after Kaji Singh's martyrdom on 3 October 1860, and Putta Ji's surrender. The British were facing much difficulty in launching any effective campaign on account of the guerrilla tactics employed by the Barwani Bhils. Meanwhile, revolts continued in the south and west. A British troop was dispatched from Mhow, but military action against the Bhils was impossible in the rainy season—it was quite evident that the tactics of warfare against the Bhils were proving to be very different from that of any other colonial battle. Newspapers such as *BG* on 12 August 1862, the *Saint James's Chronicle* on 11 September 1862 and the *Dublin Daily Express* on 15 December 1863 reported that the British Army had lost 16 officers and 273 jawans in less than a month. Bhima Nayak, too, remained active till his arrest on 3 April 1867. Newspapers of the time highlighted the beleaguered government's helplessness in the face of such resistance.

Raid at Kukshi Post, 1861

On 16 December 1861, Bhil chiefs of Barwani attacked the Malva Bhil Corps deployed at the Kukshi police checkpost. In the raid led by four chiefs—Nimla, Bisram, Ratania and Khuman—three jawans of the corps were killed and 13 injured. In a telegram sent from Indore, Keating informed Maj. Meade that, with his comrades, Nimla had surrendered unconditionally to Capt. Hanson at 6 am on 28 March 1862.[28] All four chiefs were tried and sentenced to death, but Nimla's sentence was commuted to life imprisonment. On 10 June 1862, a letter from Capt. Wood, PA, Nimar, emphasised his preference for the death sentence for Nimla.[29]

As Nimla, Bisram, Ratania and Khuman were ringleaders in their respective territories, the British faced the problem of finding their successors. Ruling the

Bhil areas or controlling the Bhils had thus far proved to be an impossible task without their chiefs' cooperation. Nimla held Doba Duggar, the most important Bhil jagir in Barwani. He had been paid a salary of Rs 20 a month. However, after the Kukshi episode, the British expressed their ire by appointing as chief his eldest son, Punjala, at a reduced salary of Rs 15 a month. As Bisram and Ratania had not commanded independent territories, no one was appointed in their stead. Instead, Dhegra Nayak, chief of Jharar, who had been of much assistance to Hanson and Keating, was appointed chief at a salary of Rs 10. He was told to maintain peace in the Jharar, Piparkund and Bokarta regions. As Kimla and Govinda had helped Keating, their salaries were raised by Rs 2. Dhan Singh, Khuman's son, was also appointed chief.[30]

Ramla Bhil, 1864–1865

In 1864–1865, as disruptions by the Bhils of Indore were constant, the Holkar Army was dispatched to subdue the rebels, leading to several clashes between the two sides. Ramla Bhil, the chief was arrested, but his comrades managed to escape to the forest. The chief was sentenced to 20 years RI. As the king was critically ill at the time, subjugating the Bhils had become all the more difficult, reported *GA* on 14 May 1864 and *BG* on 25 January 1866.

Ramla belonged to Hanuwantia in Jhabua district, in the Holkar state. A letter written by the BA on 12 February 1864 to the AGGCI reveals that Ramla, with a band of 30–

40 Bhils, frequently ravaged the Hanuwantia area. Months earlier, this band had looted a large consignment of opium in Dhar. They had also enlisted a few thakurs of Jhabua and some residents of the Holkar state. In a letter sent on 9 January 1864, the then officer had requested the establishment of a thana in Hanuwantia with at least 15 sepoys to halt Ramla's depredations, but the demand was rejected.

Ramla had been active in the preceding five to six years, and his band was expanding. One reason for his rebellion was the brutal murder of his son. Ramla was arrested in 1859 and lodged in Mandaleshwar fortress. With help from other prisoners, he had killed Capt. Hawes and escaped. Bart had granted him clemency in May 1861. In December that year, Ramla had cooperated with Cumming at Roati but that had not stopped him from organising a raid in the state of Mahi. In a letter to the AGGCI on 23 February 1864, the BA disclosed that three letters of complaint had been received from the vakil of the king of Jhabua, stating that Ramla and his comrades had looted property worth Rs 1,024 from the patwari of Rampuria. They had attacked the Kunbers of Sarangi and Chabwin in Ratlam. Of the culprits, Bor Ji, Ramla's nephew, and his comrade, Munjathia Kaliya, had been identified. The king of Jhabua was ordered to hold Ramla's arrested comrades in his custody until a thana was constructed. Nine individuals of Ramla's band were arrested for another raid in Dhar. The Indore state announced a reward of Rs 500 for Ramla's capture and urged a thakur of the Jhabua court to apprehend him.

Itiya Bhil, 1864

One of Bhima's collaborators, Itiya, a rebel chief from the village of Sakunda in Muthwar, in the Dasana hills, was a threat to the local thakur as well as the British. Itiya ravaged and terrorised his own and neighbouring areas. In October 1864, the king of Badripur requested the British Government to allow him to send his sepoys to Muthwar to eliminate Itiya. Cumming, who did not favour the plan, instead asked the chiefs of Muthwar and Rajpur to tame Itiya. The thakur of Muthwar was unable to subjugate Itiya as his own Bhils were loyal to the Bhil chief, who was also receiving assistance from the Bhils of Dasana. The source of dispute between the two parties was the 'rights' received by Dasana Bhils from Muthwar.

In one incident, about 50 Bhil chiefs of Muthwar raided Sakunda and in the skirmish that followed, Itiya's hand was injured and 20 heads of his cattle were stolen. On the other side of Sakunda, Itiya crossed the Narmada near Bhusha, in Khandesh. The village lay in the Akrani pargana, with a troop of Bhil Corps stationed nearby at Dhadgaon. At Itiya's request, the *patel* of Bhusha and some sepoys counter-attacked the nayaks of Muthwar and rescued about half of his cattle. The *patel* and one sepoy were killed in this encounter. A furious Cumming summoned the thakur of Muthwar, an indication of his soft corner for Itiya. On 15 December 1864, he summoned the Bhil chiefs of Dasana, Muthwar, Dahi and other nearby areas to Sardarpur to help persuade Itiya to renounce crime. Cumming also suggested that the Holkar state establish a thana in Dasana, which could help control Jugatia—one had already been established in Dahi.[31]

Amaria, Gujaria, Bhalchand, Bajaria and Other Nayaks

Amaria, s/o Sukla Bhil Mankur, was from the village of Boralia and yet another Barwani Bhil chief who had organised some raids. He was sentenced to three years RI on 23 November 1869. In 1864, Bhil chief Gujaria and 14 of his band were tried and sentenced.

In 1864, Mangalia Mahadev and Rupchand were also tried by the government for raids. Both Bhalchand, s/o Bheela, and Bajaria, s/o Lal Singh, belonged to the village of Lonsara in Barwani. They had organised a raid on 30 December 1867 and looted goods worth Rs 1,800 but were only fined.

The British Government was apprehensive about the spread of the Barwani Bhil revolt to the Bhils of Rewa Kantha under Rupa Nayak's leadership.[32]

Jugatia, Bandaria, Railla and Ananda

Jugatia, s/o Bhikia Bhil, one of the leading chiefs of Barwani, had been previously associated with Bhima's band in 1860. After the amnesty received from the Holkar state, Jugatia returned to his village where he murdered his wife on the suspicion that she was a witch. Although his band was not large, the British, the Holkar state, the thakurs of Dasana and Alirajpur, among others, were constantly harassed by him. For the plunder perpetrated in the Indore region, the

Holkar state sentenced him to imprisonment for 20 years. He was incarcerated in Indore Jail, but in 1871, managed to escape along with other prisoners. At the governor general's bidding, the Holkar state pardoned him on 21 June 1872 on the condition that he would, henceforth, live peacefully. The king had granted this pardon on the mediation of the priest Nathu Rao, a Brahmin of Dharmarai, a small state in the Dasana hills. Nathu Rao had a fair amount of influence among the Bhils. But Jugatia continued his raids in Holkar territory and Khandesh. In one incident, Jugatia and his son, Bandaria, raided a village in Khandesh, and the latter was caught and jailed. A letter from Col. Gordon on 23 June 1872 reveals that Jugatia had submitted an application for clemency for his son but the PA, on 6 July, had pleaded helplessness as it was out of his jurisdiction.

On 27 January 1871, the sessions court at Dhule sentenced Bandaria to four years RI, which the PA, for some reason, misinterpreted as two years. He was imprisoned in a jail in Khandesh and later shifted to Poona Central Jail. When the request for clemency reached the governor of the Bombay Government, it was rejected. The Bombay Government admonished the AGGCI that Bandaria was no child but a youth aged 32; also emphasising that the Bhil rebel had been sentenced to not two but four years of RI. In his application, Jugatia had pleaded that Bandaria had participated in the raid at the bidding of others.[33] However, he was not pardoned and was compelled to complete the four-year jail term.

On 21 January 1873, personal animosity led Jugatia, along with 50 other Bhils, to raid the house of Cheema Nayak in the village of Semli in Barwani. They looted goods worth Rs 50 and abducted three women and a girl. The local feudal chiefs tried to effect a compromise with Jugatia. Nathu Purohit, *kamdar* (goverment official) of Dahi, and the king of Dharmarai held peace negotiations with Jugatia in January 1873 at the village of Nareem Pal on the banks of the Narmada. Meanwhile, Holkar sent his sepoys to capture Jugatia. Daulat Singh, the prince of Dharmarai, along with 100 jawans joined the Holkar Army and established a police post near Jugatia's house. This enraged Jugatia and the other Bhils, and they attacked the Holkar troop on 10 February 1873, injuring a few sepoys. They also killed Munoba, a Brahmin, who belonged to the Holkar state; he was the patwari of the villages of Arda, Rolagua, Dahi and Dasana in Barwani. Led by Imamuddin, a police officer, Holkar's police laid siege for the next two months.

On 30 March 1873, Jugatia surrendered to Raja Rao Bahadur Venkat Rai, the native superintendent of Barwani and was sent to Barwani Jail. He was tried in the court of the DBA and sentenced to life imprisonment on 7 May 1873 at Yeravda Central Jail (now Yerawada Central Jail), near Poona.

The judicial department of the Bombay Government issued an amnesty to 186 prisoners on 31 December 1892. Jugatia was to serve his jail term for seven months and 24 days, on the completion of which he would be released.

Railla Bhil, Jugatia's brother, was active in the Barwani region as well. After Jugatia's surrender, Railla, too, was apprehended on 8 August 1873 and sent to Sardarpur Jail. Bandaria continued his reign of plunder after his release from jail.[34]

On 10 October 1874, Sarwan Bhil confessed to British officers that his band had looted a *kulal* (member of a potter caste) and a banjara two years earlier near Sadar Drain, located between Than and Cheetwal in Holkar territory. The raid was led by Ananda Nayak, a prominent chief of Barwani and brother-in-law of Bhima Nayak. Notwithstanding an annual income of Rs 2,500 from the state, Ananda's ravages had continued. Tutahu Bhil, a member of the group, had distributed the spoils amongst Munshi Nayak, Mangalia, Ramla, Sarwan, Dewla and himself, with each receiving eight annas. As Tutahu and Mangalia had appropriated some stolen ornaments without giving the others a share, this led to discontent within the group, precipitating Sarwan's betrayal of the band. The *mahalkuri* of Pati investigated the matter and the Barwani state tried the Bhils involved.

Over the months of 1874, 49 such cases came to light in the Barwani region alone, with goods worth Rs 6,000 looted. But the culprits were punished in only one case, which was why, with consent from the king of Barwani, the British Government decided to bring the Bhils to book. The king was disinclined to punish Ananda, but six others were penalised. As Sarwan was the informer in this case, he was pardoned.[35]

Revolt in Dasana, 1872-1902

The Bhils of Dasana remained a terrifying presence for about 20 years in the hills around Indore. Worried, the Indore state urged British officers to discipline them. On 9 May 1872, BA Maj. William Keening wrote to BA A.D. Daly that he had ordered the thanadar of Chikli to investigate. The investigation revealed that Buchia, Salamia, Khema, Bhauria, Kania and Gasu were prominent among the rebellious Dasana Bhils.

Beginning at Dhar and working their way through Barwani, Dasana Bhils entered Khandesh and looted goods worth Rs 87 and 12 annas in the village of Bhailri. Thanadar Habib Khan informed the king of Dhar that even though Jamadar Chhote Khan had made some arrests on 2 April 1877, the Bhils had denied their involvement. On 6 April, Chotte Khan escorted 11 Bhils to the village of Dabhani to which they belonged, where he was attacked by them. Buchia, the chief culprit, was killed, while some others were injured. The looted goods were recovered from Gusia Bhil, who was then tried and punished.[36]

On 14 April 1902, *HM*'s report held the famine responsible for the deterioration of the situation over the preceding years, as a result of which the entire province was being subjected to raids. Bhil rebels were in hiding in the Satpura hills south of Indore and in south Nimar. The Bhil chiefs of Dasana were once again becoming troublesome. The Indore state made several attempts to repress them, with cooperation from the British Government. The Malva

Bhil Corps and the police of Indore state were dispatched to Barwani and Alirajpur. A battle ensued between the police and Bhils, after which several Bhils were captured. Some surrendered but 42 still managed to escape. The Malva Bhil Corps raided several places in Dahod and Jhabua. Some days previously, a Bhil band had raided the police post of Pitol, 19.8 mil. from Dahod and freed a comrade. These rebels had been trying to reach their own areas of operation in British territory, all the while being prevented by the police of Jhabua.

Bhil Revolts in Alirajpur, 1870-1883

Alirajpur was a small Bhil state, the ruling king of which claimed links with the Sisodia clan. Barwani and Alirajpur were situated on the borders of Khandesh but were distinct entities, and the ruling family was controlled by the PA, Bhopawar, headquartered at Sardarpur. Although the Bhil chiefs had revolted in Bari in 1824, it was not until 1870 that the Bhils of Alirajpur engaged in any radical rebellion.

After the advent of the British, some attempts at financial reforms were made from 1820 to 1880, but these merely served to intensify the exploitation of the Bhils. The British had the villages of Alirajpur assessed by the patwaris. For centuries, the Bhils had been using the forests without paying any tax—heavy taxes were now imposed. Controls were enforced on the practice of mahua distillation. The disgruntled Bhil chiefs of 12 villages in the parganas of Rath and Takarbada submitted a list of their grievances to the PA of Alirajpur in 1883. They commended the late king as a considerate ruler who had taxed cultivators based on their implements—the rate in his time was Rs 3 or 4 per plough, and the farmers had been content. But with the incumbent king's new taxation regime, traders had instituted a new system of calculation that harmed the interests of Bhil cultivators, who were unable to pay the arrears. The excise duty and taxes on forests meant Bhil exploitation, even as they were already being exploited by moneylenders. A writ petition had been submitted in 1869, followed by more such petitions, but the fact is that the Bhils received certain concessions only after they intensified their rebellion from 1870 onwards.[37]

The Bhils of Khushalpur and Barwani regularly raided Jhabua, forcing the British to shift the Malva Bhil Corps to Thandla. The Bhils of Dasana plundered Chikalda (Alirajpur) on 9 May 1872.[38]

Chitto's Revolt

On 6 February 1883, the *Western Daily Press* reported a horrendous uprising in Alirajpur, in January to February 1883.

> The feudatory State of Ali Rajpur, where serious disturbances are reported to have broken out among the Bheel, is perhaps the smallest and least important native principality in India retaining the name and rights of semi-independence. Thanks to its isolated position on the western spurs of the Vindhya range, it escaped many of the dangers of Maratha

incursions, and some of the consequences of the extension of English power. The early records of the State have been lost, and its origin has not been rescued from the myths of history; but the ruling family retain the proud remembrance of their descent from the great house of Udaipur. The area of Ali Rajpur is as limited as its pretensions to fame—its surface not exceeding 800 square miles. The population, mostly Bheels, numbers some 30,000 persons, and the Rana enjoys a personal revenue of some £3,000 a year. His military force is composed of 150 policemen and two guns; but the occasion has not arisen for employing either it or the Malwa Bheel corps, to the maintenance of which the Rana contributes, in any serious way. In fact, Ali Rajpur has always been considered a progressive little State in its way and caused no trouble to the administration of the Central India Agency. If the Bheel was advancing anywhere in the scale of civilisation by means of education and a provident government, it would have been admitted that he was doing so in Ali Rajpur under the guidance of the Prince of the Sisodia Rajput. Ali Rajpur was many years ago the tributary of the larger State of Dhar, but in 1821 the rights of the latter were transferred to us. In the capacity of suzerain, we have been several times called upon to intervene in deciding the difficult question of family succession; but although the principality has passed through its crisis and been, like other Indian territories, the sport of fortune and the plaything of ambition, the intervention has always been attended by happy results. The present Prince Rupdeo was placed in the seat of power in 1871, on his brother's death, and has never given cause of dissatisfaction. It is probable, therefore, that the present outbreak within his brothers has been caused, not by say disloyalty towards his person or dislike for his regime, but by some fresh ebullition of that discontent and rebellious inclination among the Bheels which first revealed itself some two years ago and which does not yet seem to have been quelled or removed.

Alirajpur's population, comprising mainly Bhils and Bhilalas, was governed by the Bhopawar Agency. Its ruler had somewhat limited rights as compared to other Central Indian principalities and could do little about the serious crimes committed in the state unless authorised. When King Rup Dev Singh died in 1881 leaving no successor, the British placed the minor Bage Singh on the throne and administered the state headed by the PA of Bhopawar. But with the headquarters of Bhopawar Agency some 60 mil. away in Sardarpur, complete control of the state proved to be a challenge. The chief minister (CM) Khan Bahadur Najaf Khan looked after day-to-day affairs in the main, while the minor king was sent to Residency College, Indore to be educated.

Upon the king's death, officers held consultations about his successor. At the time, the weightiest claim was that of the king of Dharampur who requested that one of his sons be appointed king of Alirajpur. But the Bombay Government dismissed his request, as reported in the *Times of India* (hereafter *TOI*) on 4 August 1883.

In 1881, following Najaf Khan's appointment as CM, Barwani, Venkat Rao was appointed CM, Alirajpur. As several Bhil revolts had taken place during his tenure, Najaf Khan was reinstated at Alirajpur, while command was entrusted to the thakur of Jokhwara, brother of the thakur of Bori. Both Najaf Khan and the thakur of Bori had made statements during the trial of Chitto, continued the *TOI* report on 4 August 1883.

Chitto Bhil (Bhilala) led the revolt that raged here in 1882–1883. He belonged to the village of Sorwa, where he had amassed much wealth. His band consisted of 7,000 armed members, including Afghans.

To contain Chitto, Maj. Biddulph, PA, Bhopawar Agency travelled from Sardarpur to Alirajpur, with jawans from the Malva Bhil Corps and Central Indian Horse. The troops repulsed Chitto's attack and managed to drive him back to the southern hills of Rajpur. When the Bhils reopened a front, army troops were dispatched from two directions: Mhow and Sardarpur. The *Globe* on 12 February 1883 and *TOI* on 4 August 1883 reported that the disturbance was so intense that AGGCI Sir Lepel Griffin arrived post-haste on receiving the news.

Chitto Bhil's revolt may be reconstructed from the depositions made during his trial that commenced on 16 July 1883 in the sessions court of AAGGCI Capt. Robertson. Three Indian pleaders cooperated in fixing the charge against Chitto in Mhow. Biddulph, the first witness, deposed that while at Sardarpur, he had received intelligence on

19 January 1883 that several hundred Bhils led by Chitto had plundered Nanpur on 7 January 1883, injuring many and looting goods worth Rs 1,700. Subsequently, Chitto had plundered Chhaktala on 9 January, Bhawra on 11 January and Chandpur on 16 January. At Nanpur on 23 January, Biddulph discovered that several residents had been injured by sword attacks, their houses razed to the ground and set on fire. The Bhils had looted a thana and killed a man on 23 January, but Chitto's involvement remained unconfirmed. The *TOI* carried articles on these incidents on 26 July and 4 August 1883.

While at Nanpur, Biddulph was informed that 5,000 to 10,000 Bhils, Makranis and foreigners armed with guns, swords, and bows and arrows had surrounded Rajpur, the capital of Alirajpur. On reaching Rajpur, he found that the siege had continued for two and a half hours. The Bhils were preparing to plunder the state treasury, residents were being robbed and complete anarchy prevailed in the town. In an unprecedented move, its frightened queen had even come out of purdah to meet Chitto. The officers were helpless, the roads were closed and communications had broken down. Armed groups were active in broad daylight.

In view of the grave situation, Biddulph appealed to Chitto through a messenger on 25 January, urging Chitto and Bhavani, his lieutenant, to meet him to present their grievances, while guaranteeing their security. Chitto returned the appeal, attaching an annexure demanding the king be reinstated in Alirajpur. But as the annexure had no signature, Biddulph rejected its validity and returned it to the chief. Chitto then sent Biddulph another letter signed by the thakur of Phulmal, Bhavani, several *patel*s and himself. The letter demanded that the king be reinstated in court, as the existing form of governance, with British interference, was not recognised.

On 1 February 1883, Chitto sent verbal messages to Biddulph, through the *patel*s of Sorwa, asking to meet Najaf Khan. On the same day, Biddulph sent a delegation of five Indian officials led by the thakur of Bori and Najaf Khan to Doblajhiri, 4 mil. from Rajpur where Chitto and his men were camped. Najaf Khan noticed that Chitto, the thakur of Phulmal, Bhavani, the Makranis and foreigners were all carrying arms. The Makranis and foreigners were led by Dost Muhammad, a Makrani jamadar. Najaf Khan invited Chitto to Rajpur to present his grievances, but the chief declined as he feared arrest. He shared some of his grievances with Najaf Khan, particularly that Venkat Rao had failed to honour their due rights. Rao had displaced all the *patel*s and imprisoned them in chains. The forest meeting continued overnight but with no resolution, reported *TOI* on 26 July and 4 August 1883, after which Najaf Khan returned to Rajpur.

Soon after, Chitto raided several villages around the village of Sorwa, where he lived with his family. On 3 February, Biddulph set out for Sorwa, 11 mil. from Rajpur, with troops from the army and cavalry. Biddulph and Chitto engaged in an encounter on 5 February; Biddulph was surrounded and fired upon by Makranis when trekking through the forested hills. Dost Muhammad was killed in the return fire. A soldier of the Central Indian Horse was also killed, while the major himself had a narrow escape. Dost Muhammad's death was a critical success for the government, draining strength from Chitto's revolt.

Griffin reached Rajpur on 14 February 1883. A *firman* (edict) was issued on 16 February, promising general amnesty for all Bhils except the thakur of Phulmal, Chitto, Bhavani and the Makranis. Some armed Bhils then dispersed, but soon regrouped and opened up a front at Amkhut (Madhya Pradesh). When the army left Alirajpur for Amkhut, Chitto took to the forests with his family and comrades. Capt. Bignell of the Malva Bhil Corps and Maj. Isari Prasad, risaldar of the Central Indian Horse, were deputed to arrest those members of Chitto's band not covered by the general amnesty. Reports of these events were published in the *Daily Telegraph & Courier* (London) on 12 February 1883 and in *TOI* on 17 April, 26 July and 4 August 1883.

Besides Isari Prasad's troops, the army was also summoned from Panchmahal to help capture Chitto, then hiding in the forest. Holland, SP, Bombay district; ASP Spence and district police inspector (DPI) Khan Sahib Abbas Ali Khan led the siege. On 4 August 1883, *TOI* noted that the government viewed Abbas Ali's contribution as the most vital. However, the army was unable to move beyond Dhar as three Bhil chiefs, including Chitto, continued to resist, reported the *Morning Post* on 14 February 1883.

Chitto tried to escape through Berar with his principal comrades and family, making several abortive attempts to instigate the Bhils of Akola and Amravati. Capt. Bignell continued to search for and pursue Chitto's men in the forests, arresting them one by one. Beleaguered, Chitto received no reprieve, with his wife and horses hunted down during the last week of February and all of March. By the beginning of April, his mother-in-law was his only companion.

Holland's repeated attempts at persuading Chitto to surrender finally succeeded at Godhra in the second week of April 1883. The *TOI* on 26 July and 31 December 1883, the *Bangalore Spectator* on 30 April 1883 and the *Friend of India and Statesman* (hereafter *FIS*) on 27 February 1883 carried reports of the viceroy's gratitude to Holland on this achievement.

Although the Bhils had dispersed after their encounter with the army, the government had little choice but to give up its repressive policy and focus on the causes of and remedies to Bhil unrest. This served to pacify the Bhil leaders and thus, the insurrection was crushed in this area, reported *HMICE* on 17 April 1883.

The court, the proceedings of which began in July 1882, viewed the major events thus:

I. Large-scale plunder and destruction of property by the rebels;

II. Refusal to meet Maj. Biddulph at Rajpur;

III. Refusal on 1 February to meet the delegation sent to Doblajhiri, despite its request;

IV. Dost Muhammad's refusal to recognise Bage Singh as king; the king of Dharampur as the rightful claimant to the throne;
V. Attack on the PA on 3 February;
VI. Chitto's confession that he had gone to Dharampur at the bidding of the thakur of Phulmal, and his belief in the king of Dharmapur as the rightful claimant to the throne, not Bage Singh.

Nevertheless, despite the many excesses perpetrated by Venkat Rao, the court refused to pardon Chitto's crimes. Capt. Robertson was of the view that some of Chitto's rights had indeed been curtailed, but then he was not the only such victim. Robertson maintained that Chitto's aim was to see someone on the throne whom he could influence. That Venkat Rao had allowed only Banias and Rajputs to trade and burdened the Bhils with unnecessary taxes was indisputable. On 4 August 1883, *TOI* reported that Chitto's refusal to allow the CM to hoist the state's flag at the palace was tantamount to an overthrow of authority.

Biddulph also informed the court that Venkat Rao's unpopularity was the main cause for Chitto's and the Bhils' rebellion. In the preceding four years, Rao had imposed heavy taxes on forest produce. Ten years earlier, the state had granted Chitto some concessions, which Venkat Rao had dishonoured. When Chitto plundered grain meant for sale during the famine, Rao had him arrested and jailed. Thus, the whole state seethed with discontent because of state officials, reported *TOI* on 26 July 1883.

Biddulph, however, had dissociated himself from all responsibility, shifting the blame on to state officials. In fact, since the king was a minor and Biddulph was managing the state's affairs, he was equally culpable.

Biddulph informed the court that Chitto had merely wanted the removal of Venkat Rao, not the crowning of another king. Both the thakur of Phulmal and Chitto believed in the legitimacy of Dharampur's claim to the throne. At the thakur's bidding, Chitto had also visited Dharampur, where chiefs from all over the state had been invited, and the claim to the throne of Alirajpur was presented.

Khan Bahadur Najaf Khan, too, deposed at Chitto's trial. He claimed that the Bhils were not dissatisfied before 1873, as they were getting their dues. Chitto received 10 per cent of total income, including a monthly allowance of Rs 20 from the state. It was Najaf Khan's opinion that discontent had spread in the state during the preceding eight years, as the *patel*s were not receiving their legitimate dues. Some unjust taxes had also been imposed on the Bhils. For instance, if Rs 1–5 per plough was being charged for a piece of land in Barwani, the charge in Alirajpur was Rs 8–9 for a similar piece of land, reported *TOI* on 26 July 1883.

The third witness in Chitto's trial was the thakur of Bori; seven more witnesses testified. Three *patel*s deposed on behalf of the defence—all of them denounced Venkat Rao's misrule. Chitto's clerk produced a register which showed that Makranis were employed by the chief, settling their dues was impossible unless Chitto was given his own.

After the hearing, the following charges were levied against the accused:

I. Rebellion by a massive crowd of armed Bhils against the state administration in December 1881 and January–February 1883: Section 121 IPC;

II. Robbery, with five other persons in Nanpur on 17 January 1883: Section 395 IPC;

III. Instigating the Bhils to raid Baradbara on 12 January: Section 109, 395 IPC; State Law of Alirajpur;

IV. Loot of Rs 1,000 from Mangal Lal, between February and August 1882; loot of Rs 125 from Bohra Nurudddin on 30 December 1882: Section 411 IPC; State law of Alirajpur.

The overall charge was one of waging war against the government of the state. The trial ended with life imprisonment for Chitto and Bhavani, and confiscation of their property. According to articles carried in *TOI* on 26 July and 4 August 1883, the case of the Makranis was heard separately. The 16 Makranis, who had fired at the army during the battle in Sorwa, were tried in Biddulph's court on 2 August 1883. These included Nankiya, a companion of Bhavani. He had plundered Bhawra, where a trader was killed. The hearing was resumed on 9 August 1883, and the sentences were pronounced on the following day. Along with thousands of Bhil warriors, Makranis had surrounded Rajpur for more than 24 hours on 1 and 2 February 1883, when their leader, Chitto, was encamped at Doblajhiri. Of these 16 Makranis, there was insufficient evidence against three, while one was a young man of 19; they all were acquitted. Reports in *TOI* on 20 August and 31 December 1883 reveal that the court declared two Makranis—Allah Hasan and Bahram—to be notorious and sentenced them to death.

On 11 August 1883, *FIS* carried an article about yet another case in which some goods plundered by Chitto were recovered from Kalu Ghanchi, a Bhil chief of Bharuch, for which he was given a 10-year sentence.

PART II

7
RAJPUTANA, REWA KANTHA AND MAHI KANTHA AGENCIES: GENERAL INTRODUCTION

Rajputana

The British Government was responsible for the administrative unit (agency or province) of Rajputana. It included the principalities of Jaisalmer, Jodhpur (Marwar), Bikaner, Alwar, Shekhawati, Jaipur, Bharatpur, Dhaulpur, Karauli, Bundi, Kota, Jhalawad, Pratapgarh, Banswara, Dungarpur, Udaipur (Mewar) and Sirohi as well as the British districts of Ajmer, Kishangarh and Tonk.[1] Rajputana included, besides Rajasthan, some regions of present-day Madhya Pradesh and Gujarat. Of these, Udaipur, Banswara, Jodhpur, Dungarpur, Kota, Pratapgarh and Sirohi were termed Bhil areas. By some accounts Bansia Bhil, Dungariya Bhil, Kotya Bhil and Mandya Bhil had founded Banswara, Dungarpur, Kota and Mandalgarh, respectively.

Bhils and Rajputs of Rajputana

Before the advent of the Rajputs, a large chunk of eastern, southern and south-eastern Rajasthan was ruled by Bhil tribes. Bhils are said to have made important contributions to the development of the Ahar Civilisation, contemporaneous with the Indus Valley Civilisation. The Rajputs invaded this region between the 7th and 14th centuries. The influx was particularly heavy during the 11th and 12th centuries when, driven out of Sindh by Muslims, they entered these areas on horseback and established themselves in the plains. In the struggle for power that followed, the Bhils fled to the hills and dense forests when the Rajputs captured the plains. It is believed that powerful Bhil groups once inhabited the areas around Bhillmal (known today as Bhinmal). In the course of time, the Guhilauts (the Mewar ruling family) battled the Bhils and Pratihars in order to establish their rule in Mewar, slaughtering thousands of Bhils. The Bhils continued their crusade against them in the subsequent period.[2] While it is generally acknowledged that the Rajput invasion of Bhil territories dates to the period between the 7th and 14th centuries, there is no unanimity. However, it may be safely assumed that the Rajputs arrived after the 7th and before the 14th century.

The Rajputs gave due regard to the Bhils as the erstwhile inhabitants and landholders of these territories. This is evident from the custom of anointing the forehead of a Rajput chief when he ascended the throne by the blood of a Bhil chief, a custom that continued up to the middle of the 20th century. James Todd, an English administrator, tells of Goh, an ancestor of the Sisodia Rajputs, who had received the state of Idar from a Bhil king. The prevailing story is that Goh, when young, often visited the Bhils in the forests and endeared himself to them. When the Bhils decided to select a king for themselves, they chose Goh. A young Bhil pierced his thumb and with his blood, anointed Goh's forehead as a mark of his sovereignty. Bhil chiefs then gave their assent to this gesture. Goh subsequently murdered the very Bhil who had made him king.

While the anecdote does not point to the motive of the aforesaid murder, it does highlight the Rajput defeat of the Bhils of Idar and the latter's dispossession. Interestingly, the account also indicates that the Rajputs considered their victory over the Bhils as the beginning of their rule and the establishment of the source of their power as derived from the deeds and silent acquiescence of the tribals. Perhaps, the Rajput adoption of Bhil deities as their own protector gods and goddesses could well have been one means to that end. Having usurped Bhil lands, Rajputs began the custom of having their kings anointed with Bhil blood as a means of pacifying them. In Russell's time, too, Bhil landowners of Ogun and Undari claimed the privilege of anointing the Sisodia kings of the states of Udaipur, Dungarpur, Banswara and Pratapgarh. The Bhil chief of Ogun pierced his own thumb and with his blood, anointed the king's forehead as a mark of the latter's power and escorted the king to the throne, while the Bhil chief of Undari held a plate with saffron and rice used to anoint the king's forehead. On 10 October 1878, the *Times of India* carried a report on the custom of anointment of Udaipur rulers with Bhil blood begun centuries ago during the reign of Rana Bappa to whom a Bhil named Balneo had ceded the throne.

In view of the Bhils' rebellious disposition, Rajputs in their own states acknowledged Bhil chiefs as autonomous chiefs of their respective areas and conferred upon them honourable titles such as Rawat, Bhaumia and Garasia. At places where jagirs continued to remain autonomous, Bhil chiefs continued as autonomous jagirdars. These Bhil jagirdars collected a *lag or bolai* (tax) from the travellers and traders passing through their territories in return for protection. They also collected another tax—*rakhwali*—for the security of agricultural fields and properties in their territories. They received revenue-free lands as well, in return for their duties as watchmen in the plains.

The use of Bhils as village guards strengthens the opinion that they were the oldest inhabitants of these areas. In Nimar and Berar, Bhils worked as *mankar*s, the finest guards of their villages. Grant Duff has observed that the Marathas appointed the Ramosi, a Bhil tribe, as village guards. The Ramosis, a caste of professional village watchmen, were descended possibly from either Bhils or Kolis.[3]

In retrospect, the Bhils had been in a far better position under the Mughals. In *Ain-e-Akbari*, Abul-Fazl described the Bhils as law-abiding and hard working. With the decline of Mughal power, the Marathas began to invade Rajasthan, turning the Bhils increasingly rebellious. If the Bhils of Mewar had revolted, it was because of the ban on the tax which they levied on traders and wayfarers passing through their territories.[4]

The issue of blood relations and succession among Bhils and Rajputs had always been contentious. In the course of time, certain Bhil gotras of Rajasthan began to share similarities with those of the Rajputs. This tendency to claim links with the Rajputs could well be attributed to a subaltern class desire for upward mobility as well as an expression of its frustration. Some authors have dwelt on the thesis that Bhilalas were born of Bhil–Rajput cohabitation. Another claim is that Garasia blood is Rajput and Bhil in equal parts. According to *Veer Vinod* by Kaviraj Shyamaldas, the Bhils of Kalyanpura claimed descent from the Pawar Rajputs of Dhar. Similarly, the Bhils of Devpura, Paduna, Kharwad Mandva, Jawar, Chinavda, Saaru, Limboda, Singatwada, Amarpura and Derwas claimed descent from Sisodia Rajputs. That every caste or tribe has mixed blood to some degree is true. There was some degree of intermarriage between Rajputs and Bhil chiefs, but these ought to be treated as exceptions. The Bhils of Rajasthan had always been guided by their own independent traditions and socio-political ties.

The murder of Bhil tribals was quite common during Rajput suzerainty. Bhils were also sacrificed in the name of various customs and rites. In the old capital of Amber, near Jaipur, stands a Shiladevi temple where one tribal was sacrificed every morning. This custom continued till the beginning of the 19th century, i.e., till the establishment of British rule. In Sirohi, in November 1876, it was announced that the anointment ceremony would be accompanied by the custom-dictated killing of seven Bhils. On 27 May 1877, the *Cornish Times* reported that the Bhils of the state fled en masse as soon as this announcement was made. Such customs or beliefs emphasised traditional cruelty vis-à-vis the Bhils—and such acts compelled the Bhils to react with barbarity and violence.

The *Udaipur Gazetteer* of 1908 reveals that the Marathas treated the Bhils like wild animals. They staged encounters to kill the tribals, sometimes skewering them with lances or setting them on fire. On occasion, they were even known to tie a red-hot iron rod to a Bhil's body. An excess of such atrocities turned the Bhils into criminals and vandals.

However, like the Bhils of Madhya Pradesh, Gujarat and Maharashtra, the Bhils of Rajasthan had inhabited the region well before the arrival of the Aryans or Dravidians. They were the original inhabitants of the area and lived in freedom till the advent of the Rajputs in the 7th century.[5]

Rewa Kantha

Rewa Kantha was a political agency in Eastern Gujarat during British rule, through which the British maintained their control over the territories of several indigenous princes. Named Rewa Kantha owing to its location along the banks of the Rewa (Narmada), it also extended up to the banks of the Mahi.

Rewa Kantha was formed in 1811 under the aegis of the Rajputana Agency but was directly controlled by the Foreign Office. This agency had an area of 4,980 sq. mil. and in 1891, its population was 7,33,506, although it had declined to 4,79,065 by 1901, as a consequence of the famine of 1899-1900. Its borders touched Mewar, Dungarpur and Banswara in the north as well as the Bhalod subdivision, Dahod (Panchmahal), Alirajpur, some small principalities of Bhopawar Agency and some parts of Khandesh. It adjoined Gaekwad territories and the Mandvi subdivision of Surat in the south, Ankaleshwar, Bharuch, some Gaekwad areas, Godhra and Kalol (Panchmahal), Thasra and Kapadwanj (Kaira), and part of Ahmedabad in the west. The PA of Rewa Kantha was also the collector of Panchmahal, the neighbouring British district. The borders of Rewa Kantha surrounded the district of Panchmahal on virtually all sides. After Independence, Rewa Kantha was merged with the Saurashtra region of Gujarat.

Rewa Kantha covered a total of six large and 66 small principalities. The largest of these princely states was Rajpipla, which was situated in the south. The smaller states included Baria, Chhota Udaipur, Lunawara, Balasinor, Sunth, Kadana, Bhadrawa, Sanjeli, Umeta, Jambughoda, Sankhera, Mehwas, Pandu Mehwas, Narukot, Mandwa, Gad Boriyad, Sanor, Wajiriya, Vanamla, among others.

Rewa Kantha and Mahi Kantha (the second agency) were first governed by the Bhils and Kolis. The Rajputs built their first palace in Rajpipla. After defeating the Rajputs in the 12th-14th centuries, Muslims settled in Champaner. They defeated the Chauhans in 1484, and Ahmedabad became part of a Muslim sultanate. An extensive area of Rewa Kantha was then part of the Ahmedabad sultanate.

After the fall of the Champaner, local Rajputs once again held sway but the Mughals soon established their rule, followed by the Marathas. After the Rewa Kantha Agency was formed, J.P. Willoughby was appointed its first PA on 6 February 1826. The position was abolished in 1829, but revived on 12 January 1842, following an order from the board of directors.[6]

Mahi Kantha

After the success of Kathiawar's administrative system in Gujarat under the Bombay Presidency, the political agency of Mahi Kantha, covering some princely states, was formed in 1812. To the east, Mahi Kantha adjoined the territories of Rewa Kantha, Dungarpur and Kaira. Its northern borders touched the states of Mewar and Sirohi and on the western side were the territories of Kheralu, Vijapur and Gaekwad. It adjoined Balasinor, Kaira, Ahmedabad and Lunawara. With an area of 3,124 sq. mil., the agency covered six districts— Chotta (Nani) Marwar (Talukas Idar and Ahmednagar), Rehwar (Rajasthan), Sabar Kantha, Watrak Kantha, Bavisi and Katosan. Idar was the largest state, while Pol and Danta were smaller. Mahi Kantha's population of 5,17,485 in 1881 was reduced to 3,61,545 in 1901 in this disaster-prone hill tract following famine.[7] The Mahi Kantha Agency was directly governed by the Foreign Office. In 1820, Col. Walker was placed in charge after he returned from the Kathiawar expedition in 1819. By 1818, the area had come under the Bombay Presidency and most Rajputs had accepted British suzerainty. After Independence, it formed part of Gujarat in 1960.[8]

After entering into treaties with the Rajputs, the British directed their attention to political domination over the Bhils. Interference in the internal affairs of Bhils grew during the British dispensation, turning this previously autonomous society rebellious. It is from this point onward that written testimonies of Bhil rebellion are available. Before the British entered Gujarat, they made repeated attempts to win over the Bhil chiefs of the area. On 27 December 1806, the *Lancaster Gazette* reported that they had reached beneficial agreements with the Bhil tribes living in Gujarat, Malva and other mountainous areas. Controlling the Bhils had been a constant challenge for the British Army, which is why they fell back on their experience in Khandesh by forming the Mewar Bhil Corps in Mahi Kantha in 1841.

On 13 January 1818, the state of Mewar entered into a treaty with the East India Company and transferred all its external affairs to the Company's management. Similar treaties were entered into with the other Bhil preponderant areas—with Dungarpur on 11 December 1818, Banswara on 25 December 1818, Pratapgarh on 5 October 1818, and Sirohi on 11 September 1823—after which the British began to collect tribute from those states and manage their external affairs. In order to meet this expense, these states had little choice but to increase tax collection from their subjects.[9]

Under British suzerainty, Mewar covered 13,674 sq. mil., with 6,030 villages. The population in 1901 totalled

10,18,805. The state was directed to deposit a fourth of its total tax collection with the British Government for five years, after which its share was to be raised to three-eighths. However, the transfer was fixed at Rs 3 lakh per year in 1826, although it was reduced to Rs 2 lakh in 1846. Following these treaties, the British Government deputed its PAs in all the states.[10]

In order to meet British demands, Mewar enhanced the taxes levied on its subjects. Thus far, the Bhils had not been covered by any taxation system or had paid merely nominal taxes but were now subjected to increased demands. Understandably, this led to unrest. Col. James Todd, a British administrator, disbanded the jagirdars' armies, creating discontent amongst Bhil jagirdars with their own armies. They were divested of their right to collect *rakhwali* and *bolai* taxes. Revolts then erupted in the mountainous southern and western areas of Udaipur, and the Bhils imposed an embargo in their territories in 1818. All of Todd's attempts at pacification failed. In 1820, the army attempted to crush the Bhil revolt but failed. From January to December 1823, British troops tried desperately to subjugate the Bhils.[11]

The state of Dungarpur, with an area of 1,447 sq. mil., covered 762 villages. Its population was 1,59,192 in 1911. Bhils numbering approximately 75,000 accounted for about half. The Mangarh Hill of Dungarpur adjoined the borders of Sunth in Gujarat and Banswara in Rajasthan.[12]

The rebellion of the Bhils of Dungarpur and Banswara was protracted. On 12 May 1825, Bhils of Limbarabaru entered into an agreement with the Company—it was, in fact, imposed by the British. Under the treaty, Bhils were to surrender their weapons, return assets looted in the past, desist from further plunder, refuse shelter to any individual inimical to the Company and follow the Company's orders. They were to charge no more than the taxes fixed from thakurs and *rawals* in villages. Their annual tax payment to the *rawal* of Dungarpur was non-negotiable. It was incumbent upon them to provide protection if an employee of the Company visited their village. The Bhil chiefs of Simur Waru, Deval and Nandu Pal also entered into similar agreements.

Formation of Mewar Bhil Corps
Controlling the Bhils living in the hills, forests and valleys was proving impossible for the British Army—a lesson learnt from their Khandesh experience. In 1837, Col. James Outram, then PA, Mahi Kantha, had presented to the Bombay Government his proposal for the formation of the Mewar Bhil Corps. The corps was meant to meet the requirements of military police on the one hand and provide employment to Bhil chiefs in order to draw them into the Bhil Corps, which would be used in the Company's interest, on the other.

The king of Mewar had already endorsed the plan and agreed to bear the expense. While Dungarpur, Banswara and Pratapgarh were to pay Rs 70,000 annually for the purpose, Mewar's annual share was settled at Rs 50,000. The AGG in Rajputana and PAs of Mewar and Mahi Kantha sent a joint memorandum to the governor general, following which the latter's advisory council sanctioned the formation of the corps in April 1841. Following the sanction, Outram proceeded to form the Mewar Bhil Corps in 1841, on the pattern of the Khandesh Bhil Corps.

The corps was headquartered at Kherwara in Udaipur, with W. Hunter as its first captain. Of its 10 battalions, three were initially stationed in the village of Kotra. Later, when the efficacy of this force was questioned, it was reduced to eight battalions in 1861. Of these, six were stationed in Kherwara and two in Kotra. On 22 August 1848, the *Liverpool Standard and General Commercial Advertiser* reported that along with the formation of the Bhil Corps, the British also handed over responsibility for the maintenance of law and order to the Bhil chiefs.[13]

8
BHIL REVOLTS AND THEIR HEROES IN RAJPUTANA, REWA KANTHA AND MAHI KANTHA

Baroda, 1804

Baroda (Vadodara) in Gujarat was the seat of the Gaekwad state. A British Army troop stationed there after the establishment of British rule was used to deal with insurrections in nearby areas. Agencies such as Rewa Kantha, Mahi Kantha and Rajputana had not yet been established in 1804.

On 22 September 1804, Bhils attacked Lt. Herd when he was returning to Baroda Cantt. from Chhawni with his assistant, Williams and six-year-old James Urquart. Williams was fortunate to find shelter in a bush by the roadside, but Herd and the child were captured. The Bhils then tried to extort whatever money the group had, even searching Herd's person, but found little. Herd immediately informed the CO, Grummont, on his return to Baroda. Grummont organised a search by his sepoys, but the Bhils remained elusive and continued to raid Baroda Cantt., which had often witnessed such episodes despite everyday patrolling. A report of this incident was published in the *Calcutta Gazette* on 1 November 1804.

Jagga Rawat and Others

Around 1817–1818, Bhil chief Jagga Rawat and some others reigned supreme in the Banswara and Pratapgarh principalities that bordered Gujarat, Rajasthan and Khandesh. Here, Rawat Bhils inhabited the hill tracts in large numbers, with Jagga the most powerful and wealthy of all chiefs. Once an autonomous ruler of the area, he began plundering the entire region when deprived of his hereditary jagir by Rajput machinations and consequently, refused to recognise Rajput authority. When the British established their dominance in the region, they initially adopted a policy of compromise in view of Jagga's influence and strength. However, this policy was not followed for very long. On the recommendation of the Res., Indore, Jagga was arrested and lodged as a state prisoner in Asirgarh Fort on 27 February 1826.[1]

On 22 May 1819, Brig. Gen. Sir John Malcolm forwarded to Metcalfe, his secretary, letters from his assistant, Capt. Macdonald. On 31 March 1819, Macdonald had written to report that his discussion with Nathu Rawat, chief of Mowra Kairee, was satisfactory. Nathu commanded a band of about 5,000 Bhils, who lived in the hill areas to the north-east of Banswara district. In the past, his jagir had comprised 12 villages of Kairee. But a battle with the Rajput king of Banswara two years earlier had compelled his soldiers to seek refuge in the hills. The state had then attacked Mowra Kairee and captured Nathu's fairly prosperous jagir by force. Nevertheless, Nathu flatly denied launching an offensive against anyone. In Macdonald's view, Nathu's claim for the restoration of his jagir ought to have been accepted. He had assured the authorities that if his jagir was restored to him, he would take responsibility for the security of the road from Guntati to the Mahi river bank, a 12-or 13-mil. stretch. The captain wanted a bond issued for the purpose, adding that atrocities against a sizeable chunk of population would continue otherwise. Macdonald categorically stated in his letter that the Rajput king had deprived Nathu of his hereditary rights.

Macdonald had written yet another letter on 5 April 1819, apprising the authorities of the adoption of a policy to end the plunder of Bagar and Kauntel and to enhance the security of the Banswara–Pratapgarh road. On 2 April, he addressed the villagers of Sadilpore (Sadalpur), Jagga Rawat's village. Macdonald invited Jagga to his camp for a meeting, but the chief declined, pleading a recent injury sustained in an encounter with a Rajput who had seized his property in Banswara. Macdonald went to meet Jagga instead. At the meeting he assured Jagga and his associates of British protection and freedom from oppression if they pledged not to raid Bagar and Kauntel.

Macdonald then wrote to say that Jagga Rawat had made some gestures of compromise. He had agreed to refrain from plundering Kauntel if he was allowed his right to the *jowar* (sorghum) harvest (*paunk*, in Gujarati). Macdonald recommended that Jagga's right to the *jowar* harvest be recognised in writing, nor ought he be prevented from the purchase of *jowar*. The vakil of the king of Pratapgarh was in agreement as well. Macdonald also demanded protection for Jagga's wealth. As travellers on the Pratapgarh road would pay him a tax, Jagga was assured of receiving his regular dues. Macdonald also recommended a written bond regarding Jagga's future behaviour.

However, Maha Rawal Lakshman Singh, the Rajput king of Banswara, and Thakur Brahma Singh were sceptical, as it was their contention that the Bhil chiefs had repeatedly foiled any state attempts to end the plunder. They agreed on a compromise, based on Macdonald's assurance, that Jagga would be punished in case of any violation of the agreement.

Kushalpura and Suribeah were the two main centres where Bhils of nearby areas made their daily purchases. As mahua distillation took place in Kushalpura, Jagga was anxious to include it in his jurisdiction—he was allowed to do so once he signed a bond. He guaranteed the security of eight villages as well. On the same day, agreements with four more Bhil chiefs were signed. One was Khema Nayak of Padmund, who commanded 500 Bhils. The villages of three others were situated along the Pratapgarh road: they were Maji Rawat of Chikli, Hiral Rawat of Mundari, and Devadeh Rawat of Renda. Thus, after the agreement with Jagga Rawat on 22 April 1819, Macdonald successfully convinced the Bhil chiefs of Bangar, Dungarpur and Banswara to agree to give up plunder for a peaceful existence. These agreements gave them the right to collect Rs 2 per 100 carts and entrusted to them the security of the road from Pratapgarh to Deola Ghat.

However, the 22 April 1819 agreement between Jagga Rawat, local Rajput kings and Macdonald failed to hold, reasons for which remain obscure. But it appears that the kings of Banswara and Pratapgarh continued to harass the Bhils, which was why Jagga continued to plunder these states for nearly seven years and challenge Rajput interference in Bhil affairs.

More information available from the correspondence of the political department of Bengal reveals that indigenous and foreign powers failed to subdue Jagga Rawat between 1819 and 1825. The British Army attacked him and forced his surrender at the beginning of 1826. He was jailed in Asirgarh Fort on 27 February 1826. Not much is known about his imprisonment between 1826 and 1829. However, the Rajputs of Banswara, who had earlier been hostile, submitted an application from the *rawal* of the state to Maj. Stewart, Acting Resident (AR) of Indore, for Jagga's release when he was in Banswara on an inspection tour. The application explained that Jagga was labelled a rebel because of injury marks on his body. The *rawal*'s letter was presented to the south court. The abstract political letter from Bengal, dated 26 December 1829, indicates that, on 1 April 1829, the south court had enquired about Jagga's past record from the AR, Indore. Stewart responded that there was nothing to imply that Jagga had been arrested on the basis of injury marks. In fact, he was convinced that Jagga's relatives had bribed the *rawal*, which was why the latter had requested Jagga's release that was being forcefully opposed by the king of Pratapgarh.

On 8 February 1830, Stewart wrote to Chief Secretary Swinton in London that it was quite clear from Macdonald's letter to Wellesley on 30 May 1825 that all attempts at a compromise with Jagga had been unsuccessful. Jagga, who was expected to be well-behaved, honour the agreement and desist from wreaking terror in the neighbouring territories, had defied all such expectations. Left with little choice, the British conducted an army operation, forcing Jagga's surrender. While soliciting his release, the *rawal* of Banswara assumed responsibility for Jagga's conduct and assured the administration that the latter was still best suited to protect Bhil territories. Stewart, suspecting the *rawal* of mercenary motives, insisted that his application be sent to the governor general, through the council, so that the latter could hear the king of Pratapgarh's version of events as well.[2]

Jagga Nayak remained incarcerated in Asirgarh as a state prisoner till February 1830. Practically nothing is known about him thereafter, strengthening the suspicion that he was wrongfully imprisoned, more so because no other battle with him was reported after the agreement.

Kur Vasava: Rajpipla (Gujarat) and Sagwara
Between 1820 and 1822, Kur Vasava was a terrifying presence in the state of Rajpipla, as was Kalia Chamar, whose village, Koliwara, was situated on the border of Khandesh. Both Bhils were fighting an ancestral war for the control of Khunti (Nawapura).

Kur Vasava belonged to the village of Sagwara in Rajpipla. In a petition, he claimed that his father, Umed, a Bhil king, had governed Khunti, Nawapura and Dastan until certain devious Brahmins had forced his father into a settlement. Reysingh Ji, Kur Vasava's father-in-law, had established a Bhil jagir in Rajpipla in 1763, and his rule had continued till 1785. A wealthy jagirdar, the annual income of Sagwara touched Rs 50,000 during his reign. He had enjoyed some privileges since Mughal times, which were curtailed at the very beginning of British rule. When Kur Vasava was evicted from his ancestral village, Bhil jagirdars rose in rebellion against Rajpipla. With the king unable to subjugate him, his reign of terror was such that the mountainous parganas of Rajpipla were rendered desolate.[3]

Kur Vasava's band had been strengthened by Arab and Sindhi elements and consequently, it was not easy to crush him with force. Although J.P. Willoughby, the assistant resident of Baroda, had harassed the chief using armed strength, British officials thought it prudent to enter into a truce. The correspondence between James William, Res. Baroda, and Willoughby makes it clear that negotiations with Bhil chiefs were preferred for the maintenance of peace in Rajpipla. On 6 January, Kur was invited to Nanded in Maharashtra to discuss his curtailed privileges. Willoughby assured him that his past crimes would be condoned if he helped maintain peace, and himself lived in peace. Kur maintained that crime was not his hobby; rather, he had been driven to it. He was asked to submit a petition regarding his claim, whereupon he submitted eight demands on 26 January. At the time, Kur's band comprised 20 Sindhis, including his loyal jamadar, Buruk, and 30–40 Bhils. Willoughby had earlier attempted to negotiate with him at Nanded in November 1821.

The proposal thus prepared was sent to the Bombay Government for endorsement. It stated that Kur Vasava would not accept any compromise that did not include his comrades. Therefore, he ought to be allowed to have his men with him but in limited numbers, and to live in Sagwara. Later, Kur made yet another demand—that seven of his comrades, in prison for the preceding year and a half, be released forthwith. The government accepted virtually all these demands and a bond was signed on 7 March 1822. Kur was to pay only a nominal tax per hutment. Twenty-five members of his group were to be employed by the king of Rajpipla. He was allowed three horses and would receive an annual allowance of Rs 125 per head for himself, his brother and some of his comrades. A thana, with 50 horsemen and 100 infantrymen, was established in Sagwara to bolster security. F. Warden, Chief Secretary (CS), Bombay Government; W. Chaplin, Commissioner Deccan, and Capt. Briggs consented to the proposal. These measures effectively quelled Kur Vasava's rebellion.

Kur Vasava, Kalia Chamar and the king of Rajpipla entered into an agreement on 4 January 1824. These efforts led to the conclusion of peace deals with all Bhil chiefs of Rajpipla by 1823–1824. Subsequently, Maj. Robutram, PA,

Khandesh, entered into a separate agreement with Kur Vasava, which finally settled the issue.

In a letter to William Newnham, CS, Bombay, dated 16 January 1824, William referred to the agreement reached between Kur Vasava and Kalia Chamar on 4 January 1824. It was in fact reached between four parties, the other two being King Warisal of Rajpipla, and Willoughby. The main clause of the agreement stipulated that the road to Khandesh via Sagwara would be reopened so that traders could safely travel on the Lakhwara road. Robutram had also consented.[4]

In 1846, led by Kunwar Jiva Vasava, the Bhils of Gujarat raised the banner of revolt. The Banswara state sent its vakil Kothari Kesari Singh to the British agent in western Malva. On 22 August 1848, an article in the *Liverpool Standard and General Commercial Advertiser* reported that with British help, this revolt had been crushed by the end of 1850.[5]

Sagwara had been an autonomous Bhil territory for centuries, ruled by its Vasava. When the border dispute between Dam Ji Vasava of Sagwara and Rajpipla intensified around 1890, the Bombay Government had deputed acting collector of Ahmednagar, A.F. Woodburn, to settle the issue.[6]

The kings of Rajpipla looked upon the Vasavas of Sagwara as their subordinate talukdars. The Bombay Government, however, recognised the Vasavas as independent entities. Therefore, when the native princes were granted privy purses soon after Independence, Karan Singh Ji and Fateh Singh Ji, Vasavas of Sagwara, were each granted life-long allowances of Rs 2,000 a month on 16

November 1950. The Bhil revolt continued in Bhilwara in 1823–1824. At the time, the rebels had captured Hamirgarh Fort by ousting Brig. Gen. Carmichael.[7]

Etcha Puggi

The king of Lunawara paid tribute to both Gaekwad and Scindia, rendering him a subordinate. Therefore, the British Government was, in turn, entitled to revenue from those kings subordinated to Gaekwad. In January 1823, the Lunawara army camp consisted of 80 soldiers, one subedar, one jamadar, five hawaldars and five nayaks. At around 11 pm on 22 January 1823, Lt. George Richard Stoven Fenwick from the Second Battalion, First Regiment of Bombay NI, and also PA, Mahi Kantha, ordered his own troops as well as several jawans of Gaekwad's cavalry to proceed to Semaria. Gaekwad's Army was modelled along the lines of the army of the East India Company, based on an order from the Res., Baroda, and as per an agreement between Gaekwad and the Bombay Government. However, no such agreement existed between the king of Lunawara and the Bombay Government.

Semaria, a village of about 400 Bhils in Lunawara (Mahi Sagar), was notorious for its insurrections, and a thorn in the side of local feudal lords. Articles published on 27 December 1824 in the *Morning Post* (hereafter *MP*), and in the *Star* (London) (hereafter *SL*) refer to the king of Lunawara's scathing denouncement of Etcha Puggi, the *patil* of the village, as a 'bloody bastard'.

At 4 am on 23 January, Fenwick's troops reached the vicinity of Semaria and launched an attack at daybreak. Bhils of the village were slaughtered, their homes set on fire, and the village vandalised. After the battle ended, Fenwick informed Subedar Sheikh Abdullah that he had captured two Bhils, one of whom he referred to as a barbarian—it was none other than Etcha Puggi.

It is clear from the details of the battle that local feudal elements had incited the British to launch this attack. Later in the day, when the king of Lunawara met Subedar Sheikh Abdullah on the road near Semaria, the former had reportedly commented that of the many British officers he had observed, none had performed as efficiently as Fenwick. Pointing to the captured Bhil chief, the king said that if it were he who had captured Etcha Puggi, he would have immediately killed him.

The army then proceeded towards Lunawara Lines. The subedar entrusted the two prisoners to security guards and recounted the king's derogatory comment to Fenwick. Later that evening, Fenwick informed the subedar of his intention to hang the captured Bhil chief. The subedar was quick to point out that such an action could only be sanctioned by the British Government and that British law forbade such treatment of prisoners—but Fenwick remained unmoved. At around 10 pm, Fenwick ordered that Etcha Puggi be brought in a *doli* (palanquin) to a mahua tree about 100 paces from the Lines. There, the prisoner was hanged from a branch. A peon named Jagga Gogul cut the body down eventually, and it was thrown into the river on Fenwick's orders.

This illegal act reached the Supreme Court for hearing, and statements from Lt T.R. Belmore, Subedar Abdullah, Mansa Prasad, and several other officials and employees were recorded. Justices Oyyer and Terminor ratified the Company's jurisdiction in the matter. Next, they outlined the difference between war killing and cold-blooded murder. In its verdict pronounced on 30 July 1824, the Supreme Court held Fenwick guilty of the Bhil chief's death. The chief justice deemed it premeditated murder as the accused had himself ordered the hanging. However, as recorded, 'The Jury retired, and after an hour's consultation returned a verdict of Guilty, accompanied by a strong recommendation to mercy, on account of the inexperience of the prisoner, and the peculiarity of the circumstances under which he was placed.' Besides being carried in both *MP* and *SL* on 27 December 1824, this episode was mentioned in the *Asiatic Journal and Monthly Register for British India and its Dependencies* in 1825.

The causes of the Semaria massacre of Bhils were never brought to light. The role played by the local king was more than evident in the extermination of an entire Bhil village, which could well have been an issue of tax collection.

Daulat Singh and Govind Raya

Daulat Singh and Govind Raya (Govindra), with a troop of Bhils, began their revolt against the Udaipur state in January 1826, raiding police posts and killing some sepoys. They attacked a troop of 100 with matchlocks and drove off the king's surviving soldiers. The British Army failed to crush the rebellion, bringing an end to the peace brought about by the treaties signed with various Bhil chiefs in 1825. Bhils everywhere turned mutinous. The British failed to capture Daulat Singh and in 1828, the government entered into prolonged negotiations with him to secure his surrender. Along with generous allowances, he was granted the village of Babulwara for his maintenance. The Bhil jagir of Jawas, which had been confiscated in 1823, was also returned. Bhil chiefs were now allowed to collect the *bolai* tax.[8]

The Bhils of Risabhdev rebelled against the king in 1826, after some jagirs to the south-west of Debar Lake were confiscated. The British Army was called in to stamp out the uprising. Apparently, a sadhu belonging to Risabhdev had incited the rebellion for which he was later sentenced to life imprisonment. Capt. Kobe, a British officer, reached an agreement with the Bhils, with some minor conditions, but the rebellion continued. In 1826, when the Bhils rampaged through a thana in the Garasia hills, the king brought in Kobe to take charge but to little effect. Along with the Bhils of Garasia, Daulat Singh proved to be a veritable headache for the regime. Under such circumstances, the British were faced with two choices—to either leave matters to the king and withdraw or face the insurgents. The king was reluctant to assume that responsibility but committed to the entire expense that would be incurred for suppression of the revolt and to also hand over control of mountainous Bhil regions to the PA, Mewar. While decisions were to be taken in the king's name, his officials were forbidden to interfere in the process, thus allowing the British to establish full control over the hill tracts of Mewar.[9]

Akbar Shah

On 8 February 1830, the Bhils engaged in an encounter with the 20th Cavalry, then on patrol, 3 mil. from Jirpur, some 35 mil. to the east of Harsol in Gujarat. Akbar Shah, the area's Bhil chief, frequently gathered some 400 to 500 Bhils to raid the Kaira collectorate. On 24 March 1830, the *Bombay Gazette* (hereafter *BG*) carried a report of this encounter in which five jawans of the British Army lost their lives and a dozen suffered injuries.

The British and Udaipur state continued to follow a soft policy towards the Bhils up to 1838. However, there is evidence of a Bhil uprising in Banswara in 1836, and its suppression by the armed forces of the king of Banswara.[10]

Revolts during 1833–1835

In 1833, Bhil insurrections continued in the Mahi Kantha areas adjoining Khandesh. These principalities were near the borders of Khandesh and Rajasthan. Before Outram demitted office in Khandesh in 1835, the Bombay Government had ordered him to prepare a detailed report on the disturbances in Mahi Kantha. In collaboration with William, Outram prepared the report once he reached Ahmedabad, which was completed at Baroda on 14 November. The report stressed that Mahi Kantha would never be free from such disruptions until the rebellious chiefs were subdued by British bayonets.

Sir John Keane, commander-in-chief, Bombay Army, then requested Outram to take command of the military, but the latter refused the appointment and proceeded on leave. He assumed the position of PA, Mahi Kantha, on his return. With his long and varied experience in Khandesh, Outram succeeded in suppressing the insurrections in Mahi Kantha as well.

An incident involving John Gordon was reported from Chikli on 2 May 1833. Gordon, an officer of the British Civil Service, was camping at Ankaleshwar, near Bharuch. Along with some of his cavaliers, Gordon left his camp to open negotiations with a Bhil band. Proceeding with only one horseman, Gordon instructed the other cavaliers trailing behind not to fire, while urging the Bhils to lay down their arms. But unable to comprehend the reason for his presence, the agitated Bhils released a volley of arrows, three of which struck Gordon. On 20 September 1833, *MP* reported that he was brought to Ankaleshwar where he died a few days later. Several newspapers published the news of Gordon's death in 1833, but at least one British paper hinted that the news was false.

The Bhils of Dungarpur were still in rebellion in 1833 according to a report carried in the *Sherborne Mercury* on 7 October 1833.[11]

Surajmal, March 1835

Capt. Morris had planned an attack on Bhil chief Surajmal. On 17 March 1835, the army, stationed at Derol, set out for

Pinora (possibly Pinodra), a village of Saraimal, reaching an intractable mountain pass after 15 mil. Bhils and Makranis had, by then, taken up positions on nearby hills. On the afternoon of 18 March, while the captain was en route, with Pinora a mere 8 mil. away, bullets came raining down. Fortunately, most of the bullets passed over the army's head. With cooperation from the Light Infantry, Capt. Shaw of the Ninth Regiment dispersed the rebels. The army then marched towards Pinora and Maunpur. Pinora, Surajmal's village, had a large stock of food grain. After capturing the grain stocks of these two villages, they were set on fire.

The army remained on high alert all night, but there was no further attack by the Bhils. But some 500 Bhils, still entrenched on the hills, launched an attack when the army began the return trek to its camp, forcing it to halt time and again. Lt. Cruickshank of the First Regiment and 15 other British soldiers suffered injuries during the attack, while Bhil casualties numbered 350.

The Makranis later deserted Surajmal, whose position had already been undermined by the large-scale slaughter of his Bhil comrades. In view of his diminished position, Surajmal proposed a compromise to Ershine, which the British rejected. This episode was reported in the *Evening Chronicle* on 27 August and 17 September 1835 and in the *Belfast Commercial Chronicle* on 31 October 1835. When his companions deserted him, Surajmal fled into the forest.

The situation deteriorated rapidly after the chief sought refuge in the forest. With the severity of the Bhil attacks that followed, the British Army had little choice but to confine itself to Aurangabad. Plunder, murder and anarchy were the order of the day in Ahmednagar as well. On 18 September 1835, the *London Courier and Evening Gazette* reported that the British Army was no match for the rebels, and troops from other places had been summoned as reinforcements.

Revolt in Derol (Mount Abu)

A dreadful famine stalked Bhil territories, forcing the starving Bhils to revolt. In view of the extensive Bhil rebellion, the army, camped at Derol, had planned to march from Idar, led by Lt. Pottinger and Lt. Mallet, on 17 August 1835. The area was covered with dense forests and hills in which famine-stricken Bhils had positioned themselves. In the skirmish that followed, the army used about 8,000 rounds till stock was exhausted and was then forced to retreat to Idar. The *Atlas* on 12 July 1835 and the *Hereford Journal* on 26 August 1835 reported that Lt. Pottinger of the 17th NI laid down his life in this campaign.

The Bhils of southern Malva had responded positively to Sir John Malcolm's policy of compromise. But those in the north, particularly in the Udaipur area, were still violent and unyielding. In a macabre incident, British officials sent a message to the Bhil chiefs of the area, conveying that their crimes would be condoned. In response, the chiefs beheaded the messenger and hoisted his head on a bamboo pole. The officials heard of the grisly act the next day.[12]

Revolts during 1837–1838
Joint Action against the Bhils of Palgaon
The rulers of Mewar, Pratapgarh and Gwalior, and Holkar, were extremely harassed by the Bhil insurrection in Palgaon in the district of Neemuch. Since the subjugation of the Bhils was not possible for any one of them singly, British officials, through repeated correspondence, persuaded these rulers to engage in joint action.

The army troops of two districts in Udaipur state under the unified command of Mehta Sher Singh, general superintendent of the minister, joined this campaign—one troop was led by Amir Singh, and the other by Bal Govind. These troops moved into Palgaon through two passes on the northern and the south-western sides. Led by Nanu Pant Apte, the Gwalior–Holkar Army entered through the eastern pass. The army of Pratapgarh state, led by the thakur of Dhamotar, entered through a fourth pass on the south-west. The officers of these troops had decided to march overnight through their respective territories in order to reach Palgaon at a pre-determined hour the next morning to launch a joint attack. Unfortunately, the lack of punctuality and coordination on the part of the Indian troops put paid to this fine plan.

The Pratapgarh troop was the first to reach Ghyaspur Pass. Palgaon was a mere 2.5 mil. from Ghyaspur. The Bhils fought determinedly against this sudden attack, in which one *gameti* (village elder) and one Bhil were killed. As the other troops had failed to reach at the appointed hour, Bhil resistance forced the overwhelmed Pratapgarh troop to retreat 3 mil. from Ghyaspur.

The two troops from Udaipur, led by Mehta Sher Singh, were the next to arrive. They invaded the village of Palgaon and set it on fire. Seven Bhils and 40 mules were captured, and 48 animals beheaded. After this successful operation, and mindful of their own security, the Udaipur troops retreated 9 mil. to Dhariabad.

The worst showing was that of the Gwalior–Holkar troops, led by Nanu Pant Apte. A thakur of Barol (Mewar), Apte, charged with guiding the troops overnight, led them to Dholapanija instead. When accused of deliberately misguiding the troops, because he was in league with the Bhils, he claimed that he had lost his direction. Apte accused the troops of lacking the necessary enthusiasm and of failing to show any inclination to reach the destination. The British officer questioning him retorted that if the army was unenthusiastic it was because the thakur had misled it.

After the action against Palgaon, a contingent from Pratapgarh was deputed to secure the open forest route. Mehta Sher Singh's large contingent of 100 cavalry and 400 infantry jawans was asked to cooperate with the Pratapgarh troop to prevent the Bhils from resorting to any further plunder.[13]

The British administration completely found itself at a loss in 1838, owing to Bhil insurrections, plunder and violence in north India. According to *BG* on 28 March 1838, the British were weary of the incessant plunder. The Baroda army troop, with 600 jawans of all categories, was sent to deal with the rebellions, but the campaigns proved ineffective against the Bhils in their thousands. Two British officers were severely injured during the campaigns of 1837–1838.

Revolts during 1844–1856

Banswara witnessed sporadic Bhil revolts in 1844. The Bhils of Banswara collected the *rakhwali* tax from the nearby Malva areas, which had ceased following their agreement with the British, thus inciting rebellion. At the same time, the Bhils and Garasias of Posina (Gujarat), and of the state of Sirohi, were also on the warpath. However, with his force of 600 men, Capt. Wallace, PA, Mahi Kantha, managed to contain them. The epicentre of the revolt was Banswara, on the Gujarat–Rajasthan border, and any rebellion in Banswara was bound to impact Gujarat as well, reported *LSGCA* on 22 August 1848.

The Bhils of Kalibas in Udaipur state had rebelled in 1855. The king dispatched Mehta Sawai Singh on 1 November 1856 to quell the uprising. The Udaipur Army reduced the villages to cinders, slaughtered several Bhils and captured many. The severed heads of many Bhils were brought back to Udaipur.[14]

Revolt in Chandap, 1857–1858

In 1857, the army was summoned twice to quell Bhil insurrections in Chandap. On the first occasion, the army confiscated some insurgents' arms. A strong force was then dispatched under Maj. Grims, which confiscated 310 weapons from 588 villages. But the tribals of the village of Dabhora in the Kharalu subdivision, in Gaekwad territory, refused to part with their arms. They collected their men atop a hill called Taranga where they fortified themselves. The army laid siege to the hill and demanded their surrender, but their chief refused. In view of the deteriorating situation, a troop comprising the Second Grenadier Regiment, NI and Gujarat Irregular Horse attacked the Bhils on 31 May 1858. In the skirmish that ensued, some 80 Bhils were killed or injured, and 10 were captured. The British Army suffered losses as well, with two of its jawans killed and some injured.[15]

Thakur's Revolt in Mundeti (Rajasthan)

Thakur Surajmal of Mundeti was a suspect at the time of the Chandap revolt in 1858. Rebellious by nature, he had been granted clemency in 1836. The government had taken over his jagir and sanctioned him an allowance. With this allowance, Surajmal recruited Makranis and captured some hills. The army evicted him from Mundeti on 22 August 1858 and captured the town.

Revolt in Rewa Kantha, 1857-1858

Apart from sporadic incidents of Bhil rebellion, Rewa Kantha witnessed three major insurgencies by Naykara Bhils in 1837, 1857 and 1858. The Naykara Bhil chiefs of Baria, Chhota Udaipur, Jambughora and Godhra had also mutinied in 1838. In February 1838, the PA, Mahi Kantha, organised a force, led by Maj. Forbes, which was sent to subdue the rebels. Jawans deputed at border posts surrounded the rebels to force their surrender. By the end of that year, with cooperation from the chiefs of Baria and Chhota Udaipur, the primary Bhil chiefs had been hauled in and imprisoned, with some subsequently released for good behaviour.

One of the two Bhil chiefs prominent in this revolt was Kewal Dama from the village of Bara in Baria district, who was aided by his brother, Jalam Singh Nayak. His lieutenant, Omkar Singh, had formed a separate band helped by the Makranis. Some of its members in Udaipur and Jambughora had looted cattle and other property belonging to the king of Udaipur. The other band was led by Viram Nayak and his brother, Mahadev Nayak, and was aided by Amar Nayak, who had devastated the Rajgarh region of Baria. To prevent disturbances in the Sagtala subdivision, the armed forces of Baria were brought in under the PA, and the deserted villages were gradually repopulated.[16]

The Bhils of Rewa Kantha, too, were up in arms at the time of the 1857 Uprising. Surajmal was one such chief. He was divested of his position as chief of Lunawara in June 1857. In retaliation, he raided the town in July 1857 but encountered stiff resistance from the British. He then slipped into Salumbar, in Mewar. When the king of Udaipur made him a generous offer, he agreed to maintain peace.

Another rebel was Jamadar Mustafa Khan, a foreign mercenary in Sontha, who had demanded Rs 4,674 of his salary that had been withheld. On the PA's orders, a troop of Gujarat Irregular Horse was sent to arrest him.

There followed a fierce skirmish in which Mustafa was killed, while his associates fled. In Rajpipla, Syed Murad Ali attempted a rebellion in the middle of August 1857, followed by those of Kewal Dama and Rupa Gobar, both Naykara Bhil chiefs, in Panchmahal state, in 1858. For a full eight months, the British Army tried in vain to suppress the two.

After 1 November 1858, when sovereignty was transferred from the East India Company to the British Crown, some reformative laws were attempted in Bhil territories, although they were fiercely contested by the freedom-loving Bhils.[17] On 12 December 1858, news arrived from Godhra of Bhils who gathered in protest on the banks of the Anas, as the king of Kushalgarh had halted the grain supply in the direction of the river.[18]

Revolt in Rewa Kantha, 1859

Rajputs and Bhils were the main inhabitants of Rajpipla, with the comparatively better-off Kunbis comprising some part of its population in the lower reaches of the state. All of Rajpipla was dotted by hills and dense forests. Naykara Bhils lived in Baria and Chhota Udaipur, where the sheer density of the forests made it impossible to ascertain their numbers. Cases of plunder by Naykara Bhils had so multiplied in 1838 that the British had to send an army to subdue them. Sagtala, where the tribals were mainly centred, was under the direct control of the Rewa Kantha Agency. The Bhils of Lunawara and Sonth were ruled by Rajputs. Mehwasis lived between the banks of the Narmada and the Mahi.

The Rewa Kantha region was controlled by 52 Bhil chiefs in all, generally called thakurs, each governing a particular group and a maximum of 12 villages. In 1822, Gaekwad control over these chiefs ended when they came under British rule. The interference in their internal affairs now grew, turning the Bhils increasingly mutinous. The Bhils of Balasinor were Muslim by faith but lived much like their brethren of the neighbouring states. Of these chiefs, the powerful ruled their respective territories autonomously, but were governed by the PA, who also dealt with their mutual disputes.

The Naykaras and Dhamkas of Rewa lived mainly in the dense forests, while the Kolis and Rajputs practised cultivation. The plight of the Kolis often turned them rebellious. With the worsening of the economic situation, Bhils rose in protest all over Rewa Kantha. The army, whose units were drawn from Dhora, Khudadi (Khudwali), Jambughora, Palanpur and Panchne, was dispatched under Maj. Wallace to stamp out the uprisings but with little success.

Around the same time, Shivrajpur witnessed a fierce battle between Capt. Bonnor's troop and insurgent Bhils. While Lt. Hayward, of the 17th NI, was injured, 13 jawans were killed or wounded. The Bhils, too, suffered some losses, with two lives lost and half a dozen injured.

On 13 February 1859, Capt. Collier, of the 26th Regiment, attacked a Bhil stronghold, killing several rebels. His own troops suffered minor losses; some jawans were injured, reported *Bell's Weekly Messenger* on 9 April 1859.

In 1859, Bhils took some horsemen of the prince of Rajpipla by surprise, forcing them to hand over their arms. The Rewa Kantha Agency intervened, and the 14th NI, led by Capt. Francis and Lt. Keys, was dispatched to control the situation but failed. On 20 December 1859, the *Empire* (Sydney) reported that four years previously, the PA had intervened to get the prime minister of Rajpipla, Daneshwar Vishwanath Ji Bahadur, dismissed, which had soured Rajpipla's relations with the agency. Thus, all of Rewa Kantha had become a battlefield, according to the *Adelaide Observer* (SA) on 28 May 1859.

In 1859, Bhils from the district of Pol raided the districts of Panchmahal and Dahod. On 18 February 1859, they injured 18 individuals and stole 170 heads of cattle. According to APA Capt. Buckle, the Bhils of Pol and Dahod were beyond the king's control. They had raided Panchmahal, which belonged to Scindia, on eight occasions, and killed three individuals. The total loss amounted to Rs 1,657. Although the king of Jhabua enjoyed cordial relations with the British, Maj. Wallace, PA, Rewa Kantha, was of the opinion that the state of Jhabua ought to pay the compensation. The most notorious village was Palsdor, whose *kanji* (rao) Hari Singh, who belonged to the Damor tribe, had provided to the British a list of the villages of Jhabua and Dahod ravaged by the Bhils.[19]

As reported by the *Englishman* on 23 July 1860, Bhil rebellions continued in Mewar in 1860, where several Bhil bands, led by Rao Sahib, were active. The Bhils remained rebellious in Rewa Kantha till 1865, according to news carried by the *Age* (Melbourne) on 11 September 1860 and 27 June 1865.

Revolt during 1861–1863

Several instances of Bhil insurgency were noted in Kherwara, near Udaipur, in 1861.[20] In 1862, Bhil chiefs continued their agitation for autonomy in the mountainous border tracts of Maharashtra, Khandesh and Rewa Kantha. This led to conflicts in the hills and forested areas of Toranmal, Jhand and Dang. In 1863, the Bhils of Kotra and Kherwara joined forces. In 1864, the Bhils of Karwar, Parsad, Nathara and nearby areas began their raids, attributed by British officials to their neglect by district authorities.

Towards the middle of 1863, the Bhils of Banswara and Kushalgarh were making predatory incursions into the districts of Jhabua, Thandla and Petlawad. On 8 August 1863, in a letter written to Maj. Gen. Lawrence, AGGCI, Rajputana, W.S. Eden, PA, Mewar, pointed out that it was incumbent upon the king of Banswara to control the rebels in his territory.[21]

A Bhil band living in the forests of Pratapgarh and Banswara organised a massive raid in 1863. The thakur of Sonkhera pursued them and gunned down four Bhils, and then informed the British. On 27 October 1863, Lt. R.C. Bradford apprised Maj. R.I. Meade, the Indore-based AGGCI, of the thakur's fear that the Bhils would seek to avenge the deaths of their comrades. Hence, a request was made for the dispatch of a Central Indian cavalry troop to ensure his security.[22] The Bhils of Pratapgarh and Banswara had been regularly plundering villages in the district of Mandsaur for the preceding two years and ravaged Bhalod, claiming their entitlement to some villages of the district.[23]

Depradations during 1864–1867

One interesting incident, published in *BG* on 24 February 1864, concerns Mrs W., the wife of a British officer, travelling from Ahmedabad to Neemuch in a bullock cart escorted by mounted sepoys. Bhils attacked this travelling party when it was 6 mil. from Udaipur, and 67 mil. from Neemuch. They dragged down the riders and injured the bullocks with their arrows. Mrs. W. was released when a loyal Indian sepoy urged them to spare her life, offering them her belongings instead. The Bhils broke open her travel chests and plundered their contents. The lady was taken to Udaipur by a mounted sepoy and then sent on to Neemuch under escort.

Still mutinous at the beginning of 1865, Bhils raided some villages in the Bokhla region, in Mewar. On 22 February 1865, *BG* reported that the Mewar Army was dispatched to deal with the rebels.

Mehta Raghunath Singh was given charge of the district of Magra in 1866. A corrupt officer, he was responsible for the Minas' revolt in 1851. In a written complaint, the CO, Mewar Bhil Corps, accused Mehta of arbitrarily fining the Bhils and taxing them at double the rate. Such complaints led to Raghunath Singh's removal.

In 1867, the Bhils of Dewalpal causing disruptions between Kherwara and Dungarpur were overcome with the help of the Mewar Bhil Corps.[24] Dhoria, a Bhil chief from the state of Sirohi, had been raiding the villages of Idar. On account of his cordial relations with the rao of Sirohi, he spared his own state. The rao was asked to turn in Dhoria so that he could be tried but refused.[25]

Sunth, 1867

The Sunth–Mewar border witnessed some incidents of Bhil insurrection in 1867. The Sunth state had directed one Bhundiya to take charge as jagirdar of Bhanasimal, a Bhil village located close to the Dungarpur border. As Bhundiya did not originally belong to Bhanasimal, the Bhils of Bhanasimal and other villages rose in protest against an outsider as their chief. Joined by the Bhils of Kherapur, they torched the police posts of the state and attacked the Sebandi guards. The state police attacked Bhanasimal and Kherapur, but the Bhils resisted fiercely. Several policemen were injured, leaving the PA with little choice but to intervene. On his arrival on 1 April 1867, the Bhils apprised him of their complaints and explained the reasons for their rebellion.[26]

Naykara Revolt in Panchmahal, 1868

Perhaps no other tribe has made as many sacrifices in the history of British India as the Bhils in order to protect their lands, with many such chiefs from the Deccan. One heinous uprising took place in the southern part of Panchmahal state where Naykara Bhils fought the British in the village of Warrick (or Wurreck), 6 mil. from the British territory of Jambughora, to the south-east of Baroda. Covered by the forest expanse of Khandesh, the area was part of Chhota Udaipur. Its location leads to the inevitable conclusion that the rebels of Khandesh and Gujarat often slipped into one another's territories, as published in *MP* on 7 April 1868, and in the *Homeward Mail* (hereafter *HM*) on 23 March 1868.

In 1868, Bhil chief Rupa Singh led an uprising of Naykara Bhils. He had harassed the British Government in 1859 as well but had subsequently been granted the village of Bar as his jagir by the British on account of his cooperation. Rupa Singh, Mulla Manik and a Brahmin, Parmeshwar, attacked the Rajgarh thana on 2 February 1868, killing the thanadar and looting government funds worth Rs 1,500. Next, they ransacked the cash chest at Jambughora. On 6 February, they raided Jaitpur and Chhota Udaipur, but there they met with defeat.

According to British officers, Parmeshwar, who claimed to be an incarnation of god, and his associates had been inciting religious frenzy among the Bhils. Himself a non-Bhil, he nevertheless identified with the Bhils and claimed that together they were as one soul in two bodies. Parmeshwar, Rupa Singh and Mulla Manik had caused upheavals in four or five villages and killed two soldiers deputed to guard the treasury. They also threatened the town of Halol. Propert, AGG, Panchmahal, along with Capt. Seagrave, Lt. Westmacott and 50 jawans of the Bhil Corps, marched

40 mil. to provide security to the town. When informed of the uprising, Maj. Barton, PA, Rewa Kantha, rushed to the border area to provide support to Propert's troops. Two battalions of NI and one of the Gaekwad's cavalry were also hurried to Halol, under Propert's command, according to the *Homeward Mail from India, China and the East* (hereafter *HMICE*) on 10 and 23 March 1868.

In order to deal with the uprising in Panchmahal, Capt. MacLeod reached Halol on 9 February 1868. Lt. Burnes was already camped there, along with 100 armed jawans of the 26th NI. On 11 February, leaving a troop of 25 jawans at Halol under an Indian officer, MacLeod marched with the rest of the 26th NI via Champaner to Shivrajpur. While at Halol, he had sent another troop of 25 jawans to Barton at Rajgarh. At Shivrajpur, two troops, one led by Lt. Reay, and the other by MacLeod, along with 60 jawans of the 26th NI, combined forces. A troop each of Makranis and the Gaekwad's cavalry also joined the force. MacLeod set out for Jambughora on 14 February, where the army camped in open space.

Warrick, from where the insurrection was reported, was a mere 6 mil. distant. On 16 February, MacLeod proceeded to attack the Bhils, joined in his campaign by Propert. Moving cautiously, the troops approached Warrick around 7:30 am. Surrounded by high hills and dense forests, the village could only be accessed through a narrow passage. On reaching the entrance to the village, the British instructed the Makranis to climb the summit to carry out reconnaissance, and to establish control of the point of entry into the village.

Leaving the main part of the troop under Burnes, MacLeod moved closer to the village to observe the Bhils' activity, only to discover them escaping from the village's rear into the dense forest. He then rushed the cavalry round to block their escape, while the main troop invaded the village. The attacking troop included the Bhil Corps led by Seagrave and Westmacott and about 100 jawans of the 26th NI. Several Bhils were killed or injured, while the others fled into the forest. According to an initial report, Parmeshwar had been killed, but it later transpired that he had survived. He was subsequently caught and imprisoned in Jambughora, from where he made an abortive attempt to escape. Rupa Singh, too, was initially reported killed but was later apprehended. In all, 50 Bhils were taken prisoner, detained in Jambughora Jail and tried.

The village was burnt down after the battle, following which the officers returned to base camp. While still at base camp, they received intelligence on 16 February that, on the preceding night, Bhils had attacked a troop of 50 jawans, including some Makranis, who had been left at Shivrajpur under Subedar Sheikh Sultan. The skirmish had claimed five lives, while 25 were injured. The British Government later admitted in parliament that the deaths of Rupa Singh and Parmeshwar had been falsely reported. The episode was published in various newspapers such as *HM* on 23 March 1868, *MP* on 7 April 1868 and *BG* on 11 April 1868.

On 11 May, five Bhil ringleaders captured during this campaign were hanged to death at Jambughora, with a large crowd gathered to watch the spectacle. Addressing them in Gujarati, Barton emphasised that the ruffians were being punished so that the others could live in peace. On 18 June 1868, the *Glasgow Herald* published the death of Mulla Manik and four of his associates in Kathiawad, near Porbandar.

Banswara, 1872–1875
From 1872 to 1875, Banswara witnessed a number of Bhil insurrections. The main underlying causes were:
I. The 1868 treaty between Banswara and the British that gave the latter the arbitrary right to crush the Bhils;
II. A hike in barar tax. In addition, Bhils were burdened with land revenue for the first time;
III. Makranis and foreigners (i.e., the Pathans of Afghanistan) who were recruited to crush the Bhils. They would lend money to the Bhils at usurious rates and mortgage Bhil children in writing. In case of default in payment, these children were taken as slaves;
IV. The appalling famine of 1868–1875 that had plunged the Bhils into starvation and thus, on the warpath;
V. The inspiration derived from the rebellions of Bhil chiefs in Gujarat.

Dalla, the Bhil chief at Sodalpur, mutinied against the *maha rawal* (king) of Banswara on the issue of barar. The *maha rawal* had demanded Rs 2,000; Dalla, however, was prepared to pay just Rs 900. When the state issued him a notice for Rs 2,000, Dalla fled to Pratapgarh where he raised an army of 8,000. When worried British officers pressured the *maha rawal*, a compromise was effected on Dalla's terms. Bhil guerrilla activity continued in the Chilkari and Shergarh villages of Banswara. In 1873–1874, when these guerilla tactics spread to the states of Sailana and Jhabua, the PA of Bhopawar dispatched a company of Malva Bhil Corps to subdue them. In 1875, the mutiny by Bhil chiefs Deva and Omkar Rawat of Bhurukhera dissipated on its own after mutual bickering between the Bhils of Bhurukhera and Pipalkhunt.[27]

On 7 February 1873, the *Times of India* (hereafter *TOI*) reported that at the beginning of 1873, PA Capt. Bar had used the Bhil Corps to attempt to capture a Bhil band that had been regularly vandalising the Manpur district of Rajasthan. In 1873, the British Government contemplated deploying the Mewar Bhil Corps to repress an insurrection by Bhuta, a Bhil chief of Sirohi.[28]

The *Sydney Mail and New South Wales Advertiser* (hereafter *SMNSWA*) carried an article on 7 August 1875 on the rebellions by Bhils and Meenas that continued in Mewar and Marwar in 1875, where the two tribes had for long harassed the locals with their hereditary calling of plunder and murder.

On 28 October 1875, *BG*'s correspondent reported from Baroda on rumours of Bhil plans to plunder Baroda and the nearby states. The news alerted the administration, which deputed about 100 jawans at the Clock Tower in Baroda. From the state's army, 50 horsemen and 100 jawans were deployed under British officers in the towns where disturbances were anticipated, with troops in camps on high alert.

Anup Ji had been harassing the cultivators of Kuddi, in the district of Patan, for the last seven years. The *SMNSWA* on 1 January 1876 reported that he was eventually apprehended by Lt. Ballantine, along with his Bhil comrades.

Mewar, 1881

The Mewar revolt of 1881 occupies a place of distinction in Bhil history. There are reports of horrendous encounters which took place between the royal army of Udaipur and the Bhils in March and April 1881. These incidents were published in the *Sheffield Independent* on 12 April 1881. The root of one such dispute makes for interesting reading. A *kallal* (trader) had been distilling wine for the preceding four or five years under licence in Barapal, a Bhil village on the Udaipur–Kherwara road, 14 mil. south of Udaipur. He had priced the wine at four annas per bottle for the Bhils. Deeming this amount extortionate, the Bhil chief began to distil wine himself. The trader complained to the Mewar officials, leading to the chief being fined, which triggered the subsequent revolt.

On 25 March 1881, Akbar Husain, a *sowar* (mounted soldier), was dispatched by the thanadar to summon the Bhil chief of Paduna to appear before him regarding a land dispute. Paduna was located some 9 mil. to the south of Barapal on the Udaipur–Kherwara road. When the chief refused to respond immediately to the summons, Akbar Husain tried to capture him by force. This cavalier treatment of their chief infuriated the Bhils, who attacked and killed Husain. Moreover, enraged by the thanadar's audacity, Bhils of Paduna arrived in Barapal on 26 March and, along with 300 local Bhils, attacked the thana. The policemen faced the Bhils till their ammunition was exhausted. No timely help seemed forthcoming from Udaipur. The incensed Bhil crowd set the thana on fire and killed the thanadar. Next, they entered a trader's house where they killed his brother and three women. This trader had been trying to increase liquor sales in collusion with some shopkeepers, whose shops were also set on fire. The attack claimed 16 lives, including that of the thanadar, 11 *sowar*s and sepoys, among others. The Bhil crowd, later swelling to between 3,000 and 4,000, blocked the Udaipur–Kherwara road.

When news of this incident reached the Udaipur court on 27 March, King Sajjan Singh responded with 500 infantry, 150 cavaliers, two cannons, a deputation of court officials as well as the British commandant employed for his security. But by the time his army reached the spot, the Bhils had melted into the forest, stated a *TOI* report on 19 April 1881.[29]

On 27 March, the Bhil mob moved towards Alsigarh where they were joined by the Bhils of Pai. The two groups raided the Alsigarh thana, killing Dul Ji Kamdar and one of his assistants as well as two or three *sowar*s. On receiving this report, 50 *sowar*s and sepoys arrived post-haste from Bhainsorgarh, but the Bhils had escaped by then. On the same day, the Bhil mob set fire to the thana in Kewra ki Naal, but sepoys managed to kill three Bhils.

There were several reasons for this revolt. Shyamal Das, the administrative officer of the court, had suggested stringent action against the Bhils, who reacted violently to any manipulation of their traditional rights (Shyamal Das is also known as Kaviraj Shyamal Das. Sajjan Singh had deputed him to assist Col. Todd with archaeological investigations). For instance, in 1880–1881, the Udaipur court had prohibited the Bhils from the distillation of alcohol from mahua, which they had been doing for centuries. Another key reason was that the Census, which had begun in 1881, was accompanied by several rumours amongst the Bhils, one of which was that the sturdiest of them would be sent off by the government to fight in the Afghan War. Among the other reasons were rumours that new taxes would be imposed to meet the cost of war, the apprehension that the royal court would institute a count of livestock and tax them accordingly, and the sharp increase in the price of salt. Furthermore, the Bhils did not want any police or customs posts in their territories.

When the Bhils gathered in a temple at Jawar, in southern Mewar, the British Government, sensing yet another potential crisis, halted the survey work of the Census in February 1881. In April 1881, the Bhils presented their demands, consistent with their traditional culture, to the

Udaipur court—their objection to the Census, the removal of checkposts in their territories, and the protection of their right to kill witches and resolve mutual disputes. C.R. Blair, CO, Mewar Bhil Corps, had written to Probyn stressing that the Bhils of Mewar were undoubtedly far more impoverished than their brethren in other states. Even so, the British Government did nothing to prevent the Udaipur court from imposing fresh taxes. The Bhils retaliated by plundering the nearby states, ransacking railway property and attacking police posts.

Besides Barapal, the volatile situation that prevailed in Rishabhdev prompted the court to dispatch armed troops on 27 March. Rishabhdev was situated some 40 mil. from Udaipur on the Udaipur–Kherwara road. In the four days it took to reach Rishabhdev, the troops were attacked by Bhil bands at many places en route—it was rebellion all the way from Barapal to Rishabhdev.

At Rishabhdev, royal soldiers waged a tough war on the Bhils, who nevertheless fought back with determination. On 21 April 1881, the *Star* (hereafter *Sr*) reported that, in all, 80 Bhils lost their lives in this battle. Of the royal soldiers, 17 were killed and two injured. The king's officials began to consider a compromise with the Bhils as the more prudent option. Through the priest of the Rishabhdev temple, Shyamal Das attempted to contact the Bhil chiefs in the first week of April.[30]

The services rendered by Probyn were particularly valuable during the revolts of 1881. On 23 July 1883, *HMICE* reported that he had persuaded the Bhils to compromise, after which a special commission was instituted.

In a letter, dated 30 May, Political Superintendent Col. C.R. Blair informed Dr J.P. Streshan, PA, Mewar, that he had reached Udaipur on 1 April, soon after receiving intelligence of the Bhil uprising, for a discussion with the king. As political representatives of the British Government, on 15 April Blair and Wingak left Udaipur for Kherwara where they were to negotiate a compromise on 17 April with the Bhils of Barapal and Paduna, dubbed criminal villages. All along the route, the two British officers noted that the Bhils seemed willing to compromise. At Rishabhdev on 17 April, Blair sensed that the Bhils were wary of Shyamal Das. On 18 April, Blair invited the Bhil chiefs to present their problems and demands before Shyamal Das at 5 pm, at a pre-determined location.

During these negotiations, Blair and Wingak were monitoring the situation from about three-quarters of a mile. But, quite unexpectedly, a stampede ensued after a Bhil's gun accidentally went off. Frightened by the gunfire, the Bhils, running helter-skelter, began baying for battle from the hilltops. The royal soldiers, then on standby as instructed by their British officers, opened fire. Large numbers of Bhils began to gather when they heard the cries of their comrades. By then, Burns had already been sent back to Kherwara. Blair and Wingak, sensing that the Bhils were gathering in strength, escaped to Kherwara, leaving the royal soldiers to their fate in Rishabhdev. They also left their camp unattended, which was soon ravaged by the tribals. In Kherwara, the two officers considered soliciting army assistance from Ahmedabad. But, in the meantime, by the following morning, i.e., 19 April, negotiations had been reopened between Shyamal Das and Bhil chiefs of Rishabhdev and the neighbouring areas;[31] these included Nima of Biluk, Khema of Pipli and Jyota of Sagtari. Shyamal Das and Bhil mukhia Amar Singh tried to persuade the Bhils to reopen the Udaipur–Kherwara route, while court officials gave a patient hearing to the Bhils' complaints.

To end the insurrection, the Bhils proposed a pardon for all their comrades involved in the uprising, and the revival and respect of their traditional rights. Court officials had little choice but to concede to their demands. While about 100 Bhil chiefs participated in the negotiations, 6,000–7,000 Bhils watched the spectacle from hilltops.[32] On 30 May 1881, the *Nottingham Evening Post* reported that a 21-point agreement was reached on 19 April 1881, after which the Bhils returned to their forests (this agreement has been reproduced in Appendix 4).

The agreement was, in a sense, a resounding victory for the Bhils. They were even pardoned for the murder of 16 individuals, including the thanadar in Barapal. Meanwhile, the British Government took a dim view of Blair's cowardly flight to Kherwara, having abandoned the royal sepoys in Rishabhdev.[33]

The Bhima Khera region in Rajasthan witnessed a powerful Bhil revolt in 1881–1882. Here, the Bhils killed some employees of the Rajputana State Railway. Abu was no longer safe for tourists—European tourists were being attacked. An officer's bag was snatched when he was returning from Abu with his wife, reported *HM* on 27 February 1882.

The Bhils of Rajpipla rebelled once more in 1890. The dispute of jurisdiction between Dam Ji, the Bhil chief of Sagwara, and the state was now assuming violent dimensions. The Bombay Government deputed A.F. Woodburn on 21 January 1890 to settle the issue, which he did with success.[34]

Pol, 1881

Achchheram Mitharam, APA and in-charge of Idar state, had written to apprise Lt. Col. G.R. Goodfellow, PA, Mahi Kanta, of the peace that prevailed in Idar in the 20-mil. stretch from the border areas of Mahi Kantha to Shishod in Kherwara, as well as in Dungarpur. Bhil chiefs of the Mahi Kantha border areas had not supported the Mewar uprising. On the morning of 25 April 1881, 50 cavaliers from the Gaekwad's Army reached the border areas. The Sirbandi of Idar arrived with his officials, as did Achchheram Mitharam on 27 April. No disturbance had been reported after the Kherwara agreement between the Bhils and the Mewar court, effected through the mediation of the king of Dungarpur and the rao of Jawas. But this report from Achchheram was, in fact, inaccurate, as all of Pol was then in turmoil.

At the beginning of May, Bhil chiefs had compelled the rao of Pol to sign a 38-point agreement, with a reduction in taxation being key. The other important issues concerned the imposition of just fines for criminals, the cancellation of any arrears of fines and the release of prisoners. This agreement was reached between the Bhils, *patels*, wine dealers, carpenters, goldsmiths, potters, bards, weavers and the people of Vijaynagar Petta. When Goodfellow, who had gone to Pol to probe events, took the unusual decision of signing the agreement on 4 May 1881, the Bhils, quite naturally, assumed that the British Government had endorsed the agreement.

At the meeting between Goodfellow and the rao of Pol on 1 June, when the former was camping in the state, the rao complained that Bhil insurgents were ravaging his territory and that he had been pressured to support the 38-point agreement. As revealed by the Bombay Government's letters, numbered 9P, dated 17 June 1881, and 11P, dated 23 June 1881, the Bhils of Mahi Kantha and Nimar were linked. Another letter, dated 17 June 1881, from C. Gonne, CS, Bombay, discloses that Bhil tribals assembled at Ghorde were raiding and torching shops. On the same day, Goodfellow reported on the Bhil uprising in Pol—it had been instigated by Banias and was influenced by the success of the Mewar rebellion.

Subsequently, the British Government, realising that the 38-point agreement was a blunder that would greatly harm its own interests, sent its officers to rescind it. Nevertheless, the government was willing to consider the Bhils' problems. A number of Bhils arrived from Mewar in July 1881 to join those gathered at Ghorde. The police post of Gulpura swung into action to disperse the assembled Bhils, and this clash with the police claimed 20 Bhil lives. The government, which was under the impression that the Bhils had been instigated by claims made by certain Banias that Bhil debts would be cancelled, reported that the disturbance was quelled without army help.

The AGG, Rajputana Agency, arrived in Ahmedabad to explain the government's directives, and deputed Blair and Probyn to investigate the causes of opposition. On 25 July 1881, the *Aberdeen Evening Express* reported that, consequently, the government had decided to hold a meeting of British officials and Bhils in December 1881 or January 1882.[35]

In Mahi Kantha in 1881, the Bhils were once again confronting state police—it was as if their rebellion had never subsided. According to the British, the Bhils of the eastern and northern districts of Mahi Kantha were particularly barbaric.[36]

The Siyol Rebellion of Mewar, August 1881
A correspondent writing from Dungarpur provides details about the Siyol rebellion in Mewar (now in Udaipur district, near Nathdwara). Bhils from Mond Pal, led by a *gameti*, attacked and killed two Makrani soldiers, then advanced toward Sadulbur, near the Dungarpur border.

Terrified by the consequences, the Bhils initially surrendered and agreed to a peace settlement, vowing to stay out of the Dungarpur area. The DIP was instructed not to enter the Bhil zones, but this only escalated tensions. Later, the Bhils gathered in large numbers and attacked the inspector and his team, killing six men. The inspector narrowly escaped, the *TOI* reported on 7 September 1881.

The September 1899 Incident
In September 1899, a large armed Bhil group launched an attack near Khedgam, Gujarat. The encounter with an Indian Infantry Battalion at Bodel resulted in around 100 Bhils killed, many injured and 29 guns recovered reported the *Scotsman* on 30 September 1899.

The Chhappnia Famine and Revolt in Rajputana
In 1900, the *Church Missionary Intelligencer* reported that in 1899–1900, the entire region of Khandesh and Rajputana was ravaged by a devastating famine. This famine was more widespread than that of 1887, covering all of Rajputana, Central India, the south-eastern states of Bombay Presidency, Baroda, and parts of Hyderabad, stated the *Evening News* (Sydney) (hereafter *EN*) on 28 June 1900. The famine was a death-trap for the Bhils. The disaster was so profound that officers of the colonial power were indeed moved, although it must be noted that Indian princes did almost nothing to mitigate the calamity. On 21 November 1899, the *North Devon Gazette* highlighted the humanitarian efforts of Maj. and Mrs Hutton Dawson, stationed in Kotra during the famine, who postponed their London visit to see their only son and issued an appeal to the public for assistance.

The Chhappnia famine—so named as it occurred in the year chhappan, i.e., 1956 (CE 1899)—took a massive toll, killing Bhils and cattle in droves. Indigenous traders had raised food prices during the famine and plunder further worsened the situation—many were killed while protecting their homes, and the survivors were left to starve. The CO, Mewar Bhil Corps, recorded that every palm tree had been felled, its pieces ground with stone and eaten—only blackened rocks and sun-baked earth remained. Most of the wells had dried up. Cattle had died or were being eaten. Charles Stewart Thompson, the first medical missionary in Kherwara Chhaoni, in Rajputana, who had hurled himself into relief operations, later died of cholera.[37] His schools, famine relief centres and medical service transformed care in the region.

From Ealing in Britain, Col. Jasper Burns wrote a letter on 28 March 1900, which was published in *Sr* on 24 April 1900, detailing the miserable plight of the Mewar Bhils. He urged the government to step in and save the Bhils, as dead bodies were to be seen all around Mewar. He pointed out that for 40,000 famine-stricken Bhils, the Kherwara state was spending a measly Rs 350, and Mewar still less—merely Rs 200. This, said the letter, was just a drop in the ocean. In January 1900, 120 deaths were reported from the tiny Cantt. area alone. Rows of live skeletons could be seen waiting for death in Bhil shanties. The immediate requirement for famine relief was Rs 60,000, continued Burns' letter, as no improvement in the situation was expected till the following September.

Two Christian missions stepped forward with assistance during the famine. By May 1900, they were running 12 'famine kitchens' that provided food to about 5,500 Bhils, mainly children, reported the *Surrey Mirror* on 22 June 1900. The *EN* on 28 June 1900 reported that the government had announced its plan to spend 46,00,000 pounds sterling on relief operations up to December 1900 and had also postponed land revenue collections.

It requires little imagination to visualise the starving Bhils' reaction. The *Bradford Daily Telegraph* reported that on 13 September 1899 the Bhil uprising took many lives in Panchmahal and the army had to be dispatched from Baroda. On 3 May 1900, questions were raised in the House of Commons about famine deaths among the Rajputana Bhils. Sir Donald Maclean, a British Liberal politician in the UK, asked the secretary of state for India for news of Bhil deaths in Mewar. At the rate the Bhils were dying, his apprehension was that a mere 10 per cent would survive by July if the existing situation continued: What was the government doing to save them? In response, Lord Hamilton gave an assurance that the Government of India would loan the state Rs 5 lakh for famine relief. If the king required more assistance, said Hamilton, the government would immediately provide it. On 5 May 1900, *HMICE* published his disagreement with the contention that Mewar had been callous with regard to Bhil lives and property.

In the states of Sunth and Jhalod Mahal, Bhils demanded grain on credit. Those who had sold their produce to traders now wanted grain at fair prices. The astronomical hike in grain prices by traders enraged the Bhils, and two large bands began to loot grain stocks from the villages of Sunth and Jhalod Mahal. They raided Limri on 10 September 1899, where the villagers drove them back with help from the local police force. On 11 September, Bhils ravaged several villages in Sunth, decamping with gold and silver jewellery as well as cattle. The collector sent telegrams and requisitioned troops as well as two companies of the Ninth Bombay Infantry from Baroda. These companies reached Dahod by 12 September and small army troops were posted wherever disturbances were expected. The main troop was deployed under Lt. Hoshyns at Rampur in Sunth, apart from a larger one at Fatepur. On 12 October 1899, the *Englishman's Overland Mail* (hereafter *EOM*) reported that Bhil raids had decreased only thereafter.

In 1899, near Khergam in Gujarat, a large Bhil band looted substantial quantities of grain stored in warehouses. Troops of NI, dispatched from Baroda to assist the district police, pursued and attacked the Bhils near the hills. In the deadly skirmish that followed, about 100 Bhils were reportedly killed or injured. After the battle, just 39 bodies were to be found on the spot, as the Bhils had evidently removed the other dead bodies as well as their injured comrades. They had achieved their objective at the cost of 39 lives—and they were able to take away their spoils. This episode found mention in the *Yorkshire Post and Leeds Intelligencer* on 30 September 1899, and in *HMICE* on 16 October 1899.

In January 1901, the Bhils of Mewar stole some heads of cattle from Modasa Mahal, near Saira, in Ahmedabad district. The Res. asked the Mewar court to arrest the culprits and recover the stolen livestock. Maj. Dawson, the political superintendent of hill tracts in Mewar, who was then camping at Kherwara, dispatched the tehsildar and some cavaliers to the village of Watelia. The troop started their journey not in daytime, as instructed, but at night, lost their way and reached Dabaycha Patia instead. There, they were attacked by about 200 Bhils. About 250 heads of stolen cattle were recovered by the tehsildar. On his return to Kherwara, Dawson instructed the tehsildar to proceed to Udaipur, under the supervision of an officer of Mugra, to search for the cattle stolen from Khalsa Pals. On 22 February 1901, the Ahmednagar collectorate asked the Mewar court to apprehend the culprits and recover the stolen animals. The court provided the officer of Mugra with a large force, cavaliers, guns, etc. Most of the villages of Bhil raiders were located in Mewar, with some based in Idar. The primary culprits belonged to the Khalsa villages of Mewar, which were governed by the court. A total of 61 animals—32 buffaloes, 15 cows, eight calves, three bulls and three goats—were eventually recovered.[38]

The first decade of the 20th century passed fairly peacefully, which could be attributed to Christian missionary activity among the Bhils. Furthermore, under the influence of the Bhakta movement spreading among them, the Bhils had begun to abstain from violence and liquor.

Govind Guru, 1913

Bhil chief Govind Guru belonged to a tribe of nomadic Bhil banjaras from the village of Bedsa in the erstwhile princely state of Dungarpur. A cultivator to begin with, he eventually became an ascetic of the Bundi Dashnami sect. Influenced by Christian missionaries, he promoted the Bhakta or Bhagat movement among the Bhils of Mewar between 1908 and 1913. His aim was to reform Bhils living in Dungarpur, Banswara, Idar and Sunth.[39] His close association with a Hindu Giri is also the reason he is also referred to as Govind Giri. In recent years, attempts have been made to present Govind Guru as a Hindu ascetic and preacher and as a leader of the Bhagat (Bhakta) movement. Virtually all historians believe Govind Guru to be the initiator of the Bhagat movement and spokesman of monotheism among the tribals, but this is debatable.

Kherari Surmal Ralia, or Sur Ji, a Bhil belonging to the village of Lusadia, some 4 mil. from Samlaji in Gujarat, had declared himself a guru in 1869, and he, too, propagated One God. He began a cult for the reformation of Bhils, which may be termed a Bhakta or Bhagat sect. The *HMICE* on 11 March 1872, the *Pall Mall Gazette* (hereafter *PMG*) on 3 April 1872, and the *Edinburgh Evening News* (hereafter *EEN*) on 11 January 1876 carried reports on the formation of his sect as well as the government's enthusiastic support of his ideas which were aimed at weaning the Bhils from violence. Surmal was influenced by Kabir's sect (or Nath sect), which was opposed to animal slaughter, and both sects—Govind

Guru's and Surmal's—had borrowed the philosophy of non-violence from Buddhism (followers of Kabir or Gorakh in large numbers were once prevalent in Gujarat and Rajasthan).[40]

Like Buddhism, Surmal, too, rejected animal slaughter. He advised the Bhils to desist from any kind of crime or violence. He forbade alcohol, and the consumption of food before bathing. A yellow cloth tied around his turban became an insignia of his sect. His followers, sporting a red mark on their foreheads, were called *bhakta*s and included 400 Bhils of Idar and some 1,000 Bhils from the Gujarat–Mewar border areas. However, they were treated as outcasts by the other Bhils of Mewar.

Lt. Col. J. Black, PA, Mahi Kantha, once attended a meeting at Lusadia with Surmal, the aim of which was to pit the guru against insurgent Bhils. At Lusadia, Surmal requested Black for protection from inimical Bhils for his family and supporters, which the latter asked the state's chiefs to ensure.

Consequently, it is apparent that Govind Guru was not the first Bhil saint to preach monotheism. His ideas were mainly derived from Surmal's Bhakta sect, which had already become prominent in 1869. Among Govind Guru's teachings were bathing before Sunday worship, fire worship and filial responsibility. He urged the Bhils to shun killing, theft, debauchery, bitterness and deceit. Other teachings included eschewing animal slaughter and their belief in ghosts, witches and sorcery, and the practice of meditation before the holy fire and agriculture. He equated the Bhils with upper-caste Hindus, such as Brahmins and Rajputs, but considered Bhil women far superior to their Brahmin and Rajput counterparts. Bhil widows were allowed to remarry, which the other upper castes did not permit. The Bhils of Dungarpur, Banswara and Sunth found Govind Guru's teachings simple and practical and therefore, by November 1913, his sect had gathered 5 lakh Bhil devotees, reported the *Belfast Telegraph* (hereafter *BT*) on 25 February 1914.[41]

In 1905, Govind Guru formed a socio-religious organisation known as Sampa Sabha in the state of Sirohi, which functioned much like the panchayat system of ancient days. It boycotted foreign goods and promoted cottage industry.[42]

Stephen Puchs regards Govind Guru as a Nath ascetic. In his youth, when the Bhil tract was devastated by the famine of 1900 in which much of the population perished, Binda lost his wife, children and cattle. The indescribable agony caused by the loss of his immediate family and livelihood aroused in him a religious fervour and, with his surviving family members, he moved to Sunth–Rampur and Godra where he settled incognito and married his brother's widow. Soon he came in contact with Rajguru, a Hindu Gosain, and changed his name to Govind Giri. In or around 1909, he returned to Bedsa with his family to devote himself to religious activity. Declaring that God had deputed him to reform the Bhils, he swiftly won the faith of the community. His intention was to create a Bhil society free of all evils, but Brahmins were not allowed to participate in his sect's rites. He held aloof from Hindu customs and rituals. His fame spread far and wide to Dungarpur, Banswara, Sunth–Rampur, Idar, Panchmahal, and nearby areas. The number of Bhil devotees swelled such that Govind Guru began to dream of a Bhil Raj.[43]

From 1907 onwards, as Govind Guru began to attract a large number of Bhil followers, the Rajput kings of Rajputana and Rewa Kantha viewed his mediations and campaign for reform as injurious to their own interests, which were served by keeping the Bhils perpetually backward and superstitious. Govind Guru's teachings against the consumption of alcohol and narcotics were adversely affecting the revenues of these states—for instance, Sunth lost about Rs 6,000 per annum. Wine merchants were particularly agitated in 1912 and 1913, as the Bhils had begun to boycott liquor in response to their guru's teachings. In view of the considerable financial losses, the king imprisoned Govind Guru on concocted charges of cheating and misleading his subjects. He forfeited Govind Guru's savings and brought pressure on him to forsake his religious ideas by imprisoning his wife and children. On 27 December 1913, *HMICE* reported that it was precisely against such oppression that in October–November 1913 Govind Guru summoned his congregation to Mangarh Tekri (hilltop).[44]

Govind Guru's Entrenchment on Mangarh Tekri
In view of the growing unrest among the Bhils, the king released Govind Guru in April 1913 but exiled him from

Dungarpur. From then onwards until October 1913, the guru and his preachers wandered from village to village, while state officials continued to harass them. Govind Guru's missionaries continued to highlight Bhil oppression by Rajput rulers—in other words, their religious sermons brought political awareness to the Bhils.

When the king of Idar ordered the guru's arrest from his residence in Rajoda in October 1913, an enraged Govind Guru ensconced himself, along with his supporters, on Mangarh Tekri, situated on the border of the states of Dungarpur and Sunth. His occupation of the hilltop, in accordance with Bhil tradition, was meant to draw the state's attention. Punja Dheer Ji, Govind Guru's lieutenant, who belonged to Sunth in Dungarpur, represented the protesting followers who were preparing to confront and rid themselves of Rajput oppression in order to restore the Bhil Raj destroyed by the Rajputs some 800 years earlier. Thus, at the guru's summons, a large crowd of about 4,000 illiterate Bhils, armed with traditional weapons, gathered at Mangarh under his banner.

Govind Guru's offensive began on 31 October 1913 with the capture of a police jamadar and a constable of Sunth who had been sent on reconnaissance to Mangarh. On 1 November, he attempted to invade Pratapgarh Fort in Sunth, but was thwarted in the attempt by state police. He then raided some villages along the Sunth–Banswara border. When the head of the village of Bhramari in Banswara refused to come to his aid, Govind Guru ravaged Bhramari as well. Soon, some 300 Bhils from Amja in Banswara arrived at Mangarh to join their guru, who had threatened a Bhil revolt in the states of Kushalgarh, Banswara and Sunth, which was reported by *BT* on 25 February 1914.[45]

The Bhil occupation of Mangarh Tekri created a great deal of trouble for the states bordering Gujarat and Rajasthan. On 6 November, therefore, the combined armies of Banswara, Dungarpur, Sunth and Baria laid siege to Mangarh Tekri. R.P. Barrow, commissioner, Northern Division, and C.W.M. Hudson, PA, and district police chief, Rewa Kantha, proceeded towards Mangarh from Sunth. On 25 February 1914, *BT* reported that Maj. Hamilton had approached Mangarh from southern Rajputana. In addition, a troop of the 104th Rifles of Baroda was led by Wellesley, a senior officer. As reported in *HMICE* on 27 December 1913, Capt. Ayscough led a troop of the 7th Rajput Machinegun, while two troops of the Mewar Bhil Corps from Kherwara, led by Maj. Stockley and Capt. Leckie, joined the campaign.

On 12 November, Govind Guru's deputation carried a letter to Capt. J.P. Stockley, CO, Mewar Bhil Corps, and Hudson. The letter urged them to compel the kings of Banswara and Sunth to address Bhil grievances. Among Govind Guru's demands were that these kings desist from demanding *begar* (unpaid labour) from the Bhils, that they stopped their interference in the forests, that his followers be allowed to follow their religious injunctions, that excise and revenue policies be amended to stop the sale of alcohol, and that there be no compulsion to consume liquor. Other demands related to the quashing of cases lodged against Punja

Dheer Ji and 10 followers, who he believed to be innocent—these cases involved sedition, the killing of a sepoy and the torching of the Gadara check post in Rajasthan. One other demand involved his own appointment as CM, Sunth, with permission to collect tax from all classes for his maintenance.

Stockley responded to only one of Govind Guru's demands, with a promise of British protection to Bhils regarding the free observance of their religious rites in all states—he conceded to no other demand. He expressed much appreciation for Govind Guru's reformative ideas but insisted that the latter evacuate Mangarh immediately, adding that the gathering of a crowd that heavily armed was reprehensible, a detailed report of which was carried in *BT* on 25 February 1914.[46]

Hamilton, Hudson and Barrow made several attempts through their messengers at communication with various Bhil chiefs to settle the dispute. Govind Guru was given 24 hours to surrender and evacuate Mangarh, failing which the army would eject his followers by force.

Govind Guru, who had not been attacked thus far, ignored the threat. His followers regarded this miracle by their guru as an affirmation of the sahibs' fear of their divine guru's powers that would protect his devotees from bullets.

In the meantime, news of the Bhil gathering at Mangarh Tekri had reached the neighbouring states, and the Bhils of Banswara, Kushalgarh and Dungarpur grew restive. In view of this development, British officers ordered the army to surround Mangarh Tekri on the morning of 17 November

1913. Machine guns were used to disperse the Bhils, killing 12. About 900 Bhils were reported to have been arrested. (English newspapers of the day, however, put the number at 300, which appears accurate.) The arrested Bhils included Govind Guru and Punja Dheer Ji. The *HMICE* on 6 December 1913 and *BT* on 25 February 1914, reported that barring the primary leaders, most Bhils were released on the same day and sent off with a stern warning from the commissioner against armed gatherings.[47] Besides Govind Guru and Punja Dheer Ji, who were incarcerated in Ahmedabad Jail, 28 others were also arrested. Documents from Dungarpur reveal that those imprisoned included 15 Bhils from that state.[48]

In those days, the British Army used carbines or machine guns loaded on mules in order to disperse crowds. Although often off the mark, they served to create chaos and panic in crowds.[49] Tales recounted by the residents of Amalia, Khuta, Tikma, Bhongapur and Temwara put the number of Bhils killed by carbines on mules, used to break the siege, at more than 1,000. Notwithstanding actual numbers, one may safely assume that several Bhils were killed at Mangarh Tekri, several others were arrested, and the rest dispersed.

When within 48 hours news of the arrest of Govind Guru and other Bhil leaders reached Bhil territories, the tribals began protesting at various places. The government constituted a special court to try the rebels. The court held Govind Guru and Punja Dheer Ji guilty of waging a war against the states of Sunth and Banswara and of the murder of Gul Muhammad, a Sunth sepoy. It sentenced Punja Dheer

Ji to imprisonment for life, and Govind Guru to a 10-year jail term.[50]

British newspapers of the time as well as the *Banswara Gazetteer* (hereafter *BGaz*) published varying accounts of the punishments meted out to Govind Guru and Punja Dheer Ji—for instance, on 14 February 1914, the *Daily Herald* (hereafter *DH*), the *Birmingham Mail* (hereafter *BM*) and the *Western Mail* (hereafter *WM*) reported that 300 Bhils (not 900) were arrested from Mangarh Tekri. They also claimed that Maj. Bayley, CO, 104th Rifles, had arrested Govind Guru in Santpur (Gujarat), where the government had constituted a special court to try both the accused. In February 1914, the court sentenced Govind Guru to death, under Section 121, and Punja Dheer Ji to life imprisonment, under Sections 121 and 302. Twenty-eight Bhils were each sentenced to three years RI, under Sections 148 and 149. One British newspaper also asserted that after pronouncing the death sentence on Govind Guru, the Santpur special court had strongly recommended that his life be spared. The court held that Govind Guru was a venerable religious leader and social reformer of Bhils living in Central India and Rajputana well before the advent of the Aryan. According to the paper, Govind Guru's movement opposed the evils of liquor consumption which was then common among Bhils. He had resorted to sedition only after he was jailed for his anti-liquor stance and other such reforms. Only then had he staged the abortive raid on a police check post in Bombay Presidency and commanded his supporters to gather at Mangarh Tekri.

Following the judge's noting, Govind Guru filed an appeal with Barrow, who commuted his death sentence to life imprisonment. Punja Dheer Ji's sentence remained unchanged. Five of the other 28 convicts were released, while the sentences of each of the remaining 23 were reduced to six months RI. According to *BGaz*, Govind Guru died in jail, a claim contradicted by some documents. Reports regarding such claims are to be found in *DH*, *BM*, *WM* and the *Globe* on 13 February 1914, the *Londonderry Sentinel* on 19 February 1914 and *BT* on 25 February 1914.[51]

Tiha, a Bhil from Temarwa, who played a notable role in Govind Guru's Sampa Sabha, was killed at Mangarh Tekri. Six Bhils carried his body back to his village and buried him in a nearby forest, where a small monument stands even today.

Some years ago, *India Today*, too, had probed the Mangarh Tekri insurrection. Its report concluded that Govind Guru was sentenced to life imprisonment. A habitual user of marijuana, he had grown quite frail in jail. But, as his conduct was exemplary, he was released from Hyderabad Jail in 1919, although the then existing states had debarred his entry. Released after spending less than 10 years in prison, Govind Guru settled at Kamboi, near Limbari, in Gujarat, where he died in 1931.

Thus ended the life of a Bhil hero who attempted to rid his society of social evils and superstitions and who dreamt of the restoration of a Bhil Raj. A large number of Bhils of the Nath sect can still be found in the Bhil tract of Dungarpur. Govind Guru's *samadhi* (shrine) still stands in Kamboi.

Punja Dheer Ji was banished to the Andamans, where he died.[52]

On 25 March 1939, the *Dumfries and Galloway Standard* reported that after Govind Guru was imprisoned, Christian missionaries were deputed in the region to baptise the Bhils in order to blunt their rebellious tendencies.

Another Bhil reformer of Govind Guru's ilk was Gulia Bhil of Western Khandesh, commonly addressed as 'Maharaj'. Gulia's mission was to wean the Bhils from liquor and other intoxicants, and he kept his sermons free of Hindu ideas. At one time, he had a following of 75,000. Wine merchants, enraged by his sermons against alcohol, had him murdered.[53]

Udaipur And Sirohi
Eki Movement: Motilal Tejawat, His Reforms, and the No-Tax Campaign, 1921–1922
In August 1921, the Bhils of Begun, who had rebelled from time to time, once again grew restive against the state of Udaipur. From past experience, the state deemed it prudent to negotiate with the Bhils immediately. The negotiations pacified them by addressing their grievances.[54]

The rebellion led by Govind Guru had been confined to Dungarpur, Banswara, Sunth and Idar. In roughly the same period, Motilal Tejawat gave direction to the Bhil-Garasia revolts in the states of Udaipur and Sirohi. Bhils of Pahara Jagir (Mewar) rose in rebellion in 1917 against *begar* and a tax raise. The king announced some concessions in November 1918, but these were unacceptable to the

Bhils—the latter opposed *begar* altogether—and by 1921, the agitation had spread to several areas. The Bhils of Jharol, Koliyari, Madri, Magra, and of Bhaumat in Mewar, united amongst themselves against the native states and the British Government, which had come out in support of these states. Motilal Tejawat assumed leadership of these agitations.[55]

In 1921, Tejawat formed the Eki, an organisation of Bhils in Bhomat, Sirohi and other parts of south-west Mewar. He was influenced by Vijay Singh Pathik, the initiator of the Bijaulia peasant agitation. Ramakant Malviya, the elder son of Madan Mohan Malviya, was CM, Sirohi, at the time when Tejawat had successfully mobilised the Bhils on the issue of taxes. Subsequently, at the bidding of the AGG, Rajputana, Malviya succeeded in reaching an agreement similar to that reached in Bijaulia through the mediation of Vijay Singh Pathik, but the regime later reneged on the agreement.[56]

Motilal Tejawat, of the Oswal Bania caste, hailed from the village of Kolyari in the Jhadol taluka of Udaipur. After Sitaram, he was the second non-Bhil to lead the Bhils amongst whom he was venerated as a reformer and rebel leader. Quitting his job in Jhadol over differences with the jagirdar, he subsequently worked as a peddler of spices, bringing him in close contact with the Bhils. Moved by their plight, Tejawat attempted to forge a reform movement amongst them. He directed the Bhils to eschew liquor, meat and stealing, to avoid illicit relations with a widow or a married woman, to encourage widow remarriage and to avoid dowry. Tejawat's endeavours closely resembled those of Surmal

Ralia and Govind Guru, and it may be safely assumed that he was influenced by these past reformers. These reforms brought him immense popularity among the Bhils. He was also influenced by the circumstances of his time.

In 1920, the Non-Cooperation Movement, led by Mahatma Gandhi, swept the entire country. Tejawat was profoundly impressed by Gandhi's charismatic personality. In 1921, he motivated the Bhils to unite and oppose exploitation by jagirdars—thus was born the Eki movement.[57] A precedence for the Eki movement may be found in the Eka movement of Awadh, led by Madari Pasi in Hardoi and its neighbouring districts, in 1921–1922.[58] The Eka movement had urged the peasants of Awadh to oppose *begar*, to pay no taxes and to settle their disputes through a panchayat, virtually paralleling the profile of the Eki movement. Both Eki and Eka share the same meaning: unity. In both may be seen attempts to form parallel governments. Both Madari Pasi and Motilal Tejawat influenced their supporters by religious precept, social reform and personal charisma, and both, ultimately, became rebels, thus alarming the princely states.

On 19 August 1921, Tejawat was arrested by the thakur of Jhadol. The news incensed the Bhils, who gathered in their thousands and succeeded in getting him released. Drumbeats carried the message to all Bhil villages, commanding the Bhils to pay no taxes. The Bhils pledged to honour Tejawat's decision and to ostracise violators. Charismatic like Gandhi, Tejawat attracted large crowds of Bhils who gathered to pay their respects. His influence spread so far and wide that there developed a parallel government. In December 1921, Tejawat organised about 200 Bhils, beat up and arrested three officials of Jhadol and confiscated the funds collected as taxes. On 31 December 1921, the Udaipur state ordered jagirdars not to allow any congregation of more than 50 individuals and to apprehend Tejawat on sight. An award of Rs 500 was announced for his capture. The Bhil uprising, however, refused to subside. In Udaipur, the peasant movement of Bijaulia, at its height during the same period, served to influence the Bhils.[59]

Revolt on 8 March 1922

On 7 January 1922, two constables on patrol duty in Danta were beaten up and their guns seized. On 15 January, thousands of armed Bhils staged a march along Abu road in Sirohi and held meetings in the neighbouring villages. Crops in the Sirohi region were all harvested without the payment of any tax. A patrol party, deputed to provide security to the pilgrims of Amba Ji on Abu road, was captured. A thana, where grain was stored as part of taxes collected, was demolished. In February, Garasias and Bhils pledged to maintain their unity. The Bhils, led by Motilal Tejawat, fired on the APA, Mahi Kantha, in the middle of February. A sepoy of Idar was humiliated on 3 March.

The Bhils of Mewar launched an armed revolt at the beginning of 1922, aimed mainly against the levy imposed on the supply of goods and the custom of bonded labour.

At the time, Bhil chiefs, too, were influenced by the Non-Cooperation Movement raging all over the country. Tejawat, who identified with Gandhi's principle of non-violence, called for a halt to government taxes. Led by him, thousands of Bhils, armed with guns, swords, and bows and arrows, marched through Sirohi to the state of Idar. The *PMG* on 11 March 1922 and the *Women's Dreadnought* (hereafter *WD*) on 15 April 1922 viewed the incident as the beginning of a rebellion.

On 7 March, Tejawat organised a firing on the political superintendent of the hill tracts. In response, the Mewar Bhil Corps, led by Maj. Sutton, took Tejawat's followers by surprise on 8 March 1922. The crossfire in the battle claimed 22 Bhil lives and injured 29. The army suffered no losses, but Tejawat managed to escape. The Bhils later alleged that 200 compatriots had been killed. The British countered with their justification for the attack—that the Bhils, unduly influenced by the Non-Cooperation Movement, had further intensified their revolt.

The Eki movement became a visible reality from 5 April 1922 onward. On 6 April, Garasias from 40 villages assembled at Siawa (Rajasthan). Along with a political officer (PO), and supported by the 6th Battalion, the CM went to Siawa to broker an agreement. The Garasias, however, were adamant that their problems be addressed before they paid any taxes. In retaliation, the CM and PO appropriated all the grain stored in the leading Bhil chief's house. Infuriated, the villagers entrenched themselves on hilltops and began to beat their war drums. Armed Garasias engaged in a verbal dual with the CM, and one of them threatened the PO. When the British officers arrived, the Garasias attacked them. The CM and PO both beat a hasty retreat under escort. That night, the villagers manhandled an excise contractor and looted his shop. Mungthala road was blocked with large boulders. On 7 April, Garasias assembled in large numbers and squatted on Abu road and, by 8 April, the gathering had grown to 7,000. On 11 April, the CM and PO sent a joint letter to the chiefs, proposing an agreement. That evening, a patrol party from Sirohi was fired upon, injuring one member. When the Garasia chief of Siawa did not respond to the proposal, some parts of the village were set on fire at 3 am on 12 April.[60]

The Garasias then escaped to the hills, and the armed force ultimately returned to Abu road. British officers claimed that three Garasias had been killed, but the chief rebutted the claim—only one of his men had been killed, and one injured. However, even the incineration of several Bhil and Garasia villages failed to bring the situation under control. A few rebel bands were still seen loitering on the main road.[61]

Revolt on 5 May 1922

The Bhils and Garasias of Waloria, Bhula and Nawawasa villages in the Rohera tehsil of Sirohi were not prepared to pay the taxes imposed by the state. They also demanded that the thanas that had been built in their villages be removed. The Bhils of Waloria were particularly incensed and intensified the Eki movement under Tejawat.

The Sirohi state opened negotiations with the rebels. According to the report sent to the British Government by Lt. R.L. Bazelgette, an officer of the commanding force, about 600 Bhils and Garasias had assembled in Waloria. They had also summoned the Bhils of Mewar and Bhakar in Gujarat.

On 30 April 1922, Bazelgette dispatched a letter to the Bhil chiefs of Waloria, Bhula and Nawawasa, jointly signed by the CM of Sirohi and himself. The letter stated that although the court had asked the Bhils several times to clear the tax arrears, they had deserted their villages and escaped into the hills, leaving the taxes unpaid. They had blocked the Kotra road and summoned large numbers of Bhils from other places. This, said the letter, was tantamount to holding the court hostage. The letter invited them to Rohera on 3 May to respond and promised them safe passage irrespective of the negotiation's outcome. The court, it said, was soliciting their cooperation but could hardly be blamed for the Bhils' non-cooperation.

The chiefs, however, refused to respond. On 3 May, the army of Sirohi and the Mewar Bhil Corps were summoned to Rohera. Officials of the British Government and Sirohi, including Bazelgette, reached Rohera on 5 May. Another letter was sent to the chiefs of the three villages, demanding their surrender.[62] The rebels were informed that the army would launch punitive strikes in their villages if the taxes were not paid.

The chief of Waloria informed the British that his people were holding talks with those of other villages, and they would all act as mutually decided since they were religiously bound to their community by a bond of unity. Upon receipt of the officials' response that they had been instructed to break that pledge, the villagers sensed that their apprehension was not unfounded. From past experience, the Bhils knew that the state would eventually deploy the army. They had, therefore, been hiding in the hills for the preceding six or seven days, confident that the jawans of the state army would, at most, appropriate the grain or other goods equal in value to the tax under dispute from their deserted homes. Thus, all tax collection efforts made by the state and British officials went in vain.

A panchayat was convened at Waloria to reach a community decision on the payment of taxes. Bhils from villages in Mewar, Danta, Idar and Sirohi were already present, while others were summoned by the drum. On 15 July 1922, *WD* reported that in view of the volatile situation, British officers had planned a series of attacks: at Waloria on 5 May, Bhula on 6 May and Nawawasa on 7 May.[63]

On 5 May, the force was in place on Wasa road, about 500 yards north of Rohera. It was divided into several troops and dispatched to Waloria via Wasa under Lt. Bazelgette, Maj. Pritchard, Maj. Walker, Subedar Siddha Nath and Jamadar Hira.[64] Waloria was about 2 mil. distant, with Bhils entrenched on hilltops all along the road. In order to get the hills evacuated, a troop of Mewar Bhil Corps, led by Bazelgette, and two platoons under Walker, forged ahead. The CM of Sirohi also accompanied the army.

When the army reached Rohera, yet another letter was sent to the chiefs of Bhula and Nawawasa, demanding their surrender. Their villages were to be set on fire in case they failed to comply. The force set out for Bhula on 6 May, where some 200 Bhils had assembled. In the battle that followed, some Bhils were killed, and Bazelgette chased the remainder into the hills, but most remained out of firing range. The village was razed to the ground. The force then marched to Nawawasa, where several Bhils were killed and the village torched, after which it returned to Rohera.

Thus, in all, 24 Bhils were killed in the two villages, with an almost equal number injured. According to the *WD*'s report of 15 July 1922, British–Sirohi troops had burnt down the villages of Waloria, Bhula and Nawawasa, including the grain.[65]

British and Sirohi officials pressed a few Bhil villagers to sign statements in the government's favour. On 9 May, Rupa Singh, a Garasia from Bhula, was forced to depose to tax payments of $1/_6$ of the rain-fed crop, $1/_5$ of the winter crop (irrigated by an unlined well) and $1/_4$ of the crop irrigated by a lined well. But when Tejawat and some of his supporters visited Paba, Dantral, Upla, Khejra, Tankia, Garh, Samaiya, Warli, Dang, Moras, Bahimana, and other villages of Idar and Sirohi states, they sanctioned a payment of just 25 pounds (i.e. about 11.3 kg) of maize on the rain-fed crop, and a rupee and four annas on the winter crop.

The army action in Waloria, Bhula and Nawawasa mounted intense pressure on the Bhil chiefs. In the PA's presence, the CM of Sirohi and the tehsildar of Rohera sent a message to the villagers on 10 May, informing the Bhils of their availability on 11 and 12 May to hold talks. On 12 May, British officials held negotiations with the Bhil chiefs at Sanwara— Bhil chiefs Rupa, Pitha, Mana and Dalla of Bhula, Puniya and Oria of Nawawasa, Wiria of Pitha ki Padar and Jumla of Sadaphali participated in the talks. They were informed by the officers that the Bhils of Waloria had quit the Eki and that they, too, ought to follow suit. There could be no negotiation until they did so. The chiefs acquiesced reluctantly and were later made to surrender their swords head down in a bucket, signifying their oath to quit the Eki. These events were also covered in the *WD* report of 15 July 1922.[66]

The Ajmer-based Rajasthan Sewasangha (Servants of Indian States Society) took a serious view of the torching of Waloria, Bhula and Nawawasa, and the massacre of hapless Bhils. The society dispatched a team, which included Sant Satya Bhakta and Ram Narayan Chaudhari, to investigate this barbaric incident, continued the *WD* report.[67]

In May 1922, the society published a 25-page monograph, titled *The Second Bhil Tragedy*, detailing the barbaric repression of Bhils and Garasias in Sirohi.

A summary of the report is as follows: There were 325 families in Bhula and Waloria, with a total population of 1,800. A total of 640 villages had been incinerated. The army had either destroyed or confiscated 7,085 maunds of maize,

600 cartloads of dry grass and 180 livestock. The combined loss was estimated at Rs 10,000.

The CM of Sirohi and tehsildar of Rohera had threatened the tribals in the presence of the PA on 11 May. The population was terrified, which was sufficient justification for the Indian States Society to conduct an independent investigation. When the team reached Waloria, it found that the terror-stricken Bhils were in hiding in the hills. The Bhils were persuaded to return to the village to give their account of the incident. The information collected by the investigative team presented the following picture.

The Bhils were to hold a panchayat in Waloria on 5 May 1922 to which other chiefs and villagers from nearby areas had been summoned. But by 7 am, the army had already reached Waloria and demanded their surrender. The army's machine guns and rifles began to roar soon after. The terrified villagers had taken refuge in the hills and in ditches. One Britisher stood near a tamarind tree with a flag, indicating the direction in which bullets were to be aimed. The Bhils hid in ditches while bullets down rained from all sides. Kanha, son of the chief, was one casualty. When his brother, Lakha, came to retrieve his body, he took five bullets and fell down dead. Dimti Bhil from Ida was shot dead as well. Several Bhils from the neighbouring villages received bullet injuries. The bodies of many Bhils were retrieved by their comrades. After 8 am, army jawans ravaged the village, throwing cloth soaked in kerosene on Bhil huts for quick combustion. Weapons, grain, pots and utensils, clothes and other items were all set on fire or thrown into nearby wells. The summer crops were loaded on camelback and swiftly spirited away. This savagery continued till 2 pm, after which the army retreated.

When the Bhils returned to the village the next day, on 6 May, an appalling sight met their eyes. The village was still smoking—everything had been reduced to cinders. With difficulty, they recovered some half-burnt grain and stayed in the village during the day but repaired to the hills at night for their security.

On 8 May, the CM, two European officers and the tehsildar of Rohera arrived at Sanwara, along with 100 to 150 soldiers. They ordered the villagers of Sanwara to persuade the inhabitants of Waloria to return to their village or else they would be shot dead. The hapless Waloria villagers obeyed out of sheer fright. One European officer boasted that his troops had slaughtered 50 Bhils and injured 150 and that still more would be killed if they defied orders. The CM recommended the Bhils renege on their pledge. The Bhils refused outright, as the pledge was a religious and social commitment, and its violation would invite ostracisation from the community. The European officer then threatened to shoot them dead if they refused to do so and return to their villages. The Bhils replied that although they had no compunction in raising their swords to defend themselves, they would not, under any circumstances, violate the pledge.

Faced with this stoic and heroic response, British and state officers left the village, along with their troops, while the

Bhils retreated to the hills. However, even as they departed, the officers threatened to torch the Bhils alive if they refused to comply with the order. They also threatened to burn down Bhula. However, the Bhils of Bhula categorically refused to pay anything more than one rupee and four annas in addition to 12.5 seer of grain per plough as the tax. Any more tax payments, they held, would have to be sanctioned by their community.

The terrified Bhils then escaped to the hills along with their families and cattle. The army made good on its threatened retaliatory action by burning the homes of Bhula down to the ground and spirited everything else away on bullock carts and camelback.

On 10 May, the villagers received the following letter through a messenger:

To
The Headmen, Grassias, and Bhils of
Bhoola and Nanawas, etc.

Now no harsh measures will be taken against you. We have been sent by the English Government to help you in getting redress of your grievances. We shall meet at village Wasa tomorrow at 10 a.m. You can bring with you all those Grassias of Bhoola, Nanawas, etc., who want to hear our friendly advice. A Government officer, the Diwan of Sirohee, the Tahsildar of Rohera and ten orderlies shall be with us. There shall be no hindrance in your coming up to or going back from Sanwara.

Dt. Camp Rohera, 10 May, 1922 (Sd.)
H. R. N. Pritchard, Major
Secretary to the Agent,
Governor General in Rajputana

At 4 pm on 11 May, 100 to 150 Bhils arrived in Sanwara where two British officers, the CM, the tehsildar of Rohera and 10 orderlies were already present. The following dialogue ensued:

The Diwan (D): Who do you side with—Gandhi or the government?

Bhil Panch (BP): With Gandhi.

D: Tell us if you've seen Motilal.

BP: We haven't seen him.

D (in a harsh voice): Will you side with Gandhi or the government?

BP: With Gandhi.

D: Why did you join the Eki? What's the problem with you?

BP: We're suffering injustices. That's why we joined the Eki. What's it to you if we have joined the Eki? After we joined the Eki, we have given up stealing, liquor and flesh eating. Our problems are:

I. Whatever we produce, the king takes away a part of it as the tax;

II. Right or wrong, we're accused of stealing;

III. The police and tehsil officials wrongly accuse us of forced collection. They keep us in iron chains.

D: Why didn't you give a petition to the king about your problems? Why did you join the Eki?

BP: We didn't give a petition to the raja as the officers would harass us still further.

D: Then you should have gone to Abu to tell the Bara Sahib (political agent, a British officer) about your complaints.

BP: We didn't go there as they would have hauled us up and tortured us further.

D: We shall come again after eight days and redress your grievances. Whenever you want, you may come to Rohera and meet me, but you won't create any trouble. Go and get settled in your villages.

The Bhils returned to Bhula after this interaction. There, they unanimously decided that none of them would pay the additional tax, even if their children's lives were at stake. It was decided that until they received justice, they would pay for one harvest, but no tax arrears. The state, they felt, was subjecting them to innumerable hardships; such brutality was unheard of even where taxes had not been paid for four years—Sirohi, they concluded in despair, was a living hell.

The investigative team found that all their houses needed to be rebuilt. Most of the Bhils did not have any clothing left, except that on their backs. Their maize stocks had either been destroyed or were half-burnt and were, therefore, inedible. Their grinding stones and agricultural implements had either been destroyed or confiscated by the army.

Naveen Rajasthan, a newspaper published from Ajmer, carried the Rajasthan Sewasangha's report of the investigation. Its editor, Vijayi Singh, was a renowned Indian revolutionary. Incensed, the British Government condemned the report as baseless and defamatory and proposed action against Vijayi Singh under Section 124A. On 11 December 1922, the political secretary informed L.D. Wakle, secretary of the political department at India Office, London, that Vijayi Singh had tendered an apology for publishing the report. Thereupon, the foreign and political department instructed him through a letter on 11 December to disseminate the apology widely in Indian and foreign newspapers. It was thus that the *Statesman* (London) published the apology on 17 December 1922, captioned 'Pamphlet Allegations Entirely False: Ajmer Editor's Apology'.[68]

The Bhil rebellion of Mewar had now been finally quelled. Motilal Tejawat made one more abortive attempt to revive the revolt. In his absence, the Bhils compromised with the state of Sirohi in 1927. Tejawat was arrested on 3 June 1929 and released on 3 April 1936 on the condition that he would not leave Udaipur state without permission and that he would refrain from inciting any further rebellion. He was granted a monthly allowance of Rs 30. In January 1945, he was arrested once more when he tried to enter the Bhaumat region and was released in February 1947.[69]

PART III

9
TANTYA BHIL: THE GREAT INDIAN MOONLIGHTER

Quite different from all the known Bhil chiefs, there arose in the Khandwa–Nimar Bhil region a warrior whose daring deeds and tales of generosity to the public resonated both in India and abroad. Remarkably, in an age of limited means of communication, his fame reached all quarters of the globe on account of his masterful evasion of the British Government for a full 11 years. Anglo-Indian newspapers and those in Australia, New Zealand and the United States prominently published tales of his daring exploits. He was eulogised for his humane and generous treatment of the impoverished, and his anti-feudal stance. British documents dubbed this venerated Bhil chief a 'notorious dacoit', while, paradoxically, offering grudging praise for certain traits of his character. So much so that, in 1886, the *Times of India* (hereafter *TOI*) on 1 May reported that even the viceroy of British India was said to have referred to Tantya's fame in a letter to the secretary of India. Enshrined in the British psyche as the Indian Robinhood, British newspapers and documents referred to him as 'Tantya'.[1]

On 23 September 1889, the *St. James's Gazette* reported that, as far as the British were concerned, Tantya was a dacoit who would appear and disappear as if by magic, such that the local population attributed divine powers to him. British officers, who had engaged with Tantya, also reminisced about their encounters with him. In the digital newspapers preserved in Australia are fascinating accounts and extensive coverage of Tantya's legendary exploits. The *Leader* (Melbourne) published a serialised account on 5 May 1906 titled, 'Some Adventures with an Indian Dacoit'. These reminiscences were penned by Thomas Stuart Gurr, an Australian born in India, who changed the names of certain individuals and places while dramatising events. Describing Tantya as 'wicked', 'cunning', 'bandit' and 'plunderer', among other epithets, could well have been a means to give vent to the white man's rage and the colonial media's way of blunting the sting of the colonial power's failure. Nevertheless, the content on Tantya was so popular that publishers advertised their proposed publications well in advance, reported the *Mercury* on 18 June 1936, and the *Age* on 22 June 1936.

Venerated as a messiah by impoverished and hapless Bhils of Central India but described as a plunderer or dacoit by the British, scholars have accepted him as a rebel who successfully challenged the British in Central India for an extended period after the Great Uprising of 1857. This uneducated, illiterate Bhil, who was not a jagirdar or from a feudal family, detested moneylenders, revenue collectors and the British. With his guerrilla style of warfare in the

Satpura range, and his organisational capacity and daring, he successfully harassed the British and their huge armies. Living in hiding in forests and hills, Tantya and his band provided succour to the impoverished by seizing the wealth of the rich which they distributed among the resourceless.

In those days, *patils* and *malguzars* (revenue farmer) were the power centres in villages. *Malguzars* were deputed to collect revenue on behalf of the government, and, along with the wealthy and moneylenders, were infamous exploiters of impoverished Bhils. Tantya, a bitter opponent of these exploiters, looted rich moneylenders, *malguzars* and *patils*, and distributed the spoils among the poor. In turn, the Bhils expressed their gratitude by providing food and shelter to Tantya's band when they were in hiding. Tantya was not one of what the British dubbed 'criminal castes' spread over India— rather, he was an opponent of exploitation and oppression, according to *TOI* on 16 August 1884. Providing food to the Bhils of Central India during horrendous famines and bearing the wedding expenses of the daughters of impoverished Bhils, 'Tantya Mama' is still duly honoured in the folk songs of Nimar.[2] An article carried in *TOI* on 21 August 1885 stated that when he occasionally appeared at a Bhil's wedding ceremony, he blessed the bride with money instead of looting her ornaments and just as quietly melted away.

Early Life
Tantya Bhil was born in 1842 in the village of Birada in Nimar district in the Central Provinces. Birada was some

distance from the village of Palgaon, which was situated in the Satpura range, to the west of Burhanpur. Bhau Singh, his father, depended on agriculture for their livelihood and had been earlier cultivating ancestral land in the village of Pokhar, which was some distance from Biradi.[3] While S.C. Verma dates Tantya's birth to 1844, the year more widely accepted is 1842.[4]

Tantya's grandfather had contracted some loan from the *patil* of Pokhar and had mortgaged his land in Pokhar for the purpose. In lieu of interest and to prevent the loan from compounding, he laboured in the *patil*'s fields. When he died, the *patil* seized the mortgaged land. Aggrieved, Bhau Singh, his son, left Pokhar with his wife, Jivani, to settle in Biradi. The couple leased some land from the *patil* of Biradi and began cultivation. Tantya, while working alongside his father on the land, played with bows and arrows, plucked fruit and hunted birds.[5] He was a promising lad and soon developed into an expert archer.[6]

Tantya was raised in penury. Whenever there was a drought, peasants working on leased lands were left with practically nothing after rent payment—thus, Bhau Singh and Jivani often starved. While Tantya was still a child, his mother died of illness and deprivation. When he turned 24, Bhau Singh taught him to plough.[7] One legendary tale of his physical prowess concerns his mastery of a bull gone berserk—his courage left the villagers dumbstruck.

After the *patil* of Pokhar had seized Bhau Singh's ancestral land, he began to cultivate some leased land jointly with Shiva Patil. The fields, in fact, belonged to *patil*, which Bhau Singh was cultivating as a tenant. Bhau Singh died when Tantya was 30 years old and soon the *patil* of Biradi evicted him for non-payment of rent. Tantya then returned to Pokhar to work as Shiva Patil's servant, looking after his cattle. But when Shiva lost no time in taking advantage of his plight, Tantya's attitude changed.[8]

First Imprisonment

In childhood, Tantya was married to Bhikki (or Bhikai) of Pokhar. While working for Shiva Patil, Tantya had expressed his desire to pay the arrears of rent for his ancestral land seized by the former. But the *patil* was not inclined to let go of the land. Tantya lodged a complaint at the Khandwa tehsil, but as British Government policy was to avoid antagonising the landholder, the tehsil's decision favoured Shiva Patil. Infuriated by this outcome, Tantya beat up one of the *patil's* servants.[9]

The incident, which took place in 1871, alarmed the *patil*s. Himmat Patil, a zamindar of the village of Bhuiphal, near Pokhar, and a relative of Shiva Patil, had close contacts with the police. At his bidding, Shiva implicated Tantya in concocted cases of theft and pilferage. The police apprehended Tantya, and he was tried in the court of the assistant commissioner (AC), Nimar, under Section 411. Himmat Patil made a false deposition in court, following which Tantya was sentenced to two years' RI. The lower court's verdict was later quashed by the sessions court.

In 1873, when Shiva Patil once more charged Tantya with theft, the police apprehended the 'rowdy' Tantya. Himmat Patil repeated a false deposition, and the lower court, once more, sentenced him to one year RI. Tantya was then sent to Nagpur Central Jail.

To the north of Pokhar was the tomb of Nau Gaza Pir, a Sufi saint patronised by the needy and the troubled, where, after he was released from prison, Tantya offered fervent prayers for the restoration of his father's lost land. He committed to Shiva Patil the full payment of rent arrears for the land on its return. Meanwhile, Tantya was persuaded to work on Shiva's land by the latter's avowed good intentions. However, Shiva's widowed daughter Jasoda (or Jashoda), who would supply Tantya with food on the sly, suspected her father's intentions with regard to Tantya's land.[10]

Barely had three months passed after Tantya's return from jail when the village was ignited by gossip about his illicit relationship with Jasoda.[11] Outraged villagers summoned a panchayat meeting to discuss the forbidden relationship between a Bhil and a Hindu Rajput's daughter. Shiva Patil was at first ostracised, but re-inducted into the caste after paying a penalty of Rs 100.[12]

Tantya Turns Rebel

As the situation in Pokhar was tense, Tantya decided to leave the village, which was part of the Khandwa tehsil under British jurisdiction. Close by was the village of Hirapur, in Holkar territory, where Tantya settled with his family and worked as a labourer. Here, he befriended Bijania, a cruel-natured villainous-looking fellow, who belonged to the nearby village of Khajuri.

In 1878, the police arrested Tantya and Bijania on suspicion of theft in the village of Bari—police records already showed Tantya as a criminal. Although they were brought to Khandwa and tried, the charge of theft could not be proved. Tantya and Bijania were each sentenced to three months imprisonment for a brawl with the police—Tantya in Jabalpur Jail, and Bijania in Khandwa Jail.[13]

It was the second time that Tantya had faced imprisonment—the two events prepared the ground for his future life as a dacoit. He attributed his poverty and ill fortune to his repeated implication in false cases by the *patils*. He now decided to quit British territory altogether for the village of Siaro in the Holkar state. Here, he found a new friend and companion—Daulya. But the *patils* of Pokhar and other nearby villages, still harbouring enmity, continued to hatch conspiracies to implicate him.

One incident involved a theft in the house of Subhan Bhil, in a village near Pokhar. Although the stolen property was recovered from one Zalim in another nearby village, Himmat Patil and the other Rajputs prodded Subhan to state that Tantya had given him the stolen goods for safekeeping. When Tantya learnt of the conspiracy, he, who already had suffered two jail terms, decided to escape. He left Siaro to shelter in the dense Satpura forests and hills, where he was joined by Bijania and Daulya. Tantya had come to the unhappy realisation that no Bhil would ever be allowed to live his life honestly, as the *patils*, unable to stomach any manifestation of Bhil independence, would not allow him and his people to live in peace.

Tantya now took to plunder and dacoity. His companions and he began to carry out minor burglaries for their survival. Bijania, however, continued to live in Khajuria with his family and occasionally came to the forest to meet Tantya. From time to time, Tantya and his companions burgled homes in Pokhar—their anger against the villagers of Pokhar was understandable. They also kidnapped villagers from Pokhar travelling through the forest, who were released only after being ransomed. This way of life and means of survival continued for an extended period.[14]

In another incident, Tantya abducted Kalu, the brother of Bhika Patil of Pokhar, as he was still incensed with the Pokhar villagers. Kalu was kept captive for six days till his father, Sardar Patil, and Bhika Patil ransomed him for Rs 100.[15]

It seems fairly clear that Tantya and his companions took to crime as a result of the oppression perpetrated by Shiva Patil and Himmat Patil. It was equally clear that they were not inclined to let their oppressors rest in peace. At the time, Tantya was in hiding in a cave near the Shiva Baba temple on the banks of the Sukta.

Third Imprisonment and Jailbreak

The Kalu episode left Shiva Patil and Himmat Patil shaken, and they began to plot to incarcerate Tantya once more. In an elaborate ruse, Sardar Patil, a relative of Shiva Patil and Himmat Patil, deputed his son Mohan to lure Tantya out of the forest to Pokhar with a concocted tale of ill treatment by family members. Mohan begged Tantya to intercede with his parents. Falling prey to the plot, Tantya and his comrades arrived in Pokhar, where Sardar Patil deceived him with an offer of help in getting all his past crimes condoned. An unsuspecting Tantya arrived at Sardar Patil's house to sign papers to the effect.[16] But policemen waiting there ambushed Tantya and marched him off to Khandwa Jail. On the same day, Daulya and Nahal, another of Tantya's companions, were also arrested and taken to Khandwa. Bijania was arrested the next day on the charge of housebreaking and taken to Khandwa as well. Thus, in 1878, Tantya was arrested once more from Pokhar on a criminal charge.[17]

On 24 December 1878, Tantya was produced before a magistrate in Nimar, along with Daulya, Nahal and Bijania. At the very first hearing, the magistrate pronounced the accused guilty but postponed the verdict to the next day, and sent them all back to jail. But to Himmat Patil, who had made a false statement against him, Tantya openly said in court: 'Patil Daji, my name is Tantya. Remember it. Today, you got me implicated by cunningness but keep in mind, my name is Tantya.'[18-9]

Back in jail, the incarcerated friends decided to break free. With help from one Dopia, another prisoner, they made a hole in the ceiling and used a dhoti to climb out. The prisoners broke through the security cordon, scaled the 15-ft high wall and escaped in the dead of night on 24 December 1878. While escaping, Tantya taunted the policemen on duty: 'See, Tantya is taking his friends away. Let he, who has savoured his mother's milk, catch me!' Tantya was a completely changed man—he was now a rebel of the Satpura forests.[20]

The jail's emergency bell sounded in vain for hours. Bells also rang at far-flung police posts, horses covered many miles of ground in search but to no avail. By morning, the prisoners had covered a 60-mil. distance through hills, forests and valleys. Walking all day, they camped only in the evening. In one village, on hearing Tantya's name, a cloth merchant and his wife immediately sewed some clothes for the escapees. Daulya brought back the garments, along with some liquor and meat. A few years later, Tantya, in a characteristic gesture, rewarded the merchant for his generosity. It was typical of Tantya that he invariably helped the villages from where he received food and other assistance. It is little wonder that he was revered by the Bhils.[21]

Subject to feudal oppression for centuries, the people of Nimar had been unconscionably looted by first the Rajput and Muslim chiefs, followed by the Marathas, Scindias and Holkars. Bhils had been exploited in the region for centuries, with feudal lords building their mansions over the bodies of the original inhabitants of the land. After seizing this region from the Marathas, the British divided it into Nimar East (Khandwa) and Nimar West (Khargone), which were ruled by the British and Holkar, respectively. The British

Government had labelled Tantya a fearsome robber—a robber, without a doubt, but by no means a rascal. With looted money, he provided relief to thousands of orphans and the downtrodden and spelled death to their enemies. He performed his acts of wonder in the very midst of his enemies, despite the presence of police.[22]

Every village without exception now resounded with the name of Tantya Bhil, the hero of a rebel robber band that freely roamed the hills of Satpura. The band's strength soon increased to 20 members.[23] In the forests, Bhil tribals arranged for food and shelter for Tantya's band. Occasionally, Tantya went to meet his family to make arrangements for them.[24]

Tantya now grew even more daring. From Siwna, he sent a message of his contempt for the police to the DC of Khandwa. The band robbed a goldsmith in the village of Chikheli. Jesu Patil of Harbanspur sheltered Tantya in his fields for a week, even giving him money. In Kelwan, Tantya purchased a gun for Rs 19 from Nabi Bakhsh, a mechanic and gunsmith.[25]

First Loot, 6 April 1879

On 6 April, carrying guns, Tantya and his comrades were on their way to the bazaar in Khandwa via a jungle track that was little used. En route, near the Panali River, they spotted a bullock cart headed their way, stocked with various items for a wedding. Alarmed at the sight of the armed band, the two riders accompanying the cart fled, abandoning the cart. Tantya divided the spoils among his companions—it was his first raid. The band continued travelling for several days, visiting various parts of the territory to meet Bhil supporters. Another raid on a cart followed. The police did its utmost to apprehend the culprits but in vain. Six individuals were arrested on suspicion but were acquitted by the magistrate for want of proof.[26]

Himmat Patil's Murder
One night, Tantya burnt down the houses of Shiva Patil, Sardar Patil and a few other Rajputs. At about 9 pm on 25 April 1879, Tantya entered Bhuiphal; one of the band was carrying a gun, while the others were armed with swords. While his aim was to teach Himmat Patil a lesson, he had instructed his comrades not to harm the *patil*'s wife and children. Tantya's band forcibly entered Himmat Patil's house and, at Tantya's command, the *patil* was dragged out of his bedroom. With eyes full of rage against the false deposition made by the *patil* against him in court at Nimar, Tantya ordered Bijania to gun him down. Next, they ravaged and set fire to Lun Ji Patel's house. Thereafter, Tantya made his way to the village of Bori where Nana Patel, the lumberdar, was his well-wisher. The band escaped before daybreak on 26 April 1879. The injured Himmat Patil was brought to Khandwa, where he died the following day.

The administration took serious note of the incident. Nevertheless, its intelligence had failed to help apprehend Tantya, even though Chhegaon thana was barely 3 mil.

from Bhuiphal. Bijania was eventually tried and hanged for this episode, while Nana Patel was sentenced to life imprisonment. In 1881, Nana Patel tried to break out of Jabalpur Jail but was gunned down by the police. The incident at Bhuiphal was followed by 18 similar incidents in just one month.[27] Tantya and Bijania reappeared on 19 December 1879 and looted the *patil*'s house in Chichkheda. They took him hostage, but he managed to escape near Bagmar. On 17 January 1880, the band arrived at Haraswada, near Chhegaon thana, where Tantya searched the houses of some influential individuals and robbed a trader.[28] The villagers mistook the band for a police posse as they were dressed in dark-coloured coats and red turbans.

Daulya's Arrest, January 1880

In January 1880, a *malguzar* informed the police that Tantya had been spotted asleep in a nearby forest, along with dozens of his comrades. A police officer, with 100 jawans, managed to effortlessly capture the sleeping Bhils, jubilant that they had apprehended Tantya. As they were taking the Bhils to court, they learnt to their dismay that it was Daulya who had been captured, not Tantya. Enraged at his comrade's arrest, Tantya arrived at the *malguzar*'s house, along with some of his comrades.[29]

After Daulya's capture, Mahdia took his place in the band. Bijania and Mahdia usually raided together, but independently as well on occasion. Mahdia carried out robberies in Jamthi on 7 February 1880, in Jirawan on the 12th, in Kalpat on the 14th, in Lachora on the 19th, and in Nawra on the 20th. Bijania plundered Kala, in Hoshangabad, on the 23rd, Padalia on the 27th, and Hapla, in Nimar, on the 28th. Tantya raided Aulia and Koladit, in Nimar, on the 25th and 29th, respectively, and Pabai, Pachamba, Takli and Bhandaria on 2 March.[30] He carried out more raids at Belthar and Gondari on 7 March. Mahdia was arrested in April 1880, but Bijania and Tantya managed to escape.[31]

British officers, at a complete loss, were unable to ascertain Tantya's whereabouts. Towards the end of February 1880, Insp. Ibrahim Beg was posted on special duty in Nimar and charged with apprehending Tantya. He arrested 96 Bhils in March 1880; 80 of them were tried. One admitted his involvement in a score of burglaries, and a number of Bhils were apprehended on the basis of his confession.

Daulya was sentenced to life for the murder of Himmat Patil and sent to Jabalpur Jail. On the day this sentence was pronounced, Tantya raided the *malguzar*'s house in Bhuiphal, murdered him and looted all his property. As ever, the police were in the dark despite all efforts.[32]

Through a letter written on 1 September 1880, after Daulya was sentenced to life imprisonment, the DC, Nimar, informed the commissioner of Narmada Division that Govinda, son of the slain *malguzar* of Bhuiphal, had succeeded his father. Rs 37.50 was the total revenue from the village, of which the *malguzar* was entitled to half, and that Himmat Patil's widow, three sons, their wives and seven children were the remaining members of the household, continued the letter. This reference clarifies that Daulya had been sentenced in 1880, or even earlier.[33]

Daulya Breaks Out of Jail, May 1880
One night in May 1880, the alarm bells of Jabalpur Central Jail began to ring frantically.[34] Next morning, the jailor made the unhappy discovery that Daulya and seven other prisoners had escaped. Three, including Daulya and Hiria, ran day and night until they reached their chief, Tantya, whose happiness knew no bounds.[35]

Daulya's arrival in Nimar brought new energy to the band. Tantya now expanded his area of operations and began to organise raids in Indore and in the districts of Ellichpur and Hoshangabad. He divided his band into several groups, each led by one of his trusted companions. He would plan these raids beforehand—if a group was to raid one area, another did the same miles away.

Strenuous efforts to apprehend Tantya were made under the supervision of Sir Lapel Griffin, but he continued to remained elusive. A reward of Rs 500 was announced for help in his arrest, which remained unclaimed. The scheme was a dismal failure on account of complete lack of support from the Bhils. Thanks to Tantya's generosity to the poor, he received all the information he required to stay one step ahead of the administration.[36]

Bijania's Arrest, 13 September 1880

On 23 June 1880, Tantya and Bijania arrived at the village of Barur, some 3 mil. from Chhegaon thana. There, they made inquiries about the location of the *malguzar*'s house. The police swung into action once they got wind of these inquiries, but the band escaped into the forest as soon as they learnt that the police had been informed.

Soon after, Tantya and his men, clad in police uniform, made their way to the village of Hansbara, only a mile from Chhegaon thana. There, they plundered the house of a trader known to exploit the poor. When the villagers rushed to Chhegaon thana, they learnt that it was Tantya in police uniform. Circling back to Barur, Tantya ordered the *malguzar*'s family out of their house, following which he set it on fire. Mortally afraid of Tantya and Bijania, the *malguzar* withheld the information from the police chief of Khandwa. His explanation was that the house had caught fire because of a faulty kerosene lamp.[37] After this incident of arson in Barur, Tantya and Bijania proceeded to Khargone.

Ibrahim Beg had deployed a police force at the border of the Holkar state, as he had received intelligence that Tantya was to visit Shivna where he had cordial relations with the village's *patil*. Shivna was situated near Khajuri, Bijania's village, which was also under police surveillance. Tantya had planned to target the *malguzar* of Kundwara, which lay outside Holkar territory. On 23 July 1880, along with 10 armed men, he raided the malguzar's house and looted Rs 900.[38]

Tantya raided Shalipura on 30 July and Segwal on 31 July 1880. The SP of the district now himself assumed command of the anti-Tantya campaign. Fifty jawans were added to the Nimar police force and the Holkar court was ordered to cooperate. Following a few days of fragile peace, there were burglaries at Paretha on 27 August, and at Raipura the next day. Ibrahim Beg had, by then, been replaced by Insp. Sher Ali, who reached the spot on the following day and launched a search for the band. He succeeded in capturing one member and in recovering some of the plunder. The rest of the band had fled into the forest.[39]

In 1880, a catastrophic drought brought disaster upon the cattle and Bhils of Khandwa. The government was slow to provide relief to the people of Nimar, and, taking advantage of the situation, opportunistic traders began selling grain at exorbitant prices. Tantya plundered the grain-laden carts of a Khandwa trader and distributed it among the grateful villagers.

Two of Tantya's band, Bijania and Mahdia, had been spotted in conversation in the village of Sangwara on 13 September 1880. When the police was informed, Sher Ali immediately set out with an armed troop. With his constables, Imam Khan, Badri Khan, Sihori, Ram Dayal and Umed Ali, among others, he attacked the two Bhils. Both fought back determinedly with swords. Mahdia was injured and arrested. Bijania, with his extraordinary strength, held off his attackers for two hours. Head Constable Suraj Prasad, Constables Basant Singh and Jaggar, and Amir (son of

Chief Constable Muhammad Husain) overpowered him in a concerted attack, after which he was arrested. Both Bhils were put in iron chains and brought to Khandwa.

News of the arrest spread like wildfire. Bhils from all round thronged the railway station to see their hero, Tantya, who it was rumoured had been apprehended. Sher Ali, who was being congratulated by many for this significant arrest, eventually made the crushing discovery that it was not Tantya that he had arrested, but Bijania, who had been impersonating him.

The British Government awarded each of the *malguzar*s of the three villages with Rs 500, including the *malguzar* of Bhuiphal, as well as individuals whose information had led to Bijania's arrest. All three *malguzar*s were also given a gun and a sword from the armoury, with life-long licenses. Constables Basant Singh, Jaggar and Amir were awarded a month's salary as bonus. Constables Imam Khan, Badri Khan, Sihori, Ram Dayal and Umed Ali were each sanctioned two months' salary as bonus for having captured Bijania.[40] Mahdia and Bijania were tried in court at Khandwa, which sentenced the former to life imprisonment and the latter to death. As Bijania had murdered Himmat Patil of Bhuiphal, the British decided to hang him in the village.[41]

One night, Tantya and his companions raided the house of a miserly trader in the village of Chichgaon, 3 mil. from the Indore road. The Holkar police, aware that the raid was Tantya's handiwork, could do nothing. Tantya's trusted lieutenent, Bijania, was hanged only a few days after this event.[42] It was after Bijania's arrest that Commissioner A. Howell, Narmada Division, wrote to the chief commissioner (CC), Central Provinces, on 28 September 1880, to suggest that a reward of at least Rs 1,500 be announced for reliable information about Tantya.[43]

Tantya soon reappeared in Nimar. He raided Devala on 11 October 1880 and robbed the *patel* of Himgir on 20 November. The *patel*, carrying a gun, was then guarding his crops. On 27 November, he robbed some ornaments from a *gavli* (a Hindu caste) near the Balwada forest and looted a trader of Chichgaon on 7 January 1881.[44]

Bijania's Execution

On 28 February 1881, Bijania was hanged from a tree to death. Thousands of his Bhil supporters were present in Bhuiphal on the occasion. His body was left hanging for two days as a deterrent to others. Tantya was devastated. The government had managed to capture and punish some of his most trusted lieutenants, although it had failed to apprehend him thus far. The British Government was now compelled to seek the Holkar state's assistance to capture Tantya.[45]

In 1880, the judicial administration (criminal) in the Central Provinces reported that Tantya's and Bijania's areas of operation extended out of Nimar up to the Rajputana border. On 26 April 1881, *TOI* reported 37 raids, of which 21 were perpetrated in Nimar alone by Bijania and Tantya in 1880. A reward of Rs 500 was announced for Tantya's arrest in 1880 and raised to Rs 1,000 in July 1882. In addition, the Holkar state announced another Rs 500 as reward, raising the total to Rs 1,500. The king of Dhar provided Rs 1,000 to the AGGCI, as the state's share of the reward meant for Tantya's arrest.[46]

In 1880, the police raided several areas in quick succession seeking Tantya's arrest. Maj. M.M. Bowie, IGP, Central Provinces, was informed by certain former officers that Tantya seemed to have lost his influence and lacked support. Moreover, going by the data, the region witnessed merely 13 robberies in 1881, but of them seven took place in Nimar, Tantya's home district, stated the *Dublin Daily Express* (hereafter *DDE*) on 24 July 1884.

It was Insp. Sher Ali who had brought Bijania to the gallows—his enthusiasm to apprehend Tantya now doubled. A crucial breakthrough towards this end was his meeting with an elderly man at the Khandwa rest house, who claimed to be from Khajuri, Bijania's village. The man heaped curses upon the dacoits and promised to reveal Tantya's hideout, if Sher Ali cared to accompany him.

With some sepoys, and the old man in tow, Sher Ali started out at daybreak the next day. The group travelled beyond the Pandhana police station, right up to the start of the hills. Where the road ended, Sher Ali continued on horseback, dismounting at the start of a valley, from where he began to walk. Sher Ali was now trekking from one valley to another, exhausted by the heat, while the old man strode ahead like a youth. The sepoys trailed far behind. Soon, a rather cryptic conversation took place between the old man and Sher Ali.

'How far is the hideout, Chacha?' Sher Ali asked in irritation.

'You see that rock...in the ditch behind it,' replied the old man.

The old man stopped by the ditch. 'Sahib, may I ask you something?' he said. His tone and tenor had changed. Sher Ali regarded him with surprise.

'What will you do if Tantya comes out of the ditch now?'

Before Sher Ali could grasp what had been said, the old man had snatched the inspector's pistol. 'Tantya, I am. Now, what would you do, Sahib? How should I reward you? If I throw you in the valley, dogs and wolves will devour you. But I won't do it. If you care for your life, take your clothes off and put them down and run away without looking back!'[47]

Thus ended Sher Ali's dream of apprehending Tantya Bhil on that occasion!

The *patel* of the village of Kodbar, a police informant had plotted against Tantya. In order to teach him a lesson, Tantya raided his house on 1 April 1981 and also robbed his relatives. The villagers complained to the police, but it was a futile exercise. Tantya spent the next two days in peace in a forest on the banks of the Tawa, and carried out several burglaries in and around the village of Mandla on 4 April. Sher Ali was unable find any clues to these robberies, but he did manage to arrest three Surwari villagers who had sheltered Tantya. They were soon tried, and each was sentenced to three years RI, as the court had deemed them Tantya's accomplices.

On the same day, 4 April, the band reached Sahejla where the *malguzar* gave them Rs 50. Informers reported this incident to the police, who arrested the *malguzar*. The latter denied knowing the men, or even giving them any money. On the basis of the informers' statements, the deputy commissioner (DC) sentenced the *malguzar* to six months RI.[48]

An article published on 2 May 1881 in *TOI* stated that, in the last week of April 1881, Tantya had carried out daylight burglaries in two villages of Khandwa; both villages lay close to the GIP (Great Indian Peninsula) Railway line. Most of the villagers fled in fear. When the *malguzar*'s wife refused to part with her keys, Tantya branded her with a hot iron rod. Terror-stricken, the villagers held their peace.

After a month in Holkar territory, on 4 May 1881 Tantya and his band carried out a burglary in the village of Bagda in Nimar. A few days later, an informer at the Beria checkpost reported that an armed Tantya had been sighted passing through the village of Amba. After consultation with the *malguzar*, the head constable reached the spot to ascertain the information, but by then the band had disappeared, stated *TOI*.

Soon thereafter, continued the article, there was a theft at the house of the *malguzar* of Amba. A constable had been posted at Amba following the last incident. When the constable stood his ground, Tantya had his hands and legs tied and seized his gun, only untying him when the band prepared to leave.

After Amba, there were thefts in the villages of Gawligaon, Belthat and Dertalai on 22 May 1881. There was another, in Kamalkhar, east of the Berar border. The police conducted searches, but, as always, it was a futile exercise. Finally, reported *TOI*, they arrested two Bhils who had sheltered Tantya in the village of Heora.[49]

Incident at Khagra

On 6 September, Tantya arrived at the house of a barber working as a police informant in the village of Khagra, in Holkar territory. The barber's son was divested of Rs 25 and kidnapped for a ransom of Rs 250. After a week in the Satpura hills, he was finally brought to Gawligaon and kept captive in a house from where he escaped to tell his tale to the police. The police began to harass Tantya's well-wishers. Checkposts were created in the villages which Tantya frequented, and the expenses incurred on these checkposts were extracted from the villagers.

After Holkar had ordered his officials to apprehend Tantya, the search brought them to the village of Bhilkhedi, where Tantya had approached a local goldsmith for a loan. When Tantya arrived to collect the loan, the goldsmith allowed him and his men to rest undisturbed in his house. However, on the excuse that he was going to fetch the funds, he slipped away to inform the king's officers. The officers captured Tantya and his band with no trouble and hauled the dacoits before the king in ropes. The joy of the king and his officials knew no bounds, as they began to dream of handsome rewards from the British. The British Government instructed the king to hand the captives over, Tantya in particular, to the Nimar police. But their joy evaporated when the prisoner was brought to Nimar, where they learnt that it was not Tantya who had been captured, but Daulya, who had escaped from Jabalpur Jail in 1880, reported *TOI* on 8 June 1883.[50] Nevertheless, on 24 October 1881, *Reynold's Newspaper* and *HMICE* published the (false) news of Tantya's arrest near Indore.[51] In October 1881, Daulya and eight others were arrested, tried and sentenced to 14 years RI each, according to *TOI* on 13 June 1885.

The year 1881 witnessed 13 robberies in all—23 less than in 1880. The Nimar region accounted for seven of these, as against 29 in 1880. Thus, even if the police had failed to apprehend Tantya, they were encouraged by the reduction in the number of such incidents, stated *EOM* on 3 June 1882.

Daulya's arrest left Tantya shaken. In retaliation, in Bhilkheri, Tantya torched eight houses including that of the goldsmith who had informed on him, and of those who had helped the Holkar officials. Bhilkheri was ravaged, and Anjangaon and Birul were next. At Anjangaon, continued the *EOM* report, the patwari's records of revenue collected from several villages were set on fire in November 1881. Till such time that Tantya had felt safe in Holkar's territory, he had refrained from committing robberies there. Now, Tantya vowed to wage a bloody war against the king who had plotted thus against him.[52]

Hiria's Arrest

Informers from Ijiral had helped Holkar officials to arrest Daulya. Tantya laid waste to this village and burnt it down. On the night of 17 December 1881, he was spotted in the village of Jamathi in Nimar, where he forcibly extracted money already promised to him by peasants. But when the police arrived to capture Tantya, they found that he had already escaped with his band. Hiria was subsequently injured in an ambush and captured. He was tried in a magistrate's court and sentenced to life imprisonment.

Despite the joint efforts by British and Holkar officials to apprehend Tantya, they were unsuccessful in 1881. After he was caught, Hiria had confessed that the band moved from place to place and avoided resting at any location for two consecutive nights, except during the rains. They usually rested a mile or two from where they cooked, refrained from lingering too long in any district and sneaked into Holkar territory after carrying out a raid. Hiria stressed that Bhils of the entire district sympathised with Tantya and provided him with information.[53]

The anti-Tantya campaign now decided to follow a different tack. In 1882, the police summoned Tantya's relatives, supporters and all others related to him in Khandwa and dangled the bait of a reward for his arrest. Some of those summoned pledged to discover Tantya's whereabouts. The 20 selected for the task discovered that Tantya was then living in the village of Tinasia, in Holkar territory. The police set out for Tinasia, with its *malguzar* as guide. En route, they found that the *malguzar* had disappeared—he had slipped away to warn Tantya about the expedition to apprehend him. It came as no surprise to the police that Tantya and his comrades had vanished from Tinasia.

Himgiri Ravaged

On 8 June 1883 and 21 August 1885, articles in *TOI* reported on Tantya's revenge on the villagers of Himgiri for their deposition against Daulya and Hiria.[54] Certain villagers of Himgiri had deposed against Daulya and Hiria, leading to the latter's life sentence. On 16 December, along with several sepoys, a police officer reached the village of Hirapir to capture Tantya's band but found no signs of them. Presently, he noticed a fire raging some distance away. It was the village of Himgiri, whose *malguzar*, Jabbar Singh, was a police informant. On approaching Himgiri, the officer found that the entire village was engulfed in flames. In that atmosphere of terror, the village had been plundered. Some Rajputs had opened fire on the assailants, killing the *malguzar* in the cross-firing.

The year 1882 had passed, but Tantya remained at large. Holkar officials Insp. Nathe Khan and Capt. Mansa Singh arrested 30 individuals, who were either Tantya's relatives or informers, but the trying magistrate set them free.

In January 1883, Tantya caried out two thefts in the jurisdiction of the zamindar of Melghat, in Ellichpur. In 1883, a Hyderabad police report mentioned both incidents and orders were issued to the neighbouring districts to curb his depredations. On 21 February, Tantya decided to raid the house of a police informant, Pittu, the *malguzar* of Rohini in Nimar. Based on prior intelligence, the police prepared to ambush him in Pittu's house. Tantya was a mile away from Rohini when his informers warned him of the police's plan. Tantya waited patiently until the police had retreated from the village and then proceeded to rob Pittu's house. When the police began investigating the two burglaries in Melaghat, Tantya ransacked the village on 26 May 1883. On 8 June 1883, *TOI* reported the incident and the police's futile pursuit of the band.[55]

In the first half of 1883, Tantya was spotted in police uniform in the village of Siharu in Nimar, where he posed as a police inspector and availed of the *malguzar*'s services. That evening, he demanded Rs 1,000, which the *malguzar* promised to bring to the police headquarters in the next day or two. An enraged Tantya demanded the money immediately. When the *malguzar* refused, Tantya assaulted him and escaped into the forest. On 7 July 1883, *TOI* reported that Insp. Chandrika Singh from Nagpur was dispatched to investigate the incident.

On 12 July 1883, Tantya, with 20 of his men, arrived at the *malguzar*'s house that stood adjacent to the thana in Beri Sarai, Hoshangabad. Although the *malguzar* was away at the time, his wife brought all her ornaments to Tantya. But as he believed it was unjust to deprive a woman of her ornaments, he left. He was spotted in Dholgaon, near Kalyanpur, on 21 July, and in Jharp on 6 August. He was sighted in Kishanpura on 12 August, and on 10 September was observed travelling towards Chiraptla in Betul.

On 18 July 1883, Maj. Saurin Brooke, DC, Hoshangabad, wrote to inform Insp. Jiwan Singh that Tantya was extracting levies from three villages in Hoshangabad and was reportedly based in Beri Sarai. At the time, the villages of Pargana Charua were awash with stories about Tantya. One tale, reported in *TOI* on 20 August 1883, concerned a Brahmin sepoy travelling in a train, who, in the course of conversation with his co-travellers, remarked that he had heard much about Tantya's generosity, and that he was in search of the latter to request help with his daughter's wedding. When one of the travellers asked how much he would require, the sepoy mentioned a sum of Rs 500. The traveller then told his companions to give the sepoy Rs 1,100. The sepoy was left in no doubt that his fellow traveller was indeed Tantya. Another story, narrated by impoverished, superstitious peasants, believing him to be divine, held that he had once broken out of jail in the form of a fly. Tantya was now the Robinhood of the Charua forests.

The reward for his capture, or help in it, was consistently enhanced. Rs 500 in 1880, it was increased to Rs 1,000 in July that year. The Holkar state announced an additional Rs 500. A letter on 17 July 1883, from Capt. Donald Robertson to the secretary and to the CC, Central Provinces, reveals that the government had partially accepted Maj. Bowie's suggestion and enhanced the reward to Rs 1,500. In response, the Holkar state proportionately raised its share to Rs 750.

Thus, by 1883, Tantya carried a reward of Rs 2,250 on his head. However, policemen were still remarkably unenthusiastic about capturing him and the British Government was forced to depute European or Eurasian officers for the purpose.[56] On 6 November 1883, *TOI* carried a report on the apology tendered by the CC to the government for the failure to apprehend Tantya. The reason cited was that the Central Provinces were geographically cut off from British territory. However, the anticipated cooperation from the Holkar and Berar administrations was expected to provide the solution to Tantya's escape from one territory to another.

Throughout 1883, Tantya organised raids from his hideout. On 23 September, he threatened and robbed some residents of Keli and raided Ghoti in broad daylight. His ability to constantly evade and humiliate the police confounded the administration. But if Tantya managed to dodge the police year after year, it was because the Bhil community as a whole regarded him as its protector, messiah and god. His generosity and goodness may be illustrated by the incident at a wedding in the village of Arkheda, where he blessed the couple and left after reassuring the gathering of his good intentions, reported *TOI* on 21 August 1885.

Tantya was sighted in Nandgaon on 11 November 1883. In December 1883, he organised more raids, including one in the village of Karada on 10 December. From Kalu Gawli's house he seized ornaments worth Rs 500, buried in six metal pots, and Rs 2,500. He also robbed a *patel* and a cultivator. During another burglary in Birapur in Hoshangabad, he kept

Lakshman Singh tied up till the latter surrendered ornaments worth Rs 25 as well as Rs 5. He pillaged the village of Mohta in Betul on 26 December, and Mathani in Nimar on 28 December. At Mathani, he robbed a goldsmith named Kanhai of ornaments worth Rs 30. The alarming situation in the area prompted the commissioner of Hyderabad to write to the Res. on 7 January 1884, demanding the deployment of a special police force in Melaghat.[57]

In his report on police administration in 1883, Bowie recorded that the history of India would remember Tantya as Robinhood, stated *DDE* on 24 July 1884. Soon, intelligence was received that his band had split in two in January 1884. Even though both groups were reportedly at loggerheads, it put no restraint on Tantya's activity which continued unabated. But this division of the group for a time appeared to be a covert strategy employed by Tantya. His informants were jawans of the Bhil Corps that recruited no other community but Bhils. Paid barely Rs 7–8 as salary, Tantya gave generously to them to encourage their support. (Appendix 5 reproduces in full an item in the *Times of India*, 21 August 1885.)

On 20 January 1884, Tantya committed burglaries, first in Uskalli, followed by another in Kapasi, involving a dacoit named Pandu. After the Uskalli raid, he moved on to Kapasi along with the patwari, *kamdar*, and a villager named Sant Narayan, where he robbed Kapasi's *malguzar* of goods worth between Rs 3,000 and Rs 4,000.[58] The patwari of Uskalli was apprehended after an inquiry. It soon came to light that he was an agent of the Uskalli *patel*'s wife and had invited Tantya to raid Kapasi.

On 14 May 1884, a letter written by the DC, Nimar, stated that goods worth Rs 1,400 had been recovered from the Bhils of Tembhi, Dabhi, Chichkheda and Bhaggarh. Certain principal members of Tantya's band lived in these villages; the goods were part of recent raids in Nimar and Berar. A resident of Dabhi informed the DC that Tantya had been sighted at the village on 20 March 1884.[59]

Robbery in Amdhna

On 24 March 1884, Tantya raided the village of Amdhna, where he also had a close shave with the Berar police. The village lay between the Melaghat zamindari and Khilchipur. Many of the raiders suffered injuries—Lakshman Singh, too, was severely injured and died later. Tantya ravaged the village and escaped in the dead of night.[60]

On his deathbed, Lakshman Singh confessed that Jhadu and Pandu, two dacoits of Bakhar in Nimar, were also involved in the incident at Amdhna. Although this information was immediately conveyed to the Nimar police, they failed to conduct an investigation. It was well known that that members of Tantya's band had been visiting the villages around Amdhna, and some in Nimar, to stash money and jewellery with their relatives for safekeeping. But the SP, Hoshangabad, failed to apprehend them. En route to the Amdhna raid, some of the band had visited their relatives in Bakhar. A search conducted later in Bakhar yielded large amounts of cash from the Kapasi raid. The relatives were arrested, tried and jailed.

On 13 June 1885, *TOI* reported that, overall, the death of Lakshman Singh was the principal police achievement of 1884, credited to the Berar police. On the basis of Lakshman Singh's statement, efforts were made to arrest eight Uskalli dacoits also involved in the Devalia raid.[61] The DC's letter of 9 June 1884 indicates that only five of the eight had been arrested and had confessed their involvement in the Rohankheda and Tamli burglaries.

The rapidly deteriorating situation forced the commissioner of the Narmada Division to concede on 16 July 1884 that the public was losing faith in the government. On 11 August 1884, intelligence was shared about Tantya's presence on the Khandesh-Nimar-Holkar border. The IG's letter of 16 October reveals that Tantya had pillaged the village of Borpani the preceding August. On 23 February 1888, *TOI* reported that Tantya had extracted Rs 300 from Gudri, the muqaddam, and Rs 5 from Harchand, Devchand and Bucha Gawli.[62]

In November 1884, Col. M.M. Bowie, IGP, Central Provinces, and Col. Brockney, DC, Hoshangabad, made a thorough inspection of the Charua area. Their aim was to protect it from plunder and to develop a strategy to apprehend Tantya. Presenting his report on police administration in the Central Provinces in 1884, Bowie remarked that while the strategies had not been as effective as expected, they had, nevertheless, managed to prevent Tantya from entering

Hoshangabad. Unconfirmed reports of his passage through Nimar trickled in on occasion. He was also said to move through Holkar territory, but that information could not be vouched for with certainty. The SP, Nimar, seemed satisfied with arrangements for the capture of dacoits entering the district. Bowie believed that the number of Tantya's hideouts had dwindled ever since the arrest of relatives of Bhil dacoits in Bakhar and nearby villages, and hence not much was heard of Tantya's activity in the preceding months. Rumour had it that he had sought refuge in Holkar territory and in the forests of Khandesh. In an earlier report, Capt. Muhammad Khan had stated that Holkar had made elaborate arrangements to restrict the entry of Bhil rebels in his jurisdiction, all of which was reported in articles in *TOI* on 6 January and 13 June 1885.[63]

Despite the many elaborate official arrangements, Bhil rebels attacked the village of Behir in Hoshangabad at 10 pm on 27 December 1885. The house of the *malguzar*, who had fled in fear, yielded Rs 352. At 3 am (28 December), they raided Charua. ASP Dina Nath failed to make any headway in his inquiry. It was rumoured that the raid had been carried out by Tantya's band. A dacoit named Bhog Chand was arrested in connection with the Behir robbery. He confessed to the involvement of six Bhils and Bhilalas but denied Tantya's participation in the raid.[64]

The Holkar administration held up Muhammad Khan's efforts as praiseworthy. When Sardar Ratan Singh, who had once served under Khan, was appointed SP, Nimar, it was hoped that Capt. Khan and he would jointly work to apprehend Tantya. But relations between the two officers soon soured, and little headway was made because of lack of coordination. Bowie believed that Khan, with his greater sense of responsibility, was the better officer and deserved more respect. The bickering between Khan and Rattan Singh prompted Bowie to urge the king to appoint some other officer. Subsequently, Holkar replaced Khan.

In 1884, Commissioner A. Howell, Narmada Division, recommended that the anti-Tantya campaign be conducted under an officer of the rank of deputy inspector general of police (DIG). In 1881, the then commissioner, too, had made a similar suggestion, which had been ignored. On Howell's order, a new post of DIG was created, with Khandwa as headquarters. On 13 June 1885, *TOI* reported that Hamilton, SP, Hoshangabad, was appointed the first DIG to conduct the anti-Tantya campaign, with cooperation from ASP Playfair.[65]

In sum, continued the *TOI*'s report, the anti-Tantya campaign of 1884 proved ineffective because of the bickering between Holkar officials. Lt. Col. P.D. Henderson was then the general superintendent of the operation being conducted against thugs and dacoits. On 9 September 1884, he wrote to apprise C. Grant, secretary of the Government of India's foreign department, of Bowie's conviction that Tantya had been bribing the Central Provinces policemen to provide him with privileged information. Henderson suggested that one officer of the Central Provinces be attached to the

Thugee Dacoity Expedition Agency, in Indore, and efforts to apprehend Tantya be made with the cooperation of Holkar officials. Col. Berman had agreed with the suggestion, he added.[66]

On 14 January 1885, the CC sanctioned police deployment in the villages of Tembhi, Chichkheda and Dabhi. After the Behir–Charua robbery, based on a letter on 22 January from the CC sanctioning the reorganisation of the police force in the Cherua region, one chief constable, five head constables, one lance constable and 32 constables were deployed. On 16 February, the commissioner informed the CC that of the 200 residents of Behir, only one had a sword and were, therefore, unable to defend themselves.

On 26 February 1885, at 6 pm, a group of 15–16 armed robbers believed to be part of Tantya's band arrived at the village of Kutlai (Kotlya) under the Attar police station. There, they asked the landlord about the richest person in the village and were directed to the house of Ram Gopal. When they could find nothing there, they set the house on fire. The robbers stole jewellery and cash worth Rs 120 to 1258 from the other villagers. Later, at 9 pm, they committed another robbery in the village of Atud.

A letter written to L. Neil by Robertson, first AAGGCI, reveals that Isari Prasad, a former risaldar, had been deputed, along with the Bhil Corps, to assist the police force of the Central Provinces in anti-Tantya operations.

In the first half of 1885, Tantya raided Ellichpur and escaped into the reserved forest, taking shelter on Kali Dev hill on the Hoshangabad–Nimar border. Supervised by the DIG, the operation to apprehend Tantya included 50 jawans of the Bhil Corps and several men of the local police and forest departments. A large force was deployed on the banks of the Tawa, on the Hoshangabad border, to prevent Tantya's escape into Holkar territory. This river separated Ellichpur from Nimar. But, by sheer chance, torrential rain caused the river to rise, which forced a change in the armed forces' tactics. Taking advantage of the situation, Tantya slipped away, reported *TOI* on 3 July 1885.

Robberies in 1885

Following raids in Nimar in March 1885, a letter from the IG on 9 April 1885 suggested that Hamilton be deputed as DIG on special duty, operation dacoity and the recruitment of six head constables and five constables at monthly salaries of Rs 3 and Rs 2, respectively. Hamilton was given one-fifth of his regular monthly salary as deputation allowance. These suggestions were accepted on 17 April.

At 7 pm on 21 March, about two dozen of Tantya's band reached the village of Surgaon Banjari where Bapu Mang, the constable responsible for the arrest of Bhavalya and Olia, two of Tantya's men, was present in the *malguzar's* compound. Bondarya, who had joined Tantya's band in 1885, tied Bapu Mang to a wooden pole after which Tantya severed the constable's nose.

The band beat up Devthara, a *malguzar*, and robbed him of cash and goods worth Rs 1,226. From information received from another *malguzar* inimical to Devthara, Tantya knew exactly where the *malguzar* had buried his valuables.⁶⁷ Of the group, Bondarya, Unkar (Omkar) and Bhavalya were armed with swords and guns. Hamilton assumed charge at the Khandwa headquarters on 27 April 1885. Tantya arrived at Khaigaon with 14 of his men, shot dead Constable Bapu Ram who was deployed at the village and went straight to the *malguzar*, Lakshman Gujjar. He extracted Rs 467 from Govind Teli and his brother, to whom the *malguzar* had led the band. Tantya also addressed the villagers. Subsequently, Hamilton arrested the *malguzar* who was sent to Khandwa Jail. Bapu Mang was rewarded with Rs 100 and promoted as head constable. The widow of Bapu Ram, the other constable, was sanctioned a pension.⁶⁸

The system of 'red disks' was instituted by the government in 1883–1884. These were slips of red paper given by village guards to the police as warning of Tantya's impending arrival in the area. There were days when red disks had warned as many as 18 police stations of his imminent arrival. But Tantya had made this system the butt of ridicule—if a 'red-disk' robbery was expected to be perpetrated in a certain village, in fact, it took place in another. The government eventually discarded this ineffective mode of communication in 1886.⁶⁹

Through an order, dated 26 May 1885, the IG reorganised the Nimar police force; he now deployed one chief constable, six head constables and 130 constables. The district was divided into four areas—Mortakka, Pandhana, Burhanpur and Piplod—with each area to be patrolled by a head constable, 20 high-ranking jawans and 50 constables. A chief constable, two head constables and 50 constables were deployed with Hamilton. In addition, certain influential *malguzar*s were deputed as honorary inspectors. No less than 110 breech-loader guns were distributed. For the individual who captured Tantya, or helped in it, a reward of Rs 3,250 was announced, in addition to proprietary rights to the *malguzar*.

Tantya, while assessing the current situation, travelled along the Tapi and through the South Nimar forests to Devri. When Hamilton received this intelligence, he instructed the district's SP to dispatch the Burhanpur patrol party under Insp. Gulzari Mal to Devri. For reasons that are obscure, the order was not carried out.

On 26 May 1885, Tantya robbed Sukhram Gawli of goods worth Rs 620, and Rs 630 from Jamuna Bai, a *malguzar*. On 1 June, he raided Salia Khedi in Ellichpur, near the Narmada, and looted goods worth Rs 2,000 from the villages of Didamda and Lawada on 7 June.[70] Tantya spent the monsoon in the hills of Kalia Baba, in the Gondwana Reserves, but slipped into the Berar region when 50 jawans of the Bhil Corps began an encirclement—at least, that was what Hamilton was led to believe.

At 6 pm on 1 September, with 10–12 of his men, Tantya looted the *malguzar* of Bhakrada in Nimar. From Chain Singh, he seized ornaments worth Rs 500 and some cash and dragged the *malguzar*'s brother to the forest. Then it was the turn of Lumberdar Khadag Singh, an honorary inspector. Tantya severed his mother's nose and set fire to his house. According to Hamilton, Tantya's band had been egged on by Padam Singh, another *malguzar*, who was inimical to Khadag Singh. But Padam Singh's version was quite different. Khadag Singh, he said, had promised Tantya Rs 500 but went back on his word when the government appointed him honorary inspector. Padam Singh claimed that, in reality, it was his house which was set alight, not Khadag Singh's. On 17 September, nine individuals, including the patwari and *kotwar* (watchman), were punished because of their failure to inform the police about the Bhakrada raid.

In mid-1885, Tantya, with 25 of his men, robbed the village of Bukhara of goods worth Rs 2,000, after which he slipped into Holkar territory. Hamilton dismantled the checkposts built in Roshia and Khard and summoned a risaldar and 25 jawans from the Dorwa check post. He strongly suspected that the men at the checkposts had been helping Tantya enter Holkar territory. Unnerved by the British Government's displeasure, Lt. Munna Singh of the Holkar state wrote to the GGCI on 25 September, assuring him of the strenuous efforts being made to apprehend Tantya.

After the special forces were withdrawn from the borders, Hamilton was released from the anti-Tantya campaign and deployed for routine duty in Nimar from 15

September onwards. These measures reduced the efficacy of the anti-Tantya campaign. Meanwhile, Tantya's raids in the Holkar state continued unabated, with one at Pipalgaon on 15 September. A policeman and two dacoits were injured in this raid; one injured dacoit died the next day.

On 1 October, the IG once more put forth a proposal to strengthen the Nimar police force. He recommended the deployment of three head constables, 50 constables and 30 *sowar*s from 1 November onwards. Isari Prasad and 50 jawans of the Bhil Corps were to be deployed with the IG.

The proposal was accepted on 15 October, and it was decided that the DC and District Superintendent of Police (DSP), Nimar, would maintain direct contact with Holkar officials. On 23 November, the CC announced rewards for those helping to apprehend Tantya, Bondarya, Bhavalya, Thakur Nukar, Phool Singh and Renku; clemency for their past crimes was also promised. On 26 November, the reward was enhanced to Rs 3,000. The advertisement, reported *TOI* on 2 October 1885, was widely publicised in Nimar, Hoshangabad, Betul and Berar.[71]

The Advertisement

The advertisement issued in this connection stated the following:

> According to the order of the Chief Commissioner, the following persons have committed robberies and at least two of them have committed murders. It is believed that they are committing robberies together and are declared offenders:

Tantya s/o Bhau Singh Bhil
Bondarya s/o Harchand Bhil, Tembhi, Khandwa, Nimar
Devalya s/o Banga Bhil, Dabhi, Khandwa, Nimar
Bhavalya s/o Ugharya Bhil, Tembhi, Khandwa, Nimar
Unkar (Omkar) s/o Vithal Bhil, Tembhi, Khandwa, Nimar
Lachhman s/o Vithal Bhil, Tembhi, Khandwa, Nimar
Bhavalya s/o Hira Lal, Chichkheda, Khandwa, Nimar
Thakur s/o Narayan Kunbi, Takli, Khandwa, Nimar
Unkar (Omkar) s/o Banya Bhil, Chichkheda, Khandwa, Nimar
Phool Singh Banjara, Manjrod, Khandwa, Nimar
Rengu Korku, Sonkhedi, Hoshangabad

Everyone has a right by law to nab a declared criminal and use every tact to get him captured. Further, there won't be any punishment if there is a murder [at the hands of the nabber], in trying to catch a person who has committed a serious crime like the ones committed by the above mentioned criminals who deserve execution or life sentence, if he resists arrest or tries to run away. The Queen's Government informs all the subjects that if a person captures one or more of the abovementioned declared criminals, alive or dead, and hands him over to the government, he would be rewarded by the government as below.

Reward

Anyone who captures Tantya will get three thousand (3,000) in cash and the proprietary rights over the revenue of one thousand (1,000) bigha land in village Nandgaon of

Hoshangabad district. Anyone who captures Bondarya will get three thousand (3,000) in cash and the proprietary rights over the revenue of five hundred (500) bigha land in village Nandgaon of Hoshangabad district. Anyone who captures one of the following accomplices of Tantya, will get a reward of five hundred rupees:

Devalya s/o Banga Bhil, Dabhi, Khandwa, Nimar
Bhavalya s/o Ugharya Bhil, Tembhi, Khandwa, Nimar
Unkar s/o Vithal Bhil, Tembhi, Khandwa, Nimar
Lachhman s/o Vithal Bhil, Tembhi, Khandwa, Nimar
Bhavalya s/o Hira Bhil, Chichkheda, Nimar
Thakur s/o Narayan Kunbi, Takli, Khandwa, Nimar
Unkar s/o Banya Bhil, Chichkheda, Khandwa, Nimar
Phool Singh Banjara, Manjrod, Nimar
Rengu Korku, resident of Sonkhedi, Hoshangabad

It is also announced that all the crimes of the following will be condoned:
Devalya s/o Banga
Bhavalya s/o Ugharya
Unkar s/o Vithal Bhil
Lachhman s/o Vithal Bhil
Bhavalya s/o Hira Bhil

Provided they present themselves to the government and give the details that leads to anyone or all of the declared offenders.

The persons who have sheltered or helped anyone or all of the above mentioned declared offenders or prevent someone from giving information to the officials, will be tried under Sections 212 and 216 IPC. From this advertisement it is informed that no one will be tried if he helps the officers in the capture of anyone who helps the officers to arrest the declared offenders.[72]

Tehsil Bhikangaon, in Khargone, was the epicentre of the anti-Tantya campaign. On behalf of the British Government, Isari Prasad appointed certain Bhils as informers. Capt. Muhammad Khan and Lt. Munna Singh represented the Holkar state.

Madhav Rao, *patil* of Shivna, in the Holkar state, was Tantya's well-wisher. While Tantya was in hiding, Madhav Rao solemnised the marriage of Tantya's son. Plainclothes policemen were on hand to seize Tantya if he appeared at the wedding. When a bullock cart entered the village, the police conducted a search but found only two women inside. After the marriage was solemnised, one of the women threw off her sari, blessed the couple, jumped into a nearby drain and disappeared—it was indeed Tantya. His wife, Bhikki, shed tears of joy. The policemen had, yet again, been outfoxed.[73]

Crosthwaite was recalled from Burma for one year (1885–1886) and appointed CC, Central Provinces, by the government, which had hoped to avail of his experiences in Burma. On 23 February 1888, *TOI* reported that being unsuccessful in his endeavour, Crosthwaite returned to Burma.

Main Events and New Officers, 1886

The year dawned with more robberies in Betul and Hoshangabad. Col. Ward, who had been in charge of Nimar for some months, was now given command of the anti-Tantya campaign. He was appointed special commissioner (SC) for the suppression of dacoity in the Narmada Valley. Three police officers—Hawkin, Sardar Ratan Singh and Morris—were deputed in Hoshangabad, Betul and Chhindwara, respectively. They took charge of their respective districts immediately and deployed honorary police forces, as did Hamilton in Nimar. Ward visited Bhopal to meet AGGCI Griffin, who concurred with the CC's view that Ward ought to be allowed to wield the same authority in Holkar territory as he had in the Narmada Division.[74]

Meanwhile, on the night of 11 January 1886, a group of 40–50 men, led by Tantya, arrived to raid Nakwara in Hoshangabad. The village patwari and muqaddam were tied up with ropes but were later released unharmed. On the same day, the homes of three influential residents of Jijgaon were raided. The loot from Nakwara amounted to Rs 43 and Jijgaon to Rs 2,538, which included ornaments and cash. The *malguzar* of Jijgaon hurried to the Magardha check post, which was 3 or 4 mil. distant. At the same time, the residents of Nakwara sent a message to their *malguzar*, who was then in Harda, and he, too, informed the police. With two constables and 12 gun-wielding villagers, the head constable of Magardha reached Jijgaon immediately, but the raiders had escaped an hour earlier via the Makrai road.

Along this route, the police retrieved a bag with part of the Nakwara spoils but little else. The head constable made the unhappy discovery that Kanhaiya Karku—a former dacoit, whom the government had released on the condition that he would assist in Tantya's arrest—had misled them.

On 13 January 1886, the DC urged the Holkar police to help apprehend Tantya. On 22 January, Tantya attacked the village of Chuna Hujuri in Betul. Reaching the village at 5 pm, he made inquiries about Ramchand and Kohar Gawli. Here, he bifurcated his band and one group raided Kohar's house for cash and ornaments worth Rs 900. The other decamped with goods worth Rs 300 from Ramchand's house. Both the groups reunited outside the village within the hour and slipped into the Nimbiya forests. They also dragged along the village hawaldar for some distance but freed him unharmed. The Chicholi police station was informed as well. The police reached the village at 10 pm, but by then, as always, it was too late.

Tantya was spotted near Dhakochi on 11 March. Ratan Singh and Hawkin launched a search, accompanied by Hamilton. Unsurprisingly, just five of 20 policemen of the search party were willing to enter the cave where Tantya was believed to be in hiding—the others kept a safe distance. Interestingly, whenever a dangerous campaign against Tantya was launched, some policeman feigned illness and hastened to get hospitalised, while others quit their jobs immediately.

On 27 March, Tantya organised a retaliatory raid on the village of Bandi, about 18 mil. from Charua. He set fire to 27 houses and grain stores in the village because the village *malguzar*, Tamla Patel, had refused to supply him with provisions. Ratan Singh, who reached the spot the next morning, returned empty-handed.

On 11 April, Tantya raided the village of Debrabandi in Rajaborari and looted goods worth Rs 700. This incident took place when both the SPs of Hoshangabad and Betul were on leave and an SC was in charge. Hawkin was able to reach the spot only two days later. The arrival of a small police party from Betul the next day also proved fruitless. Tantya decamped to the Khampur forests of the district after the incident.

On 13 April, Tantya's band reached Ghorpad, some 9 mil. from the Khampur checkpost. There, they came across a police party comprising a head constable and three constables, and nine village landowners. The police fired upon them, but the band, well out of firing range, remained safe in a drain.

One reported incident, regarding the torching of the Makrai royal palace, could well have been Tantya's handiwork. Ratan Singh had discovered a grain store in the forest, which the king of Makrai had left unprotected, a clear indication that the latter was surreptitiously aiding Tantya. It was also rumoured that Tantya was hiding in the Makrai forests, while an intensive search for him was underway in the forests of Charua and Kalibhit.

SC Ward's next step was to deploy policemen in all the villages of the district. After consultation with the SPs, Isari

Prasad concluded that the campaign to apprehend Tantya would be successful only after the supply of provisions to him was completely withdrawn. Some 50 jawans of the Malva Bhil Corps were deployed at the three places in Makrai where the dacoits were known to shelter. Constables were positioned in villages, and the DC issued orders to the *malguzars* and village chiefs regarding their security. After the deployment of constables at Betul, Charua and Rajaborari, 80 constables were deployed at Harda. The CC himself assumed charge of the police in Makrai. With the tightening of the net, the supply of provisions to Tantya was made virtually impossible.

Ward had also devised a plan, revealed in his letter of 17 May 1886, regarding the complete reorganisation of the police force in the districts of Betul, Hoshangabad and Nimar. According to his proposal, special police would be deployed at Khanapur for the surveillance of areas such as Punasa (west), Kason (north) and Bhagwanpur, where the dacoits retreated after their raids. The special police deployed at Asirgarh would control the areas of Dhaulkot and Diwal, and the contingent in Ghatakhedi would guard the Sendhwal and Manjrod regions. However, on 23 June, the CC rejected the proposal—a clear indication of his awareness of assistance to Tantya from landowners like Dadu Patel, Shobha Patel and Raja Patel.[75]

In May 1886, Isari Prasad arrested three banjaras and recovered some of the goods looted from Jijgaon. Meanwhile, Muhammad Khan's loyalty was in question.

An inquiry revealed that Khan and Munna Singh had had altercations on at least two occasions, with each accusing the other's men of providing Tantya-related information to the British.

Ward was transferred well before the CC had turned down his 17 May proposal of police reorganisation along military lines, and was replaced by Col. Hammond. The anti-Tantya campaign continued to be supervised by the IG.

On 16 August 1886, the DC, Betul, was informed of the arrest of Daryav Gond, a member of Tantya's band. Daryav was granted clemency on the condition that he would cooperate in Tantya's arrest. On 6 September, Col. Ricketts, Commissioner, Narmada Division, called a meeting of the officers engaged in the anti-Tantya operation at which a reorganisation of the police in the three districts, the formation of an espionage team and tightening of the patrolling system was approved.[76]

When Tantya's band appeared in Mulgaon in Nimar, a constable, deputed there for village security, attacked the raiders with the cooperation of some villagers. He was shot dead and the raiders left after their job was done. Mukunda, a Bhil informer, met a gory end at Tantya's hands soon after he gave the Holkar state information about Tantya.[77]

On 3 September, along with 20 of his men, Tantya arrived in Barur, near Chhegaon police station. Enticed by the reward announced by the government, the *malguzar* had been collecting information about the band. Tantya ravaged the *malguzar*'s house, held his only son, Madho Kunbi, to ransom and demanded Rs 1,000 within the hour. A chief constable and four constables arrived in Barur when this information reached Chhegaon police station. One of Tantya's band took a bullet during the cross-firing that followed, but the group managed to escape along with the injured member and the abducted boy under the cover of darkness.

Madho returned to the village on 17 September but, petrified, he refused to divulge any details of Tantya's hideout—he claimed he had been blindfolded throughout his abduction. A report on the incident in *TOI* on 25 January 1887 and in *HMICE* on 15 February 1887 stated that the policemen who took part in this encounter were promoted.[78]

Tantya's elusiveness caused much embarrassment to the IG. He deputed two reliable inspectors to disguise themselves as traders so as to make discreet inquiries at the markets of Hoshangabad, Betul, Khandwa and Indore. The report, which the two inspectors submitted after they had toured the Satpura–Vindhya belt, stated that Tantya had a strong hold on the entire region. Peasants and tribals had great respect for him and, consequently, were unhelpful to the police—many were the youths who would sacrifice their lives for Tantya.[79]

On 30 July 1886, *Colonies and India* published an interesting story about Tantya.

TANTYA

Many curious stories have been told of the duplicity and cunning of the Kaffirs in South Africa, the Malagasies, the blacks of Australia, and the natives of all castes in the East, but it may be questioned if anything more cunning than the duplicity exhibited in the following narrative has ever come within the knowledge of Western readers. It is said that a police Sahib, who had been told off on special duty to catch Tantia, while he was enjoying a pipe, surrounded by a large camp full of followers and spies, heard an altercation, and, on asking the reason, found his native policeman had stopped a man from approaching the Sahib. The Sahib ordered him to be brought forward. He was brought forward, having first been searched to see he carried no arms. He was a common Bhil coolie with a loin cloth on, and another rag about his shoulders, but bareheaded. He said he wished to speak to the Sahib alone and impressed upon the Sahib (with possibly various lies) that he had some important grievance to lay before him. The attendants were ordered to retire, and the coolie, in a low voice, said he had heard, as all Bhils know, that Government had offered a reward for Tantia, that he knew where he was asleep under a tree and quite alone, that no amount of torture would make him confess, for his life would not be worth five minutes from Tantia's friends, but if the Sahib would pay him 500 rupees down, and would take his rifle and come with him alone, he would show the enemy asleep under a tree; the Sahib could shoot or capture him, and he, the coolie, would make off; no one would know he had played the spy; and he would get his 500 rupees, and so on. After some communing with his inner self, the Sahib agreed to the terms. He mounted his horse, and with loaded rifle went off with his guide. They marched for several miles through jungles and ravines, and the coolie said, "I will bury my rupees under this tree." He did so. At the end of another mile the coolie requested the Sahib to tie his horse up and come on foot. The advice was followed. After another short distance the Bhil coolie suggested that as it was very hot, he would, if the Sahib pleased, carry the rifle, walking only one step in advance of the Sahib, as they had some difficult climbing to do in the ravines. This idea, though not agreed to at first, was eventually also carried out, for the coolie seemed a poor sort of nervous little fellow. Shortly after the coolie stopped and said the Sahib had better stop while he reconnoitred to see if Tantya was still asleep, and he proceeded to place the rifle against a tree, where the Sahib could see it by a look sideway. The coolie went forward as silent as a tiger, and a little time elapsed. When the Sahib, becoming impatient, went forward to take up his rifle, the rifle was gone, the coolie never returned, the horse had disappeared. Next morning the Sahib found his way out of the ravines, and, the strangest part of all, the coolie sent word to the Sahib that he hoped he had convinced him it was no use trying to catch Tantia, for, he added, the coolie was the dacoit Tantya himself!

On 24 March 1886, *HMICE* reported the government's mortification at being unable to apprehend Tantya even with a large troop of 200 cavaliers and infantrymen. Even an espionage expert like Puggies had failed.

Another apocryphal tale, carried in the *Boston Guardian* on 14 May 1887, involved an SP riding through a forest track where he came upon a hill wayfarer, tired and scantily clad, carrying a bundle of wood on his head. The SP informed the villager that the government had declared a reward for Tantya's arrest. The villager directed him to an alternate forest track, which he assured the officer would lead straight to Tantya. The SP took his advice but failed to find Tanya. A few hours later, he was informed of a raid on a neighbouring village. The officer then correctly concluded that the wary villager who had misguided him could well have been Tantya himself.

The year 1886 was drawing to a close and Tantya continued to remain out of reach. In November 1886, Griffin was entrusted with the responsibility to apprehend Tantya.[80] He sought permission from his superiors to take action against Tantya in winter. On 30 November, F.C. Anderson, office secretary of the acting CC, Central Provinces, informed the Government of India that acting CC Fitzpatrick, by a letter sent to Griffin on 22 October, had wholeheartedly endorsed the strategies suggested for Tantya's capture. Griffin, however, was convinced that there were two main reasons for failure in this regard. One was the territorial mentality of the Central Provinces police force, which did not want to give the other forces a chance to seize Tantya. The second reason was cowardice.

Fitzpatrick had, in fact, failed to find any basis for Griffin's reasoning. He emphasised that he had given the DSPs of Nimar and Hoshangabad permission to enlist jawans from other districts as well. Ward had pointed out earlier that as there had been several occasions when the police had missed Tantya by a whisker, the accusation of cowardice was perhaps unjust. Fitzpatrick put forth three reasons for the failure to apprehend Tantya. First, the paucity of resources for intelligence. Second, the Bhils, who eulogised Tantya, refused to cooperate with the police. Third, Tantya was able to shelter with ease in Holkar territory. Fitzpatrick, therefore, was in favour of deploying Indian police officers. He said that the number of informers was being increased and recommended that Griffin directly contact the administrative officers for other assistance. Towards the end of 1886, Griffin deputed Isari Prasad to capture Tantya.[81]

On 26 December 1886, Tantya was spotted in the district of Betul where he raided Dholgaon. As reported by *TOI* on 25 January and *HMICE* on 15 February 1887, a few villagers and policemen reached the spot at once and engaged his band in a futile skirmish. However, his raids continued with impunity into 1887; in Sankheda on 5 February, where goods worth Rs 1,200 were looted and in Singot on 12 April to the tune of Rs 1,800.

In his sanction sent to the IG, Central Provinces, the Commissioner, Narmada Division, endorsed the proposal to provide free pasture for 1,000 livestock for five years to any individual who arrested, or helped in the arrest of, Tantya—dead or alive. This sanction was widely publicised in the districts where Tantya took refuge. In a letter written from Pachmarhi on 20 April 1887, C.W. Doveton, assistant conservator of forests, offered the services of the forest department.[82]

On 21 June and 15 August 1887, *TOI* carried reports of Tantya's fame which was by then so widespread that at a cultural programme held in the railway institute, Khandwa, one Asim presented a song titled 'Tantya Bhil'.

At the beginning of 1887, the responsibility for Tantya's capture shifted from Griffin to Isari Prasad. But, despite all of Isari Prasad's efforts, and the Holkar state's vigilance, Tantya managed to execute two robberies, reported *TOI* on 5 April 1887. Disgruntled by his lack of success, Isari Prasad surrendered this responsibility on 27 October 1887 and was dissociated from the anti-Tantya campaign. Tantya and his men lost no time in raiding Pokhar on the same day.[83]

Nehar was then appointed SP, Khandwa. His report to the Commissioner, Narmada Division, emphasised that every move of the local police was known to Tantya. There appeared to be no option but to appoint a British inspector.

The appointed inspector boarded the train from Bombay in a first-class compartment. At Patalpani railway station, near Mhow, two coolies entered his compartment. One of them asked for the inspector's permission to carry his luggage to the police lines, which was granted. In the course of conversation en route to the police lines, the coolie mentioned that a peasant, who Tantya visited off and on, lived by a hillock in the vicinity. Loathe to lose an opportunity to capture Tantya, the inspector offered him the government reward sanctioned for Tantya's capture. The coolie feigned nervousness but eventually agreed to help the inspector on the condition that half the reward be given in advance to the peasant. The money changed hands, as agreed, and they set out the next morning. In a repeat of many such previous instances, the poor inspector was led a merry dance over hill and dale by the coolie, who was, needless to say, none other than Tanya. Eventually abandoned in the forest, his weapons appropriated by Tantya, the inspector returned, quite unable to believe that Tantya had, in fact, released him unharmed.[84]

Raid on Pokhar's Patil: The Great Indian Moonlighter
In his youth, Tantya was alleged to have had a relationship with Jasoda, the widowed daughter of Shiva Patil of Pokhar, and it was at Pokhar that the *patil* had humiliated him. Mohan, Sardar Patil's son, had been the cause of Tantya's arrest in 1878. The widows of Sardar and Mohan lived together in Pokhar, receiving a pension for their husbands' services to the government. There was much tension between Gajia, Mohan's mother, and Jasoda, who faced constant humiliation from the former on account of her past relationship with Tantya. On 27 October 1887, Tantya arrived in Pokhar with his men to terrorise the *patil*'s family. British newspapers gave much prominence to the incident. For instance, the *North-Eastern Daily Gazette* reported the following on 7 October 1889.

THE REVENGE OF AN INDIAN DACOIT: A WOMAN'S NOSE CUT OFF

Tantya Bheel has been committed for trial in India charged with causing grievous hurt. The case was investigated by the Assistant Commissioner at the Jabalpur Court. The surrounding grounds were densely crowded from an early hour. Tantya was heavily manacled and guarded by an armed police force. The evidence showed that about ten years ago Tantya Bheel, known to be intimate with Jashoda, daughter of his employer, a native of the village of Pakar, was, by the machinations of Mohan Chowdhri, a near relative of Jashoda's, lodged in Khandwa Jail for two months on a charge of theft. After serving his term, Tantia, bent on reprisals, returned to Pakar, and proceeded to harass his enemies by slaughtering cattle and destroying agricultural implements. Mohan Chowdhri, to whom Tantya was indebted for his two months' imprisonment, enjoyed naturally a large share of the dacoit's attention, so much so that he resolved at any risk to capture his enemy. A clever snare was laid, and Tantya at last was run to earth and confined in Khandwa Jail. Pending his trial Tantya escaped, and began the wild career which has made him known to us as the most desperate dacoit in India. In October, 1887, Tantya Bheel made his way to Pakar. On the 27th he visited the house of Mohan Chowdhri, and enquired for his old enemy. He was informed by Mohan's mother that he had died some days before. Tantya refused to believe the story, and proceeded to beat the mother of Mohan Chowdhri, demanding the

100 rupees which Mohan had been awarded a year before for capturing Tantya and claiming also 500 rupees, the sum which the father of Jashoda had been fined by the village panchayat for the misconduct of his daughter. The woman refused to give the money to Tantia, whereupon she was seized, dragged out of the village, stripped of her jewellery, and mutilated by having her nose severed from her face with a hunting knife. At his trial Tantia, who was undefended, did not contradict the above allegations, except in minor particulars. He acknowledges having mutilated the woman, but denies having robbed her. He also acknowledges having claimed 600 rupees, but maintains that he had a right to the money. The other charges will be tried later.

On 6 December 1887, the *Globe and Traveller*, another British newspaper, published a piece on ignorance in India, highlighting the abduction of two women and the nose-severing of one and comparing it with the deeds committed by Roger and Captain Moonlight. It also compared Tantya with Ireland robbers Pyne and Gilhooly, sarcastically adding that the National League ought to honour this 'Great Indian Moonlighter' with honorary membership. The piece is reproduced here.

PARNELLISM IN INDIA

The National League should certainly confer honorary membership on Tantya Bhil, the great Indian "moonlighter." This worthy's methods of carrying on a "constitutional movement" against the law are precisely those which now obtain in Ireland. Take, for instance, the description given by a native paper of his latest exploit. "With a body of five followers, he proceeded to a village, seized two women who had incurred the displeasure of his band, dragged them into an adjoining jungle and cut off their noses." Quite like dear Captain Moonlight. But the similarity does not stop there. As usual, the people of the village, it is reported, "permitted the dacoits to act just as they pleased." So do the villagers of Blatherskite permit the Irish dacoits to act just as they please in robbery, mutilation, and murder. Again, this Tantya Bhil is an outlaw like Mr. Pyne, Mr. Gilhooly, and the other hide-and-seek players in Ireland, dodging the myrmidons of the law from place to place precisely as they do. So far, the resemblance is complete, but note the difference of attitude taken up by the national press in the two countries. In Ireland, dacoity is extenuated, if not actually praised; it is the "wild justice of revenge," and so forth. Very different is the tone of the native papers in India; some of them even go so far as to advocate the punishment of any villages that do not make resistance to Tantya Bhil. A happy idea: what if it were applied to Ireland? In that case, the bold Irish peasant might not think it a manly part to remain passive while innocent people are being mutilated or murdered before his eyes.

On receiving intelligence of the incident at Pokhar on 27 October 1887, the SP left no stone unturned to apprehend Tantya, but his effort was, needless to say, in vain. In the meantime, Tantya masterminded a burglary in the village of Banjhargaon, near Khandwa, and looted property worth Rs 3,000. After these two episodes, he slipped into Holkar territory. He reappeared in Bhuiphal in November 1887 at the house of Himmat Patil whom he had killed years ago and extracted Rs 200 from his widow and son.

Encounter in Gangradhna

Between November 1887 and 15 June 1888, Tantya and his men raided the villages of Dhankot, Bhogaon, Gangali, Bistar, Kodri and Roshni, while constantly evading the police and varying their areas of operation.

On 28 June, the 20-member band engaged in a significant encounter with the police at the village of Gangradhna in Hoshangabad. A modest force of a head constable and four constables dispatched messages to all the nearby checkposts for reinforcements, while the villagers maintained a night-long vigil, waiting for a police force that only arrived the next morning. Tantya's band, under the impression that a large police contingent had arrived, abandoned their weapons and food items and fled to safety. The Gangradhna encounter prevented Tantya's foothold in Hoshangabad and the district was spared several raids in the future.

Tantya's next raids were on the villages of Bhuriasot, Padar and in Holkar territory. The raids followed more or less the same pattern of retaliation against his enemies, and loot of cash and goods.

Nevertheless, the police now noticed a significant change. Before the Uskalli and Kapasi raids on 20 January 1884, and even after that, he had received safe harbour in the Gangradhna forests. Then, the villagers had refrained from informing the police. By 1888, the situation had changed—the villagers were now volunteering information.

In one incident, when sheltering in the forests of Betul, Tantya came face to face with a constable. Tantya took the man prisoner, seized his gun, divested him of his uniform and after severing his nose, drove the mutilated policeman away. It was as if severing noses had become his favoured pastime.[85]

Between 1878 and 1886, Tantya was responsible for some 400 raids in Nimar, British and Holkar territories but was never caught. The cream of police officers, British and Indian, were deputed on the job, but he managed to consistently outwit them all.[86] In 1887, Central India reported 150 cases of dacoity, to the tune of Rs 2,10,000.

Despite the extensive security arrangements and despite train and telegraph facilities, Tantya was spotted in Indore, right under the very noses of Holkar officers—the CM, Indore, was convinced that Tantya visited relatives in the city. Some of these relatives were, therefore, arrested and tried in the sessions court, reported *TOI* on 11 and 17 April 1888. The manager of the Indore court in Khargone, who was responsible for instigating Tantya to carry out raids, was dismissed in April 1888 at Griffin's insistence, according to a report in *TOI* on 4 May 1888 and in *HMICE* on 4 June 1888.

According to the 1888 report of the Central Provinces police, the Nimar region witnessed five raids that year, with Tantya's involvement reported in four, a claim sometimes dismissed as dubious. But his involvement in two of these raids was indeed indubitable—one at Gangradhna and the other at Padar.[87]

10
PROTECTION TO TANTYA BHIL AND PUNISHMENT

The British Government was convinced that the infamous Tantya Bhil was receiving covert assistance from certain powerful individuals of the Holkar state. Whenever pressure on him mounted in the British dominion, he sought refuge in Holkar territory where he was assured of safety. The question was: who were these powerful individuals?

According to reports in the *Times of India* (hereafter *TOI*) on 8, 9, 13 and 30 June 1888, chief among them was Khema Nayak, who provided Tantya with shelter and help for five long years. Originally hailing from the Deccan, Khema had settled in the village of Satwara in Nimar. He was an *ijradar* (revenue collector) of the Holkar state and *patel* of the villages of Rosa, Mordad and Warkla—a man of undoubted importance. A cattle trader in the main, trading 1,000 heads each year, he travelled to Malwa, Khandesh and Hyderabad Deccan every year. He commanded a large army, weapons and horses and several warehousing facilities. During the monsoon, he camped in the *gowalia*s (wild pastures) of Ikla, Kakra and Khedra, where he sheltered

Bhil chiefs like Tantya. At one time, Tantya and Khema belonged to neighbouring villages. Tantya's association with him greatly enhanced his own strength, increasing his trade and profits manifold. Consequently, he viewed any assistance to Tantya as his obligation.

The charge of collusion was soon proved against Khema Nayak. In mid-1885, he was looted of goods worth Rs 1,800, for which he held four of his men—Taja, Ramu, Chandra and Mayaram—responsible. Damodar Pant, the thanadar of Bamnala, arrested all four accused, who lost no time in informing officials that Khema was in league with Tantya. Pant was a relative of Khema's bookkeeper. One of the accused alleged that Tantya had brought plunder worth Rs 7,500 from a raid, wrapped in two blankets and loaded on a bull's back, to be stashed in Khema's house, which included British coins and Halu-Holkar coins. Khema, Chandra, Sakri and Sukya had unloaded the loot.

When the four accused made bail, they promised to return the stolen money in a week but failed to honour the pledge. Khema then lodged another complaint with Rajaram Vishwanath, a class three magistrate. When the four accused appealed to Tantya, who was then in hiding, he assured them that Khema would receive his funds. Khema and Tantya subsequently met in Cheep Khal (Churi Khal) and after the latter's assurances, Khema moved an application withdrawing his complaint. An agreement was drafted in the presence of the magistrate, in which Khema accepted the fact of theft. But the agreement failed to mention that Tantya had guaranteed return of the money. Nor did Khema accept that Tantya had given him silver coin, as alleged by the four accused. The court was suspicious of Khema's withdrawal of his complaint for a second time, leading to the inescapable conclusion that he was in league with Tantya. The depositions made by Khema's men proved the allegations against Khema of sheltering Tantya. When the four accused agreed to turn government approvers, and to cooperate, the lower court quashed the charges against them and ordered a trial to uncover the truth of Khema's alleged protection of Tantya.

At the end of April 1888, Isari Prasad brought a charge against Khema that was to be tried by Ganesh Krishna, a class three magistrate. The lower court took the charge against Khema as proved. By the end of May, his advocate, Atmaram Chimna Ji, filed an appeal in the sessions court at Indore, seeking to overturn the lower court's verdict. However, K.G. Acharya, the sessions court judge, endorsed the punishment of seven years RI meted out to Khema.

Khema's advocate then filed an appeal in the sadar court, the royal court of Indore, also known as the high court. At the Indore Sadar Court, Chief Justice Baijnath and Justice Dhurandhar heard Khema's case for two days and decided to examine the four witnesses who had not been produced by the prosecution before the sessions court. The pleader for the four witnesses was hopeful that British judges would hear their cases anew, which could possibly disclose valuable information about the hideouts of notorious dacoits.

Khema Nayak's appeal in the Indore Sadar Court was heard on 19 June 1888, but of the four witnesses summoned only one appeared. Isari Prasad and Bhavani Prasad were pleaders for the British Government. After the hearing, the verdict was reserved for 25 June, reported the *TOI* in its editions of 8, 9, 13, 21 and 30 June 1888.

Regarding Khema Nayak's appeal, the chief justice specified the following charges:

1. Khema had sheltered, fed and provided other amenities to the notorious bandit, Tantya Bhil: Section 160, Indore Penal Code;
2. Despite his position as an *ijaradar* and *patel*, i.e., a government servant and thus obliged by law, he had failed to arrest Tantya: Section 163;
3. He had shielded a criminal despite receiving a reward: Section 161.

It was under these sections that the sessions court had taken these charges as proved. Khema moved the high court on the ground that the evidence presented had failed to corroborate his collusion with Tantya. For instance, regarding the charge that he had received goods worth Rs 7,500 from Tantya, he claimed that he had been in the Deccan at the time, continued the report in *TOI* on 30 June 1888.

The chief justice was of the view that Khema was well aware of his obligations. His son, Prem Nayak, also an *ijradar*, had signed two muster rolls on 26 June 1886 and as per Section 26 of Indore Criminal Procedure Code, he was obliged to inform the police whenever Tantya entered his village. Hence, Khema's guilt stood proved, continued the *TOI* report of 30 June. On 25 June 1888, Chief Justice Baijnath and Justice Dhurandhar sentenced Khema Nayak to seven years RI, according to reports in *TOI* on 26 and 30 June 1888.

If Tantya Bhil had gone scot-free for such an extended period, the main reason was the unstinted support he had received from the entire Bhil community. Of these, the protection provided by Khema Nayak was critical, stated the *Colonies and India* on 4 July 1888.

On 27 June 1888, *TOI* had alleged that in native states, such as the Holkar state, local influential individuals like Khema Nayak acted as the main shield for dacoits like Tantya. Ever since Tantya had trained Khema's son in archery, he had developed a rapport with Khema's family. The cattle trader had not only provided weapons and horses but also protected Tantya's band from the administration's reach and even concealed plunder received from him. The British had entrusted the task of capturing Tantya to Khema Nayak, but the latter had steadfastly refused to betray a hero of his own community—rather, he had preferred to deceive the British. The *TOI* hailed Khema's arrest and punishment as just albeit belated. His harsh punishment was meant to serve as a warning to others sheltering criminals in Indore–Gwalior and other native states.

The Khema Nayak case had necessitated a reconsideration of the contracts made for Tantya's arrest. The *TOI* report also commended the determination of the

Indore High Court judges who had punished Khema in a separate case but criticised the state of lower courts in the Holkar state as unsatisfactory, as some of its officers had knowingly created various obstacles for the prosecution. A deputy magistrate chastised the four accused who had deposed against Khema, who claimed that they had been pressured to retract their depositions—which proved Khema guilty—made before the committing magistrate. The *TOI* expressed the hope that those corrupt individuals would be punished, so as to discourage conspiracies against the administration. The king, too, would have to honour his promise of good governance, so that Tantya and other criminals did not escape unpunished.

British officers at Indore believed that the Holkar state, a veritable nest of criminals, needed to discipline several officers, including imprisoning several high-ranking ones, as perquisites to streamlining its administration. They were determined to bring these conditions to the king's attention, and his allowance was contingent on the assurances he made to the viceroy and his council, continued the *TOI* report of 27 June 1888.

The affair took several interesting turns after the verdict on 25 June 1888 against Khema Nayak. When Khema was sent to serve his sentence, some of the witnesses in the case lodged a complaint in the royal court. It was heard by a special court of law constituted by the durbar. *The Homeward Mail from India China and the East* (hereafter *HMICE*) published an article on this 'alleged torture' on 21 September 1888, based on a correspondent's report from Mhow on 31 August. The sequence of events, as recounted in the *HMICE* report, is reproduced here:

ALLEGED TORTURE

A correspondent writes from Mhow, Aug. 31: Rajaram, Class Three Magistrate, and Damodar, Thanedar of Bamnala, who were accused by some witnesses in Khema Naique's case of torturing them, have been placed on trial before Mr. Kesheorao Acharya, who has been specially appointed by the Durbar to hold the inquiry into the charges of torture and giving purwana to Khema Naique for carrying arms. On the 11th instant both the accused were brought before the special magistrate, who, without recording any evidence, examined them at length, although an objection was raised by Rajaram's counsel to that procedure. Sirdar Bahadur Isriprasad, of the Central India Horse, is in charge of the prosecution. After offering some evidence, the prosecution produced as witness Khema Naique, who is undergoing imprisonment in the city jail. He stated that before he was brought in court to give evidence, he had been taken from the jail to the Residency Bazaar, and there questioned about Tantya Bheel, and that the object of this was now confessing his complicity, and that of Rajaram with Tantya Bheel, notwithstanding his appeal to the durbar against his conviction by the Saddar Court, was his desire to see Rajaram share with him the fruits of his crime, as Rajaram failed to bring about Khema's release. Khema Naique also admitted that after his conviction, witnesses for the prosecution had visited him in Jail. On the 23rd Isriprasad, the prosecutor, presented an application to the court for permission to send Damodar, one of the accused, to the village of Bamnala to bring some papers from there, but was ordered to apply next morning in the presence of both the accused. On the 24th, however, Damodar and Isriprasad did not put in an appearance in Court, and Rajaram's pleader objected to the prosecutors taking a co-accused without the Court's permission. On the 30th the case was called, but Isriprasad and Damodar were still absent from Court, and on Damodar's surety being asked where Damodar was, told that as the surety was not consulted when Damodar was sent away, he had no knowledge of his whereabouts. Rajaram's pleader informed the Court that Damodar was seen at Sanawad on the 25th in company of the prosecution witnesses, and that he had been sent to a village to collect evidence for the prosecution. The case was adjourned till the 3rd of September.

11
TANTYA BHIL'S DEMISE

Tantya Bhil was now over 45 years of age. Years of rough living in the forests, of nights spent in hills and caves, and living on wild fruit and often going hungry—of living a life of great uncertainty, in other words—had taken its toll. He was now growing old and frail, and his eyesight was failing. The days when he could board a running train, when he could throw down bags of grain and then himself jump out, the days when he could travel 60 mil. a day were long gone. He began to seriously consider approaching the government for clemency.

In May 1889, Isari Prasad was once more deputed to head the anti-Tantya campaign. Tantya was regularly supplied with provisions by a Rajput, Ganpat (or Ganpati), who belonged to the village of Baner in Holkar territory. Mangi Bhagwant, thanadar of Warla, had once suggested that Isari Prasad involve Ganpat and his men in the campaign to capture Tantya. He had also suggested that Khargone be made the headquarters of anti-Tantya operations. Isari Prasad acted on the suggestions and appointed Ganpat Singh Rajput as a government informer—Ganpat now began to receive government funds. Ganpat soon informed Tantya, who was then living in Sabalgarh, that he had discussed the issue of clemency with Isari Prasad.[1]

Isari Prasad was sceptical of Ganpat's claim that Tantya was to be found in Sabalgarh, dismissing it as yet another trick by the dacoit. But when he realised that Ganpat was indeed cooperating, he made his way to Khargone on 15 May 1889. On 9 June 1889, Ganpat and he met at Khargone for discussions, followed by another meeting on 29 June. Isari Prasad's proposed meeting with Tantya was arranged by Ganpat. Sabalgarh was located some 20 mil. to the southeast of Baner in the Satpura range. At about 8 am on 30 June, Tantya was spotted standing atop a hill while, Isari Prasad, along with 300 sepoys, including Bhagwant Singh, was positioned in the valley below. Bakhshi Singh, and Bajrang Singh of the Bhopal Battalion, had also accompanied Isari Prasad. Although Tantya was well out of firing range, Isari Prasad and he were able to hold a conversation from their respective positions. Isari Prasad assured Tantya that he would take the latter's case to the government, which was expected to grant clemency in a month. Isari Prasad's contingent then returned to Khargone. Bakhshi Singh, of the Central India Horse from Bhopal, later conducted a thorough search of the hills, but Tantya was nowhere to be found. Isari Prasad then correctly surmised that Ganpat had already informed Tantya about the search by security forces. Ganpat admitted to it but claimed it was because he wanted to retain Tantya's faith in him.[2]

A month later, Ganpat invited Tantya for the festival of Raksha Bandhan but also informed the police on 7 August 1889 that Tantya was to visit his home on 11 August. An army troop reached Jamli, south of Khargone, on 9 August and camped there, reaching Baner the next day.

Oblivious to any perceived threat, Tantya arrived at his Rajput friend's house at about 10 pm on 11 August, to have his rakhi tied by Ganpat's wife. At the time, Ganpat informed Tantya that while clemency had indeed been granted, Isari Prasad had not delivered the paperwork. Treating Tantya hospitably, Ganpat invited the latter to rest but ingeniously separated him from six of his men. As soon as Tantya put away his weapons and lay down to rest, Ganpat signalled the police waiting in a neighbouring house. Nayaks Bajrang Singh, Bakhshi Singh, Pancham Prasad, Mirdar Khan and Nand Singh charged in and pounced upon the defenceless Bhil. On 19 August 1889, the *St. James's Gazette* (hereafter *SJG*) reported Tantya's arrest, which had spread like wildfire on the night of 11 August 1889.[3]

Controversy soon dogged claims of credit for the arrest. The newspapers rejected the claim of the British police. J.W. MacDougall, DC, Nimar, contradicted the report in *TOI* on 25 September, declaring that Isari Prasad deserved the credit for capturing Tantya with cooperation from the secret police. But on 6 October, in a counter claim, a letter published in the *Indian Mirror* claimed that the Holkar police had seized Tantya and that Isari Prasad was nowhere in the vicinity during Tantya's arrest—in fact, Khandesh policemen reached the spot post factum, after Ganpat had conspired to have him arrested by the Holkar police.[4]

Ganpat was rewarded with Rs 400, the injured Ekiya Bhil, Rs 75; and Shambhu, Madhiya and Govinda Bhil each received Rs 50. Each of the 17 security force men who had captured Tantya was given Rs 30, and the other members of the force were each awarded Rs 15. Thanadar Mangi Bhagwant received Rs 280.[5]

How an ever-alert rebel like Tantya was captured demands an analysis of his psyche and situation at the time. The fact is that, in order to stay out of the British Army's reach, Bhil rebels like Tantya never slept without sentries who, day and night, took turns to guard their chief, stated the *North London News and Finbury Gazette* on 9 June 1894.

According to a news item published by the *Colonies and India* (hereafter *CI*) on 28 August 1889, there was some difficulty in the identification of the famous Bhil chief whose arrest had been published the week before. Local men and women were first called in for identification. He was then identified by those whose nose he had severed and finally, his barber.

On 19 October, the *Kadina and Wallaroo Times* (SA) published an article titled, 'Capture of A Great Indian Robber Chief.'

> A prominent Bhil dacoit chief, whose name is Tantya Bhil, has been arrested in Indore in the Holkar territory. The Bhil who had sheltered him was the one who got him nabbed.

[Here Ganpat has been said to be a Bhil while other documents say he was a Rajput.] He was then sleeping in Baner, a hill village in the Holkar territory, on the border of Khandesh and close to Nimar. For hearing, his case was brought to the court of Rajaram, a magistrate under Holkar. The paper added that lower castes regard him as one of their heroes, and folksongs dub him as a great warrior of the tribal people. He was much renowned in the lower classes, and love stories too are replete with his references. He has been described as the "Rob Roy of India." He headed a group of bandits and roamed through the sprawling Khandesh territory while all efforts to nab him went in vain. So much so that policemen were getting mad with despondence. From the way he was arrested, it is obvious Roy the Indian bandit couldn't have been caught without some treachery. When he was enjoying the hospitality of a person of his own tribe, in full security and confidence, the carrot of a big reward enticed the host and he gave that renowned bandit to the custody of Holkar's police. The British Government ran after him for ten to twelve years, but he always dodged even the most efficient officers. Often, whole areas were surrounded, but his people always brought him the news. The tighter the siege was, the more ineffective it proved to be. How and which way Tantya escaped always remained a mystery for the administration. Every month Tantya successfully committed a robbery over a hundred miles radius, and this hide and seek greatly dented the credibility of the police. If the British police, equipped with facilities like rails and telegraph, couldn't nab Tantya, it proves beyond doubt that he couldn't escape without his fame among the common people and his thousands of wellwishers. Tantya undoubtedly rewarded whosoever gave him shelter. He stood with his Bhil community in all their happiness and sorrows, and took care of them. Even the ones troubled by him didn't inform the police as it was impossible to get away from his colleagues. Thus, a wide territory was witness to his fame and his terror regime. At intervals, he used to appear in the eastern parts of the Bombay Presidency, sometimes in Berar, but he mostly lived in the Central Provinces. He always threw a challenge to the administration and police. Therefore, the treachery committed by a wellwisher is a matter of concern for the administration as well. He was no thief-in-the-night. He didn't do such things for himself either. He was a leader of his tribals. To the Bhils, plunder was the means of livelihood, and he did plunder for his own people. His community was called a criminal tribe and robbery was their occupation, which occasionally involved murder. There are several such criminal castes in India, but their number is gradually dwindling; else they are changing their profession. The worst of them are the thugs. Tantya's arrest has undoubtedly weakened the Bhils, and their suppression will be all the easier now. But timebound rehabilitation schemes must be launched. Progress is needed. We shouldn't forget that several policemen hail from the Bhil community. In this case, a thief was used to nab a thief. But so far Bhils haven't ditched their people. So much so that Bhil policemen provided security to the Bhils. A whole book it will make if the tales of Tantya's valour were collected.

This Australian paper also mentioned a basket trick. It said:

> Often it appeared that Tantya would be netted, but every time he managed to escape. Once he was chased for several days at a stretch, and his arrest seemed imminent, while he was living in a thatched mud house below a pipal tree. But there was no Tantya when the place was searched. He had entered a basket. When the basket was inspected, it was all empty. A giggling sound came from the sky, but nothing was to be seen. It was Tantya who was laughing even in the face of death. Yet his own face was not visible; it was only the hot sun shining in the sky.

One may well imagine how Tantya's arrest would have exhilarated the police. Isari Prasad organised an identification parade, and on 15 August, Harchand (Tantya's brother-in-law), Keshav (a relative), Ramji (husband of his wife's sister), and Siladar Patil were summoned to Khargone for the purpose.

The following day, Tantya was produced in the court of Rajaram, a magistrate of the Holkar state, and his relatives were brought in to confirm his identity. Once confirmed, instructions were awaited from superiors about his trial, which was to be conducted either at Khandwa or at Indore.

On 19 August, he was brought to Indore via Sanawad under army escort. The next morning, he was first produced before King Shivaji Rao Holkar, and then before a first-class magistrate where yet another round of identification was organised. The magistrate noted that the accused was born in British territory and had committed most of his crimes there—hence, he ought to be tried in a British court. Ganpat, Isari Prasad and others made their depositions before the magistrate. Tantya expressed his desire to surrender before Holkar. He admitted to severing noses and looting moneylenders, but flatly refused to recognise the authority of Judge Rajaram. On 21 August 1889, *CI* reported that the proceedings were completed on the same day and Tantya was handed over to the AGG, who incarcerated him in Central India Agency jail.

On 22 August, the court recorded the statement of Tantya's former paramour Jasoda, now aged 40. She identified him but denied any special attachment. Another deposition was that of Gajia (Gajri, according to Baba Bhand) of Pokhar, now aged 60, whose nose Tantya had severed.

Much thought was then expended on court jurisdiction—British police wanted to try him in Khandwa. Through an order dated 26 August, L.K. Laurie, secretary to the CC, took the accused on remand, to be produced before a judge in Jabalpur. Under Section 344 of the Code of Criminal Procedure (CrPC), Tantya was lodged in Jabalpur Jail. Laurie thereupon declared that the British Army had arrested Tantya and handed him over to the government and ordered a strict vigil of the accused during the investigation and court proceedings. Doubtful about the efficacy of a trial in Nimar, in accordance with the law, the SP, Nimar, was asked to bring all proof and evidence to the court in Jabalpur.

On 26 August, Laurie's order was wired to Col. Hammond, IG, Khandwa; it required Tantya to be sent to Jabalpur under Section 541 and preparations made to try him for all his crimes in the preceding 11 years.

On 28 August, Tantya was brought by train from Indore to Jabalpur Central Jail, via Khandwa. Huge crowds of Bhils thronged every station to get a glimpse of their beloved hero. On 29 August, Tantya was produced before a judge, who ordered 15-day police custody. Capt. Hamilton, SP, Jabalpur, who had been in charge of the anti-Tantya operations of the Narmada Division in the past, was entrusted with the responsibility of the trial. ASP H.P.K. Skipton was deputed to collect evidence of the crimes committed in his district. The government appointed a renowned barrister, H.J. Steon, to plead its case. On 13 September, Steon, in a detailed letter to Hamilton, stated that Tantya was arrested in the Holkar state and later handed over to the Central Provinces. According to the CrPC, an accused ought to be tried in the very area where the crime had been committed, and therefore, Tantya could be tried under the jurisdiction of Ismay, DC, Jabalpur. Steon asked Hamilton to apprise Laurie of this legal imbroglio and to consult a law expert like Gurthweit. The barrister believed that the case ought to commence in Khandwa and then shift to Jabalpur. Another option was to have a Khandwa judge handle the case but added that he thought the first option was preferable. The government ignored Steon's opinion, as it was determined not to hold the trial in Khandwa.[6]

On 26 September, Tantya was brought to Ismay's court, under tight security, where he was charged with robbery and dismemberment. The court compound was packed with Tantya's supporters and the room in which the case was heard was packed to capacity as well. Next, eight witnesses were produced on 28 September, and their statements attested to the Pokhar robbery and Gajia's dismemberment. Tantya, who had refused a lawyer, presented his own case. Replying to a question, he disclosed the reason for Gajia's dismemberment. The witnesses were cross-examined on 29 September. Hamilton produced proof on behalf of the government. Ismay held Tantya guilty under Sections 395 and 397 CrPC and referred the case to the sessions court.[7]

Tantya's case was to be heard at the sessions court on 5 October, but the hearing was postponed on account of the festival of Durga Puja. On the same day, a new charge was slapped on him—the murder of Himmat Patil and plunder of the latter's house.

Court proceedings began early on 9 October, with the courtroom filled to capacity, and a large crowd eagerly waiting for the court's stand. The judge was assisted by two assessors. In Case 32/1889, Tantya was sentenced to life for dismemberment and robbery. But the government, dissatisfied with the verdict, wanted nothing less than Tantya's execution. Tantya was therefore brought before the Deputy Commissioner of Police (DCP), and the charge of murder and robbery made against him on 5 October was re-examined. The DCP examined some of the evidence, heard the witnesses, and once more referred the case to the sessions court to try Tantya in Case 33/1889, for Himmat Patil's murder.[8] This was a calculated move to bring him to the gallows. On 16 October 1889, *CI* claimed that the murder charge against Tantya appeared insubstantial.

Bijania, Tantya's trusted lieutenant, had already been executed in the Himmat Patil murder case. Four cases of robbery had been first proved against Bijania for which he was sentenced to life. He was subsequently charged with Himmat Patil's murder, held guilty and executed. The argument now was that in a murder case, under Section 391 IPC, all members of the said culprit's group would be held responsible. The court collected statements of 18 witnesses, including Hamilton. The others were: Ganpat Singh (Khargone); Govind (Himmat Patil's son); Narayan (kotwal of Bhuiphal); Lungi and Rukri (Himmat's brothers); Gopal (Himmat's nephew); Daulat Singh (Maigaon); Bhika, Jasoda and Gajia (Pokhar); Lakshman (Dabhi); Sirdar, Sikdar, Maikum, Zalim, Madan and Posika.[9]

On 19 October 1889, Sessions Judge Lindsay Neil pronounced the death sentence on Tantya. It could hardly have been otherwise, with so many British officers inimical to Tantya. The British were ecstatic with the verdict, while the Bhils mourned their beloved hero.[10]

On Tantya's behalf, some lawyers petitioned Laurie as to why Tantya was being held responsible for a murder for which Bijania had already been executed. They demanded a commutation of the death sentence. On 19 November 1889, in Jabalpur Jail, Tantya affixed his thumb impression to the petition, which was presented to the judicial commissioner on 21 November by A.H.H. Hallet, the jail superintendent. As the judicial commissioner was then on leave, Lindsay Neil—the very man who had pronounced the death sentence—was deputising for him. The petition was, quite naturally, rejected.

Barrister T.W. Dhikkan, who practised in the Nagpur High Court, was a member of the Nagpur Bar. Along with Gopal Rao, Balwant Rao, Hory and other lawyers, Dhikkan sent a joint petition to Laurie, but this, too, was rejected. The date fixed by Laurie for Tantya's execution was 4 December 1889. Tantya's last wish to see his wife and children, Nathu and Kishan, was not granted, even though the superintendent of Jabalpur Central Jail had written to Laurie on 24 November to request a postponement of the execution so that his family could be brought to Jabalpur. But as the government was in a tearing hurry to ensure Tantya's end, his last wish was not honoured.

On the night of 3 December, Jabalpur swarmed with Bhils carrying bows and arrows. In view of the immense crowd, Tantya was executed within the jail premises on the morning of 4 December.[11]

Although several lawyers had made genuine efforts to have Tantya's sentence commuted, they failed dismally against the British judicial system. On 11 December 1889, *CI* reported that Tantya's relatives, who were present on the occasion, had expressed dissatisfaction with the sentence and had refused to accept his body for the last rites.

The Indian Robin Hood, Tantya Bheel, notwithstanding the endeavours made in many quarters to obtain mitigation of the capital sentence recently passed upon him, was executed at Jubbulpore on December 4. He persistently affirmed his innocence of the murder with which he was charged. Some of his relatives were present, but they declined to dispose of the body, on the ground that Tantya had been outcasted and rendered impure by execution. They expressed great dissatisfaction that he had accumulated no loot for the family.

Folklore has it that Tantya's body was either buried or disposed of in the jungle at Patalpani, where a Tantya temple still stands by the railway track. It was claimed that trains stopped there to salute the fallen Bhil hero. Both claims are highly debatable—no documents exist to corroborate the said disposal. The body of a renowned Bhil like Tantya could not have been so cavalierly discarded, as it would have hurt the sentiments of the large body of his supporters gathered to bid him farewell. Regarding trains stopping at Patalpani—the steep ascent is responsible for trains moving at slow speeds or halting briefly.[12]

Thus, from 1878 to 1889, all of Khandesh and other parts of the country resounded with tales of Tantya the bandit, who had rendered helpless the British Government, feudal lords, *malguzar*s and moneylenders alike. Tantya's daredevilry continued to astonish and confound British officers. His valour, generosity and commitment to the masses has resonated in popular culture, such as a film made about him and several folk songs. The great Bhil warrior's rebellious character and lofty humane values vis-à-vis the oppressed bestow on him a distinct identity. On 13 August 1890, the *Taunton Courier and Western Advertiser* published a piece, first carried in the *Pall Mall Gazette* on 23 June by a Bengali writer, titled 'Biography of an Indian Outlaw', which illustrates Tantya's greatness. An excerpt follows:

> He was no common outlaw, this Tantya; he had stuff in him of which through developing and refining agencies greatness in the best sense of the term is forged. Tantya set at nought and defied the constitutional authorities of the land—authorities whom a gracious providence has in his infinite mercy ordained as the saviour of India, but barring this sole circumstance, Tantya, when weighed in the moral balance, will hardly, we may say it without exaggeration, be found wanting. He had almost all the greatest virtues of which the entire body of human morality is composed. He had, first of all, disinterestedness, on which the whole edifice of morality is reared, and then justice and mercy, which dropping like the gentle rain, and verity and forbearance, and fortitude and courage, which cast out fear, and friendliness and reverence—in short, he had a heart filled with every excellency. His ear had heard the eternal melodies that are ceaselessly chanted forth by the spirit that is of sea and land, and the light of the setting sun and the deep heart of man. The life of such

a person is a study fraught with the most precious and ennobling instructions. Tantya was reckoned one of the principal Bheel outlaws in Central India. He committed many a dacoity at many a place, he set fire to many a village, he cut off many persons' noses and, standing at a distance, laughed merrily over their confusion and agony; he assisted at the murder of many a man and pillaging many a village he reduced many a man to the most abject poverty, yet we cannot restrain our tears for him, still we cannot repress the emotion that heaves and swells in our bosom. Whose heart will not be wrought up with an intense and burning grief at the sight of one ranging woods and free as a bird brought to such a plight at the treachery of a common man? From whose eyes tears will not trickle down in copious streams?

Pall Mall Gazette, 23 June 1890;
Taunton Courier and Western Advertiser, 13 August 1890

The dread of Tantya Bhil, and tales about him, haunted the British psyche for decades. Newspapers and journals in the United States, Australia and England were replete with news and anecdotes about him. On 29 November 1889, an article in the *Western Mail* compared him to Rob Roy of Scotland, who had successfully eluded the administration. The *SJG* published the following news on 9 September 1889, reproduced in the *New York Times* on 10 November 1889, briefly encapsulating Tantya Bhil's eventful life up to his last arrest.

ROBBER TANTYA BHEEL: INDIA'S ROBIN HOOD MAKES A FULL CONFESSION OF CRIMES

Tantya Bheel, the bold Robin Hood of the Central Provinces in India, who was recently captured, has just made a full confession, according to the *Pall Mall Gazette*. 'Fifteen years ago he left his village and took up the occupation of cultivator of land. He committed some minor police offense and was sentenced to a year's imprisonment in the Nagpur Jail. He was subsequently imprisoned in Jubbulpore Jail, and on his release settled in Holkar's territory, but was forced to take refuge in the jungle to escape arrest consequent on a false charge of robbery. He carried on petty depredations for a year, and was arrested and imprisoned in Khandwa Jail, whence he managed to escape. He then formed a dacoit band and commenced robberies on an extensive scale. His first dacoity was accompanied by murder, and his men next pillaged and burned a village. In one of his raids a policeman's nose was cut off. Subsequently Tantya raided Pokur, where he cut off the nose of a woman who had helped to betray him, and he robbed her daughter-in-law of all her jewels. At a robbery in the Behut [Betul] district he again cut off a policeman's nose. For the last two years, being much harassed by both the Central Provinces and Holkar's police, he got tired of his jungle wanderings; he was growing old, and his eyesight was failing. On commencing his career, he could travel sixty miles at a stretch, but now not more than twenty. The greater portion of his time was spent in Holkar's territory. He had never killed anybody himself, but had robbed the rich to help the poor.

Last year he distributed 6,000 rupees among the poor on the banks of the Narbada. He had frequently purchased bullocks for poor people.

He was eventually arrested through the treachery of a Gumpoot [Ganapat] Rajput, to whom he had frequently given large sums of money, with which the latter had promised to purchase him a pardon. He had latterly suffered severely from want of food and malaria through sleeping without shelter in the rain. He states that other bands are now committing extensive robberies in his name. Rajaram, a native magistrate accused of participating in Tantya's robberies, has been convicted by the Session Judge and sentenced to seven years rigorous imprisonment and fined 5,000 Rupees.

Tantya's popularity was so great that as early as 1889, B.L. Roy of Calcutta published a book in Bengali titled *Tantya Bhil* by Priyanath Mukhopadhyay.

The Gond state of Nagpur lived in terror of Tantya. On 7 June 1888, the House of Commons discussed a petition moved by Rani Moti Kunwar and Rani Basant Kunwar, widows of the late Gond king, Suleiman Shah of Nagpur. In this petition, the queens had alleged that the state's income had dwindled because of the notorious Tantya Bhil. He virtually ruled the northern Deogarh area of the state, they contended.[13]

On 20 May 1907, the *Evening News* published an article on Tantya:

THE THUG'S TREASURE:
AN ANCIENT SYSTEM OF MURDER

India has many false delusions, one of them being that crimes practised in days gone by are now extinct. I have seen it written, says a contributor to the 'Field,' that thuggee has been eradicated. It has been generally accepted that the fearful method of making away with mankind disclosed years ago by Mr Taylor in 'The Confessions of a Thug,' has disappeared but, in my opinion, as long as India is India, that ancient system of murder will remain as an heirloom to the race of Asiatic prone to that peculiar crime. The story I have to relate is indirectly connected with the dacoit Tantya and his followers.

It was in 1884 that I searched a certain watercourse in the Asseerghur jungles for tracks of tiger. I found them about five miles from a village called Kakria, in surroundings that suited my methods in every way for the erection of a machan, and I called upon my followers to tie up the buffalo and prepare the place for a kill. Near at hand was a temple, ancient and moss-bound. Much to my surprise, my men refused en masse to help me in any way. They at first offered all sorts of feeble objections to the position, which did not deceive me. I felt that there was some strong superstition or other feeling of repugnance which made them hostile to a machan being erected on that particular spot. I went to my tent and pondered, and whilst so doing my head shikaree approached me, and told me that he would explain matters to the best of his ability.

What the shikaree said to me I will endeavour to repeat in his own words. 'Sahib,' he said, 'Tantya the dacoit is in these regions. He is a friend of the poor, but bitter enemy of the Feringee sahib and the rich. He has murdered many men, and the riches he has gathered are hidden in many places. Cheetoo, one of his followers, has served you well and he once knew what I am saying is true.' It became known that Tantya Bheel had hidden half a lac of rupees in the vicinity of the temple near where you wish us to erect a Machan. Cheetoo, your late hunter, knew it also, and he communicated the news to his brother. They both resolved to gather the wealth whilst Tantya was elsewhere, and, having collected some digging implements, they set out at sundown for the temple. The treasure was actually buried beneath the temple idol. Cheetoo and his brother Rugoo never returned to their homes, and when two of their relatives set forth to find them, they likewise returned not. 'Some days after these events a brother of mine was hunting for thatch in the neighbourhood of the temple, and came across four dead bodies. Two of them were skeletons, the third was partially devoured, but the fourth, which was inside the temple, was—owing to the incident having occurred about Christmas—in a fair state of preservation. There were no wounds on the body, but simply a dark blue mark round the neck, proving strangulation by the thug's knotted handkerchief, and a bruise at the nape of the neck.' The shikaree added that Tantya had in his employ two renowned thugs, who could kill their victims before they reached the ground, and those experts watched Tantya's treasure. I was not surprised that the shikarees avoided the spot, though it was known that Tantya had long since lifted his ill-gotten gains and planted elsewhere.

A long poem, titled 'The National Congress Resolution and the Arms Act', referred to the manner in which Tantya's very name had terrorised the British. It was published in the *Homeward Mail from India China and the East* on 6 February 1888. An excerpt follows:

> But the Indian Government, always keen to please,
> Also gave parwanas to horrid men like these: —
> Yar Mahomed, Yusufzai, down to kill or steal,
> Chimbu Singh from Bikanir, Tantya the Bhil.

Within a year and a half of his execution, the *Border Watch* (Mount Gambier, SA) on 27 April 1892 published an article about him that described him as a thief extraordinaire. An excerpt follows:

THIEVING EXTRAORDINARY

As thieves, the Bheels still maintain their old prestige as the most adroit professionals in that branch of industry in India, and abounding in many types of roguery. Endless tales are told of their skill in stealing, and in escaping pursuit by tricks which would put the most knowing thieves of Europe to blush. They have been known to steal the blanket from under a sleeping man, who had been put on his guard that this would be attempted. The feat was simply accomplished by the thief tickling the face of the sleeper, and as involuntarily he turned himself under the slight titillation, the blanket was gently pulled bit by bit from under him.

Naked and oiled all over they move about noiselessly, and if grasped will eel-like slip out of the captor's grasp. If not, he will probably feel drawn across his wrist the sharp, razor like knife, which is always hung suspended round the thief's neck by means of a string. They have a trick of dropping poison on the leaves of the plantain bushes among which the cattle that they are not able to capture are grazing. In the morning the cattle being found dead, the carcasses are thrown away by the Hindoo owners. This quite suits the thieves' designs and calculations, for they immediately return, flay the dead animals, and sell the skins, which were what they were desirous of obtaining. The Bheels, on being pursued, have been known to escape among the burnt stumps which, owing to the prevalence of forest fires, cover considerable tracts of country in certain parts of India and allow the pursuing parties to pass them within a few yards by the expedient of throwing their black, sinewy, limbs into such attitudes that they would be mistaken for the scorched stumps among which they were hiding.

An amusing (and possibly even true) story in reference to this trick of theirs is often related. An English officer with a troop of cavalry was on one occasion pursuing a party of thieving

Bheels. The soldiers almost overtook the savages, when suddenly they lost sight of them behind a rock, and though a strict search was made until dusk they failed to find them. The day had been hot and the sun exhausting. The officer, imagining that in an open space like this the Bheels could not escape very far, ordered a halt near a clump of blackened stumps. Exhausted, he threw himself on the ground, hung his helmet on a scorched branch, and leaned his back against a stump. To his astonishment the stumps seemed to be coming alive before his eyes, loud chuckles came from them; in about a second or two he found himself thrown to the ground by the stump on which he was leaning, and his helmet seized by the very branch on which he had hung it. At the same time the other stumps became as suddenly metamorphosed into men, and before he or his men could recover from their astonishment, they had disappeared, carrying off the officer's helmet as the reward of their exertions! What he had taken for a clump of blackened stumps was the party of Bheel thieves, who had skilfully, after their usual manoeuvres thrown themselves into the attitudes which had imposed on their pursuers in so ludicrous a manner.

EPILOGUE

The Bhil tribes inhabiting the greater part of Indian soil once ruled over kingdoms in the hill tracts of Central India, Gujarat and Rajasthan. Their chiefs were the kings of those regions. Horse-riding invaders, driven out of Afghanistan and the neighbouring areas by Muslim aggressors, uprooted the Bhils from the plains of Rajasthan and Gujarat. Till then, the Bhils, an extremely simple-hearted and peace-loving people, lived contented lives with no private property. Upon displacement, they sought refuge in the Satpura hills.

The decline of Bhil power may be dated to this period. With their feudal orientation, Rajputs seized Bhil lands, compelling the Bhils to abandon their millennia-old way of life. Growing rebellious and violent in retaliation, the Bhils waged a bitter war against feudal chiefs, moneylenders, traders and finally, the British. For their own defence during the hard survival struggle, they brought the mountain passes under their control. For their livelihood, they collected taxes from traders and travellers passing through, or robbed them outright. Gradually, hunger turned the landless Bhils into plunderers and killers seeking safety in hills, valleys and forests, where it proved almost impossible to overcome them. Recognising the rebellious disposition of the Bhils, the British, on assuming control of Central India, conducted an assessment of the geostrategic importance of Bhil territories. They believed the British Empire had little to gain from Central India and Rajputana, where trade routes would remain unprotected as long as Bhil chiefs controlled the hill passes. Preferring to adopt the policy of appeasement, jagirs were restored to some Bhil chiefs, some were sanctioned pensions, while others were deployed at frontier checkposts. Finally, through the organisation of the Bhil Corps, the Bhils were metamorphosed into a disciplined army and incorporated into British armed might. In the second-half of the 19th century, Christian missionaries were encouraged to work among the Bhils to temper their rebelliousness. These missionaries attempted to bring Bhil communities into the mainstream through the spread of education, service and social work.

But while these measures brought some of the Bhils closer to the administration, new rebel groups continued to appear. The Bhil revolt thus began around 1800 and with some vicissitudes, continued incessantly till 1925— Bhils continued to fight and die. In addition, there were unimaginable deaths as a result of hunger and famine. However, when the nationwide Non-Cooperation Movement under the Congress and Mahatma Gandhi intensified, independent Bhil initiatives gradually petered out.

The atrocities committed by the Marathas and Rajputs against the Bhils before the advent of the British are counted in history as amongst the most ruthless of genocides, when tens of thousands of Bhils were done to death. Very little data are available about these genocides, although the present work has mentioned some of these cases. History records several episodes in which up to 15,000 Bhils were killed in one fell swoop, with record-keeping of such genocides making an appearance only after the arrival of the British. The Marathas treated the Bhils no better than wild animals; their ruthlessness and tyranny knew no bounds—the use of hot iron rods and chains on captured Bhils, and even burning them alive. It is hardly surprising, therefore, that the incensed Bhils had little compunction in committing heinous criminal acts against them.[1]

There were two jails in South Konkan before 1835—in Malwan and Malwan Bay—where the Bhils were incarcerated. In the latter was an island, with a fort—Sindhu Durg—where, before 1835, more than 60 Bhils were jailed, mercilessly beaten and subjected to inhuman treatment that claimed several Bhil lives. There was no appeal against it—the dead Bhils were simply thrown into the sea—as nobody was allowed to visit the island. It was the British who decided to shut down Butcher's Fort—as Sindhu Durg Fort Jail was commonly known—reported the *Bombay Gazette* on 18 February 1837.

From the very dawn of human civilisation, the 'civilised' have subjected tribals to unbounded atrocities, plundered their wealth, forests and lands and converted their cheap labour into handsome profit. Raw data from the 20th century reveal that, on average, 273 Bhils were killed every year in the three Bhil-preponderant districts of Madhya Pradesh—i.e. one Bhil was slaughtered every 32 hours—at a time when the entire Indian population numbered about 25 crore.[2] This gruesome culture of killings is ancient.

A section of the Bhil population threw in its lot with the British Government. But the marked cultural, social, physical and linguistic differences between the two races remained an insurmountable barrier, even though it was the British who made provision for permanent dwellings, education and employment for the Bhils. A section of the Bhils, who were not restored their authority and property, continued their insurrection. Seeking to subdue the Bhils, the British employed a combination of persuasion and repression. Wherever suppression failed, they employed the policy of reform, settlement, education and employment. Bhil settlements were created; the tribals were incorporated into the army and used against their rebellious brethren. As reported in *BG* on 21 May 1836, 'Mr Elphinstone converted the Bheels of the Deccan from robbers and murderers, into good subjects and preservers of the peace to retain in our pay or otherwise secure the interest of one or two of the most influential chiefs, making them responsible for the good behaviour of the rest.'

The British Government was responsible for drawing the Bhils out of forests and hills and integrating them in governance and administration. Using such enticements as salaries, lands and jagirs, it attempted to keep them from the path of rebellion. Emerging from the forests, Bhils now began to frequent the towns and bazaars. The Rajputs, too, came to the realisation that friendly relations with Bhils were to their own advantage. Several Bhil Corps were formed, a first important move. The second was to engage the Bhils in agriculture and the third was the restoration of some of the jagirs to their erstwhile holders, with partial autonomy. The rise of the Bhakta cult amongst them contributed significantly to the decline in criminality and violence. The propagation of Christianity by missionaries was another important factor, reported the *Belfast Newsletter* on 7 May 1915. Originally based in Calcutta, these missionaries established their headquarters at Indore and worked to effect social reform among the Bhils through Christianity, reported the *Newcastle Chronicle* on 13 April 1889. The combined effect of these factors as well as the rise of the national liberation movement contributed to the decline in Bhil insurgency after 1925. Documentation of any Bhil revolt before 1800 does not exist.

This book attempts to acquaint readers with more than 200 Bhil chiefs or rebels who were active between 1800 and 1925. Nevertheless, credit for their heroism still continues to elude Bhil heroes like Kaji Singh, Bhima Nayak and Tantya Bhil. The history which we read is, by and large, a history of suppression of a marginal people's interests, of their oppression by hegemonistic, elitist and tyrannical powers. But this is not the last word, as hundreds of Bhil heroes and their sacrifices are waiting to be discovered by future researchers—many of the darkest cellars are still to be opened.

NOTES

Prologue
1. W. Gordon Gordon-Cumming, *Wild Men and Wild Beasts: Scenes in Camp and Jungle*, 2nd edition (Edinburgh and London: Edmonston & Douglas, 1871), 181–82.
2. Bipin Chandra et al., *India's Struggle for Independence* (New Delhi: Penguin Books, 1989).
3. Charu Chandra Mukherjee, *The Life of Tantia Bhil: The Renowned Bandit Chief* (Calcutta: B.H. Dutt, 1890).
4. Baba Bhand, ed., *Jan Nayak Tantia Bhil and the Peasant and Tribal Movement: Source Material* (Bhopal: Swaraj Sansthan Directorate, 2001).

PART I

Chapter 1—Bhil Tribes: General Introduction

1. William Gordon Gordon-Cumming, *Wild Men and Wild Beasts: Scenes in Camp and Jungle*, 2nd edition (Edinburgh and London: Edmonston & Douglas, 1871), 180.
2. Subhash Meena and Nitesh Pal Singh Meena, 'Historical Perspectives of Different Tribal Groups in India,' *International Journal of Interdisciplinary and Multidisciplinary Studies* (IJIMS) 1, no. 10 (2014): 50.
3. Braj Kishore Sharma, *Tribal Revolts* (Jaipur: Pointer Publishers, 1996), 5.
4. M.A. Ansari, *Tribals in Criminal Web* (Jaipur: Publication Scheme, 1987), 69.
5. https://trci.tripura.gov.in/bhil; reserchgate.net/Bhil in Pakistan/ Hussain Ghulam, Bielefeld University/August 2020.
6. Braj Kishore Sharma, *Rajasthan Mein Kisan Evam Adivasi Andolan* (*Peasant and Tribal Movements in Rajasthan*), in Hindi, 9th edition (Jaipur: Rajasthan Hindi Granth Academy, 2019), 1, 3.

7. Sharma, *Tribal Revolts*, 1–2.
8. Meena and Meena, 'Historical Perspectives,' 50.
9. D. Graham, *A Brief Historical Sketch of the Bheel Tribes Inhabiting the Province of Khandesh* (London: British Library, Historical Print Editions, 1843), 1–2.
10. P.C. Jain, *Christianity, Ideology and Social Change among Tribals* (Jaipur: Rawat Publications, 1995), 76.
11. *Imperial Gazetteer of India*, Provincial Series, Bombay Presidency, vol. I (Calcutta: Superintendent of Government Printing, 1909), 149–52.
12. R.V. Russell and Hira Lal, *The Tribes and Castes of the Central Provinces of India*, vol. II (New Delhi and Madras: Asian Educational Services, 1993), 293.
13. Meena and Meena, 'Historical Perspectives,' 50–51.
14. London Church Missionary, *Society, Battling and Building amongst the Bhils* (London: Salisbury Square, EC, 1914), 11.
15. Ansari, *Tribals in Criminal* Web, 71–72.
16. Meena and Meena, 'Historical Perspectives,' 50–51.
17. Russell and Hira Lal, *Tribes and Castes*, 293.
18. National Archives of India (NAI), Foreign Department, Notes, file no. 2212/1869, *A Short History of the Mewar Bhil Corps* (August 1890).

Chapter 2—Khandesh and Its Bhils

1. William Wilson Hunter, *Imperial Gazetteer of India*, vol. XV, 1908–1931 (Oxford: Clarendon Press, 1908), 225–26.
2. D. Graham, *A Brief Historical Sketch of the Bheel Tribes Inhabiting the Province of Khandesh* (London: British Library, Historical Print Editions, 1843), 1; A. K. Prasad, *The Bhils of Khandesh Under the British East India Company*, Thesis (Poona: University of Poona, 1986), 8–10.
3. Evans Bell, *Memoir of General John Briggs of the Madras Army; With Comments on Some of His Words and Works* (Picadilly: Chatto and Windus, 1885), 82.
4. Baba Bhand, *Jan Nayak Tantia Bhil (Tantia Bhil: A People's Hero)*, in Hindi, (Delhi: Prabhat Prakashan, 2014), 5.
5. Hunter, *Imperial Gazetteer of India*, 225–26; Stewart Gordon, T*he New Cambridge History of India*, vol. II, no. 4: The Marathas 1600–1818 (Cambridge University Press, 2008), 139.
6. *Gazetteer of the Bombay Presidency*, vol. XII (Government General Press, 1880), 1; Prasad, *Bhils of Khandesh*, 3.
7. Maharashtra State Archives, Mumbai (MSAM), vol. 14/398 (Mumbai: Political Department, 1830); Prasad, *Bhils of Khandesh*, 3.

8. Bell, *Memoir of General John Briggs*, 75–76.
9. *Gazetteer of the Bombay Presidency*, vol. XII, 252, 254.
10. A. H. A. Simcox, *Khandesh Bhil Corps* (Bombay: Thacker & Company Limited, 1912), 1–2.
11. D.C. Graham, *A Brief Historical Sketch of the Bheel Tribes Inhabiting the Province of Khandesh* (British Library, Historical Print Editions, 1843), 1–4.
12. Graham, *Brief Historical Sketch of the Bhil Tribes*, 4–5.

Chapter 3—British Policy Towards the Bhils of Central India and Khandesh

1. *Imperial Gazetteer of India*, Central India (Calcutta: Superintendent of Government Printing, 1908), 1.
2. *Gazetteer of the Bombay Presidency*, vol. XII (Government General Press, 1880), 254; Evans Bell, *Memoir of General John Briggs of the Madras Army: With Comments on Some of His Words and Works* (Picadilly: Chatto and Windus, 1885), 41, 53–54; A. K. Prasad, *The Bhils of Khandesh Under the British East India Company*, Thesis (Poona: University of Poona), 8–10.
3. Bell, *Memoir of General John Briggs*, 41, 53–56; A. H. A. Simcox, *Khandesh Bhil Corps* (Bombay: Thacker & Company Limited, 1912), 15; Prasad, *Bhils of Khandesh*, 38–39.
4. Bell, *Memoir of General John Briggs*, 75, 78; Prasad, *Bhils of Khandesh*, 3.
5. Bell, *Memoir of General John Briggs*, 56, 61; N. Benjamin and B. B. Mohanty, 'Imperial Solution of a Colonial Problem: Bhils of Khandesh up to c. 1850,' *Modern Asian Studies* 41, no. 2 (Cambridge University Press, 2007), 343–44.
6. Bell, *Memoir of General John Briggs*, 77–79.
7. *Maharashtra State Gazetteers*, Jalgaon District, revised second edition (1962), 104–105; Prasad, *Bhils of Khandesh*, 146–55.
8. Bell, *Memoir of General John Briggs*, 56, 61, 78–81; Benjamin and Mohanty, 'Imperial Solution of a Colonial Problem,' 343–44.
9. D.C. Graham, *A Brief Historical Sketch of the Bheel Tribes Inhabiting the Province of Khandesh* (British Library, Historical Print Editions, 1843), 1–5.
10. Maharashtra State Archives, Mumbai (MSAM), Political Dept., vol. 10/193 (1825); Benjamin and Mohanty, 'Imperial Solution of a Colonial Problem,' 348–50.
11. Graham, *Brief Historical Sketch of the Bheel Tribes*, 6–7.
12. Benjamin and Mohanty, 'Imperial Solution of a Colonial Problem,' 351.
13. Benjamin and Mohanty, 'Imperial Solution of a Colonial Problem,' 351–52; MSAM, vol. 10/193; Prasad, *Bhils of Khandesh*, 36.
14. Graham, *Brief Historical Sketch of the Bheel Tribes*, 8–14.

15. *Maharashtra State Gazetteers*, 107–108.
16. *Imperial Gazetteer of India*, vol. XXII, Digital South Asia Library, 103.

Chapter 4—Bhil Revolt and Its Leaders in Khandesh and Central India

1. Braj Kishore Sharma, *Tribal Revolts* (Jaipur: Pointer Publishers, 1996), 6–7.
2. Maharashtra State Archives, Mumbai (MSAM), Political Dept., vol. 10/105 (1823); N. Benjamin and B. B. Mohanty, 'Imperial Solution of a Colonial Problem: Bhils of Khandesh up to c. 1850,' *Modern Asian Studies* 41, no. 2 (Cambridge University Press, 2007), 347.
3. *Gazetteer of the Bombay Presidency*, vol. XVI, Nasik (Bombay: Government Central Press, 1883), 194.
4. *Gazetteer of the Bombay Presidency*, vol. XII, Khandesh (Bombay: Government Central Press, 1880), 254; *Maharashtra State Gazetteers*, Jalgaon District, revised second edition (1962), 91, 94; *Maharashtra State Gazetteers*, Ahmednagar District, revised edition, (Gazetteers Department, Government of Maharashtra, 1976), 137.
5. *Gazetteer of the Bombay Presidency*, Nasik, 194–95.
6. *Gazetteer of the Bombay Presidency*, Khandesh, 254; *Maharashtra State Gazetteers*, Jalgaon District, 91, 94; *Maharashtra State Gazetteers*, Ahmednagar District, 137.
7. *Maharashtra State Gazetteers*, Jalgaon District, 93.
8. R. C. Majumdar, *The Sepoy Mutiny and Revolt of 1857*, 1st edition (Firma K. L. Mukhopadyay, Calcutta Oriental Press, 1957), 40.
9. Evans Bell, *Memoir of General John Briggs of the Madras Army: With Comments on Some of His Words and Works* (Picadilly: Chatto and Windus, 1885), 71–72.
10. John Malcolm, *A Memoir of Central India, Including Malwa, and Adjoining Provinces: With the History and Copious Illustrations of the Past and Present Condition of the Country*, (London: Kingsbury, Parbury and Allen, 1828), vol. 1, 522–25; vol. 2, 421.
11. Malcolm, *A Memoir of Central India*, vol. 1, 522–25, vol. 2, 421–22; National Archives of India (NAI), Hyderabad, vol. 556, 1–170, 1 April 1820 to 30 July 1820, 'Nadir Singh—Report on the Character' (New Delhi).
12. Arvind M. Deshpande, *John Briggs in Maharashtra: A Study of District Administration Under Early British Rule* (Delhi: Mittal Publications, 1987), 86–88; Ajay Sharika, *Being Jangli: The Politics of Wildness* (New Delhi: Sage Publications, 1998), 131, 135.
13. Bell, *Memoir of General John Briggs*, 78–79; *Gazetteer of the Bombay Presidency*, Khandesh, 257; *Maharashtra State Gazetteers*, Jalgaon District, 104–105.

14. A. K. Prasad, *The Bhils of Khandesh Under the British East India Company, 1818-1858*, (New Delhi: Konark Publishers,1991), 148-49; Alf Gunvald Nilsen, 'Subalterns and the State in the *Longue Durée*: Notes from "The Rebellious Century" in the Bhil Heartland,' *Journal of Contemporary Asia* 45, no. 4 (April 2015), 575-95; *Gazetteer of the Bombay Presidency*, Khandesh, 257; *Maharashtra State Gazetteers*, Jalgaon District, 104-105.
15. Deshpande, *John Briggs in Maharashtra*, 104; Sashi Bhusan Chaudhuri, *Civil Disturbances During the British Rule in India (1765-1857)* (Calcutta: The World Press Ltd., 1955), 158.
16. *Gazetteer of the Bombay Presidency*, Khandesh, 257; Chaudhuri, *Civil Disturbances*, 158; also see 'Bhil Disturbances', The Gazetteers Department, Maharashtra, https://www.gazetteers.maharashtra.gov.in/cultural.maharashtra.gov.in/english/gazetteer/DHULIA/his_british%20period.html
17. *Gazetteer of the Bombay Presidency*, Khandesh, 253; Deshpande, *John Briggs in Maharashtra*,104, 137.
18. 'Bhil Disturbances', The Gazetteers Department, Maharashtra, https://www.gazetteers.maharashtra.gov.in/cultural.maharashtra.gov.in/english/gazetteer/DHULIA/his_british%20period.html
19. *Gazetteer of the Bombay Presidency*, Khandesh, 257.
20. 'Bhil Disturbances', The Gazetteers Department, Maharashtra, https://www.gazetteers.maharashtra.gov.in/cultural.maharashtra.gov.in/english/gazetteer/DHULIA/his_british%20period.html
21. British Library, London, Reference: IOR/F/4/1026/28138, Papers regarding an affray which took place at Bari, a village in Alirajpur on 14 December 1824.
22. British Library, London, Reference: IOR/F/4/1021/28048, Bombay Political, Insurrection in Baglan.
23. *Maharashtra State Gazetteers*, Jalgaon District, 106.
24. British Library, London, Reference: IOR/F/4/1021/28048, Bombay Political, Insurrection in Baglan. A muqaddam was a village chief through whom the government controlled the villagers. A *mamlatdar* was a local revenue official like a tehsildar of a taluka.
25. Ibid. Gomasta (gumashta) was an Indian agent of the East India Company who supplied the Company with items prepared by the local artisans or weavers.
26. *Maharashtra State Gazetteers*, Jalgaon District, 107; Chaudhuri, *Civil Disturbances*, 159-60.
27. 'Arrow in the Skull: Conflict with the Bheels, 1833', Britain's Small Forgotten Wars, http://www.britainsmallwars.co.uk/arrow-in-the-skull-conflict-with-the-bheels-1833.html
28. *Maharashtra State Gazetteers*, Jalgaon District, 108-109.

29. Dafadar was a post in the Indian cavalry, equivalent to sargent in the British Indian Army. A risaldar was a commander in the Indian cavalry; it was a medium-level position.
30. *Maharashtra State Gazetteers*, Jalgaon District, 109; A. K. Prasad, *The Bhils of Khandesh Under the British East India Company*, Thesis (Poona: University of Poona, 1986), 147.
31. Prasad, *Bhils of Khandesh*, Thesis, 147.
32. *Maharashtra State Gazetteers*, Jalgaon District, 109–11. *Mahalkari* was a revenue official in charge of revenue collection in a *mahal*, a unit of land settlement. A *deshmukh* was a jagirdar administering and monitoring revenue collection in a certain number of villages. A *deshpande* was a jagirdar who maintained the revenue records in a certain number of villages.
33. *Gazetteer of the Bombay Presidency*, Khandesh, 262.
34. S. C. Verma, *The Bhil Kills* (Delhi: Kunj Publishing House, 1908), 14.
35. *Maharashtra State Gazetteers*, Ahmednagar District, 144–45.
36. *Maharashtra State Gazetteers*, Ahmednagar District, 145–46; *Gazetteer of the Bombay Presidency*, Nasik, 200.
37. *Gazetteer of the Bombay Presidency*, Nasik, 200–202.
38. Makranees or Makranis were a warrior caste from Makrana in Balochistan, who had settled in Gujarat, Dadra and Nagar Haveli, etc. See N. K. Singh and A. M. Khan, eds., *Encyclopaedia of the World Muslims: Tribes, Castes and Communities*, vol. 1 (New Delhi: Global Vision Publishing House, 2001).
39. Shiv Narayan Yadav, *1857 Swadhinta Sangram mein Janjatiya Balidan*, (*Tribal Sacrifices in the War of Independence, 1857*), in Hindi (Swaraj Sansthan Sanchanalaya, 2008), 205, 207, 209, 213.
40. National Archives of India (NAI), CIA, file no. 2099, 6 October 1858. Letter from the Political Assistant of Nimar, addressed to the AGGCI.
41. NAI, CIA, file no. 3907, 3 November 1858, New Delhi.
42. *Maharashtra State Gazetteers*, Jalgaon District, 112; *Maharashtra State Gazetteers*, Ahmednagar District, 146.
43. NAI, CIA, Bhopawar Agency, file no. 1427, 1858. Proceedings in the Case of Certain Bheels Concerned in the Burning of the Gujari Dak Bungalow.
44. NAI, Office of Agent Governor General for Central India, file no. 34, Bhikari Naik, 1867–68. Indore Durbar, Khandesh Bheel Naiks.

Chapter 5—Bhil Revolts in the Khandesh Frontier Region and Maharashtra after 1858

1. *Maharashtra State Gazetteers*, Ahmednagar District, revised edition (Gazetteers Department: Government of Maharashtra, 1976), 145–46; *Gazetteer of the Bombay Presidency*, vol. XVI, Nasik (Bombay: Government Central Press, 1883), 203.

2. *Gazetteer of the Bombay Presidency*, vol. XVI, Nasik, 203.
3. *Maharashtra State Gazetteers*, Jalgaon District, revised second edition (Gazetteers Department: Government of Maharashtra, 1962), 112; *Maharashtra State Gazetteers*, Ahmednagar District, 146.
4. *Ziladar (jiladar)* was a minor official. In areas where zamindari was practised, he was deputed to collect taxes in a particular territory; he also managed canals and opium cultivation.
5. *Maharashtra State Gazetteers*, Ahmednagar District, 146.
6. National Archives of India (NAI), Foreign Department, Political–B, file nos. 29–30, February 1882.
7. NAI, Foreign Department, Political–A, file nos. 294–99, 1870.
8. Charu Chandra Mukherjee, *The Life of Tantia Bhil: The Renowned Bandit Chief* (Calcutta: B.H. Dutt, 1890), 60.

Chapter 6—Bhil Revolts Post-1833: Barwani and Alirajpur

1. Shashank Kela, *A Rogue and Peasant Slave: Adivasi Resistance, 1800–2000* (Delhi: Navayana Publishing, 2012), 130–36.
2. National Archives of India (NAI), Central India Agency (CIA), Bhopawar Agency, file no. 734, 1858.
3. *Maharashtra State Gazetteers*, Jalgaon District, revised second edition (Gazetteers Department: Government of Maharashtra, 1962), 111; NAI, CIA, Bhopawar Agency, file no. 137, 1860.
4. K. S. Singh, 'The Tribals and the 1857 Uprising,' *Social Scientist* 26, no. 1 (January–April 1998), 83–84.
5. *Maharashtra State Gazetteers*, Jalgaon District, 112.
6. NAI, CIA, file no. 137, 22 October 1857. Letter from Mr Masefield addressed to the AGGCI.
7. *Maharashtra State Gazetteers*, Jalgaon District, 112.
8. Ibid.; Shiv Narayan Yadav, *1857 Swadhinta Sangram mein Janjatiya Balidan*, Hindi (*Tribal Sacrifices in the War of Independence, 1857*) (Swaraj Sansthan Sanchanalaya, 2008), 244.
9. NAI, CIA, file no. 1420, 28 June 1858. Letter from the Office of Political Assistant of Nimar, addressed to the AGGCI.
10. NAI, CIA, file no. 1420, 20 August 1858. Letter from the Office of Political Assistant of Nimar, addressed to the AGGCI; NAI, CIA, file no. 1774, 20 November 1858.
11. NAI, CIA, Bhopawar Agency, letter no. 272, 29 August 1859.
12. Yadav, *1857 Swadhinta Sangram*, 244–45.
13. NAI, CIA, Bhopawar Agency, file no. 137, 1860.
14. NAI, CIA, Bhopawar Agency, file no. 140, 26 June 1860.
15. Kela, *A Rogue and Peasant Slave*, 149.
16. NAI, CIA, file no. 743, 2 May 1861. Letter from the Political Agent of Nimar, addressed to the AGGCI.

17. NAI, CIA, file no. 3072, 12 June 1861. Letter from the leader secretary to Government of India, addressed to the AGGCI.
18. Yadav, *1857 Swadhinta Sangram*, 260-61.
19. NAI, CIA, Bhopawar Agency, letter no. 455, 24 February 1859, and letter no. 134, 1 April 1861.
20. Yadav, *1857 Swadhinta Sangram*, 248-50.
21. NAI, CIA, file no. 1422, 29 March 1860; NAI, CIA, Bhopawar Agency, letter no. 115, 28 February 1860, and letter no. 73, 11 March 1861; NAI, CIA, Bhopawar Agency, letter no. 664, 31 December 1859.
22. NAI, CIA, Bhopawar Agency, letter no. 115, 28 February 1860, and letter no. 73, 11 March 1861; NAI, CIA, Bhopawar Agency, letter no. 664, 31 December 1859.
23. NAI, CIA, file no. 1058, 24 July 1861. Letter from the Political Agent, Nimar, addressed to R. Shakespear Bart.
24. NAI, CIA, Bhopawar Agency, letter no. 399, 26 March 1861; letter no. 272, 29 August 1859; letter no. 45, 24 January1860; letter no. 115, 28 February 1860.
25. Kela, *A Rogue and Peasant Slave*, 168-70.
26. NAI, CIA, Bhopawar Agency, letter no. 33, 31 May 1867.
27. NAI, CIA, file no. 49, 11 January 1859. Letter from the Commanding Officer, 1st Cavalry, HC, addressed to the AGGCI.
28. NAI, CIA, file no. 217, 28 March 1862. Telegram from Maj. Keating to Maj. Meade; NAI, CIA, Bhopawar Agency, file no. 145, 1862-70.
29. NAI, CIA, Bhopawar Agency, file no. 144, 1862.
30. NAI, CIA, Bhopawar Agency, file no. 145, 1862-70.
31. NAI, CIA, Bhopawar Agency, file no. 508, 1864-65.
32. NAI, CIA, Bhopawar Agency, file no. 1477 & 1474, 1869, and file no. 871, 1868.
33. NAI, CIA, Bhopal Agency, file no. 510, 1872, and file no. 512, 1873.
34. NAI, CIA, Bhopal Agency, file no. 512, 1873.
35. NAI, CIA, file no. 10, 30 March 1875. Indore letter receipts. It submits the opinion of the Barwani Durbar for punishing some of the Barwani Bhils who committed robbery in Holkar's district.
36. NAI, CIA, Bhopawar Agency, file no. 509, 1872-78.
37. Kela, *A Rogue and Peasant Slave*, 208-10.
38. NAI, CIA, Bhopal Agency, file no. 1135, 1873-98, and file no. 1715, 1874.

PART II

Chapter 7—Rajputana, Rewa Kantha and Mahi Kantha Agencies: General Introduction

1. National Archives India, Home Education-B, 1889, 'Students History of Rajputana,' New Delhi.

2. Braj Kishore Sharma, *Rajasthan mein Kisan evam Adivasi Andolan* (*Peasant and Tribal Movements in Rajasthan*), in Hindi, 9th edition (Jaipur: Rajasthan Hindi Granth Academy, 2019), 2, 5, 7.
3. R. V. Russell and Hira Lal, T*ribes and Castes of the Central Provinces of India*, vol. II (London: Macmillan & Co. Limited, 1916), 279–80.
4. Sharma, *Rajasthan mein Kisan*, 7–8; NAI, Foreign Department, notes, file no. 2212/1869, 'A Short History of the Meywar Bhil Corps,' August 1890.
5. Braj Kishore Sharma, *Tribal Revolts* (Jaipur: Pointer Publishers, 1996), 8–9.
6. *Rewa Kantha Directory,* vol. I (Rajkot: Parmar Press, 1922), 1–8.
7. *Mahi Kantha Directory*, vol. I (Rajkot: Liberal Laxmi Printing Press, 1922), 2–3, 16, 22, 46.
8. *Gazetteer of the Bombay Presidency,* vol. I, part I, 'History of Gujarat' (Bombay: Government Central Press, 1896), 424.
9. Sharma, *Rajasthan mein Kisan evam Adivasi Andolan*, 9, 35–36.
10. *Rajputana Gazetteer*, vol. II–A (Ajmer, 1905), 26, 32; *Rajputana Gazetteer*, vol. I (Calcutta, 1879), 1.
11. Sharma, *Rajasthan mein Kisan evam Adivasi Andolan*, 35–37.
12. Report on the Administration of the Dungarpur State for the Samvat Year 1970–71(AD 1913–14), published by Authority Rawalpindi, printed by J. R. Thapar & Sons at the Egerton Press, 1, 4.
13. Sharma, *Rajasthan mein Kisan evam Adivasi Andolan*, 37–40.

Chapter 8—Bhil Revolts and Their Heroes in Rajputana, Rewa Kantha and Mahi Kantha

1. British Library, London, Reference: IOR/F/4/1027/28142, 'The Notorious Bhil Robber Jagga Rawat is Ordered to be Confined,' 1826, and OR/F/4/1253/50487, 'Further Information Supplied Regarding the Antecedents of the Bhil Robber Jagga Rawat,' July 1826.
2. Ibid. Malwa then had six divisions, including Kauntel (HQ: Mandsaur) and Bagar (HQ: Banswara). Other divisions were Rath (HQ: Jhabua and Jobat), Sondwara (HQ: Mahdipur), Umatwara (HQ: Rajgarh and Narsinghgarh) and Khichiwara (HQ: Raghogarh).
3. Selections from the Records of the Bombay Government, vol. XXIII, new series, part II, 'Bheel Settlements,' (Bombay Education Society Press, 1856), 701, 703–709, 715, 717, 722–723, 733; British Library, London, Reference: IOR/R/2/524/270, File 4A/144A, 1824.
4. British Library, London, Reference: IOR/R/2/524/270, File 4A/144A, 1824.
5. Braj Kishore Sharma, *Rajasthan mein Kisan evam Adivasi Andolan* (*Peasant and Tribal Movements in Rajasthan*), in Hindi, 9th edition (Jaipur: Rajasthan Hindi Granth Academy, 2019), 40.

6. National Archives of India (NAI), Foreign Department, Internal-A, file nos. 52-55, March 1890.
7. NAI, Ministry of States, Political, file no. 361-P/49, 1950.
8. Sharma, *Rajasthan mein Kisan*, 38; NAI, Foreign Department, Notes, file no. 2212/1869. 'A Short History of the Meywar Bhil Corps,' August 1890.
9. NAI, Foreign Department, Notes, file no. 2212/1869. 'A Short History of the Meywar Bhil Corps,' August 1890.
10. Sharma, *Rajasthan mein Kisan*, 38.
11. NAI, Rajputana Agency, Political (Dungarpur), 1835, file-progs. no. 1-Dungarpur 1835.
12. *Mayo Constitution*, 24 September 1838.
13. NAI, Rajputana Agency, Political 183, file no. 6-Banswara (old)-II/1837-38.
14. Sharma, *Rajasthan mein Kisan*, 39, 41.
15. *Mahi Kantha Directory*, vol. I (Rajkot: Liberal Laxmi Printing Press, 1922), 50-51.
16. *Rewa Kantha Directory*, vol. I (Rajkot: Parmar Press, 1922), 9-11.
17. G. N. Sharma, ed., *Social and Political Awakening Among the Tribals of Rajasthan* (Jaipur: Centre for Rajasthan Studies, University of Rajasthan, 1947), 12.
18. NAI, Central India Agency (CIA), file no. 4, 13 December 1858, New Delhi. Letter from Sir R. Shakespear Bart, addressed to the AGGCI.
19. NAI, CIA, file no. 382, 7 March 1889, New Delhi. Letter from the political commissioner of Gujrat, addressed to the AGGCI; NAI, CIA, file no. 594, 4 April 1859. Letter from the PA, Rewa Kantha, addressed to the AGGCI.
20. Sharma, *Rajasthan mein Kisan*, 43.
21. NAI, CIA, file no. 686, 20 August, 1863, New Delhi, Letter from the AGG, Rajputana, to the AGGCI.
22. NAI, CIA, Malwa Agency, file no. 287, 1863.
23. NAI, CIA, Malwa Agency, file no. 290, 1864.
24. Sharma, *Rajasthan mein Kisan*, 43.
25. NAI, Foreign Department, Political, file no. 90-92, May 1868.
26. NAI, Foreign Department, Political-A, file no. 38, August 1867.
27. Sharma, *Rajasthan mein Kisan*, 43-44.
28. NAI, Foreign Department, Political, file no. 2, Part B, May 1873.
29. Biswamoy Pati, ed., *Issues in Modern Indian History: For Sumit Sarkar* (Mumbai: Popular Prakashan, 2000), 75-76, 84; NAI, Foreign Department, Political-A, file nos. 313-334, August 1881, New Delhi.
30. Pati, *Issues in Modern Indian History*, 75-84.
31. NAI, Foreign Department, Political-A, file nos. 313-334, August 1881, New Delhi.
32. Pati, *Issues in Modern Indian History*, 86, 88-89.

33. NAI, Foreign Department, Political-A, file nos. 313-334, August 1881, New Delhi.
34. NAI, Foreign Department, Internal, file nos. 52-55, 1890, New Delhi.
35. NAI, Foreign Department, Political-A, file nos. 313-334, August 1881, New Delhi.
36. NAI, Defence-A, 1900-08, File Defence-A-1900-August-60-66, Delhi.
37. Rowena Robinson and Joseph Marianus Kujur, eds., *Margins of Faith: Dalit and Tribal Christianity in India*, (India: Sage Publications, 2010), 214.
    The Chappania Famine (1899-1900) hit the Bhils very hard. 'The loss of life from starvation and disease was terrible, and was made worse by looting, for many were killed in defending their homes, and the survivors were left without food or the means wherewith to buy it.' The commanding officer of the Bhil Corps wrote, 'Every palm tree has been cut down, pounded between stones, and eaten, and now only the black rocks and sun-baked mud are left. All cattle are dead or eaten, and water is dried up in nearly all the wells.' Thompson, who threw himself into relief works for the Bhils, died of the cholera that followed. The successors of Thompson continued the work and reaped fruits in the form of conversion of a number of Bhagats. Cited by Lobo, 1991: 43.
38. NAI, Home Department, Public-B, file nos. 315-317, October 1901, New Delhi.
39. V. K. Vashisth, 'The Bhil Revolt of 1913 Under Guru Govind Giri,' *Proceedings of the Indian History Congress* 52 (1991), 522-23.
    The term 'Bundi Dashnami' refers to the Dashnami sect originating in the Bundi state. Essentially, it was similar to Dadu Dayal's sect or the sect of the formless god. However, most documents refer to it as Nathpanthi. Its religious rites had no place for Brahmins.
40. Subhash Chandra Kushwaha, *Kabir hain ki Marte Nahin* (*Kabir Never Dies*), in Hindi (Allahabad: Anamika Prakashan, 2020), 77.
41. Vashisth, 'The Bhil Revolt of 1913,' 522-23.
42. Sharma, *Rajasthan mein Kisan*, 9; Rima Hooja, *Rajasthan: A Concise History* (Delhi: Rupa Publications India Pvt. Ltd., 2018), 711.
43. Stephen Puchs, 'Messianic Movements in Primitive India,' *Asian Folklore Studies* 24, no. 1 (1965), 50-52.
44. Vashisth, 'The Bhil Revolt of 1913,' 522-23.
45. Vashisth, 'The Bhil Revolt of 1913,' 523-24; *Rewa Kantha Directory* (revised edition), vol. I, (Rajkot: Parmar Press, 1922), 25.
46. Vashisth, 'The Bhil Revolt of 1913,' 524; *Rajasthan District Gazetteers*, Banswara, K. K. Sahgal, Directorate, District Gazetteers, Government of Rajasthan, Jaipur, 1974, p 34; *Rewa Kantha Directory*, 25.
47. Vashisth, 'The Bhil Revolt of 1913,' 525; *Rewa Kantha Directory*, 25.

48. *Rajasthan District Gazetteers,* Banswara, 34; 'Report on the Administration of the Dungarpur State for the Samvat Year 1970– 71(AD 1913–14),' published by Authority Rawalpindi, printed by J. R. Thapar & Sons at the Egerton Press, 4.
49. Subhash Chandra Kushwaha, *Awadh ka Kisan Vidroh (Peasant Revolt in Awadh),* in Hindi (Rajkamal Prakashan, 2018), 146.
50. Vashisth, 'The Bhil Revolt of 1913,' 525.
51. *Rewa Kantha Directory,* 26; *Rajasthan District Gazetteers,* Banswara, 34.
52. Uday Mahurkar, 'Descendents of Mangadh massacre seek recognition of past tragedy', India Today, 10 Sept. 2012, https://www.indiatoday.in/magazine/special-report/story/20120910-jallianwala-bagh-in-gujarat-brutal-tribal-massacre-gujarat-rajasthan-border-759622-1999-11-29
53. Puchs, 'Messianic Movements in Primitive India,' 53.
54. NAI, Home Department, Political, file no. 300. 'A Fortnightly Memorandum of the Internal Situation in Rajputana for the Period Ending 31 August 1921,' New Delhi.
55. Sharma, *Rajasthan mein Kisan,* 108–109.
56. Prithvi Singh Mehta, *Hamara Rajasthan* (Our Rajasthan), in Hindi (Jalandhar and Allahabad: Hindi Bhavan), 358.
57. Sharma, *Rajasthan mein Kisan,* 109.
58. Kushwaha, *Awadh ka Kisan Vidroh,* 246.
59. Sharma, *Rajasthan mein Kisan,* 110–12; British Library, London, Foreign and Political Department, file no. 954–International, Secret/1923, Reference: IOR/R/1/1/1419.
60. British Library, London, Foreign and Political Department, file no 954–International, Secret/1923, Reference: IOR/R/1/1/1419.
61. NAI, Home Department, Political, file no. 18, part I, April 1922, New Delhi.
62. British Library, London, Foreign and Political Department, file no. 954–International, Secret/1923, Reference: IOR/R/1/1/1419.
63. NAI, Foreign and Political Department, file no. 428P (Secret), 1923, New Delhi.
64. British Library, London, Foreign and Political Department, file no. 954–International, Secret/1923, Reference: IOR/R/1/1/1419.
65. NAI, Foreign and Political Department, file no. 428P (Secret), 1923, New Delhi.
66. British Library, London, Foreign and Political Department, file no. 954–International, Secret/1923, Reference: IOR/R/1/1/1419; NAI, Foreign and Political Department, file no. 428P, Secret/1923, New Delhi.
67. NAI, Home Department, Political, file no. 300/1921. 'A Fortnightly Memorandum of the Internal Situation in Rajputana for the Period

Ending 31 August 1921,' New Delhi; NAI, Foreign and Political Department, file no. 428P, Secret/1923, New Delhi.
68. British Library, London, Foreign and Political Department, file no. 954–International, Secret/1923, Reference: IOR/R/1/1/1419.
69. NAI, Foreign and Political Department, file no. 428P, Secret/1923, New Delhi; Rajasthan State Archives, Udaipur Confidential Records, file no. 40, bag no. 4.

PART III

Chapter 9—Tantya Bhil: The Great Indian Moonlighter

1. *Chand* (Hindi magazine) 1, no. 1 (November 1928). The reference is to the special Phansi (Gallows) Issue, edited by Acharya Chatur Sen Shastri (Golden Jubilee, 2009). Originally published during the British Raj, the publication featured a number of revolutionaries who were sent to the gallows. Predictably, copies of the publication were immediately confiscated by the police, and it was proscribed. Hereafter, it has been referred to as *Chand: Phansi (Gallows)*. See p. 34.
2. Ushakiran Agrawal, 'Psychological Aspects of Tantia Bheel's Revolution,' IOSR-JHSS 20, no. 10 (October 2015), 14–16, www.iosr.journals.org.
3. Charu Chandra Mukherjee, *The Life of Tantia Bhil: The Renowned Bandit Chief* (Calcutta: B.H. Dutt, 1890), 1; *Chand: Phansi (Gallows)*, 34.
4. S. C. Verma, *The Bhil Kills* (Delhi: Kunj Publishing House, 1908), 14.
5. Baba Bhand, *Jan Nayak Tantia Bhil and the Peasant and Tribal Movement* (*Tantia Bhil: A People's Hero*), in Hindi (Delhi: Prabhat Prakashan, 2014), 13–14; *Chand: Phansi (Gallows)*, 34.
6. Mukherjee, *Life of Tantia Bhil*, 2.
7. Bhand, *Jan Nayak Tantia Bhil*, 15–17.
8. Mukherjee, *Life of Tantia Bhil*, 2–3.
9. Bhand, *Jan Nayak Tantia Bhil*, 19–20, 23; *Chand: Phansi (Gallows)*, 34.
10. Bhand, *Jan Nayak Tantia Bhil*, 20–24, 136.
11. Mukherjee, *Life of Tantia Bhil*, 4.
12. Bhand, *Jan Nayak Tantia Bhil*, 22–24.
13. Mukherjee, *Life of Tantia Bhil*, 5; Bhand, *Jan Nayak Tantia Bhil*, 25, 136; *Chand: Phansi (Gallows)*, 35.
14. Ibid.; ibid. 26–27; ibid., 34–35.
15. Mukherjee, *Life of Tantia Bhil*, 6; Bhand, *Jan Nayak Tantia Bhil*, 27–28.

16. Mukherjee, *Life of Tantia Bhil*, 6-7.
17. Ibid., 7; Bhand, *Jan Nayak Tantia Bhil*, 136.
18. Bhand, *Jan Nayak Tantia Bhil*, 7-8.
19. *Chand: Phansi (Gallows)*, 35-36.
20. Madhya Pradesh State Archive and Museum (MPSAM), Bhopal, Civil Secretariat, 1886, Police Dept., Compilation, file no. 160, parts I to IV, sub: 'Thuggee and Dacoity (Narrative of the Career of the Tantia Bhil. Compiled from the records by H.P.K .Skipton, ASP)'; *Chand: Phansi (Gallows)*, 35-36.
21. Mukherjee, *Life of Tantia Bhil*, 8-10.
22. *Chand: Phansi (Gallows)*, 36.
23. Bhand, *Jan Nayak Tantia Bhil*, 32.
24. Mukherjee, *Life of Tantia Bhil*, 10.
25. Bhand, *Jan Nayak Tantia Bhil*, 32-33.
26. Mukherjee, *Life of Tantia Bhil*, 11; Baba Bhand, ed., *Jan Nayak Tantia Bhil and the Peasant and Tribal Movement: Source Material* (Bhopal: Swaraj Sansthan Directorate, 2001), 42. To distinguish this compilation of Baba Bhand from his book published from Delhi, it has hereafter been referred to as Bhand, *Source Material*, while his book has been referred to as Bhand, *Jan Nayak Tantia Bhil*.
27. Bhand, *Source Material*, 12-13, 75-76; Bhand, *Jan Nayak Tantia Bhil*, 36, 38, 136.
28. Bhand, *Source Material*, 42-43.
29. Mukherjee, *Life of Tantia Bhil*, 13; Verma, *Bhil Kills*, 14-15.
30. Bhand, *Source Material*, 43.
31. Mukherjee, *Life of Tantia Bhil*, 15; Bhand, *Source Material*, 43.
32. Mukherjee, *Life of Tantia Bhil*, 14; *Chand Phansi Number*, 37.
33. MPSAM, 1880, file no. 160, Dacoities and Highway Robberies, part II.
34. Bhand, *Jan Nayak Tantia Bhil*, 42.
35. Ibid., 42-43; Mukherjee, *Life of Tantia Bhil*, 15.
36. Verma, *Bhil Kills*, 14-15; *Chand Phansi Number*, 36.
37. Bhand, *Jan Nayak Tantia Bhil*, 43-45.
38. Ibid., 46; Bhand, *Source Material*, 44.
39. Bhand, *Source Material*, 44-45.
40. MPSAM, 1880, file no. 160, Dacoities and Highway Robberies, part II; Mukherjee, *Life of Tantia Bhil*, 15-16; Bhand, *Jan Nayak Tantia Bhil*, 48.
41. Mukherjee, *Life of Tantia Bhil*, 15-16; Bhand, *Jan Nayak Tantia Bhil*, 49.
42. Mukherjee, *Life of Tantia Bhil*, 17.
43. MPSAM, 1880, file no.160, Dacoities and Highway Robberies, part II.
44. Bhand, *Source Material*, 46.

45. Ibid., 15-16; Bhand, *Jan Nayak Tantia Bhil*, 48-50.
46. MPSAM, 1883, file no.160, Dacoities and Highway Robberies.
47. Bhand, *Jan Nayak Tantia Bhil*, 52-54.
48. Mukherjee, *Life of Tantia Bhil*, 17-19; Bhand, *Source Material*, 46.
49. Bhand, *Source Material*, 47.
50. Mukherjee, *Life of Tantia Bhil*, 20-21, 23-24; Bhand, *Source Material*, 47.
51. MPSAM, 1882, file no. 160, Dacoities and Highway Robberies.
52. Mukherjee, *Life of Tantia Bhil*, 22.
53. Ibid.; Bhand, *Source Material*, 47.
54. Mukherjee, *Life of Tantia Bhil*, 24-31.
55. Ibid., 26-27; National Archives of India (NAI), Home Dept., Police-B, file nos. 89-90, August 1884.
56. MPSAM, 1883 and 1884, file no. 160, Dacoities and Highway Robberies.
57. Mukherjee, *Life of Tantia Bhil*, 28-30; MPSAM, 1883 and1884, file no. 160, Dacoities and Highway Robberies.
58. MPSAM, 1884, file no. 160, Dacoities and Highway Robberies.
59. MPSAM, 1886, file no. 160, Thuggee and Dacoity, parts I to IV.
60. Mukherjee, *Life of Tantia Bhil*, 30.
61. MPSAM, 1886, file no.160, Thuggee and Dacoity, parts I to IV.
62. Ibid.; MPSAM, 1884, file no.160, Thuggee and Dacoity.
63. Mukherjee, *Life of Tantia Bhil*, 30.
64. MPSAM, 1886, file no.160, Thuggee and Dacoity, parts I to IV.
65. Bhand, *Jan Nayak Tantia Bhil*, 6.
66. NAI, file nos. 48-49, September 1884.
67. MPSAM, 1886, file no.160, Thuggee and Dacoity, parts I to IV.
68. Ibid.; Bhand, *Source Material*, 51.
69. MPSAM, 1886, file no. 160, Thuggee and Dacoity, parts I to IV; Bhand, *Jan Nayak Tantia Bhil*, 58-59.
70. Bhand, *Source Material*, 52.
71. MPSAM, 1886, file no. 160, Thuggee and Dacoity, parts I to IV.
72. MPSAM, 1885, file no. 160, Thuggee and Dacoity.
73. Bhand, *Jan Nayak Tantia Bhil*, 99-101.
74. MPSAM, 1887, file no. 160, Thuggee and Dacoity.
75. Ibid.; MPSAM, 1886, file no. 160, Thuggee and Dacoity, parts I to IV.
76. MPSAM, 1887, file no. 160, Thuggee and Dacoity.
77. Mukherjee, *Life of Tantia Bhil*, 31.
78. MPSAM, 1887, file no. 160, Thuggee and Dacoity.
79. Bhand, *Jan Nayak Tantia Bhil*, 62.
80. Mukherjee, *Life of Tantia Bhil*, 33.
81. NAI, file no.18-20, December 1886.
82. MPSAM, 1887, file no. 160, Thuggee and Dacoity.
83. Mukherjee, *Life of Tantia Bhil*, 33-34.

84. Bhand, *Jan Nayak Tantia Bhil*, 62–65.
85. Mukherjee, *Life of Tantia Bhil*, 34–59.
86. Chand: *Phansi (Gallows)*, 36.
87. Mukherjee, *Life of Tantia Bhil*, 55.

Chapter 11—Tantya Bhil's Demise
1. Charu Chandra Mukherjee, *The Life of Tantia Bhil: The Renowned Bandit Chief* (Calcutta: B.H. Dutt, 1890), 38–39; Baba Bhand, *Jan Nayak Tantia Bhil* (Delhi: Prabhat Prakashan, 2014), 117–18.
2. Ibid.; Madhya Pradesh State Archive and Museum (MPSAM), Bhopal, Civil Secretariat, 1889, Police Dept., Compilation, file no. 160A, 'Capture of Tantia Bheel.'
3. Mukherjee, *Life of Tantia Bhil*, 38–39, 61; Bhand, *Jan Nayak Tantia Bhil*, 119–21.
4. Mukherjee, *Life of Tantia Bhil*, 61–64.
5. MPSAM, 1889, file no. 160A, 'Capture of Tantia Bheel.'
6. Bhand, *Jan Nayak Tantia Bhil*, 122–32.
7. Mukherjee, *Life of Tantia Bhil*, 40–41; Bhand, *Jan Nayak Tantia Bhil*, 133.
8. Ibid.; ibid. 134–35.
9. Bhand, *Jan Nayak Tantia Bhil*, 136–38.
10. Ibid., 138; Mukherjee, *Life of Tantia Bhil*, 40–41.
11. Bhand, *Jan Nayak Tantia Bhil*, 140, 142, 144–45.
12. S. C. Verma, *The Bhil Kills* (Delhi: Kunj Publishing House, 1978), 14.
13. Proceedings of a Public Meeting. 'The Formation of the Northern Central,' by Northern Central, British Society. Questions by Sir Roper Lethbridge and answers by Sir John Gorst, in the House of Commons, 7 June 1888, 22.

Epilogue
1. Shrichand Jain, *Vanvasi Bhil aur Unki Sanskriti (Forest-Dwelling Bhils and their Culture)*, in Hindi (Jodhpur: Rajasthani Granthagar, 2018), 11.
2. S. C. Verma, *The Bhil Kills* (Delhi: Kunj Publishing House, 1978).

SELECTED BIBLIOGRAPHY

Agrawal, Ushakiran. 'Psychological Aspects of Tantia Bheel's Revolution.' IOSR-JHSS 20, no. 10 (October 2015): 14–16, www.iosr.journals.org.

Ansari, M.A. *Tribals in Criminal Web*. Jaipur: Publication Scheme, 1987.

Bell, Evans. *Memoir of General John Briggs of the Madras Army; With Comments on Some of His Words and Works*. Picadilly: Chatto and Windus, 1885.

Benjamin, N. and B.B. Mohanty. 'Imperial Solution of a Colonial Problem: Bhils of Khandesh up to c1850.' *Modern Asian Studies* 41 (2009), Cambridge University Press.

Bhand, Baba. *Jan Nayak Tantia Bhil (Tantya Bhil: A People's Hero)* (Hindi). Delhi: Prabhat Prakashan, 2014.

Bhand, Baba, ed. *Jan Nayak Tantya Bhil and the Peasant and Tribal Movement: Source Material*. Bhopal: Swaraj Sansthan Directorate, 2001.

'Arrow in the Skull: Conflict with the Bheels, 1833', Britain's Small Forgotten Wars, http://www.britainssmallwars.co.uk/arrow-in-the-skull-conflict-with-the-bheels-1833.html

Sen Shashatri, Acharya Chatur, ed. *Chand: Phansi (Gallows)*. New Delhi: Golden Jubilee, 2009.

Chandra, Bipan, Mridula Mukherjee, Aditya Mukherjee, Sucheta Mahajan, and K.N. Pannikar. *India's Struggles for Independence*. New Delhi: Penguin Books, 1989.

Chaudhuri, Sashi Bhushan. *Civil Disturbances During the British Rule in India (1765–1857)*. Calcutta: The World Press Ltd., 1955.

Deshpande, Arvind M. *John Briggs in Maharashtra: A Study of District Administration Under Early British Rule*. Delhi: Mittal Publications, 1987.

Gazetteer of the Bombay Presidency, vol. I, part I. 'History of Gujarat.' Government Central Press, Bombay, 1896.

Gazetteer of the Bombay Presidency, vol. XVI. 'Nasik.' Government Central Press, Bombay, 1883.

Gazetteer of the Bombay Presidency, vol. XII. 'Khandesh.' Government Central Press, Bombay, 1880.

Graham, D. *A Brief Historical Sketch of the Bheel Tribes Inhabiting the Province of Khandesh*. London: British Library, Historical Print Editions, 1843.

Ghulam, Hussain. *Bhils in Pakistan*. Germany: Bielefeld University, 2020.

Gordon-Cumming, William Gordon. *Wild Men and Wild Beasts: Scenes in Camp and Jungle*, second edition. Edinburgh and London: Edmonston & Douglas, 1871.

Gordon, Stewart. *The New Cambridge History of India: The Marathas 1600–1818, II (4)*. Cambridge: Cambridge University Press, 2008.

Hooja, Rima. *Rajasthan: A Concise History*. New Delhi: Rupa Publications India Pvt. Ltd., 2018.

Hunter, William Wilson. *The Imperial Gazetteer of India*, vol. XV, 1908–1931. Oxford: Clarendon Press, 1908.

Imperial Gazetteer of India. Provincial Series. Bombay Presidency. Calcutta: Superintendent of Government Printing, 1909.

Imperial Gazetteer of India. Central India. Calcutta: Superintendent of Government Printing, 1908.

Imperial Gazetteer of India, vol. XXII, Digital South Asia Library.

Jain, P. C. *Christianity, Ideology and Social Change among Tribals*. Jaipur: Rawat Publications, 1995.

Jain, Shrichand. *Vanvasi Bhil aur Unki Sanskriti (Forest-Dwelling Bhils and Their Culture)* (Hindi). Jodhpur: Rajasthani Granthagar, 2018.

Kela, Shashank. *A Rogue and Peasant Slave: Adivasi Resistance, 1800–2000*. Delhi: Navayana Publishing, 2012.

Kushwaha, Subhash Chandra. *Chauri Chaura Revolt and Freedom Struggle*. The Netherlands: Acumen, 2021 (Hindi: Penguin, New Delhi).

Kushwaha, Subhash Chandra. *Kabir hain ki Marte nahi (Kabir Never Dies)* (Hindi). Allahabad: Anamika Prakashan, 2020.

Kushwaha, Subhash Chandra. *Peasant Mobilisation and Revolt in Awadh, 1920–1922*. The Netherlands: Acumen: 2021 (New Delhi: Rajkamal, 2018 [Hindi]). Lobo. 1991.

Madhya Pradesh State Archives and Museum (MPSAM). Bhopal, Madhya Pradesh.

Maharashtra State Archives, Mumbai (MSAM), Political Department, 1823, 1825, 1830.

Maharashtra State Gazetteers. Ahmednagar District, revised edition. Mumbai: Gazetteers Department, Government of Maharashtra, 1976.

Maharashtra State Gazetteers. Jalgaon District, second revised edition. Mumbai: Gazetteers Department, Government of Maharashtra, 1962.

Mahi Kantha Directory, vol. I. Rajkot: Liberal Laxmi Printing Press, 1922.

Majumdar, R.C. *The Sepoy Mutiny and Revolt of 1857*. Calcutta: Firma K.L. Mukhopadhyay, Calcutta Oriental Press Pvt. Ltd., 1957.

Malcolm, John. *A Memoir of Central India, Including Malwa, and Adjoining Provinces: With the History, and Copious Illustrations of the Past and Present Condition of the Country*. London: Kingsbury, Parbury and Allen, in two volumes, 1828. Delhi: Gyan Publishing House, 2022.

Meena, Subhash and Meena, Nitesh Pal Singh. 'Historical Perspectives of Different Tribal Groups in India.' *International Journal of Interdisciplinary and Multidisciplinary Studies* (IJIMS) 1, no. 10 (2014).

Mehta, Prithvi Singh. *Hamara Rajasthan (Our Rajasthan)* (Hindi). Jalandhar and Allahabad: Hindi Bhavan, 1950.

Mukherjee, Charu Chandra. *The Life of Tantia Bhil: The Renowned Bandit Chief*. Calcutta: B.H. Dutt, 1890.

National Archives of India (NAI), New Delhi.

Nilsen, Alf Gunvald. 'Subalterns and the State in the *Longue Durée*: Notes from "The Rebellious Century" in the Bhil Heartland.' *Journal of Contemporary Asia* 45, no. 4 (2015).

Pati, Biswamoy, ed. *Issues in Modern Indian History: For Sumit Sarkar*. Mumbai: Popular Prakashan, 2000.

Prasad, A.K. *The Bhils of Khandesh Under the British East India Company*, Thesis. Poona: University of Poona, 1986.

Prasad, A.K. *The Bhils of Khandesh Under the British East India Company, 1818–1858*. New Delhi: Konark Publishers, 1991.

Puchs, Stephen. 'Messianic Movements in Primitive India.' *Asian Folklore Studies* 24, no. 1 (1965).

Rajasthan State Archives. Udaipur Confidential Records, File 40, Bag 4.

Rajputana Gazetteer, vol. I. Calcutta, 1879.

Rajputana Gazetteer, vol. II-A. Ajmer, 1905.

Report on the Administration of the Dungarpur State for the Samvat Year 1970–1971(AD 1913–1914). Published by Authority Rawalpindi and printed by J.R. Thapar & Sons at the Egerton Press.

Rewa Kantha Directory, vol. I. Rajkot: Parmar Press, 1922.

Robinson, Rowena and Joseph Marianus Kujur, eds. *Margins of Faith: Dalit and Tribal Christianity in India*. New Delhi: Sage Publications India Pvt. Ltd., 2010.

Russell, R.V., and Hira Lal. *Tribes and Castes of the Central Provinces of India*, vol. II. London: Macmillan and Co. Ltd, 1916.

Russell, R.V., and Hira Lal. *The Tribes and Castes of the Central Provinces of India*, II. New Delhi and Madras: Asian Educational Services, 1993.

Sahgal, K.K. *Rajasthan District Gazetteers*. Banswara, Directorate of District Gazetteers, Government of Rajasthan, Jaipur, 1974.

Selections from the Records of the Bombay Government, no. XXIII, new series, part II. 'Bheel Settlements.' Bombay: Bombay Education Society Press, 1856.

Sharika, Ajay. *Being Jangli: The Politics of Wildness*. New Delhi: Sage Publications, 1998.

Sharma, Braj Kishore. *Rajasthan mein Kisan evam Adivasi Andolan (Peasant and Tribal Movements in Rajasthan)* (Hindi, ninth edition). Jaipur: Rajasthan Hindi Granth Academy, 2019.

Sharma, Braj Kishore. *Tribal Revolts*. Jaipur: Pointer Publishers, 1996.

Sharma, G.N., ed. *Social and Political Awakening among the Tribals of Rajasthan*. Jaipur: Centre for Rajasthan Studies, University of Rajasthan, 1947.

Simcox, A.H.A. *Khandesh Bhil Corps*. Bombay: Thacker & Company Ltd., 1912.

Singh, K.S. 'The Tribals and the 1857 Uprising.' *Social Scientist* 26, no. 1 (1998).

Singh, N.K., and A.M. Khan, eds. *Encyclopaedia of the World Muslims: Tribes, Castes and Communities* (4 volumes). New Delhi: Global Vision Publishing House, 2001.

Vashisth, V.K. 'The Bhil Revolt of 1913 under Guru Govind Giri.' *Proceedings of the Indian History Congress* 52 (1991).

Verma, S.C. *The Bhil Kills*. Delhi: Kunj Publishing House, 1908.

Yadav, Shiv Narayan. *1857 Swadhinta Sangram mein Janjatiya Balidan (Tribal Sacrifices in the War of Independence, 1857)* (Hindi), Bhopal: Swaraj Sansthan Sanchanalaya, 2008.

LIST OF NEWSPAPERS AND JOURNALS

1. *Aberdeen Evening Express*
2. *Aberdeen Journal*
3. *Adelaide Observer* (South Australia)
4. *Age* (Melbourne)
5. *Asiatic Journal and Monthly Register for British India and its Dependencies*
6. *Atlas*
7. *Bangalore Spectator*
8. *Banswara Gazetteer*
9. *Belfast Newsletter*
10. *Belfast Telegraph*
11. *Bell's Weekly Messenger*
12. *Birmingham Daily Post*
13. *Birmingham Mail*
14. *Bombay Gazette*
15. *Border Watch* (South Australia)
16. *Boston Guardian*
17. *Bradford Daily Telegraph*
18. *Burton Chronicle*
19. *Calcutta Gazette*

20. *Church Missionary Intelligencer*
21. *Colonies and India*
22. *Congleton & Macclesfield Mercury and Cheshire General Advertiser*
23. *Cornish Times*
24. *Cumberland Pacquet, and Ware's Whitehaven Advertiser*
25. *Daily Herald*
26. *Daily News* (London)
27. *Daily Post*
28. *Daily Telegraph & Courier* (London)
29. *Derby Mercury*
30. *Downpatrick Recorder*
31. *Dublin Daily Express*
32. *Dublin Evening Post*
33. *Dumfries and Galloway Standard*
34. *Edinburgh Evening Courant*
35. *Edinburgh Evening News*
36. *Empire* (Sydney)
37. *Englishman's Overland Mail*
38. *Evening Chronicle*
39. *Evening Mail*
40. *Evening News*
41. *Evening News* (Sydney)
42. *Exmouth Journal*
43. *Falkirk Herald*
44. *Field*
45. *Friend of India and Statesman*
46. *Geelong Advertiser* (Victoria)

47. Glasgow Daily Herald
48. Glasgow Herald
49. Globe
50. Globe and Traveller
51. Halifax Courier
52. Hampshire Advertiser
53. Hereford Journal
54. Homeward Mail
55. Homeward Mail from India, China and the East
56. Illustrated London News
57. Illustrated Sporting and Dramatic News
58. India Today
59. Inquirer and Commercial News (Perth)
60. Jackson's Oxford Journal
61. Jam-e-Jamshed
62. Kadina and Wallaroo Times (South Australia)
63. Kentish Weekly Post (or Canterbury Journal)
64. Lancashire General
65. Lancaster Gazette
66. Leader (Melbourne)
67. Liverpool Standard and General Commercial Advertiser
68. London Courier and Evening Gazette
69. London Daily News
70. London Evening Standard
71. Londonderry Sentinel
72. Madras Athenaeum
73. Madras Courier
74. Manchester Courier

75. Manchester Courier and Lancashire General Advertiser
76. Mayo Constitution
77. Mercury
78. Mercury (Hobart)
79. Mid-Surrey Times
80. Monmouthshire Merlin
81. Montrose, Arbroath and Brechin Review; and Forfar and Kincardineshire Advertiser
82. Morning Advertiser
83. Morning Post
84. Naval Military Gazette and Weekly Chronicle of the United Services
85. Naveen Rajasthan
86. New York Times
87. Newcastle Chronicle
88. Newcastle Courant
89. North Briton
90. North Devon Gazette
91. North London News and Finsbury Gazette
92. North Wales Chronicle
93. North-Eastern Daily Gazette
94. Norwich Mercury
95. Nottingham Evening Post
96. Oxford Journal
97. Pall Mall Gazette
98. People and Collectivist (Sydney)
99. Poona Observer
100. Preston Chronicle and Lancashire Advertiser

101. *Queenslander* (Brisbane)
102. *Reynold's Newspaper*
103. *Royal Cornwall Gazette*
104. *Royal Gazette*
105. *Saunders's Newsletter*
106. *Scotsman*
107. *Sheffield Independent*
108. *Sherborne Mercury*
109. *St James's Gazette*
110. *Star*
111. *Star* (London)
112. *Statesman* (London)
113. *Sun* (London)
114. *Surrey Mirror*
115. *Sydney Mail and New South Wales Advertiser* (NSA)
116. *Taunton Courier and Western Advertiser*
117. *Times of India*
118. *Tribune* (Melbourne)
119. *Udaipur Gazetteer*
120. *Western Daily Press*
121. *Western Mail*
122. *Woman's Dreadnought*
123. *Yorkshire Gazette*
124. *Yorkshire Post and Leeds Intelligencer*

ABBREVIATED NEWSPAPERS AND JOURNALS

1. A — *Atlas*
2. BG — *Bombay Gazette*
3. BGaz — *Banswara Gazetteer*
4. BM — *Birmingham Mail*
5. CI — *Colonies and India*
6. DDE — *Dublin Daily Express*
7. DH — *Daily Herald*
8. DM — *Derby Mercury*
9. DNL — *Daily News* (London)
10. EEC — *Edinburgh Evening Courant*
11. EEN — *Edinburgh Evening News*
12. EN — *Evening News* (Sydney)
13. EOM — *Englishman's Overland Mail*
14. FIS — *Friend of India and Statesman*
15. GA — *Geelong Advertiser* (Victoria)
16. HC — *Halifax Courier*
17. HM — *Homeward Mail*
18. HMICE — *Homeward Mail from India, China and the East*
19. ICN — *Inquirer and Commercial News* (Perth)

20.	ILN	*Illustrated London News*
21.	IT	*India Today*
22.	LES	*London Evening Standard*
23.	MP	*Morning Post*
24.	NC	*Newcastle Courant*
25.	PMG	*Pall Mall Gazette*
26.	PO	*Poona Observer*
27.	S	*Scotsman*
28.	SJG	*St James's Gazette*
29.	SL	*Star* (London)
30.	SMNSWA	*Sydney Mail and New South Wales Advertiser* (NSA)
31.	Sr	*Star*
32.	TOI	*Times of India*
33.	WD	*Woman's Dreadnought*
34.	WM	*Western Mail*

OTHER ABBREVIATIONS

1.	AAGGCI	Asst. to AGGCI
2.	ACP	Assistant Commissioner, Police
3.	AGGCI	Agent to the Governor General of Central India
4.	APA	Acting Political Agent
5.	AR	Acting Resident
6.	ASP	Assistant Superintendent of Police
7.	ASPA	Assistant to Political Agent
8.	BA	Bhil Agent
9.	CC	Chief Commissioner
10.	CM	Chief Minister
11.	CO	Commanding Officer
12.	CP	Commissioner, Police
13.	CS	Chief Secretary
14.	DBA	Deputy Bhil Agent
15.	DC	Deputy Commissioner
16.	DIG	Deputy Inspector General
17.	DPI	District Police Inspector
18.	GG	Governor General
19.	NI	Native Infantry

20.	PA	Political Agent
21.	PO	Political Officer
22.	PS	Political Supervisor
23.	RC	Resident Commissioner
24.	Res.	Resident
25.	SC	Special Commissioner
26.	SP	Superintendent of Police

Commissioner and Collector have not been abbreviated. Others like Brig., Capt., Col., Maj., Maj. Gen., Gen., Insp., etc. are common usage and therefore, full forms have not been indicated in the text.

APPENDIX 1

To
William Chaplin Esq
Commissioner
Poonah

Sir,

I do myself the honour to submit accompanying translations of letters from the Moamlutdars [*mamlatdars*] of Baglan and Lohnece dated the 1st, 2nd and 3rd Instant. On the receipt of the first intimation of the rising reported in these dispatches, I immediately ordered on the neighbouring Lamnahs with 25 Horse from Kokurmoonda [Kukarmunda], and as many rank and file of locals from this place, to strengthen means at the Command of the Moamlutdar [*mamlatdar*] of Baglan. It is not impossible that these aides will have caused the marauders to quit their position in the fort of Moolern [Mulher], and obliged them, if not to disperse, at least to retire into the Dhang, in the fastnesses of which the assemblage of these insurgents seems to have been formed, and the body is reported to be numerous, especially as it is said not only to be headed by one Godajee, a person who formerly acted a conspicuous part in this province and is a connection or retainer of Trimbuckjee Danglia, but is also said to have been joined by foreign mercenaries, it would be imprudent to trust to these slight resources alone, since either any casual success in any encounter with the police or their being allowed to continue for any time assembled with impunity might generate a confidence that might be attended with much injuries to the country.

3rd. Viewing the subject in this light, I have addressed letters, of which the accompanying are copies, to the Officer Commanding at Malligaum and to Captain Rigby at Kokurmoonda, requesting that all the available force at those places may be directed to march, with as little delay as possible, to Baglan.

4th. If 50 to 100 more of the Auxiliary Horse could be sent to this quarter just now, they would be of the most material use. I have distributed the greater part of those now here all over the most frequented roads, where they give daily escorts to travellers and thereby prevent many of the robberies, which in such a season, would undoubtedly be perpetrated by the Bheels. With these escorts I feel the greatest reluctance to interfere, but unless you can spare some more Horse, I may be obliged to concentrate a number of them westward. Even though this should not be necessary I require some additional Horse to give the escort system full effect, and at the same time to leave a few men disposable for any contingency. You will perceive that some of the Bheels in Fauj are said to have joined the insurgents. This I shall not be surprised to hear confirmed. These people cannot resist the opportunity which anything like a disturbance is likely to afford to them, of following their favourite occupation. The great body of these people, is however, no doubt from the Dhang [Dong] situated below the Ghauts [Ghat], and beyond this jurisdiction.

5th. I beg on this occasion to mention that I often experience considerable inconvenience from the map that has been furnished to me, not including any of the territory by which this Province is bounded, and to suggest that you will have the goodness to direct this omission to be rectified as I conclude it can easily be, by the Deputy Surveyor General at the West of Khandesh from Rajpipla on the North to below Chondore on the South, might happen to be of the most material use.

Dhoolia
4th April 1825

I have the honour to be
A. Robertson
Collector

'Bombay Political, Insurrection in Baglan', British Library, London, Ref. IOR/F/4/1021/28048.

APPENDIX 2

KHANDESH REVOLT AND INDIAN AGRARIAN DISCONTENTS

To the Editor of *The Daily News*

Sir, Khandesh has expelled the Company's Revenue Surveyors, and repudiated the land tax. Troops have marched into Khandesh from all quarters—horse, foot, and artillery, and have been actively engaged in putting down the insurrection; and it is probable that the next mail will bring the intelligence of the discomfiture of the insurgents, 22,000 in number, according to the latest accounts—but perhaps not without bloodshed. What remains?

The causes of discontent remain. Horse, foot, and artillery cannot touch them. The short-sighted selfishness of the East India Company—the connivance or apathy of the Board of Control— the ignorance of parliament—in the face of these obstacles to redress, what hope can the oppressed and tax-ridden people of India have of obtaining it? They have no such hope; they have long ceased to cherish it. 'They nurse their discontents in secret, or study a fruitless, or else a disastrous revenge.' Khandesh is but one such an instance. The example is easy of imitation; and we fear that it will be imitated—in thousands of districts not less racked and ground down with taxation than the rained district of Khandesh.

Is it worthwhile, in the presence of these facts, for parliament to continue to repose a blind confidence, in the flattering but mendacious pictures of good government and contentment, which the recognised parliamentary advocates of the company are so much in the habit of presenting, as the portraiture of the past and present condition of the Company's Indian Helots? We do not ask, if it be worth the while of the company to encourage these gross misrepresentations, for we know that the renewal of their charter depends upon the degree of credit with which they are received. But is it safe or useful for parliament, the representative of that English people, which must answer with its blood and treasure, by and by, for every present hour of oppression and connivance, to accept any longer such base and contemptible pretexts, for conniving one moment more in the great oppressions endured, by one hundred and fifty millions of the Queen's subjects, at the hands of a corporation in the city?

It will not do for Sir James Weir Hogg to say the discontents are local. We have had occasion, more than once, to show that they are universal, or nearly so, throughout British India—a vast territory, rivalling in extent the whole continent of Europe. It was but the other day that we heard the groans of the wretched Bengalis, and the nobler protestations of the manly hill tribes, whom the downfall of the Sikh sovereignty had placed beneath our yoke. We are now compelled to witness, in the armed rising of the peasantry in half-conquered Khandesh, and in the sympathy everywhere expressed for their cause throughout the Presidency of Bombay, a proof, if we needed one, that the Calcutta association was not the mouthpiece of Bengal alone, nor Saadat Khan the mere avenger of some obscure grievance, hidden in the far mountains of the north-west. The Madras Presidency has never, to our knowledge, told a different tale of the real condition of its people, and their appreciation of the singular blessings of the Company's government. On the contrary, the same Indian mail which brought us the startling intelligence from Khandesh, which enables us to produce a new and striking illustration—derived the revenue system now in operation at Madras—of the sufferings of its people, and, let us add, of the danger which threatens their European masters. I, lately, drew attention to an undertaking, in which the editor of the *Madras Athenaeum* had been for some months past engaged, and which had for its object the combination of the people of the Presidency, native and European, in the cause of Indian reform. Feeling persuaded, that the only real difficulty in the way of that reform consists in ignorance of Parliament, and anxious to believe that Parliament will be only too happy to have that ignorance enlightened, our Indian contemporary had hit upon a very admirable and unexceptionable method of obtaining the newest and most authentic information, and of systematising it in a form acceptable to the curious. Circulars, printed and distributed over the Madras Presidency, have produced the required information; every question has been fully answered; and the results, digested with great industry and fairness, and accompanied with the justificatory documents, are now before the public. The following is a brief summary of the valuable evidence of two or three Madras land holders, one of them being Mr. Fischer, the respected and patriotic zamindar of Salem—on this very subject of the land-tax, or Company's rack-rent, which in the Bombay Presidency has wrought such mischief at Khandesh.

In the Madras Presidency there are two kinds of tenures—the Raiyatwari and the Zemindari. Under the former—which is nearly universal—the Raiyat or farmer holds of the Company direct and settles annually with its officers. Under the latter—where it exists—the zamindar or landlord holds of the Company at a fist or tribute, and recovers over against the Raiyats under him. Under the former tenure, again, the assessment is made on a money valuation, and the rent is paid in cash according to the assessment. This mode of assessment, which is called the government puttah, is also the mode usually followed under the zamindari tenure. There is, however, under the latter, sometimes used—but rarely—a more favourable assessment, called '*amaneevarum*', under which the rent is valued according to the quantity of produce, and is paid in kind; the crop being cut, threshed, and measured in the presence of the Company's police, and one-half of the surplus left after deducting all the village masses, being thereupon handed over to the Company, and the other half to the cultivating Raiyat. But this—being accounted much too beautiful an arrangement in favour of the said raiyat, is now nearly everywhere discontinued. Where it exists, however, it is stated to be most beneficial. 'I have stood,' writes a very intelligent land holder, 'on a ridge that divided a zamindari from government land; and when my eye roved over the most luxuriant cultivation on the zamindari side of it, nothing but wastelands presented themselves to my view, so far as I could see on the other. Inquiring into the cause of this vast difference, the answer given was that "cultivating amaneevarum lands is like eating milk and rice; but cultivating government puttah lands is like eating blood and rice!"' It is, in truth, a system of serious and short-sighted cruelty. Whether the zamindari or the Raiyatwari tenure obtain—the general system—that of rack-rents and cash collections—is gradually exterminating an industrious and frugal people, and turning a whole country of unexampled fertility, which had been cultivated for thousands of years before the Company's era began, into a howling wilderness. If zamindar be the channel of communication, he must make up his mind 'to play the tyrant with his Raiyats; fully aware that, whatever be the cause of the Irsal, or remittance, being delayed, interest at the rate of 12 per cent, will be wrenched out of him; and what is worse still, his zamindari may be attached, at the option of the collector, for the default of a single instalment'. This attachment, it appears, is a stretch of power beyond the regulations, which only authorise the attachment for the arrears of one year. The collector's 'discretion' is above 'regulation'. He adds, 'In my district the collector has a different course chalked out for him and pursues it without any regard to the regulation. A week before the due day of each instalment, he sends a circular notice to each zamindar in his district, to remind him that the ensuing instalment, of *kist* falls due on the 15th of that month, and that, if the same is not paid in time, his zamindari will be attached forthwith. This threat sets the Zamindari's people on the qui vive and the turn to and bully Raiyats, until the *kist* is raised.'

In this respect the Raiyatwari system is just the zamindari, with a slight difference. The collector, having no zamindar between him and the Raiyats, is unable to 'turn to and bully' them by deputy; and, instead of having only one reminder to threaten with confiscation, he has several thousands of Raiyats to gratify with that pleasing bit of intelligence.

What follows is so shocking, and so important, that we prefer to give it, word for word, as it appeared in the printed queries, and Mr. Fischer's written replies. The character of the man, and his long experience in the Presidency, are in every way a voucher for the accuracy of his statement: What share does the government obtain of the produce?

After paying expenses of cultivation the government's share of the produce is the whole, or nearly the whole. By produce of course is meant what remains after paying the expenses of production.

Is the assessment in theory or practice a permanent one? The assessment is too permanent by far, both theoretically and practically. It is continued even after the land ceases to be able to pay it. Consequently, it is thrown up, and hence the large tracts of fine land lying waste in every district. It is the finest lands in general that are waste from being too highly taxed.

There is some Nunjah (or wet) land in my Zamindari assessed at Rs 18.10 per acre; *Thottam* (or garden) lands at Rs 8.9; and Poonjay (or dry) at Rs 6-4:— on much of which I am obliged to remit 25 per cent, of the *kist*, to get it cultivated; making up for such remission, by bringing all passible waste into cultivation. Seeing which it was, that a late invidious and unscrupulous collector proposed to claim all lands in Zamindaries that were waste at the time of the survey as belonging to government, and actually did seize and appropriate small portions, and was supported in it by the government, and by its judge, when the question was carried before the courts. The amount of the suits precluded my carrying in an appeal to England.

Are the same lands cultivated for any length of time by the same Raiyats? The Raiyats are attached to their patrimonial lands, and will hold by them, if they will afford them subsistence.

Is the right of occupying land in your district saleable in the market, and at what price? Whether lands are saleable or not depends entirely on their locality, and whether they are lightly, moderately, or highly assessed. For the assessment throughout the country is exceedingly unequal; it is having depended entirely upon the humour and character of the men who were employed to establish it and upon the behaviour of the people at the time. If the government employee were hard-hearted and exacting, and the people of any place showed a spirit of independence or indifference, and did not propitiate the native establishment, it was laid on thick. But if the government employees were considerate and lenient, and the people were submissive and well behaved, and forked out handsomely, they were let off cheap. Hence the great inequality in the taxation between the Taluka of the same district, any, between the villages of the same Taluka. The collectors of this district have repeatedly reported that many parts of the district were much overtaxed, and strenuously advocated a reduction; but those reports have all ended, as all rich reports do, with short-sighted and parsimonious government, in smoke.

Has the quantity of wasted and increased in your district, or diminished wasted and has increased, is increasing, and ought to be diminished?

Has any land, which is highly assessed, gone out of cultivation, and poorer soils been taken up in lieu of them?—This happened to a very great extent in this district.

Is the condition of the Raiyat better or worse, than at former periods within your recollection?—My experience extends over a space of 30 years, and is considerable, from my occupations of cotton grown and indigo planter; and I should say that the condition of the Raiyat is much worse now than before; and it is daily growing worse.

Is more food and clothing consumed by the agricultural population now than formerly, within the memory of the present generation?—No, not so much.

Are remissions frequent—and are they granted on account of the Raiyat's losses, or on the score of his inability to pay?—Remissions are unknown, except on occasions of extraordinary droughts, and failures of crops; when it is only given to save the Raiyats from utter ruin, deserting lands, or running away.

When a Raiyat is unable to pay his rent, and, if either distrained upon or granted a remission, is he allowed to cultivate his fields as before?—When a Raiyat is unfortunate, and once gets into arrears, and is unable to pay his rent, he goes downhill fast. The whole system is one of depression and ruin. Nothing is done to help, except, as I have said above, on very extraordinary occasions. He is coerced in every possible way—the gentlest of which is by bringing him to the Tahsildar's *Cutcherry* and keeping him there an unlimited time, away from his family and his fields. When all such means fail, his lands are sold, if they are worth sale, by the Circar, if they are not before sold by the moneylender, from whom he has already got the utmost credit he can, to pay the government with. Then he is booked and reported as *nathady* (a beggar) and set adrift to prey on society.

Do you know instances where a remission has been granted to cultivators, who are too poor to pay, and refused to others who have been, in former seasons, more provident or successful?—Such is the common practice, and is the source of much complaint.

Is the necessity for granting remissions a consequence of over assessment, or of causes connected with the habits of the people?—The necessity for occasional remission is attributable to both causes over assessment and the improvident character of the people. This has left them little or no means of accumulation; and this perhaps is the very origin of their improvidence.

And this, we may also say, is, perhaps, the very origin of agrarian discontents and incorrectness, like that of Khandesh.

Letter to the editior, *The Daily News* (London), February 3, 1853.

APPENDIX 3

Political No. 13 copy
India Office
London 30 April 1861

To His Excellency The Honourable

1. The Government in Council the papers forwarded with the letter of your Excellency Government, No. 6, dated 26th January 1961, relating to the death of the Bheel Naik Kajee Singh and the capture of his son Pholad Singh by the hands of Rohideen, a Mukranee Jemadar, and a party of the Khandesh Police.

2. The records of your Government prove that Kajee Singh and his father before him instead of empowering the Bheels of the Satapura Range in the preservation of order and tranquillity have been for a long period of years, the main source of disturbance in the province and of detriment to its more peaceful inhabitants.

3. From the merciful consideration extended to Kajee Singh by your Government on more than one occasion he had every opportunity afforded him of a reformation. Twice he received pardon for grave offences and was restored to his

situation of trust and responsibility. But kindness and conciliation failed to reclaim him for more than short intervals; the hereditary lawlessness of his nature was too strong; and he remained to the last, as Mr. Reenes states, 'a traitor and pest of Khandesh and the Northern frontier'.

4. From the proceedings before me, I observed that his career was marked by peculiar atrocity. On one occasion he tortured some persons to confess and went to such lengths that one died and two others were maimed for life. Effects of his cruelty and just previous to the gallant and successful attack upon him by Lieutenant Atkins and Procyon, on the 1st July, he perpetrated a very cruel murder on one of his Murine followers. Mr. Mansfield writes, 'His capture or death was absolutely indispensable to the peace of the country.'

5. It was clearly incumbent on your Government to use every means in your power to uphold the supremacy of the law and give protection to the lives and properties of Her Majesty's subject in Khandesh. I do not therefore disapprove of the reward offered for the capture of Kajee Singh and in reference of the subsequent that nothing could be more carefully worded than the terms in which this offer was made known. Those terms could offer no justification for the treacherous act by which Kajee Singh was deprived of life and Her Majesty's condemnation of this transaction and in your decision negativing the proposal to give reward to Rohideen and his associates.

6. I regret to observe evidence in these proceedings that attention as does not appear to have been paid to the just and humane policy so frequently resorted to with success heretofore,

for the reclamation from their predatory habits of the aboriginal tribes of India. Mr. Mansfield remarks, 'Though an officer belonging to the Indore Residency has always been nominally in charge of the Burwanee state, no one has ever resided there for any length of time or become personally acquainted with the Bheel Chiefs of the country. In an interview I had with some of them in 1858 they told me that they had nobody to seek redress from and where obliged to take the law into their own hands.' Under such circumstances it is not surprising that the peace of the country has been disturbed and I hope that, with the view of preventing further disorder, Mr. Mansfield's judicious suggestion that Major Keating should assemble the Bheel Chiefs and then make a full report on their circumstances and means of subsistence and what measures are necessary for the future peace and security of the frontier has been adopted.

7. I feel assured that I may trust to your excellency to maleate upon your officers in Khandesh that successful results can only be obtained in their dealing with these wild and uncivilised tribes by blending conciliation with vigour and by the strictest honesty and the most scrupulous good faith.

C. Wood
Under-Secretary to the Govt. of India

APPENDIX 4

TRANSLATION OF 21 ARTICLES OF AGREEMENT BETWEEN THE DURBAR AND THE BHEELS OF MEYWAR

1. You will not suffer at any time by men and houses being counted.
2. Men and women will not be weighed.
3. Mahomedans will not be allowed to live in Rakabdeoji.
4. The murder of the Thanadar and sepoys in Padona and Bara Pal, & c., was a very great offence; still at your request it is pardoned. In future he who commits an offence will be punished.
5. Land will not be measured.
6. One-half of the Tisala fixed by the Jemadar Bal Govind, and which ever since that time has been taken from those who inhabit Pals, will be taken from you, and you are exempted from payment of the other half.
7. Arrangements will be made so that the Kamdars may not give trouble to you at the time of Koonta [when the grain is measured], but there should be no procrastination or refusal on your parts in paying the proper amount of revenue.
8. Wherever you do not pay Koonta or share of produce of Kardhna [small grain], then it will not be taken.
9. No tax will be levied on mangoes and mohwa.
10. No custom duty will be taken for mohwa which the Bheels bring for their own use.

11. The sowars of Patiya have hitherto taken the sum of twelve annas [12 Annas] for the Choki of Poonam; that sum will not be taken hereafter.

12. The Thanas will Act be increased in number.

13. Grass and wood will not be taken from the inhabitants of Pals without being paid for.

14. The amount received by the Pals of Biluk and Peepli from the Bhandar [Treasury] of Shree Rakabdeoji will ever remain the same.

15. There will be no contract for opium, salt and tobacco.

16. In the Pal hills of the Mugga Parganas there will be no contract for grass and wood.

17. During the past three years those who have been imprisoned will be set free upon a fine being paid by those who are able to do so.

18. The Dak Hurkaras [postal runners] will be taken from the respective Pals through which the Dak [post] goes. The Political agent will be addressed on this point.

19. The Sirkaree sowars will not be kept up at the Chokis at which they are now posted as protectors of the road so long as you continue responsible as you have agreed to be for the safety of the road.

20. From pilgrims going to and from the shrine of Rakabnathji and that of Shree Nathji, the Bholai will be taken according to ancient custom.

21. In the Pals, Koonta or share of grain will not be taken from the Jogis and Dhobis who have never paid it, and they must do the Raj business according to ancient custom.

Dated Baisakh Badi 5, Summut 1937, corresponding with 19 April, 1881.

APPENDIX 5

The liberty still enjoyed by Tantia Bhil, the notorious dacoit, is brought before us by a Correspondent. We have often referred to the case with which he commits his depredations, in spite of the efforts of the police to prevent him, and the still greater readiness with which he evades their futile attempts to capture him. Year by year the reports of the police administration of the Central Provinces reach us, and the burden of their song about the romantic dacoit is that he is 'still at large'. The repetition of this phrase becomes as monotonous as the ever-repeated report during the American Civil War that strenuous efforts were about to be put forth to terminate the rebellion, or the more recent tidings which used to be continuously sent from Mandalay that the 'King was still drunk', or the still more recent telegrams which almost daily have informed us that negotiations with Russia continue with the prospect of a speedy and amicable termination. Those in charge of the hunt after Tantia Bhil seem to consider it such good sport that they prolong it as much as possible. If by chance they were to capture him they would be deprived of their sport, which in up-country stations affords employment during the day and subject matter for talk over 'pegs' at night—and they would be unable to send in their periodic reports that 'Tantia is still at large'. And in the meantime the robber goes on robbing those who have anything to rob, cutting the noses off those who resist him or spy upon him, and defying the efforts of the administration to capture him. Our correspondent shrewdly, and perhaps cruelly, describes the position in the form of a dilemma—'That Tantia must be a very clever man to escape and evade the police during the last seven years; or the police are non-efficient body seem patent', and in the words of Mr. Anstey in his recent 'farcical romance', this dilemma is sounding its dread orans at the very door of the Police Administration. But it is doing more than this: it is imbueing the mind, of the people in the district with disloyalty; it is undermining the prestige of the executive; it is bringing into contempt the British raj.

Tantia Bhil having reached notoriety will no doubt in time attain the dignity of a biography, but in the meantime it is difficult to gather up the fragments of description and rumour into a consistent whole. The police reports are full of stories about his crimes, nor are his generosities omitted; but it is more than likely that incidents in which others have been the chief actors have been connected with him without just warrant. As romances require heroes to centre upon, so do heroes gather romance round them. It is thus with the dread dacoit Tantia Bhil. We find in the police reports that children being frightened by some sudden apparition of the notorious murderer stand still with fear by the wayside, but are reassured by the apparition dropping a rupee into their water pots. Then on another occasion he enters an enclosure where are gathered a wedding party in their gayest attire and wearing jewels to the value of some three or four thousand rupees. But he pardons them their wealth, assures them he has no intention of robbing or killing them, but wishes to see the owner of the village; then he presents the juvenile bride and bridegroom with a rupee each, and salaams himself away. Such stories are repeated from village to village, and as they spread they receive continual accretions, and in time reached the marvellous, and are then the more readily credited by the simple villagers. Thus the murderer becomes a hero at the cost of a little swagger and a few judiciously spent rupees. At times Tantia Bhil's activity is boundless, he follows up dacoity with dacoity, and then he becomes quiescent for a while and retires into hiding. Thus, for example, we read in the police report for 1883 that after the Hemgir dacoity on the 16th December 1882, he and his gang were next heard of in the Melaghat Zamindari of the Ellichpur district, where two dacoities were committed in January. In the following month they appeared at the village of Rohini in the Nimar district to take vengeance upon the Malgujar of the village; but he, being absent, escaped with his life, while his house was plundered and burnt. Then on the 26th May he recommenced with a very serious dacoity in the Melaghat Zamindari. In July again he showed himself for a moment only to disappear again. In the end of September he issued once from his hiding place and committed several very serious and deliberate dacoities. In December some more dacoities were committed, and again in January, when it became apparent that his band was split up into two sections which were both out on the war path. Their activity did not abate, as was apparent from the police report, an extract from which has already appeared in our columns giving the history of Tantia Bhil's doings for the year, and an interesting and valuable contribution from a correspondent in the Berar's, which was published lately by our local contemporary, gave details showing how Tantia Bhil still slashes off noses and terrifies as well as robs the community in which he finds himself.

The immunity which Tantia Bhil enjoys suggests that, however clever a fellow he may be, his cleverness partly consists in gaining over to his support the police who go out in search of him. 'The police of the Central Provinces,' we are informed by the correspondent to whom we have already referred, 'are recruited from among the very tribes which it is their duty to restrain and repress.' And it is apparent that if the pay of the policemen is about seven or eight rupees a month while he may obtain something substantial as a bribe from a successful dacoity, committed, it must be remembered, by people who are his friends and perhaps his relatives, the temptation to be unfaithful is very strong. The rural police do not enjoy the best of reputations, their ignorance and rapacity being notorious, and they are often so placed in the course of carrying out some skilfully laid plan to capture the dacoit that they are able to reveal their instructions to the criminals they are pursuing. It is not surprising that the plan should miscarry in such cases; but those in charge can hardly escape altogether from the blame of the miscarriage. The tendency in the Central Provinces is, we understand, to gradually replace the British element by native, and this process, if it be continued, must continually recruit the ranks of those who sympathise with the dacoits. The want of unity in the search, and the want of harmony between the officers, is admitted in last year's report. 'During the past year,' we read, 'it has, however, been more than ever painfully apparent that the chief causes of the failure of our operations against Tantia have been the dissensions, resulting from petty jealousy, between officers entrusted with conduct of those operations and the want of accord and cooperation on the part of the police of different districts.' It is high time that some measures were taken to cure the officers of their 'petty jealousy', and to produce a better system in which 'accord and cooperation' may be restored to 'the police of different districts'; for the daring and effrontery of the dacoit must not be allowed to remain a notorious scandal, nor mar the fair fame of the British Administration through the 'petty jealousy', of some subordinate officials.

The Times of India, 21 August 1885

INDEX

A

Abdullah, Mansa Prasad, Sub. 196
Abdullah, Sheikh, Sub. 195
aborigines 5, 21, 26
Abul-Fazl 176
Acharya, Kesheorao 328
Acharya, K.G. (J) 324
administrative system 25, 180
agitation, Bhil landowners 86
agreement, Kherwara 224
Ahar Civilisation 173
Ahir tribes 34
Ahirani 34
Ahmedabad 60, 94, 179–80, 211, 223, 226
Ahmednagar 62, 64, 67, 76, 79, 91–92, 109–10, 115, 124–25, 193, 201
Ain-e-Akbari, Abul-Fazl 176
Akrani 36, 40, 143, 151
Alcohol/drinking 29, 36, 40, 220, 235, 237, 242
Ali, Farzan 102
Ali, Meer Sahmat 144
Ali, Sher 277–78, 280–81
Ali, Syed Murad 207
Alirajpur 72–73, 117, 126–27, 143–44, 152, 157–62, 167–68, 179
Anand, Bhil chief 72
Ananda 152
anarchy 37–39, 41, 47, 71, 201
'Ancestor Ramana' 25

Andamans 133, 242
Anderson, F.C. 312
Anderson, H.L. 141
Anglo-Maratha War 33
Aniya 120
Ankaleshwar 179, 199
anti-Bhil campaign 121
anti-Tantya campaign/operations 277, 285, 294–95, 299–300, 303–4, 308, 314, 330, 338
Anup 13, 218
Apte, Nanu Pant 202–3
Arabs 11, 34, 38, 44, 63, 82, 112, 136, 191; mercenary assistance 63; merchants 63; soldiers 122; traders 38
armed groups 162
army personnel, killing of 82, 85, 100
Arthur, Capt. 95
Aryan conquest 28
Aryans 22, 24, 178, 240
Ashburner, L.R. 107
Asirgarh Fort 189
Assistant Superintendent of Police (ASP) 114, 136, 338
Atkins, Lt. 100, 104, 106, 133, 136–37, 143, 147, 401
atrocities 8, 178, 187, 354, 401
Auchit 13, 45–46, 68
Ayscough, Capt. 237
Azim Beg, Naib Risaldar Mirza 72

B

Baba, Bhudhagir 129
Baba, Kalu 90, 131
Bagga 95
Bahadur, Daneshwar Vishwanath 209
Baijnath (CJ) 324, 326
Bajirao, Peshwa 62, 64; title of 40
Bakhsh, Meer Nabi 66
Bakhsh, Nana 103
Ballantine, Lt. 218
Balneo 175
Bandaria 152-53, 155
Bangash, Wahid Wali Khan 63
Bangchund 13, 83, 109
Banias 11, 36, 166, 225-26
Banjara, Nimar Phool Singh 301-2
banjaras 155, 307
Banswara 27, 173, 175, 179, 181-83, 186-90, 193, 198, 204, 210-11, 216-17, 232, 234-39, 242
Banswara Gazetteer (BGaz) 240-41
Bappa, Rana 175
Bar, Capt.. PA 217
Barapal 218-19, 221, 223
barbaric 6, 22, 39-40, 59, 226
Barda tribe 40
Bari village 14, 267
Baroda (Vadodara) 129, 185, 191, 194, 198, 203, 213, 217-18, 227, 229-30, 237
Barrow, R.P. 237-38, 241
Bart, Hamilton, Sir 141
Bart, R. Shakespear, Sir 136
Barton, Maj. 214
Barwani 11, 126-27, 129, 132-34, 140-41, 143, 145-49, 152, 154-58, 161, 167; Durbar 354n35 365
Basevi, Lt. 100
battles: Amba Pani 131; of Assaye 62; at Dabakovari 96; of Dhaba Bawdi 140
Baugh, Maj. 136
Bawa, Sitaram 78, 101-2, 104
Bayley, Maj. 240
Bazelgette, R.L., Lt. 248-50
Beg, Haidar 113-14
Beg, Ibrahim 274, 276-77
Beg, Naib Risaldar Mirza Azim 72
beheading 201, 203; animals 77; Bills 122
Belmore, T.R., Lt. 196
Bennet, Lt. murder of 78-79
Berar 32, 64, 165, 176, 289, 291-92, 300, 335, 408
Bernier, François 37
Bettington, A. 112
Betul, DC 288, 290, 300, 304-9, 313, 320, 345
BGaz Banswara Gazetteer 240
bhagats 30, 232
Bhago 13-14, 90-91, 94-95, 109-15, 131
Bhakta, Sant Satya 251
Bhakta cult 356
Bhakta or Bhagat movement 232-33
Bhamania, Bhil chief 83
Bhand, Baba 12, 15-16, 337
Bharuch 169, 179, 199
Bhaumia 176
Bhavalya, Nimar 296-97, 300-302
Bhil agents (BA) 50, 57, 83, 107, 146, 149-50; A.D. Daly 156; Capt. Hutenison 127; J.C. Wood 134; of Khandesh 118; Lt. Evans 85; Maj. William Keening 156; Probyn 136
Bhil, Ahmad 82
Bhil, Banya 301-2
Bhil Battalion 137
Bhil, Bhavo Singh 123
Bhil chiefs: agreements with 188, 224; Ahmad, Muslim 82; amrs supplier to 95; Anand 72; Appa Nayak 110; as autonomous 176, 210; of Bangar 188; of Barwani 126-27, 129, 146, 148, 152; Bhamania 83; of Bharuch

169; Bhils loyalty to 151; Bhola
Singh 122-23; of Bhula 250-
51; Chitto Bhil 161-69; custom
of 174; of Dalla 216; of Dang
40, 75, 78, 80, 83, 116-19,
210, 250; of Dasana 151, 156;
Dhoria 212; Dhur Singh 78;
Govind Guru 232-42; Govind
Mang 78; in Gujarat 216;
Gujaria 152; Hiria 47; Jagga
Rawat 13, 140, 186-90; Jangia
121;intermarriage between
Rajputs and 177; Juba 65; of
Khandesh 130; Khundu 79-80;
landowners 86, 175; Mahadev
24, 79, 79-80; Mahi Kantha
224; marriage with Rajputs 26;
Mogir 81; monthly wages to
127; of Muthwar 151; Nadir
Singh 65-67; from Nalcha 66;
Nandu Pal 183; Nawawasa
248-51; and non-violence
246; of Ogun 175; Paduna 218;
Penchund 13, 84; pensions
353; in Rajpipla 191; Rania
78; region 12, 109; religion
and language 27-28; Re Singh
Nayak 77; rights 145; Rupa
Singh 213; at Sanwara 251;
Simur Waru, Deval 183; of
Sirohi 212; at Sodalpur 216;
Surajmal 13, 199-201, 205-6;
Tantya 323; titles on 176, 210;
treaties with 197; of Undari
175
Bhil Corps 50-56, 59, 61, 79-81,
83-85, 87-88, 90, 147, 183-84,
213, 215, 217, 295-96, 298, 300;
and cavaliers 83; chowkidars
and 37
Bhil deities 30; Rajput adoption
of 175
Bhil, Dev Chand 109
Bhil, Gulia 242
Bhil, Hiria 13, 47, 71, 122, 275,
285-86

Bhil Infantry 52
Bhil, Itoba 122
Bhil, Kania 13
Bhil, Kaniya 69-70
Bhil, Kanhaiya 124-25
Bhil kings 7, 9, 31, 63, 174, 191;
demotion to patel 7; as gameti
27
Bhil, Railla 155
Bhil, Ramla 149-50, 155
Bhil, Sarwan 155
Bhil, Seva 138
Bhil territories 5, 44, 52, 54, 190,
201, 207, 239, 353; Rajput
invasion of 174
Bhil, Tutahu 155
Bhil, Ugharya 301-2
Bhil uprising 165, (see also
rebellion): Dang 117;and
intelligence 222; at Kondhar 92;
in Panchmahal 229; in Pol 225;
in Udaipur 245
Bhil, Yadia 122
Bhilala, born of Bhil-Rajput as 27
Bhilalas 27, 31, 65, 160-61, 177,
293
Bhillmal (Bhinmal) 174
Bhil-Rajput cohabitation 177
Bill/Bheel, Tantya 12, 15-16,
108, 120-21, 261-92, 294-99,
302-6, 308-9, 313-14, 316-20,
322-28, 330-33, 336-8, 346,
348-49, 405-8; advertisement
on 300-301; and arrests 272,
275, 279-80, 283-85, 289, 292,
294-96, 299-300, 305, 307-8,
311-13, 315, 318, 332, 335-37;
assistance to 307, 323; attacking
Chuna Hujuri 305; band 271-
72, 277, 286, 291, 293, 295-96,
299, 306, 308-9, 319, 326;
birth of 263-64; case 339; in
Central India Agency jail 337;
clemency for 332; confession of
crimes 345-46; encountering
Sher Ali 281; encounter in

Gangradhna 319-21; execution 341-42; family of 336; first loot 271-72; former paramour Jasoda 337 (see also Jasoda/ Jashoda); hideouts 280, 293, 309; honorary membership on 317; Imprisonment and Jailbreak 267-71; as Indian Robinhood 261; in Jabalpur Jail 337; life sentence to 339; with Nehar 314-15; nose severing of constable 296, 320, 345; nose severing of women 299, 316-17; noses severing 320, 337, 344; noses severing of barber 333; raids Gangradhna 319, 321; raids Ghoti 289; raids Holkar state 300; raids Nimar 320; raids villages 319; revenge 286; reward on 301-7; as "Rob Roy of India" 334; as Robinhood of Charua forests 288, 290; sheltering 15, 271, 281, 283; in son's marriage 303; story about 309-11; tale on 312, 335, 342, 344; in Tinasia 285; turns rebel 266-68; witnesses against 339-40
Bhils 26, 96-97, 99, 158-60, 174, 326, 349-52, 355, 388-89, 400, 403; agitation of 126; Agreement with Durbar and Meywar 403-4; alliance with Pindaris 64; anarchist 38; and civil disobedience 9; armed 164, 168, 245; band 78-79, 111, 113, 116, 122, 124, 131, 209-10, 217, 221, 230; banjaras 232; Barwani 147; in black book 5, 9, 21-22, 35, 83, 119, 173, 176, 181, 225, 271; of Chikalda 146; of Dasana 151, 156; dialect 28; divisions of 31, 36; at Ghevari-Chandgaon slaughtering of 62-63; guerrilla activity 217; heroes 12-14, 245, 356-57; (see also Bhil chiefs); hill-dwelling 40; Hirdhi 39; of Indo-Aryan family 28; informer 308; insurgencies 105, 146, 210, 356; insurrections 198, 202-3, 212, 216; intermarriage among 27;jagir in Rajpipla 191; jagirdars 149, 176, 182, 191; of Khandesh 37-42, 50, 53, 86; at Kopargaon 62; loyalty 55; in Lunawara 194; as mankars 176; Marathas and 178; massacre of captured 71-72; men 28, 104; Mutwa 50; Nahal 39, 71, 269; oppression 236; peasants 109; policemen 335; population 34, 127, 355; power 352; prisoners 60; raids 52, 124, 230; Rajputana 8, 27, 229; rebellion 12, 78, 82, 181, 201, 205, 209, 257; as rebellious 9, 54, 56, 90, 127; rebels 60, 72, 83, 93, 110, 153, 156, 293, 333; Satmala 69; slaughtering of Gangthari 63; soldier 52; titles of 24; Turvi 39, 47, 49, 69, 83; as village guards 176; warriors 70, 168; women 28, 132, 234
Bhils of: Adawad 57, 69; Alirajpur 157; Ankush 71; Banswara 204, 238; Barapal 222; Bhaggarh 291; Bhakar 248; Bhoola 254; Chandore 46, 62; Chichkheda 291; Dabhi 291; Dahod 209; Dasana 146, 151, 156, 158; Devpura 177; Dewalpal 212; Dungarpur 199, 234; Garasia 197; Godhra 165, 179, 205, 207; Gujarat 178, 193; Idar 175, 233; Indore 149; Jharol 243; Kalibas 204; Kalyanpura, Vinod on 177; Kherwara 210; Khushalpur and Barwani 158; Koliyari 243; Kotra 210; Lunawara 207; Madhya Pradesh 178; Madri 243; Magra 243; Maharashtra

178; Mahi Kantha 225; Malva 84; Mewar 30, 176, 221, 228, 231–33, 245, 245, 248; Nanawas 254; Nandurbar 46; Nimar 225; Paduna 222; Pahara Jagir 242; Palgaon 202; Pol 209; Rajasthan 30, 177–78; Rajpipla 224; Rajputana 8, 27, 173, 178; Rawat 176, 186; Rewa Kantha 152, 206; Risabhdev 197; Sonth 207; southern Malva 201; Tembhi 291; Tripura 23
Bhomia 106
Bhopal Battalion 331
Bhopawar Agency 160–61, 179
Bhuiphal 265, 273–74, 278–79, 319, 340
Bhumiya 27
Biddulph, Maj. 161–63, 165–68
Bignell, Capt. 164–65
Bijania 267–69, 273–74, 276–80, 340; arrest of 276, 278–79; execution 279–83; imprisonment of 267
Bikarai 83, 109
'Bilawa' 24
'Biography of an Indian Outlaw' 343
Birch, Capt. 130
Bisram 148–49
Black, J., Lt. Col. 233
Blair, C.R., Col. 100, 221–23
Blair, Lt. 100
Blowers, Lt. 145
Bombay, governor of 46, 64, 139
Bombay Army 199
Bombay Gazette 8, 31, 64, 110, 132, 198, 354
Bombay Government 50, 55, 104, 109, 116, 119, 125, 130, 132, 153–54, 192–94, 198, 224–25
Bombay Native Infantry (NI) 53
Bombay Native Regiment 50
Bombay Presidency 23, 32, 43, 60, 106, 119, 180, 227, 240, 335, 392–93

Bombay–Agra road 45, 131, 144–45
Bombay–Indore road 141
Bomla, Jav Nayak 91
Bondarya 296–97, 300–302
Bonnor, Capt. 208
Boudich, Capt. 133
Bowden-Smith, Henry, Capt. 81–82
Bowie, M.M., Maj. 280, 288, 290, 292–94
Bradford, R.C., Lt. 210
Brahmin, Lakshman 144
Bribe/corruption 27, 134, 189, 211, 327
Briggs, Capt 33, 44–49, 65, 68–71, 85, 100, 192; agreement with Gumani 47, 68; agreements with Bhil 46; John,
British 12; capturing Khandesh 45; entering Gujarat 181; policy of appeasement 44, 50, 353; suzerainty 61, 181; war against Arabs 38
British Army 45, 48, 69, 71, 75, 77–78, 99, 102, 181, 183, 185, 196–98, 201, 205, 207; Ganga Nayak attack on 47;
British Government 48, 72, 75, 117, 119, 146, 151–52, 155–56, 182, 194–95, 203, 213, 215, 217, 220–23, 225, 322, 355, 409; awarded malguzars 278
British Police 125, 332, 334, 337
British Policy 43–57, 103, 139; in Khandesh 59
British Soldiers 48, 100, 200
British–Sirohi troops 250
Brockney, Col. 292
Brooke, Saurin, Maj. 288
Buckle, Capt. 209
Bundi Dashnami 232, 368n39
burglaries 49, 274, 277, 281–82, 287, 289, 319; in Kapasi 290; in Rohankheda 292; Tamli 292; in Uskalli 290

Burnett, Robert Hamilton 101, 106, 132
Burns, Jasper, Col. 228

C
Cadell, Lt. 117
Calcutta Gazette 11, 44, 64, 185; on Bhills 11
Canning 79
castes 7, 29, 31, 176–77, 266, 310; Brahmins 11, 31, 93, 120, 154, 213, 234; curse of 31; Kolis 31, 91, 119–20, 176, 179, 208; nayaks 24, 27, 31, 56, 95, 107, 113, 151–52; ordinary Bhils 31; Oswal Bania 243; Shudras 7
Census of 1901 23
Central India Agency (CIA) 43, 159, 337
Central Indian cavalry 211
Central Indian Horse 161, 164, 328, 331
Central Provinces 27, 35, 279–80, 288–89, 292, 294, 312–13, 335, 338, 405, 408–9
Chamar, Kalia 13, 190, 192–93
Chamberlain, Lt. 94
Chand, Dev 78
Chandra 12, 323
Chaplin, William 74, 192
Chapman, F.S. 91, 93
Chaudhari, Ram Narayan 251
Chauhans 179
checkposts 141–42, 221, 240, 283, 299, 304; Dorwa 299; Gadara 238; Khampur 306; Khard 299; Kukshi 148; Roshia 299
Cheel, hanging of 47
Chhanuchhiri, see Tikekar, Ramchandra Vinayak
Chhaoni, Kherwara 228
Chhota Udaipur 179, 205–7, 213
Chichkheda 273, 291, 295, 301–2
Chikli 46, 143, 156, 188, 199
Chimna, Atmaram 324
Chowdhri, Mohan 70, 269, 315–16

chowkidars 31, 37, 48, 68
Christian missionaries 232, 242, 353
Christianity 356
Clarke, Capt. 100
clemency 138, 140, 150, 153, 300, 330–32
Collier, Capt. 208
colonial/company rule 10, 35, 89, 227; Peshwas opposition to 67, see also British Government compromise 10, 104, 154, 186–88, 190, 192, 200–201, 217, 221–22
constables 91, 245, 277–78, 295–98, 300, 304, 306–7, 309, 319
Coolie Corps 111
criminals 51
Crosthwaite 303
Cruickshank 100, 200
cultural: ethos 25; expression 27; programme 314
culture 24, 30, 61
Cumming, Capt. 9, 102, 140–41, 143–44, 150–51
Cumming, W.J., Lt., Acting Political Agent (APA) 132
customs 24, 30, 39, 50, 177–78; killing by 177; and rites 177

D
Dabhi 291, 295, 301–2, 340
dacoits 261–62, 267–68, 290–91, 293–94, 300, 304–5, 307, 316, 318, 320, 324, 326, 344–45, 347–48, 405–9; Bhog Chand 293; Jhadu 291; Kanhaiya Karku 305; Pandu 93, 290–91; Uskalli 292
dafadar 73, 85, 363n29
Dahi 127, 146, 151–52, 154
Dahod (Panchmahal) 124, 157, 179, 209
Dalla 13
Daly, A.D., BA 156
Dama, Kewal 206–7
Damodar 328–29

Daniel, Maj. 120
Das, Shyamal 220–23
Dashrath 47, 70, 121; revolt against Company 70
Dashrath Bhil 69–70, 121
Daulatta 119–20
Daulya 267, 269–70, 273–75, 284, 286; arrest 273–74, 284–85; Breaks Jail 275; escaping Jabalpur Jail 284
Davidson, Lt. 94
Davies, Lt. 64, 70, 113
Davison 86, 136
Dawson, Hutton, Maj. 227, 231
Deccan Army 45
Deccan Field Force 92–94
Deccanis 113
deities 8, 24, 27, 29–30
Dengle, Goda 62–63, 67, 74–75, captured in Ahirgaon 65; in jail 64; Triayambak (Dengalia) 62, 74
Depradations 211–12
Deschamp, Maj. 72
deshmukh (jagirdar) 87, 363n32
Deshpande, Arvind M. 12, 87, 363
Deva 13
Devi 46
Dhamkas 208
Dhan 70
Dhang (Dong) 50, 387, 389
Dharampur 160, 166–67
Dharangaon 51, 55, 63, 83, 87; kachahri (court) 54
Dheer, Punja 13, 236–42
Dhikkan, T.W. 341
Dhurandhar (J) 324, 326
Diester 136
Dorepi tribes 40
Doveton, C.W. 314
Dravidians 178
drought 6, 61, 124, 264, 277; in Khandesh 123; in Rajputana 123
Duggar, Doba 147, 149
Dulla, Sheikh, Pindari chief 47, 70
Dungarpur State 27, 173, 175, 179–83, 188, 199, 224, 226, 232, 234–39, 241–42
Dysart, G.S., Lt 127, 136
Dysart, Lt. 133, 136

E
East India Company 32, 181, 194, 207
Eden, W.S. 210
Eki (Unity) 243–44, 251, 255–56
Eki/Eka movement 242, 244, 246, 248
Elphinstone, Mount Stuart 46, 49–50, 52, 355
Ennis, death 67
Erandol 47, 71, 87–88
Eurasian officers 289
Evans, Maj. 96–97, 100, 102, 131
exodus 7
exploitation 13, 157–58, 244, 263, 270

F
famine 6, 41, 60–61, 123–24, 156, 166, 180, 201, 234, 353; of 1899–1900 123–25, 179; Chhappnia 227–31, 368n37; Christian missions during 229
Fenwick, George Richard Stoven 194–96
feudal chiefs/lords 21, 25, 61, 63, 342, 352; oppression by 270
Fitzpatrick 312–13
Forbes, C. (J) 115
Forbes, Maj. 205
forests 5–7, 22, 24, 26, 28, 33–34, 59–61, 118–19, 123–24, 157–58, 164–65, 174, 207–8, 270–71, 355–56; Akrani 143; Balwada 279; Barwani 143; of Betul 320; of Charua 306; Dasana–Sultanpur 146; Gangradhna 320; of Kalibhit 306; Khampur 306; Makrai 306; Nimar 298; Nimbiya 305; Satpura 267, 270

forts/fortress: of Dhaulk 45;
Hamirgarh 194; Mandaleshwar
137, 141, 150; Moolern
(Mulher) 387; Mulher 74–75,
77; Yawal 84
Francis, Capt. 209

G

Gaekwad 33, 117–19, 180, 185,
194, 205, 208, 214, 224; army of
194, 224; territories of 179, 205
Gajia 315, 340; dismemberment
337, 339
Gallows Number of Chand 16
Gandhi, Mahatma 9, 244, 353
Garasias 24, 176–77, 197, 204,
245–46, 248, 250–51; armed
247; of Bhula/Bhoola 247, 254;
of Nanawas 254; of Nawawasa
247, 254; of Waloria 247
Ghanchi, Kalu 169
Gobar, Rupa 207
Goddard, Col. 35
Goh 174–75
Gonds 23
Gonne, C. 225
Goodfellow, Col. G.R., Col. 224
Gordon, John, Col. 153, 199
Gordon-Cumming 9
Gosavi, Manohar 62
Gough, I. Maj. 72
Govind, Bal 202
Govind, Guru 232–42, 244; Sampa
Sabha of 234, 2421
Govinda 41, 149, 274
Graham. Lt. 38, 91, 128
Grant, A.R. 138, 141–43, 147, 176
Grant, C. 294
Great Uprising of 1857 90, 128,
262; Bhil heroes 12
grievances 117, 157, 162–63, 254,
256
Griffin, Lepel, Sir 28, 161, 164, 275,
312–14, 320
Grims, Maj. 204
Gujarat 21, 23, 25, 32, 41, 44, 72,
117–18, 123–24, 126, 178–82,
230, 232–33, 240–41, 352
Gujarat Bhil Corps 43
Gujarat Irregular Horse 205–6
Gujarat-Rajasthan border 204
Gujjars 34, 36; of Nandurbar 36
Gumani (Gumania) 13, 46–48,
68, 72
Gurr, Thomas Stuart 262
Gwalior 84, 202, 326
Gwalior-Holkar troops 203

H

Hall, Lt. 117
Hallet, A.H.H. 341
Hamilton, Maj. 132, 229, 238, 294,
296–99, 304–5, 338–40
Hammond, Col. 308, 338
Hancock, J.G. 60
hangings 29, 101, 113, 195, 278,
350–51
Hankin, C. 122
Hanson, Lt. 98, 117, 148–49
Har 109–10
Hastings, Lord 64
Hatania, arrest of 13, 80
Helms, Capt. 142
Hemchand, Ganesh 115
Henderson, P.D., Lt. Col. 294
Henry, J.W., Capt. 81, 90–91,
112–13
highway robbery 6
hill/mountain passes 11, 22, 33,
37, 68, 81, 92, 200, 202, 350,
352–53; Ajanta 37; Ambhore
110; Asirgarh 64; Barwani 44;
Dhawali 107; Ghyaspur 202;
Goin 141; Morin 82; Sendhwa
47, 68, 70, 92, 131
hill ranges 25, 33, 64, 146; Ajanta
33, 40–41, 50, 56; Chandore 62,
64; Narmada Valley 21, 304; on
northern Kandesh 25; Satmula/
Satmala 25, 33, 90; Satpura 33,
40–41, 44, 51, 70, 80, 100, 106,
117, 263–64, 331; Sukhen 33;

Vindhyas 21, 146, 159
Himgiri, ravaging of 286–91
Hindu: customs 26, 235; deities 30
Hinduism 26
Hindu–Muslim discord 86
Hindus 25–26, 30, 234
Hingona 140
Hira, Wasir 94
Hiria, arrest of 285–86
Hislop, Thomas, Briggs and Sir 45
Hogg, James Weir, Sir 391
Holkar 37, 44, 101, 151, 154, 270, 279, 283, 293–94, 334, 337
Holkar Army 44, 131, 149, 154, 202; Supkaram in 63
Holkar, King Shivaji Rao 336
Holkar kingdom 66–68, 130
Holkar state 102–3, 107, 142, 144, 149–50, 152–54, 288, 299–300, 303, 322, 326–27, 336, 338; territory 129, 133, 153, 155, 282–83, 285, 293, 296, 299, 319–20, 322, 330, 333–34
Holkar, Yashwant Rao 40, 66
Horse-riding invaders 352
Hoshangabad 274–75, 287–89, 291–94, 296, 300–301, 304, 306–7, 309, 313, 319
Hoshangabad–Nimar border 296
Hoshyns, Lt. 230
Howell, A. 279, 294
Hudson, C.W.M. 237–38
human rights 5, 9
hunger 6, 123–24, 140, 352–53; see also famine; poverty
Hunter, W. 184
Husain, Akbar 218–19
Hutenison, Capt. 127, 140

I

ijaradar 322, 325
Imamuddin 154
Indian princes 59, 227
Indore Criminal Procedure Code 325
Indore Regular Cavalry 137
Indore Sadar Court 324–25
Indus Valley Civilisation 174
informers 282, 285–87, 303, 313, 330
insurgencies 9, 76, 116
insurrection 165, 185, 194, 199, 214, 217, 223, 355
investigation 73, 76, 127, 155–56, 252, 257, 291, 316, 337
Itiya 13, 142–43, 151

J

jagirdars 87, 89, 176, 182, 186–87, 191, 197, 205, 212–13, 243–44, 353, 356, 363
jail: Ahmedabad 239; Allahabad 66; Dhule 78, 83, 132; Indore 146, 153; Jabalpur Central 267, 273–75, 284, 337–38, 341, 345; Jambughora 215; Khandesh 153; Khandwa 267, 269, 297, 316, 345; Nagpur 266, 345; Sardarpur 145–46, 155; Yeravda Central/Poona Central Jail 153–54
jamadar 67, 73–74, 102, 106, 112, 122, 156, 163, 192, 194, 206; Hira 249; Chhote Khan 156; Mukranee/Makrani 139, 163, 400
Jamal, Syed 120
Jambughora 205–6, 208, 213–15
Jan Nayak Tantya Bhil and the Peasant and Tribal Movement, Baba Bhand 15
Jardin, Neil, Lt. Col. 45, 68–69
Jasoda/Jashoda 266, 315–17, 337, 340
jawans 55–56, 76, 81–82, 85, 87, 94, 110, 132–33, 136–37, 148, 204–5, 208, 213–15, 218, 298–300; killing of 116
Jawar 220
Jhabua 124, 150, 157, 209–10, 217
Jhalod Mahal 229–30
Jiva, Kunwar 85–86

Joshi, Madan Mohan 16
Jugatia 13, 152–55

K
Kaira 179–80
Kaliya, Munjathia 150
kallal (trader) 218
Kalu Baba 90, 131
Kalu episode 268
kamdar (goverment official) 154, 290, 403
Kamdar, Dul 219
Kathiawar 34, 180
Kathiawar expedition 180
Keane, John, Sir 199
Keating, Capt. K.H. 101–4, 117, 134, 138, 141–44, 148–49, 402: attacks on Bhima 141
Keening, William, Maj., BA 156
Kennedy, Lt. 130
Khajya 133
Khan, Dawood 63
Khan, Habib 156
Khan, Khan Bahadur Najaf 160–61, 163, 167
Khan, Khan Sahib Abbas Ali 164
Khan, Muhammad, Capt. 293–94, 303, 307–8
Khan, Mustafa 206–7
Khan, Najaf 167
Khan, Nathe 286
Khan, Phegi 46, 68
Khan, Sahib Ali, Risaldar 85
Khandesh 32–48, 50, 52–53, 56–57, 60–64, 70–71, 75, 83–86, 88–90, 96, 104–10, 115–16, 118, 123, 126–30, 133, 138–40, 153, 198–99, 401–2; history of 58; Muslim Bhils of 121; as 'Orchard of the West' 41; peasantry 89; policemen 332; territory 334; vandalising of 146
Khandesh Bhil Corps 35, 43, 55, 57, 90, 108, 118, 136, 184
'Khandesh Revolt and Indian Agrarian Discontents' 89
Khandesh-Gujarat frontier region 124
Khandwa 267, 269–72, 276–78, 280, 282, 285, 294, 297, 301–2, 314, 316, 319, 336–38
Kherwara 184, 210, 212, 222–24, 231, 237
Khode, Vishwanath Sakharam 16
Khuman 148
Khundu 46, 68–69, 79–80
Kier, Maj. 128
Kobe, Capt. 197
Koli (Bhilala) 12, 31; of Purandar Ghera 120
Koli Corps 91, 110, 116
Kukarmunda (Kokurmoonda) 41, 57, 70, 75, 387
Kukarmunda Agency 50
Kukshi episode 149
Kunbi, Narayan 301–2
Kunbis 207
Kunwar, Rani Basant 346
Kunwar, Rani Moti 346
Kushalgarh 207, 210, 237–38
Kutch 34

L
Lachhman, Nimar 301–2
Lakshman, Balaji 54
Lakshman, Balaji Sakharam 62
Lal, Himmal 140
Lancaster Gazette 44, 104, 181
Land Tax, Revolts against 89–90
landholders 174, 265
landowners 27, 89, 307
Langston 98
Laurie, L.K. 337–38, 340–41
Lawrence, Maj. Gen. 210
Leckie, Capt. 237
Life of Tantia Bheel, Mukherjee 15
Light Field Force 136
loans 8, 36, 42, 50, 78, 86
loots/looting 6, 123, 168, 263; Barwani 155; Datwada 140, 145; government treasury 131

lumberdar 272
Lunawara 179–80, 194–95, 206–7; army camp 194

M
Macdonald, Capt. 186–89
MacDougall, J.W. 332
Machan, Col. 91, 347–48
Maclean, Donald, Sir. 229
MacLeod, Capt. 214–15
Madhav, Nath 16
Madhya Pradesh 21, 23, 32, 41, 71, 117, 123–24, 164, 173, 178, 355
Magra 211, 243
Mahadia, execution of 115–21
mahalkari (revenue official) 87, 363, see also mamlatdar
Maharashtra 21, 23, 45, 47, 63, 65, 67, 69–70, 108–9, 111, 113, 116–17, 121, 123, 125
Mahdia 273–74, 277–78
Mahi Kantha (second agency) 14, 173, 175, 177, 179–83, 185, 194, 198–99, 204–5, 224–26, 233
Makranis 99, 105, 136, 139, 162–64, 167–69, 200, 205–6, 214–16
Malcolm, John, Sir 21, 44, 65, 186, 201: letter to Metcalfe 66
malguzar 263, 273, 275–76, 278, 282, 285–87, 290, 293, 296–99, 304, 307–8
Mallet, Lt. 201
Malligam camp 54
Malva Bhil Corps 43, 57, 84, 116, 124, 143, 148, 157–58, 161, 164, 217
Malva region 25, 33, 44, 47, 66, 68, 84, 117, 156, 181
Malviya, Madan Mohan 243
Malviya, Ramakant 243
Malwa Bheel corps 159
Malwan 60, 354
mamlatdar, of Baglan 74–75, 77
mamlatdar/Moamlutdars (revenue officer) 68, 74–75, 84, 87, 89, 138, 362n24, 387
Mand, Govind 75
Mandaleshwar 103–4, 142
Mandaloi, Raghunath Singh 104
Mandloi, Daulat Singh 101
Mandloi, Raghunath Singh 101
Mang, Bapu 296–97
Mang, Govind 74, 78
Mangarh Tekri 235–40; insurrection 241
Manik, Mulla 213, 216
Mankur, Sukla Bhil 152
Mankurs 65
Mansfield 87–89, 401–2
Maratha 11–12, 33–34, 36, 40, 45, 54, 60–62, 75–77, 176, 178, 180, 270, 354
Maratha Army, British war against 44
Maratha Confederation 33, 76
Maratha Peshwas 33, 62
Maratha war, of 1803 33, 41; see also Anglo-Maratha war
Marathas 11–12, 33–34, 40, 44, 54, 60–61, 176, 178, 180, 270, 354; defeat in Astha 45; for massacre of Bhils 62
Marwar Bhil Corps 43
Marwaris 23, 28, 36, 114
Mawasia 90, 131
Meade, R.I., Maj. 148, 210
Meena 217
Mehwasis 207
Melaghat Zamindari 291, 407
Metcalfe, Charles, Sir 66
Mewar, states of 23, 25, 27, 173–74, 176, 180–83, 197–98, 202–3, 209–11, 217–18, 221–22, 225–26, 228–29, 231–33, 237, 242–43, 246, 248, 250; treaty with East India Company 181
Mewar Bhil Corps 181, 183–84, 211–12, 217, 221, 228, 237
Mhow 65, 82, 84, 92, 105, 136, 138, 142, 147, 161, 328
Mith Sagare 110–11

Mitharam, Achchheram 224
Mogir 13, 80–82
moneylenders 8, 11, 36, 86, 93, 114, 123, 262–63, 337, 342, 352; looting 337
Montgomery, Maj. 91–92
Morin, Maj., Bhills surrender before 47, 70
Morris, Maj. 84, 87–88, 128, 199, 304
Mughals 59, 63, 130, 176, 180
Muhammad, Dost 163–64, 166
Mukherjee, Charu Chandra 12, 15–16
muqaddam (village chief) 77, 292, 304, 362n24
murder 46, 49, 79, 106, 121, 125, 128, 175, 177, 335, 339, 344–45, 347; of Gangadhar Shastri 64; of Gul Muhammad 239
Muslims 25, 40, 174, 179, 208; Bhils 64, 69, 121; chiefs 270; Hirdhi Bhils as 39; Tarvi Bhills as 39
Mutwari tribe 40
Muwasia 133

N
Naik, Bhagoji 112–13
Naique, Khema, case 328
Nanawas 254
Nanded 113, 191–92
Nandur Shingote 113
Nandurbar 32, 36, 46, 49–50, 84
Narayan, Gopal 77
Nasik 32, 34, 64, 74, 90–92, 109–10, 124
Nath, Dina 293
Nath, Subedar Siddha 249
'The National Congress Resolution and the Arms Act,' poem 349
national liberation movement 356
Nawapura 190–91
Nayak, Amar 206
Nayak, Ananda 155
Nayak, Appa 110

Nayak, Bhago 90, 94–95, 109, 114–15, 131
Nayak, Bhikhari 107
Nayak, Bhima 13–14, 90, 92, 104–5, 109, 127–43, 145, 147–48, 155; band 143, 152; martyrdom 140; mother, Sursi 142; wife Nandi 146
Nayak, Brahma 146
Nayak, Cheel 69
Nayak, Cheema 154
Nayak, Chitto 13
Nayak, Dev 69
Nayak, Dhan Singh 107
Nayak, Dhegra 149
Nayak, Ganga 46
Nayak, Gumani 68
Nayak, Har 109–10
Nayak, Isram 147
Nayak, Itoba 113
Nayak, Jagga 190
Nayak, Jalam Singh 206
Nayak, Jangia 121
Nayak, Kaji Singh 127–39
Nayak, Kalu 146
Nayak, Khajya 133
Nayak, Khala 90, 130
Nayak, Khema 13, 16, 156, 188, 322–27; sentencing RI for 326; sheltering Tantya Bhil 15
Nayak, Mahadev 206
Nayak, Mahadia 110
Nayak, Mahipat 94
Nayak, Mawasia 128
Nayak, Mohasa 146
Nayak, Nurla 133
Nayak, Pathar 91
Nayak, Prem 325
Nayak, Putta 13, 100–101
Nayak, Re Singh 13, 74–75, 77–78
Nayak, Rupa 152
Nayak, Shyam 102, 140, 144
Nayak, Sukram 113
Nayak, Viram 206
Naykaras 117, 205, 207–8, 213
Naylor 121

Neemuch 71, 81–82, 202, 211
negotiations 49, 154, 191, 222–23, 242, 248, 251, 405
Nehar 314
Neil, Lindsay (J) 295, 340–41
Newham, W. 60, 193
Nilkanth, Krishna 77
Nilma 13
Nilsen, Alf Gunvald 12
Nimar 116–17, 269–70, 272, 274, 279, 284–85, 287, 290–93, 296, 298–300, 304, 307–8, 320, 322, 337; Bhil dialect of 28; burglary in 282; Daulya in 275; drought in 277; PA 133; raids in 121, 279, 291, 296, 320; robberies in 280; Tantya in 279; Tantya in folk songs of 263
Nimla 138, 147–49
Ninth Bombay Infantry 230
Nizams 11, 33, 37, 61, 63, 90, 110–12, 120, 122, 125
Non-Cooperation Movement 9, 244, 246, 353
North Devon Gazette 123, 227
North-East Agency 51
North-Eastern Daily Gazette 315
No-Tax Campaign 242
Nuttall, Capt. 91, 93–94, 110

O

occupation: basket weaving 40; cultivation 40, 50, 54–55, 77, 116, 208, 264, 395–97
opium 72, 102, 131, 145, 150, 404
oppression 6, 13, 126, 187, 235, 263, 268, 356
Outram, James, Col. 49–50, 52–55, 57, 76, 78–80, 183–84, 198–99
Owens, Maj. 49, 78
Oyyer (J) 196

P

Paduna 177, 218–19, 222
Pakistan 23
Pal, Nareem 154

Pall Mall Gazette 125, 232, 343–45
panchayati system 22
Panchmahal 124, 164, 179, 209, 212–14, 229, 235
Pandya 78
Pant, Ragghu Ramchandra 77
Parmeshwar 213, 215
parnellism 317–21
Pasi, Madari 244
Pasley, Capt. 81
patels 56, 73–74, 151, 163, 167, 272–73, 279, 281, 289, 291, 306–7, 322, 325; of Rosa 322
Pathak, Mohan 16
Pathans 37, 216
Pathik, Vijay Singh 243
Patil, Himmat 265–69, 275, 340; extraction on 319; false statement against Tantya 269; murder of 274, 339
Patil, Naroba 63
Patil, Sardar 268–69, 272
patwari 150, 154, 157, 290, 299, 304
Paul 76
Pawar Rajputs of Dhar 177
peasants 12, 86–87, 89, 264, 285, 309; of Awadh 244; movement of Bijaulia 245
pensions (see also clemency) 46–47, 49, 68–69, 77, 85–86, 102, 144, 297, 315; to Bhil chiefs 46, 49; sanctioned 46, 51, 353
Peshwas 37, 40, 44, 61, 67, 76, 117
Phadke, Vasudev Balwant 120
Phadnawis, Nana 40
Pimpalner 50, 83
Pindaris 11, 34, 38–39, 47, 63–64; leader Bakhsh 64; looting Malkapur 63
Pir, Nau Gaza, tomb of 266
plunder 25–26, 37–38, 41, 65, 67–70, 114, 116, 129–31, 139–40, 152, 155, 187–89, 201, 203, 335; at Ahmednagar 125; Bhawra 168; Chhaktala 162; of Himmat Patil 339; Kala 274; Kauntel 187;

Kheir 147
Pokhar 264–69, 315, 318, 337, 340 incident 318, 339; patil of 264, 267
Police 73, 93–94, 130, 145, 212, 219, 269–70, 303, 305, 309, 313; Berar 291–92; Central Provinces 294, 312–13, 321; checkposts 141–42, 148; Holkar 154, 278, 305, 332–34, 345; Irregular Mounted 130; Jhabua 124, 157; Nimar 121, 277, 284, 291, 297, 300; Poona 101, 119
police informant 122–23, 281, 283; Jabbar Singh 286; raid on Pittu 287
police station: Attar 295; Chhegaon 308–9; Chicholi 305
political agents (PA) 45, 146, 148, 153, 157, 160–61, 192, 194, 197, 199, 204–6, 208–10, 212, 214, 251–52; of Rewa Kantha 179
Poona Horse 88, 94, 97, 111, 116, 136, 147
Poona Irregulars 136
Poona Regiment 44
Pottinger, James Fox, Capt. 95, 201
Powra tribals 36
Prasad, A.K. 12
Prasad, Bhavani 325
Prasad, Isari, Maj. 164, 295, 300, 303, 306–7, 313–14, 324–25, 328–32, 336–37; meeting with Tantya 331
Prasad, Pancham 332
Pratapgarh 82, 173, 175, 181, 183, 188–90, 202–3, 210–11, 217; troop 202–3
Pratihars 174
priests 29, 221
prisoners 71, 77, 83, 94, 99, 122, 125, 142, 150, 153–54, 195–96, 269–70, 275
Pritchard, Maj. 249
Probyn, Oliver, Maj. 34, 106–7, 117, 133, 136–37, 147, 221, 226

Propert 213–14
Puchs, Stephen 234
Puggi, Etcha 13, 194–96
Puggies 312
Pune–Nasik road 91
Punjala 149
Purohit, Nathu 154
Putta 13, 100–101, 109, 147

Q
Queenslander 21

R
Rahilia 46
Rai, Kirtibhanu 16
Rai, Raja Rao Bahadur Venkat 154
raids 69–70, 120, 122, 125, 127, 144, 147–48, 150, 152–53, 155–56, 272, 274–75, 291, 293, 319–21; Ahmednagar 125; Amdhna 291; Aulia 274; Balakwada 146; Banswara 146; Bhakrada 299; Bhamania 83, 123, 153; Borgaon 122; Charua 293; Cheema Nayak 154; Dahod 157; Devala 279; Devalia 292; Dholgaon 313; Ellichpur 295; Hingoni 144; Holkar territory 153; Indore 275; Jhabua 157–58; Kaira collectorate 198; Kantool 145; Kapasi 292, 320; Karada 289; Khandesh 153; Kheria Rundi 123; Koladit 274; Kukshi 148–49; Limri 230; Nakwara 304; Nimar 121, 279, 291, 296, 320; Panchmahal 209; Pokhar's Patil 315; police informant 287; Poona 120; retaliation on Bandi 305–6; Sakunda 151; Salia Khedi 298; Sankheda 313; Sultanpur 147; villages of 319
Railla 152, 155
Rajaram (J) 328, 334, 336–37, 346
Rajasthan 12, 16, 21, 23, 80–81,

173, 177–78, 180, 182, 186, 233,
  237–38, 352
Rajasthan Sewasangha 251
Rajpipla 7, 179, 190–93, 207, 209
Rajput: cavalries 6; machinations
  7, 186; suzerainty 7, 177
Rajputana 8, 11, 23, 27, 108, 123,
  125, 173, 185, 227–28, 235,
  240, 243; Bhils 8, 27, 229;
  principalities of 173
Rajputana Agency 43, 178, 226
Rajputs 6–7, 9, 12, 59, 61, 173–81,
  207–8, 234, 236, 330, 352,
  354, 356; marriage with 26; of
  Rajputana 11, 173–78
rakhwaldar 107, 127–28, 133, 144
Ralia, Kherari Surmal or Sur 69,
  232–33, 243–44
Ram 13, 45–46, 68; revolts of Bhil
  chiefs 45
Ramchander 122
Ramdas 45
Ramla, nephew Bor 150
Ramosis 67, 119, 176
Rana 46, 159
Rania 78
Rao, Atta 77
Rao, Hanumant 140
Rao, Nathu 153
Rao, Ramachandra 133
Rao, Venkat 161, 163, 166–67
Ratania 13, 138, 147–49
Rawat, Devadeh 188
Rawat, Hiral 188
Rawat, Jagga 13, 140, 186–90
Rawat, Maji 188
Rawat, Omkar 13, 73, 217
Rawat, Rao Singh 73
Raya, Govind 196–98
rebellion 12–13, 89, 115–17, 145,
  150, 197, 199, 204, 212, 216–17,
  221, 242, 246; 1818 65; 1819
  47; 1857 134, 138; against
  begar and tax raise 242; against
  oppression 13; casualties 100;
  Mewar 218, 224–25; peasants
  88; Vasava 192
'red disks,' system of 297
religious rites 29–30, 238
retaliation 62, 146, 206, 246, 284,
  319, 352
revolt: 1804 61; 1819–1820 68–71;
  1833–1835 198–99; in 1844
  204; 1844–1856 204; 1857
  90–94, 115, 145; 1861–1863
  210; 1881 Mewar 218;
  1881–1882 223; 1922 245–53;
  against Land Survey in Jalgaon
  86; in Alirajpur 157–58; Baglan
  74; in Bari 1824 72–79, 157;
  of Barwani Bhils 147, 152; of
  Bhago 90; Bhil 10; in Central
  India 58, 61; in Chandap 204;
  of Chitto 158–69; Dang 83,
  116; Dang Bhil Chief's in 80,
  83, 116; in Dasana 156–57;
  in Derol (Mount Abu) 201;
  Garasia 242; of Hatania 13,
  80; of Holkar Yashwant Rao
  40; In Barwani of Bhil Chiefs
  126–27; Jaora Jail 125; in
  Jhand 116; in Khandesh 14,
  89, 116, 126, 390–99; Koli 12;
  in Maharashtra Khandesh
  Frontier Region 119; by
  mamlatdar 84; Minas 211;
  in Nanded 113; in Nasik 91;
  Naykara Bhils in 117, 212–16;
  peasant 88–89; in Pent 93; of
  Ram Bhil chiefs 45; in Rewa
  Kantha 205; Santhal 12; by
  Shivram Nayak 74; in Toranmal
  Hills 116; at Traiyambak 93
Rewa Kantha 14, 109, 117–18, 173,
  175, 177–80, 185, 205–10, 214,
  235, 237
Rewa Kantha Agency 180, 207, 209
Ricketts, Col. 308
Rigby, Capt. 75, 78
rigorous imprisonment (RI) 85,
  128, 132, 149, 152–53, 240–41,
  265, 281–82, 284, 324, 326

ringleaders 88, 148
riots, in Burhanpur 86
Risaldar 72-73, 299, 363
Risaldar, Farzan Ali 102
Risaldar, Mirza Azim Beg 72
Risaldar, Sahib Ali Khan 85
Rishabhdev 221-23
roads 36-37, 67, 91-92, 104, 127, 130-32, 134-35, 144-46, 193, 218-19, 404; Abu 245, 247; Banswara-Pratapgarh 187; Indore 141, 278; Kotra 248; Lakhwara 193; Makrai 304; Malva- Khandesh 68; Mungthala 247; Pratapgarh 187-88; Sendhwa- Mhow 105; Sendhwa-Shirpur 128; Shirur-Mundhwa 67; Udaipur-Kherwara 218-19, 221, 223; Wasa 249
'Rob Rays' of India 35
robberies 119-21, 125, 274, 280-81, 284, 290, 295, 314, 318, 334-35, 339-40, 345-46; in 1885 296; in Amdhna 291-96; Behir-Charua 293, 295; Bukhara 299; by Daulatta 119; in Malegaon 122; Sukhram Gawli 298
Robertson, Archibald, Col. 49-50, 74-75, 161, 166, 295; writing to William Chaplin 74
Robertson, Donald, Capt. 288
Robinson, Col. 47, 71
Robutram, Maj. 192
Rohiddin, Makrani jamadar 139, 400-401
Rohillas 120, 122; of Akrani 36
Rose, Capt. 128
Royal Cornwall Gazette 105
Rupdeo 160

S
Sable, Krishna 120
Sagwara 7, 70, 118, 190-93, 224
Sakharam, Lal (Lala Bhau) 84

Salwa Judum 53
Samraichchakaha, Suri 30
Sangamner 67, 92, 110; disturbances 67
Santhals 23
Satmala 25, 33, 41, 90
Satpoora/Satpura hills 33, 40-41, 44, 51, 70, 100, 106-7, 129, 135-36, 138, 263-64
Satpura hills: Bhil rebels hiding in 156; British occupation of 41
Satpura/ Satpoora Field Force 96, 132
Satpura-Vindhya belt 309
Sauter, Frank, Sir 110-13; siege at Mith Sagare 111
Scindias (Shinde/Sindhiyas) 11, 37, 44, 62-63, 68, 84, 119, 194, 209, 270
Seagrave, Capt. 213, 215
sedition 110, 145, 238, 240
Seely, Capt. 26
Semaria massacre of Bhils 196
sepoys, killing of 124
September 1899 Incident 227
settlements 25, 70, 86, 191, 355
Shah, Akbar 198
Sharika, Ajay 12
Sharma, Braj Kishore 11
Shaw, Capt. 200
Shepherd 99
Shirpur, Rebel Activities in 105
Shivram (Sevram) 75, 77
Shobhania 78
shraddha (Hindu funeral ceremony) 25
Shripat, Bhil chiefs 118
Shyamal 13, 117
Shyamaldas, Kaviraj 177
Sibthorpe 98
Sindhis 113, 174, 192
Sindhu Durg 60, 354
Singh, Amir 202
Singh, Bage 160, 166
Singh, Bajrang 331
Singh, Bakhshi 331-32

Singh, Bhagwant 331
Singh, Bhim 63–64
Singh, Bhiman 66–67
Singh, Bhomia Bisen 105–6
Singh, Brahma 146, 188
Singh, Chandrika 287
Singh, Daulat (son of Kaji) 13, 118, 129, 131, 139–40, 146, 154, 196–97, 340
Singh, Devi 13, 118
Singh, Dhan 149
Singh, Dhur 78
Singh, Dular 90, 131
Singh, Fateh 193
Singh, Ganpat 330–34, 337, 340
Singh, Hari 209
Singh, Hira 73
Singh, Jamadar Bagga 102, 106
Singh, Jiwan 288
Singh, Kaji/ Kajee 13–14, 90, 109, 127–31, 133–39, 142–43, 147, 356, 400–401; campaign against 138; martyrdom of 139–48
Singh, Karan 193
Singh, Kira/ Keera 13, 118
Singh, Lakshman 290–92
Singh, Lumberdar Khadag 299
Singh, Madho (Madho Nayak) 136–38
Singh, Man 107
Singh, Mansa, Capt. 286
Singh, Mehta Raghunath 211
Singh, Mehta Sawai 204
Singh, Mehta Sher 202–3
Singh, Munna, Lt. 299, 303, 308
Singh, Nadir 13, 46, 65, 65–67
Singh, Nayaks Bajrang 332
Singh, Omkar 206
Singh, Padam 299
Singh, Pratap 83
Singh, Puran 73
Singh, Raghunath 211
Singh, Raja 96; as Khwaja Singh or Kaji Singh 96
Singh, Ram 86
Singh, Ram Bakhsh 73

Singh, Ratan 305–6
Singh, Rup 68, 72
Singh, Rup Dev 160
Singh, Rupa 13, 213, 215, 250
Singh, Sajjan 219–20
Singh, Sardar Ratan 293, 304
Singh, Uday 118
Singh, Vijayi 257
Singh, Yashwant 72, 129
Sirbandi of Idar 224
Sirohi, army of 248
Sirohi state 173, 177, 180–81, 204, 212, 217, 234, 242–43, 245–51, 256–57
Sisodia Rajputs 159, 174–75, 177
Sitaram 13–14, 102–4, 243
Siyol Rebellion of Mewar 226
Skipton, H.P.K. 338
Smith, Gen. 64, 67
sowars 112, 218–20, 300, 404
Spears, Capt. 72–74
spies 115, 310–11, 406
St. James's Gazette 262, 332
starvation 6, 60, 216, see also famine
Steon, H.J. 338
Stevenson, J.F. 63, 125
Stewart, Maj. 93–94, 189–90
Stockley, J.P., Maj. 57, 140, 238
Streshan, J.P. 222
Sultan, Subedar Sheikh 215
Sultanpur 50, 78, 83, 105, 109, 117, 147
Sunth 123, 179, 182, 229–30, 232, 234–35, 237–39, 242
Sunth–Banswara border 236
Sunth–Mewar border 212
Surajmal, Thakur 205
Suri, Haribhadra 30
Sutton, Maj. 246
Swanston, Capt. 65
Swinton 190

T

tactics 48–49, 148, 296
talukdars 193

Tantya Bhil (Marathi) by Nath
   Madhav 16
Tantya Bhil by Kirtibhanu Rai 16
Tantya Bhil by Mukhopadhyay 346
'Tantya Bhil' by Vishwanath
   Sakharam Khode 16
Tantya Bhill (Marathi play) by
   Shantaram Gopal Gupte 16
Tantya Bhillaya Powada by Bal
   Mohan Pathak 16
Tantya Bhill yanche Charitr (Hindi
   translation by Madan Mohan
   Joshi 16;
tax, rakhwali 204
taxation 6–7, 85–86, 157–58,
   166–67, 176, 182–83, 188, 220,
   224, 238, 242–49, 254–56, 397;
   on cultivators 158
Taylor, A.L. 91
tehsildar of Rohera 251–53, 255
Tejawat, Motilal 8, 242–46, 248,
   250, 257
Terminor, J 196
Thakur 31, 93, 114, 123–24, 150,
   152, 161, 183, 202–3, 208,
   210; of Bori 161, 163, 167;
   of Muthwara 142; revolt in
   Mundeti 205
thanadar 8, 143, 156, 213, 218–19,
   223, 323, 330, 403
Thatcher, T., Col. 91
theft 233, 265–67, 282–83, 286,
   316, 323, see also robberies
thieving extraordinary 349–52
Thompson, Charles Stewart 228
Thomson, E.H., Capt. 133–34
Thugee Dacoity Expedition
   Agency 295
thug's treasure 347–49
Tikekar, Ramchandra Vinayak 16
Todd, James, Col. 174, 220
Tope, Tantya 92, 105
traders 8, 92, 96, 123–24, 132,
   135–36, 138, 218–19, 229–30,
   273, 276, 278–79, 352
treasury (Bhandar) 93–94, 132,
   140, 142, 213, 404
Treaty: of Adgaon 62; of Bhopal
   33; of Mandsaur 44
trial 29, 125, 152, 161, 167–68,
   316–17, 324, 328, 336–38;
   Bhima Nayak 145; Chitto 167;
   to death 148; hanged Bhuiphal
   273; Hiria 285; Tantia 316–17
tribal movements, in Rajasthan 12
tribes 7, 22, 25, 30, 35, 38–40,
   53–54, 59, 175, 177–78, 205,
   207, 232, 334–35; Dangchi 40;
   Khotil 40
triial, Gusia Bhil 156
Tukia 120
turvi, sacred thread 24, 31

U

Udaipur Gazetteer 178
Udaipur state 23, 25, 173, 175,
   182, 184, 196, 198, 202–4, 206,
   210–11, 219, 221, 242–43, 245
Umed 191, 277–78
Unkar, Nimar (Omkar) 27, 297,
   301–2
uprising 75, 82, 88, 90, 92, 123,
   129, 197, 204, 206, 208, 213–14;
   1857 (War of Independence)
   61, 90, 92, 105, 129, 206;
   1857 (War of Independence),
   see also under rebellion; in
   Banswara 198; in Erandol 88;
   Mewar 218, 224–25; of Naykara
   Bhils 213; in Panchmahal 214

V

vandalism 24, 126
varna traditions, see castes
Vasava, Dam 193;
Vasava, Kunwar Jiva 13–14, 46,
   69, 85, 109, 193; plundered
   Nawapur 70
Vasava, Kur 13, 190–94
Vasavas, of Sagwara 7, 193
Vashishth, K. 12

Verma, S.C. 264
viluvar for bowmen 24
Vinod, Veer 177
violence 6, 11, 48, 178, 203,
    231–33, 356
Vishwanath, Rajaram 323

W

wahiwatdar (patron) 129
Wakle, L.D. 257
Walker, Maj. 180, 250
Wallace, Maj. 64, 208–9
Waloria 247–53; army action in
    251
Ward, Col. 304, 306–8, 313
Warden, F. 192
warfare 47, 148, 262
Warisal 193
warriors 13, 44, 261
wedding 31, 271, 289, 303
Wellesley, G. 73–74, 190, 237
Western Bhil Agency 84
Western Malva Agency 123
Westmacott, Lt. 215
Whitmore, Ensigns 76
William, James 191
Williams 185, 193, 198
Willoughby, J.P. 180, 191–93
Wilson, Maj. 66
Wingate, Capt. 88, 222
Wise, Maj. 120
witchcraft 6, 30
witnesses 115, 167, 324–25,
    327–28, 335, 339–40, 392
Wood, J.C. 134, 148
Woodburn, A.F. 193, 224
worshipp: of dead 30; of Jain
    Tirthankara Rishabh Dev 30

Z

zamindar 42, 85, 265, 286, 393–95
ziladar (jiladar) 113, 364n4